# FIVE FAMILIES

# FIVE

# FAMILIES

*Mexican Case Studies in the Culture of Poverty*

## OSCAR LEWIS

WITH A NEW INTRODUCTION BY

## MARGARET MEAD

Foreword by Oliver La Farge

A CONDOR BOOK
SOUVENIR PRESS (E&A) LTD

*For Ruth, Gene, and Judy*

# CONTENTS

# ACKNOWLEDGMENTS

*Because the field research for this volume was carried out over a long period, I have incurred many obligations. I am grateful to the American Philosophical Society for research grants for the summers of 1947 and 1948; to the Behavioral Sciences Division of the Ford Foundation for a grant-in-aid in 1952; to the Guggenheim Foundation for a fellowship in 1956–57; and to the Wenner-Gren Foundation for Anthropological Research for a grant-in-aid during the summer of 1958. Finally, I want to thank the Graduate Research Board of the University of Illinois for their loyal support of my Mexican research since 1948. They have given me research grants in 1948, 1951, 1955, 1957 and 1958.*

*To my wife, Ruth M. Lewis, I owe the greatest debt for her contribution to this volume. She has been of invaluable assistance in the field research in Mexico and has worked closely with me in the write-up of these days. I am grateful to Helen S. Kuypers for her excellent editorial assistance on this manuscript. To Dr. Nathan W. Ackerman, Professor of Psychiatry, Columbia University, Professor Fred P. Ellison of the University of Illinois, and Mrs. Dorothy K. Bestor, I also wish to express my thanks for their encouragement and helpful comments on portions of the manuscript. I am also grateful to my friends in the Asociación Psicoanalítica Mexicana—Dr. Ramón Parres, Dr. José L. Gonzales, Dr. Santiago Ramírez, Dr. José Remus, and Dr. Luis Feder—for their stimulating discussion of the materials on the Martínez family. I want especially to thank the Mexican artist Alberto Beltrán for his fine drawings.*

*Finally, I am deeply indebted to the members of the five families whose confidence and cooperation have made this work possible. To protect them, their names and place names have been changed. It was a great privilege to know these people, and I admire the courage with which they face their sometimes overwhelming problems.*

# INTRODUCTION
## BY MARGARET MEAD

*Five Families* is the best introduction to Oscar Lewis's work. It contains all of the things for which Oscar Lewis became famous— his development of the method of viewing culture through a careful, exact picture of family life, as seen through the eyes of several of its members; his sensitivity to the hardships and sorrows of the Mexican people; his concern for the poverty which industrialization was introducing all over the world; and his magnificent evocative writing.

He was the first anthropologist to insist that there was a culture of poverty which deserved careful ethnographic study, and he invented the method of seeing individuals as they presented themselves within families, which were also carefully placed within specific milieus. The short sketch of the Sanchez family is a preview of his masterpiece, *The Children of Sanchez;* the section on the Azteca family is derived from his long study recorded in *Life in a Mexican Village. Five Families* documents the degree of empathy which Oscar Lewis had for the Mexican people—an empathy which was less clear in his study of Puerto Ricans. Because he did the bulk of the field work, the interviewing and the translation, this book is more representative than his later studies in Puerto Rico and Cuba where he used more interviewers.

I knew his work almost from the very beginning, from his struggles with culture change in Tepoztlán, from the days when he went to India to do field work which provided contrast to his Mexican work, and that left him permanently weakened and physically vulnerable. In 1959 I spent some time with him in Mexico City visiting the slum settlements where people welcomed him and the visitors he brought. His warm rapport with the people, in the midst of the distressing poverty, the deep mud through which brides stepped in their rented finery, the crowded little rooms where over-stuffed furniture crowded out the people so that they had to sleep on platforms near the roof—these images are still vivid in my mind.

His work was indeed what Jules Henry called passionate ethnography, combining rigorous requirements of exactitude with a deep passionate sympathy for the special kind of suffering, suffused with pity for the self and for the other, which is intrinsically Mexican. And he combined a repudiation of much of the materialism which was spreading to Mexico from America with an ardent faith that technology, properly applied within a system of social justice, would bring relief from poverty and pain. It was in that belief that he planned to work in Cuba, where he hoped that the poor would find poverty more bearable in a system which was oriented towards a more equitable distribution of wealth. But he also gloried in the introduction of mechanized agriculture in Mexico with its 55,000 tractors, and would have found it hard to predict a recent estimate that modern, mechanized, oil fueled agriculture is less efficient than that of the Mexican peasant, working his small plot with a steel hoe, whom he pitied.

So these accounts—so vivid, so human, so revealing—must be seen as a real breakthrough in ethnographic work and in the study of the poor, especially the urban poor. But they can also be read as a record of a hope that has failed, a hope that was still alive when Lewis wrote of the increasing literacy and the change from tortillas to bread and to knives, forks, and spoons. He fully realized the increasing misery that accompanied the rush into the cities, but he was not yet alarmed by the population explosion, nor had he come to question with Ivan Illich the kind of school system which turns out most of those who attend it as identified failures, stigmatized by their inability to go further.

But although many of the hopes that were brighter when he wrote have dimmed, and his last days were shadowed by the failure of Cuba to realize those hopes, the pictures which he drew of the life of Mexican families are as vividly illuminating today as they were then. The details may have changed a little: the words of the advertisements on TV are different; the Mexican wooing of tourists has a sharper note in it than it had in 1959; the discovery of oil has placed Mexico among the "have" countries, but still tremendously burdened by under-development and less tolerant of the tourist who orders bottled water. But the conditions that created the requests for bottled water are still there. The people of Mexico still display, as they did when his book was published, a mixture of pride in, and repudiation of, the accuracy and empathy with which he wrote about them. His respect for them and their suffering led him to great protectiveness of those who helped him, and his strictures on the insensitivities of other anthropologists earned him more sporadic rejection among his colleagues than it did among those whose lot he depicted.

Oscar Lewis was a great innovative anthropologist, and *Five Families* is the place to begin to know his work. Most of the issues he raises are still with us and will be with us for the next half century at least.

# FOREWORD

For a considerable number of years Oscar Lewis has been experimenting with, and perfecting, an important technique for ethnological reportage. This is the minute and as nearly as possible total observation of the daily life of single family households in a community and in related series of communities. The fruits of his technique have been impressively demonstrated in his *Life in a Mexican Village*, a description of remarkable completeness, great interest, and thoroughly upsetting to common preconceptions of the psyche of modern, rural Mexicans.

From Tepoztlán, the Mexican village of the book just mentioned, he followed Tepozteco families that had moved to Mexico City. In the course of this, he made findings that have caused important changes in anthropological concepts of the changes inherent in the shift from rural to urban life. From studying these migrants, as part of his documentation on the village whence they came, he moved quite naturally into what is usually regarded as the preserve of sociologists when he applied his method to the sampling of the lower classes of Mexico City in general.

His technique offers one method of grappling with the modern social scientist's dilemma. Traditionally, anthropologists have dealt with primitive communities, usually relatively small in number and far more homogenous than "modern" societies. It was possible for a well-disciplined student of such groups, in time, to arrive at summations that are scientifically acceptable, even though the subjective element can never be entirely eliminated. The greater the numbers, the more complex the society under consideration, however, the more nearly impossible it becomes for the investigator to view and comprehend it all. The humanistic, face-to-face method comes up against firm limits of numbers, variety, or usually both.

Sociologists, who from the outset interested themselves more in modern, urban communities, relied heavily on statistical analysis. The longer we study human beings in their infinite variety, the more apparent it becomes that they cannot in reality be encompassed within the specified rigidities of the kinds of data that can be manipulated mathematically, even given the staggering range of present-day computers. Somewhere along the line, there must be an interpretation arising from the individual's observation, with all its weaknesses of emotion and bias.

Nowadays the student of peoples bolsters himself with all sorts of objective aids, above all a number of psychological tests (usually called, with unconscious humor, "a battery") and the greatest possible use of statistics. Even so, in the end, if his findings are to be of any use at all, someone must interpret them in humane terms, someone must inject the element of description.

These difficulties clash directly with the obvious, increasing need to have for our guidance in realistic actions of great import that understanding of the peoples of the world that the social sciences are supposed to give us. Anthropologists can no longer stay entirely, safely aloof from the great world, the world with which military men, diplomats, statesmen of all kinds are inexorably engaged. As Dr. Lewis remarks in his opening section, "It is ironic that many Americans, thanks to anthropologists, know more about the culture of some isolated tribe in New Guinea, with a total population of 500 souls, than about the way of life of millions of villages in India or Mexico and other underdeveloped nations which are destined to play so crucial a role in the international scene"—in short, about the great majority of mankind.

His study of a day in the life of each of five Mexican families is an attempt to give us a living picture of one segment of those millions by a process of sampling in depth. The treatment is as nearly objective as is most ethnological field work. The recorder points no morals, draws no conclusions, except in his separate, opening section, and then with great restraint, makes no comments. He simply lays before us five days, five perfectly ordinary days in the lives of five ordinary,

representative families. Of necessity, his families have been fiction-
alized; that detracts in no way from the value of the report. Ines-
capably, behind the eyes of the observer lies the filter of his personality, the inescapable, subjective factor in the social and in many
other sciences.

The picture we get, of course, is Mexican. It would not even apply
to all of Mexico, yet it also has universal values. As Dr. Lewis points
out, it illustrates the little recognized dynamics of poverty. To me,
among the striking things about these families are their general
*malaise,* the rarity among them of happiness or contentment, the
rarity of affection. Demonstrative affection or, except during a relatively brief courting and initial mating period, what we usually mean
by "love" are rare among the poorer, simpler peoples of the world.
Above all, where hunger and discomfort rule, there is little spare
energy for the gentler, warmer, less utilitarian emotions and little
chance for active happiness. These generalizations, however, do not
fully account for the characters of the people described for us here,
and we may note that the most dreary, the most utterly loveless,
the most hateful, are the *nouveaux riches* Castros, handled with a
magnificently brutal frankness, a family to dismay Chekhov, to stand
Zola's hair on end.

Is this reasonable? Can we believe it? Can we accept as characteristic the repeated elements of decaying or decayed religion, broken
families, unions out of wedlock, adulteries, and plain polygamy? The
answer may lie in yet another factor. All of the families in this book
consist of people whose culture is what we usually call "in transition," meaning that it is going to hell in a handbasket before the
onslaught of the Age of Technology. Here is the greatest export of
the Euro-North American family of nations—a new material culture
that shatters the nonmaterial cultures of the peoples it reaches, and
that today is reaching them all. All over the world, people are hating
the light-skinned, machine-age nations, and busily aping them. One
of the first returns they get is a cultural desolation.

Let us look again at the Castros. They have achieved a North
American material culture. They have a two-toned car and plumbing,
they even eat a North American breakfast. At the end of the day,
Señora Castro curls up with a translation of a North American best-

seller. Yet they have not entered the northern culture, they are merely uprooted, divorced from the enrichments of their own sources without having received any substitutes other than objects; they are sounding brass and tinkling cymbals, being without love, being true to nothing.

The *malaise* I am discussing extends over the whole world. A portion of the dynamics of poverty, at least, belongs to it, for in many, many instances an old, physically satisfactory, *primitive* existence is replaced by an unsatisfactory, *impoverished* existence as peoples become caught in the economic web that is inseparable from the extension of the Age of Technology. Typically, too, the cultural shock results in a breakdown of the basic social unit, the family, although in the case of the second, third, and fourth families of these five, we note with interest how strong is the continuance of the pattern of cohesion, resulting in truly curious patchings together of fragments and of parts that themselves are products of the breakdown.

Drastic culture changes, especially notable in family life and religion, are occurring as well among the nuclear nations of the new age, even though they have had a comparatively gradual transition into it over the past century and a half, from the beginning of the Industrial Revolution.

Most "whole" cultures, cultures in which the people follow a long-established set of adaptations to themselves, each other, and their circumstances, reward their participants with what can loosely be termed *satisfaction*. It is characteristic of breaking or broken cultures that they no longer give satisfaction, no longer "make life worth living," which in turn may lead to bitterness towards the original source of change, an intuitive blame-placing. Whether or not unconsciously stressed, the element of unsatisfaction is strongly apparent in Dr. Lewis's five families.

This work is more than a sampling of Mexico. It illuminates, painfully, something of the human condition of the masses, the myriad millions, who through that same technology have suddenly become our near neighbors, whose good will or enmity may prove crucial to our own survival.

Oliver La Farge

# FIVE FAMILIES

# The Setting

In this book I have attempted to give the reader an intimate and objective picture of daily life in five Mexican families, four of which are of the lower income group. My purpose has been to contribute to our understanding of the culture of poverty in contemporary Mexico and, insofar as the poor throughout the world have something in common, to lower-class life in general.

This book has grown out of my conviction that anthropologists have a new function in the modern world: to serve as students and reporters of the great mass of peasants and urban dwellers of the underdeveloped countries who constitute almost eighty per cent of the world's population. What happens to the people of these countries will affect, directly or indirectly, our own lives. Yet we know surprisingly little about them. While we have a great deal of information on the geography, history, economics, politics, and even the customs of many of these countries, we know little about the psychology of the people, particularly of the lower classes, their problems, how they think and feel, what they worry about, argue over, anticipate, or enjoy. Traditionally, anthropologists have been students and spokesmen of primitive and preliterate peoples who live in remote corners of the world and have little influence upon our civilization. It is ironic that many Americans, thanks to anthropologists, know more about the culture of some isolated tribe of New Guinea, with a total population of 500 souls, than about the way of life of millions of villagers in India or Mexico and other underdeveloped nations which are destined to play so crucial a role in the international scene.

1

The shift from the study of tribal peoples to the study of peasants and, as in the case of this volume, to urban dwellers lends a potentially new and practical significance to the findings of anthropologists. It also calls for a re-evaluation of the relationship between the anthropologist and the people he studies, most of whom are desperately poor. Although poverty is quite familiar to anthropologists, they have often taken it for granted in their studies of preliterate societies because it seemed a natural and integral part of the whole way of life, intimately related to the poor technology and poor resources or both. In fact, many anthropologists have taken it upon themselves to defend and perpetuate this way of life against the inroads of civilization.

But poverty in modern nations is a very different matter. It suggests class antagonism, social problems, and the need for change; and it often is so interpreted by the subjects of the study. Poverty becomes a dynamic factor which affects participation in the larger national culture and creates a subculture of its own. One can speak of the culture of the poor, for it has its own modalities and distinctive social and psychological consequences for its members. It seems to me that the culture of poverty cuts across regional, rural-urban, and even national boundaries. For example, I am impressed by the remarkable similarities in family structure, the nature of kinship ties, the quality of husband-wife and parent-child relations, time orientation, spending patterns, value systems, and the sense of community found in lower-class settlements in London (Zweig 1949; Spinley 1953; Slater and Woodside 1951; Firth 1956; Hoggart 1957), in Puerto Rico (Stycos 1955; Steward 1957), in Mexico City slums and Mexican villages (Lewis 1951, 1952), and among lower class Negroes in the United States.

To understand the culture of the poor it is necessary to live with them, to learn their language and customs, and to identify with their problems and aspirations. The anthropologist, trained in the methods of direct observation and participation, is well prepared for this job, whether in his own or in a foreign country. Unfortunately, in many of the underdeveloped countries the educated native elite generally have little first-hand knowledge of the culture of their own poor, for the hierarchical nature of their society inhibits communication across

2

class lines. In Mexico, for example, practically nothing of a scientific nature is known about lower-class family life. In one of the few recently published studies on the Mexican family (Bermudez 1955), the author had to rely almost entirely upon data from novels. This is not to minimize the insights of novelists; but there have been very few great contemporary novels dealing with the lower classes of underdeveloped countries.

This new subject matter calls for some modifications in the conventional research designs of anthropologists. Peasant villages cannot be studied as isolates apart from the national culture; city dwellers cannot be studied as members of little communities. New approaches are necessary, new techniques, new units of study, and new ways of reporting the data so that they can be understood by the nonspecialist.

The present study of five Mexican families is a frank experiment in anthropological research design and reporting. Unlike earlier anthropological studies, the major focus of this study is the family rather than the community or the individual. The intensive study of families has many methodological advantages. Because the family is a small social system, it lends itself to the holistic approach of anthropology. The family is a natural unit of study, particularly in a large metropolis like Mexico City. Moreover, in describing a family we see individuals as they live and work together rather than as the averages and stereotypes implicit in reports on culture patterns. In studying a culture through the intensive analysis of specific families we learn what institutions mean to individuals. It helps us get beyond form and structure to the realities of human life, or, to use Malinowski's terms (1922, p. 17), it puts flesh and blood on the skeleton. Whole family studies bridge the gap between the conceptual extremes of culture at one pole and the individual at the other; we see both culture and personality as they are interrelated in real life.

In my studies of families in Mexico over the past fifteen years, I have used four separate but related approaches which, when combined, provide a rounded and integrated study of family life. The first or topical approach applies most of the conceptual categories used in the study of an entire community to a single family. The data on the family are organized and presented under the headings of material culture, economic life, social relations, religious life, interpersonal relations, and so on. From a great mass of information based upon living with the family, interviews, and extended observation, the various aspects of the family and of the individual members of the family are reconstructed. This approach is analytical and has the advantage of permitting comparisons between the family culture and the larger culture outside the family.

A second approach is the Rashomon-like technique of seeing the family through the eyes of each of its members. This is done through long, intensive autobiographies of each member of the family. This gives more insight into the individual psychology and feeling tone as well as an indirect, subjective view of family dynamics. This type of material would probably be most useful to the psychologist. Its methodological advantage derives from the independent versions of similar incidents in family life which amount to a check on the validity and reliability of the data.

The third approach is to select for intensive study a problem or a special event or crisis to which the family reacts. The way a family meets new situations is revealing particularly of many latent aspects of family psychodynamics; it also points up individual differences.

A fourth approach to the study of a family as a whole is through detailed observation of a typical day in the life of the family. To give depth and meaning to this approach it must be combined with the other three. This is what I have done to some extent in the present volume.

The selection of a day as the unit of study has been a common device of the novelist. However, it has rarely been used and certainly never exploited by the anthropologist. Actually it has as many advantages for science as for literature and provides an excellent medium for combining the scientific and humanistic aspects of anthropology. The day universally orders family life; it is a small enough time unit to allow for intensive and uninterrupted study by the method of direct observation, and it is ideally suited for controlled comparisons. It makes possible a quantitative analysis of almost any aspect of family life. For example, one can study the amount of time devoted to the preparation of food in different families, the amount of conversation between husband and wife or between parents and children, the amount of laughter, the extent and kind of table talk, etc. One can also study the more subtle and qualitative aspects of interpersonal family relations.

The study of days presented here attempts to give some of the immediacy and wholeness of life which is portrayed by the novelist. Its major commitment, nevertheless, is to social science with all of its strengths and weaknesses. Any resemblance between these family portraits and fiction is purely accidental. Indeed, it is difficult to classify these portraits. They are neither fiction nor conventional anthropology. For want of a better term I would call them ethnographic realism, in contrast to literary realism. These days are not composites; they are real days. And the individuals are not constructed types but are real people. In a sense, these portraits of contemporary Mexican life are historical documents which may be useful for cross-cultural comparisons now and in the future. How many controversies might have been avoided and precious hours of research time saved if historians had had comparable records of ordinary days in the lives of families of ancient Egypt, Rome, or feudal Europe!

I would like to emphasize that one cannot simply knock on any door to do this kind of family study. It demands an unusual degree of rapport and confidence between the investigator and the family. Although I was a foreigner and a "norte-Americano," I encountered no hostility and very little antigringoism among these families. I have spent hundreds of hours with them in their homes, eaten with them, joined in their fiestas and dances, listened to their troubles, and discussed with them the history of their lives. They were generous with their time and good-naturedly submitted to Rorschach tests, Thematic Apperception tests, the Semantic Differential, and intensive interviews. The study of the village family was only a small part of my larger study of the community as a whole. Similarly, the studies of three of the city families were part of my study of lower-class life in the *vecindades* or tenement-like settlements of Mexico City. I have known the Martínez family since 1943 and the other families since 1950. My repeated visits to Mexico over the years to work with these families were one of the most important factors in the growth of our rapport and friendship.

The selection of the particular day for observation and recording was arbitrary, practically a random choice, except that an ordinary day was chosen rather than one marked by an unusual event such as a birth, a baptism, a fiesta, or a funeral. In four of the five days the conversations were taken down stenographically by a trained assistant. In two of the cases the assistant was a relative of the family and in a third, a close friend of many years. Rapport was sufficiently good in all so that the normal routines of family life were only minimally affected or distorted by the presence of the investigator. Although the controlled laboratory procedures of small-group studies with built-in microphones and one-way screens were not possible, these case studies give a camera-like view of the movements, conversations, and interactions that occurred in each family during one day. Of necessity this meant the reporting of some pedestrian details as well as severe restraint in manipulating the data to sharpen interest or to reveal the "essence" of the lives. Some selection of data had to be made to avoid repetition and insignificant events, but approximately ninety per cent of all the recorded data has been retained. To give more depth and meaning to the studies, descriptions of the characters and of their homes and autobiographical material, in flashbacks, have been added.

Although each family presented here is unique and a little world of its own, each in its own way reflects something of the changing Mexican culture and must therefore be read against the background of recent Mexican history. The history of Mexico since the Revolution can conveniently be divided into two periods, from 1910 to 1940, and after 1940. In the first period, which ended with the Cárdenas administration, the emphasis was upon basic institutional change—the transformation of a semifeudal agrarian economy, the distribution of land to the peasants through the *ejido* program, the strengthening of labor's position, the emancipation of the Indian, and the spread of public education. Beginning with the Camacho administration in 1940, the tempo of social change and land distribution was slowed down, and industrialization and greater production became the new national slogans.

The changes since 1940 have been impressive and far-reaching. The population has increased by over ten million to reach a high of thirty million people in 1957; this has been accompanied by a surge of urbanization, with millions of peasants and villagers moving into the cities. The growth of Mexico City has been phenomenal—from one and a half million in 1940 to four million in 1957! Mexico City has now become the third or fourth largest city on the American continent. The economy has been expanding and the country has become acutely production conscious. Leading newspapers daily headline record-breaking achievements in agriculture and industry and proudly announce huge gold reserves in the national treasury. A boom spirit has been created which is reminiscent of the great expansion in the United States at the turn of the century. The accomplishments in agriculture have been even more impressive than those in industry, especially in view of the essentially arid nature of the country. Since 1940 about a million and a half hectares have been brought under irrigation, the total harvested area has been increased by about 70 per cent, and the number of tractors has increased from 4,600 to over 55,000. To appreciate the significance of the last item for an underdeveloped country we must recall that India, with its 380 million people, had only 5,000 tractors in 1955.

The increased national wealth has made for some improvement in the level of living of the general population. More and more rural people sleep on beds instead of on the ground, wear shoes instead of huaraches or instead of going barefoot, use store-bought pants instead of the homemade white *calzones,* eat bread in addition to *tortillas,* grind their corn in the mill instead of by hand, drink beer instead of pulque, use doctors instead of *curanderos,* and travel by bus or train instead of on foot or by burro. In the towns and cities the trend has been from adobe to cement, from clay pots to aluminum, from cooking with charcoal to cooking with gas, from eating with *tortillas* to eating with tableware, from the *metate* to the electric blender, from phonographs to radios and TV, from cotton to nylons, and from cognac to whiskey.

One of the most significant trends in Mexico since 1940 has been the increasing influence of United States culture. While this influence is most marked in the large cities, it can also be seen in rural areas. The proximity of the United States, improved means of communication and transportation, increased travel by both Mexicans and North Americans, the power and prestige of the United States as a great industrial civilization, the large U.S. investments in Mexico, and the growth of a middle class which models itself after its northern counterpart are some of the more important factors responsible for this influence.

Large-scale advertising came in with recent U.S. investments and has a decidedly U.S. flavor. The major television programs are sponsored by foreign-controlled companies like Nestles, General Motors, Procter and Gamble, and Colgate. Only the use of the Spanish language and Mexican artists distinguishes the commercials from those in the United States. On the Quaker Oats program one hears the Mexican lightweight idol Ratón (The Mouse) Macias recommend Quaker Oats as the cereal of champions. Some commercials do not even trouble to translate phrases and have spread American linguistic forms or *pochismos*. Thus, beauty products are announced as "Touch and Glow," "Bright and Clear," etc. American department stores retail practices, such as self-service, attractive open display of goods, standardized and guaranteed articles, and fixed prices, have been made more popular in the past ten years by stores like Woolworth's and Sears Roebuck and Co. Self-service supermarkets, complete with packaged foods, many with American brands, are opening in the better-to-do neighborhoods of Mexico City and in some of the smaller towns. American-made clothing and shoes, or locally made articles carrying well-known American labels, are sold in the higher priced shops.

Increased employment in factories and office buildings has led to the spread of the quick lunch, eliminating the midday meal at home as well as the traditional siesta. The American style breakfast, juice, cereal, ham and eggs, and coffee, has become popular, displacing the traditional beans, chili sauce, and *tortillas*. The practice of eating stuffed turkey on Christmas eve has been adopted by some middle-class families. The same trend is seen in the substitution of the Christmas tree for the customary Nativity scene and in the giving of gifts on December 25 instead of on January 6, the Day of the Three Kings. The spread of English is also noteworthy. English has been adopted as a second language in the schools, replacing French.

Despite the increased production and the apparent prosperity, there are symptoms that all is not well in Mexico. Although the national wealth has increased greatly, its uneven distribution has made the disparity between the incomes of the rich and the poor more striking than ever before. And despite some rise in the standard of living for the general population, over 60 per cent of the population were still ill-fed, ill-housed, and ill-clothed in 1956, 40 per cent were illiterate, and 46 per cent of the nation's children were not going to school. A chronic inflation since 1940 has squeezed the real income of the poor, and the cost of living for workers in Mexico City has risen over five times since 1939. According to the census of 1950 (published in 1955), 89 per cent of all Mexican families reporting income earned less than 600 pesos a month or $69 at the 1950 rate of exchange.

The great increases in agricultural production in the past twenty years have been concentrated in only two regions of the country, the North and Northwest, where a new commercial agriculture has developed, based upon large private holdings, irrigation, and mechanization. The great mass of the peasantry continues to work its tiny subsistence holdings with traditional backward methods. The contrast between the old and new agriculture in Mexico is becoming ever sharper. Thus, whereas less than 1 per cent of the cultivated land is worked with the aid of 55,000 tractors, about 20 per cent of the land is still worked by the pre-Hispanic method of cutting and burning without benefit of plow and oxen. The production of Mexico's two basic food crops, corn and beans, has managed to keep up with the rapid population growth in the past twenty years, but the margin of security has been slight and in drought years Mexico has been forced to spend its precious dollars to import huge quantities of corn to feed its people.

It is common knowledge that the Mexican economy cannot give jobs to all of its people. From 1942 to 1955 about a million and a half Mexicans came to the United States as *braceros* or temporary agricultural laborers, and this figure does not include the "wetbacks" and other illegal immigrants. Were the United States suddenly to close its borders to the *braceros*, a major crisis would probably follow in Mexico. Mexico also has become increasingly dependent upon the U.S. tourist trade to stabilize its economy. In 1957 over 700,000 tourists from the United States spent almost 600 million dollars in Mexico to make tourism the single largest industry in the country. The income from the tourist trade is about equal to the total Mexican federal budget.

One aspect of the standard of living which has improved very little since 1940 is housing. With the rapidly rising population and urbanization, the crowding and slum conditions in the large cities are actually getting worse. Of the 5.2 million dwellings reported in the Mexican census of 1950, 60 per cent had only one room and 25 per cent two rooms; 70 per cent of all houses were made of adobe, wood, poles and rods, or rubble, and only 18 per cent of brick and masonry. Only 17 per cent had private, piped water.

In Mexico City conditions are no better. The city is made more beautiful each year for U.S. tourists by building new fountains, planting flowers along the principal streets, building new hygienic markets, and driving the beggars and vendors off the streets. But nearly two million Mexicans, or about one half of the city's population, live in slumlike housing settlements known as *vecindades,* suffering from a chronic water shortage and lacking elementary sanitary facilities. Usually, *vecindades* consist of one or more rows of single-story dwellings with one or two rooms, facing a common patio. The dwellings are constructed of cement, brick, adobe and form a well-defined unit with some of the characteristics of a small community. The size and types of *vecindades* vary enormously. Some consist of only a few dwellings, others of a few hundred. Some are found in the commercial heart of the city, in sixteenth- and seventeenth-century two- and three-story Spanish colonial buildings which have become run-down, while others, on the outskirts of the city, consist of wooden shacks or *jacales* and look like semitropical Hoovervilles.

The developments on the outskirts of the city, which do not yet have water, sewers, or electricity, are crowded with the makeshift shacks of the newly arrived peasants who cannot support themselves in the villages. When they find jobs they move into the slums; the slum-dwellers, as soon as they can afford to, escape the crowding by moving out to the edge of the city. Because decent housing is not available at reasonable rents, many people stay on in their one-room apartments long after they are financially well off. Their little dwelling fills up with new furniture, china, TV sets, refrigerators, electric appliances, and even perhaps a washing machine, until there is hardly space for the family to move about.

To introduce the reader to the members of the five families presented in these days and to help him understand these people, I will briefly sketch the background of each family and indicate some of the salient aspects of the communities in which they live. The first day describes the Martínez family, which lives in a Mexican highland village which I call Azteca, about sixty miles south of Mexico City. It is a village of peasants, artisans, and shopkeepers, with a total population of 3,500. Most of the villagers are bilingual, speaking both Spanish and ancient Nahuatl. The village culture represents a fusion of pre-Hispanic, Spanish colonial, and modern culture traits. The village has been caught up in the mainstream of national life. It was in the heart of the Zapatista rebellion during the Revolution. It has a new school, a road, a bus line, corn mills, communal and *ejido* lands, a typical Mexican plaza with a Catholic church and government buildings, and also some Protestant missionaries. In spite of these many changes, however, the agricultural economy of the village has changed very little, and the increasing population pressure on the limited land resources creates a serious problem. Azteca, along with thousands of villages in the densely populated central highland area, has not participated in the newly developed commercial and mechanized agriculture of the North or in the great hydroelectric projects of other parts of the country.

The Martínez family, like 85 per cent of the villagers of Azteca, lives on a bare subsistence level. Pedro Martínez, the head of the family, reflects some of the forces that have been at work in rural Mexico since the Mexican Revolution of 1910–20. He has moved from an illiterate peon to a political leader in his village, from speaking only the native Nahuatl Indian language to reading and writing Spanish, from an isolated provincialism to a familiarity with and participation in state and national political campaigns, from folk-Catholicism with its admixture of pre-Hispanic beliefs to Seventh-Day Adventism, and then back again to Catholicism.

Pedro and his wife Esperanza were married in Church in 1910, the year the Mexican Revolution broke out. Theirs has been a stable marriage along traditional lines in which Pedro comes close to the ideal village pattern of the dominating, authoritarian male and his wife to the ideal of the submissive woman. The children, too, fulfill the village requirements for hard work, respect, and obedience, although as they grew older they began to change in response to outside influences.

The second day deals with a family in transition from village to city life. Agustín Gómez, the father, came from a better-to-do peasant family of Azteca village, which he and his wife left seventeen years ago in an effort to improve their lot. They are now a hard-pressed working class family living in a crowded one-room apartment in a *vecindad* which I call the Casa Grande. This is a huge tenement consisting of 157 households with a total population of about 700. Although the living standards of the Casa Grande are low, they are by no means the lowest to be found in Mexico City. Monthly incomes per capita per household ranged from 23 to 500 pesos ($3–$40). Twenty-seven per cent of the households show less than 100 pesos ($8) per capita income, 41 per cent show between 101 and 200 pesos ($16), 22 per cent between 201 and 300 pesos, and 10 per cent between 301 and 500 pesos. The Gómez family is in the upper middle group with a per capita monthly income of about 300 pesos.

Our study of the distribution of selected items to measure the standard of living in this community shows that 79 per cent of the households have radios, 55 per cent gas stoves, 54 per cent wrist watches, 49 per cent use knives and forks (spoons are quite common but most eating is done with *tortilla* and the hands), 46 per cent have sewing machines, 41 per cent aluminum pots, 22 per cent electric blenders (informants refer to the traditional stone mortar and pestle as the Mexican blender), 21 per cent television sets, 10 per cent washing machines, 5 per cent automobiles, and 4 per cent refrigerators. Radios have become so common that they are no longer diagnostic of wealth. The use of tableware for eating has proved to be the single most diagnostic item for socioeconomic level. Gas stoves, TV sets, and wrist watches rank next in order.

There is a wide range of level of education in the *vecindad*, varying from twelve adults who never attended school to one woman who attended for eleven years. The average number of years of school attendance of the 198 adults of our sample is only 4.7. However, only 8 per cent of the residents are illiterate. The children of the *vecindad* show a substantial educational advantage over their parents.

About 72 per cent of our sample of 71 households in the *vecindad* are occupied by the simple biological or nuclear family and 28 per cent by some form of the extended family. Of a total of 158 married people living in the 71 households, 91 are women and 67 are men. In other words, 24 married women are living without husbands, either as heads of households or with some relative. Nine women are widowed and the remaining 15 are separated, divorced, or deserted. Twenty per cent of all marriages are of the common-law type with most of these in the lower income group; and in 20 per cent of all households in the *vecindad* there is at least one woman who has been deserted.

The Gómez family prefers city to village life and has made a good adjustment to the *vecindad*. It shows relatively little of the disorganization and breakdown which is so often associated with the urbanization process and has remained stable despite some internal conflict. The working children contribute to the support of the family, religious participation has become more important and more Catholic, and the *compadre* system continues to function with some modifications. The family maintains its ties with relatives in their village and preserves many village beliefs and customs. There also have been some striking changes in family life, however, namely: displacement of the father by the mother as the dominant figure in the family; increased freedom for the children; a steadily rising standard of living on the basis of installment buying; a higher aspiration level, added leisure, and greater opportunities for diversion; broader social contacts; and a gradual modernization of many beliefs.

The third day deals with a more urbanized lower-class family. The wife, Julia Rojas, was born and reared in Mexico City slums; the husband, Guillermo Gutiérrez, at an early age severed his ties with the small mining town in which his father had earned an impecunious living as a miner and part-time schoolteacher. Guillermo's three children by his first wife were all born in Mexico City.

The Gutiérrez family now lives in the Panaderos *vecindad,* one of the poorest slum tenements in the city. Eighty-five per cent of the households in this *vecindad* have an average monthly per capita income of less than 200 pesos, or $16; the average number of years of school attendance of those who completed their education is 2.1, and 42 per cent of the residents are illiterate. Moreover, the children have very little educational advantage over their parents. The much greater poverty of the Panaderos *vecindad* is also revealed in the absence of most of the luxury items found in the Casa Grande. In Panaderos we find an average of 1.4 luxury items per household as compared to 4 per household in the Casa Grande. The complete absence of gas stoves and knives and forks is especially diagnostic of the low standard of living.

The biological family is the predominant residence unit in the *vecindad.* Six of the thirteen families found in the twelve households are of this type. However, nine of the twelve households are related by kinship ties and constitute three extended families. Three

*14*

apartments are occupied by widowed or abandoned women living with their grown children, and two apartments are occupied by men who have separated from their wives. In only one apartment is there a true extended family consisting of a man and his wife and their married daughter and grandchildren. Forty-six per cent of the marriages in the *vecindad* are of the common-law type.

The Gutiérrez family is the poorest of the city families in this volume although by no means the poorest in the Panaderos *vecindad*. However, it shows the best adjustment to its life conditions, and there is less tension between husband and wife than in the other families described. In this family there is an almost complete absence of the middle-class values which are beginning to spread throughout the lower strata of Mexican society. The parents show little drive to improve their standard of living and do not place high value on education, clothing, or cleanliness for themselves or their children. On the other hand, they are self-employed and have a definite preference for independent business enterprises. Guillermo is a petty artisan and shopkeeper; Julia is a street-vendor, the only wife among our five families who works outside the home. Guillermo often spends time working at things that interest him whether or not they are financially rewarding. Julia works to provide food for the family, and the children are expected to work and contribute to their support as soon as they are physically able.

The fourth day presents a family which combines working-class and lower middle-class traits. The father, Jesús Sánchez, a restaurant worker who has long since lost his ties with his native village in Vera Cruz, adds to his low income by raising poultry and pigs. For the past thirty years he has lived in various one-room tenement apartments, including the Casa Grande, in the heart of Mexico City. Recently, however, thanks to his winnings in the national lottery, he built a house in a poor colony on the outskirts of the city. Here Lupita, one of his two wives, lives with their children. His younger wife, Delila, continues to live with her children in a city tenement.

The Sánchez family is a complex structure since Jesús Sánchez has had children with four women, each of whom has had children by previous marriages. This study reveals some of the relationships and conflicts that arise between half brothers and sisters, stepbrothers and sisters, and between stepparents and stepchildren. Jesús is unusual among lower-class Mexican men because of his strong sense of reponsibility to his various wives and children, none of whom he has abandoned. As in many lower-class families, his marriages have been of the free union or common-law type.

The fifth and last day gives us a glimpse of a *nouveau riche* family. The father, David Castro, is a self-made post-Revolutionary millionaire who grew up in a slum tenement and who has by no means lost all of his lower-class traits. These can be seen in his relationship with his wife and mistress, with both of whom he lives in free union, in his violence with his wife and children, in his periodic abandonment of them, in the allotment of the daily expense money to his wife, and in his punishing of her by withholding money. Isabel, his wife, came from an impoverished middle-class family with upward-striving ambitions. She married David because of his money and is now staying with him for the same reason. She would not know how to support her four children alone. Because of her need for luxury, she lacks the resourcefulness and independence of lower-class women who readily support themselves when their marriage is no longer pleasing to them or when they are temporarily abandoned. The incorrigibility of the children in this family is in sharp contrast with the behavior of children in poorer families. Also notable are the degree to which this family admires and imitates the United States; its resemblance to the American middle class; its rejection of some Mexican traditions; the presence of gadgets and the absence of true cultural interests; and the evidence of feeding problems and other neurotic symptoms.

In comparing the five families we find a number of traits that cut across rural-urban differences and reflect national and class cultural values. In three of the families the marriages were of the free union type. The fact that the *nouveau riche* family is one of the three is unusual, since common-law marriage is a predominantly lower-class pattern. However, this reveals the extent to which the father in this family has carried over lower-class patterns to his new status. In the

*16*

first two families, both from Azteca village, the marriages were formalized by law and church weddings.

Although free unions constituted approximately 20 per cent of all marriages in the nation according to the 1950 census, the children of such marriages are considered to be illegitimate by Church and civil law. Nevertheless, on the local community level, both urban and rural, these marriages are socially acceptable. In terms of lower-class standards, only children who have not been recognized or supported by their fathers are considered illegitimate.

The Mexican cultural emphasis upon male dominance and the cult of *machismo* or masculinity is reflected in at least three of our families in which the husband is clearly the dominant and authoritarian figure. All the husbands except Señor Gutiérrez have had extramarital affairs and illegitimate children and three are supporting a mistress or *casa chica* at the present time. Only in the village and Gutiérrez families is this not the case. In three of our families the wives had children with other men before their present free union marriages and were deserted by their "husbands." In addition, daughters in two of the families are deserted mothers. In all cases, except for Guillermo Gutiérrez, the children remain with the mother or her family. This practice is widespread in Mexico and contributes to a matrifocality in family life, particularly among the lower class. If we accept the interpretation of the *casa chica* pattern as evidence of *machismo*, its distribution in these families is in accord with my general impression that *machismo* is much weaker in rural areas than in the cities and weaker among the lower classes than in the middle and upper classes.

In two of the families, the Gómez and the Gutiérrez, the wives have a great deal of influence and use it, although even here they show some subservience to their husbands. It is interesting that in one of these families the husband is impotent and in the other the husband has mild homosexual tendencies. This suggests that in the strongly male-oriented Mexican culture only men who are aging, impotent, homosexual, or "bewitched" are unable to carry out the authoritarian role of the husband. The Gutiérrez family comes closer

17

to an equality of status and power between husband and wife than any of the other families, and significantly this is the only one in which the wife is a major economic support of the family.

A number of Mexican psychiatrists have pointed to the phenomenon of "the absent father" as a crucial characteristic in the psychodynamics of the Mexican family. By this term they refer to a number of things: the many children who grow up without knowing their fathers because of the desertion of women, the high incidence of loss of father due to premature death, particularly during periods of revolution, and the barriers to close emotional bonds between fathers and children due to the authoritarian status of the father. How does this trait of the "absent father" apply to our families? Of the five husbands in our families, two never knew their fathers and three have had poor relations with their fathers. Two of the wives did not know their fathers and only one of the other three wives (Julia) has had a good relationship with her father. All of the husbands and wives of our families have had closer ties with their mothers or substitute mother figures than with their fathers.

In evaluating the relationship between the parents and children in the five families we again find that the children have closer emotional ties to their mothers; however, all the children, except in the Gómez family, respect their fathers and feel affection for them. All the mothers are devoted, sacrificing, and strongly child-oriented. The fathers are more authoritarian, less child-oriented, and, with the exception of Guillermo, spend a great deal of time away from the home, although none of them have abandoned their families for any length of time. This, and other data, suggest that the younger generation in these five families enjoy greater family stability and a longer period of childhood than did their parents.

Our data highlight the sharp discrepancy between the generally low status of women in Mexico and their considerable influence in the family, both on their husbands and their children. The mother figure is a deeply internalized symbol which not only affects a man's relationship with his mother but also carries over to his wife. The result is often an ambiguous position for the son who finds that his closest ties are with the parent of lower status.

## The Setting

In the rapidly changing culture of Mexico with its increasing educational opportunities, the difference between the educational level of parents and children in particular families is one of the most revealing indices of upward mobility and aspiration level. A comparison of the five families shows that three of the mothers are illiterate, one has had three years of schooling, and another four years. Two of the fathers have had only one year of school, two have had four years, and the millionaire has had eight years. However, in all the families some of the children have had or will have had more schooling than their parents. The least improvement in level of education of children over their parents occurs in the Gutiérrez family.

*A Day in a Mexican Village:*

## THE MARTINEZ FAMILY

**CAST OF CHARACTERS**

| | |
|---|---|
| Pedro Martínez, age 59 | *the father* |
| Esperanza Garcia, about 54 | *the mother* |
| Conchita Martínez, age 29 | *the eldest daughter, married and living with her husband, Juan* |
| Felipe Martínez, age 23 | *the eldest son* |
| Martin Martínez, age 22 | *the second son* |
| Ricardo Martínez, age 18 | *the third son* |
| Machrina Martínez, age 17 | *the younger daughter* |
| Moisés Martínez, age 13 | *the youngest son* |
| Herman Martínez, age 7 | *Conchita's illegitimate son* |

# THE MARTINEZ FAMILY

THE ancient highland village of Azteca lay quiet and serene on the mountain slope in the early morning darkness. The air was cool and fresh after the long night rain. Spreading from the top of the slope to the broad valley below, eight barrios, each with its own chapel and patron saint, formed little communities within the larger village. A paved road connecting Azteca with the main highway cut across the village and ended abruptly at the plaza. Here were the municipal building, the central church, the mill, a few small shops, and a bare park. Extending up and down the slope the old terraced streets, laboriously constructed of blue-gray volcanic rock, were lined by small, one-story adobe houses with their patios of semi-tropical plants and trees set behind low stone walls.

In the barrio of San José, halfway between the highest and lowest point in the village, stood the house of Pedro Martínez, almost hidden by the overhanging branches of the native plum trees in his orchard. The tile-roofed house was typical of those in San José, the poorest of the eight barrios, and consisted of one windowless room and an attached kitchen flimsily built of cane stalks. The house site was still called by its pre-Hispanic Nahuatl name, *Tlatlapancan,* or "the place where much was broken," referring to a local legend which told how the village god Azteco, said to be the son of the Virgin Mary, had broken one of his clay toys on this site. Forty-three years before, Pedro had thought the house site would be a propitious one and had bought it for fifty pesos.

Over the years Pedro had carefully worked on the little house and its neglected plot of ground, planting guave, coffee, avocado, hog plums, and other plants, all of which contributed to the family diet. Five years ago he and his sons had built the kitchen and had moved the simple hearth of three large stones from the smoky adobe room to the more airy kitchen where the smoke could filter through the spaces between the cane stalk of the walls. For all of its simplicity, it was the best house Pedro and his wife Esperanza had ever lived in.

It was still dark on this July morning when Esperanza opened her eyes. The house was quiet and no sounds came from the street. Esperanza got out of the hard bed in which she and Pedro slept, smoothed her dress, and wrapped a thin dark blue cotton shawl about her head and shoulders to ward off the morning chill. She walked barefoot across the dirt floor, found the big clay water jug, and dashed some cold water on her face; then she dried herself with the edge of her shawl.

Kneeling at the hearth, Esperanza uncovered the ashes of last night's fire and fanned some still glowing chunks of charcoal into flames. She didn't want to use a match to light the fire for a box of matches cost five centavos and was still a luxury. Now the big clock in the plaza struck four. It was a half hour earlier than she had thought. Well, her daughter Machrina could sleep a little longer. It was the time of year when the men planted and cultivated the corn, and the women had to rise early to prepare food for them. In the winter months, during the harvest, when the men sometimes worked all night and the women had to give them food at any hour, Esperanza and her daughter had to snatch sleep sitting on the low stools. It was only in September and October when the men were harvesting plums that the women could stay in bed as late as six o'clock.

Esperanza filled the clay pot and set the cinnamon tea to boil. Over a hundred *tortillas* had to be made—twenty-five each for Pedro and for Felipe, Martin, and Ricardo, the three oldest sons who worked in the fields, and ten more for Pedro's dog. Esperanza lifted down one of the tin cans hanging from the rafters where she kept her supplies of food. It contained corn which had been ground at the mill the previous night. Before the coming of the mill, a few years back, Esperanza had got up at two in the morning during the farming season to grind soaked corn into a fine dough. Now the mill did most of that work for her; she had only to regrind the dough a bit to make it smoother and to give it the taste of the grinding stone. The men of the village had opposed the corn mill because, they said, hand-ground corn tasted better. But the women had won out; the mill was a success. Yes, it was good to have the mill. But all the same it was expensive. The thirty-four centavos paid to the miller would have bought half enough corn to feed the whole family for a meal. Machrina should do more grinding at home, Esperanza thought as she knelt before the grinding stone.

The first slapping of the *tortillas* into shape caused Pedro to stir, but the reassuring sound lulled him back to sleep. Their bed stood in the far corner of the kitchen behind an improvised wall of empty plum crates. This wall did not protect him from the noises of the kitchen but it did provide some privacy from the grown children, except during the plum season when the crates were used to haul plums. Until a year ago the whole Martínez family had slept in the other room, but Pedro had recently moved the metal, springless bed into the kitchen. It was embarrassing, he had come to realize, to lie down with one's wife in the presence of one's grown children. And the bed, which he had acquired almost as a gift from a soldier he had met when they were both patients in the military hospital, showed off to better advantage in the kitchen.

Pedro's wish for privacy, however, had been partially thwarted when Machrina announced that she too wanted to sleep in the kitchen "since it is not nice for a girl to sleep all alone with her grown brothers." Machrina and little Herman, who had shared her bed since infancy, now slept in a cold and draughty corner of the kitchen. The four sons slept undisturbed in the adobe room.

When the plaza clock struck five Esperanza awakened her daughter who quickly jumped up, fully dressed in a slip, plain cotton dress, and apron, and took her mother's place at the grinding stone. Machrina looked younger than her seventeen years. Her brown hair was parted in the middle and worn in two braids; her face was quiet and serious but during the day, when she chatted with a friend or with her brothers, it was often lighted up by a smile that revealed her tiny, childlike teeth. Now she tucked her bare feet under her short, plump body and began to grind the corn. Esperanza, too, was short and round, but she rarely smiled and her face generally had a drawn, dull expression.

Esperanza next woke Martin since it was his turn to go for water. He slipped into his soiled cotton pants and huaraches, washed his face in the cold water, and without a word shouldered the yoke with the two water cans and left for the fountain. The daily rains now watered the fruit trees and the garden, so Martin had to make only eight trips back and forth to fill the family water jug. In the dry season the boys had to make twenty trips.

Felipe, the eldest son, awoke before Martin had finished his chore. Felipe was the most fastidious member of the family and took longest to dress. At night he took almost all his clothes off under his blanket and hung them on a nail. He brushed his teeth (without toothpaste), washed his face and hands with soap every day, and used a rag to dry himself with instead of his shirttail. He had a small pocket mirror which he let no one else use. All this had come about since Felipe had found a sweetheart, a widow much older than himself. Now, seated on the iron cot frame which supported the *otate*, a hard mat made of bamboo-like stalks placed crosswise and lashed together, Felipe groped for his huaraches. His left eye was blind, due to a childhood fall from a plum tree, and he turned his head in a rather exaggerated manner to see to the left.

As the eldest son, Felipe tried to dominate his brothers and sister, but was generally unsuccessful, particularly with Martin, who was taller and stronger than Felipe and almost the same age. Martin had flatly refused to obey Felipe or to show him the respect due an older brother. For this Felipe blamed his father, who had never permitted him to exercise authority.

Pedro and his third son, Ricardo, were now getting up. Pedro was short and stocky and his paunch bulged as he dressed in his homemade, dirty, patched shirt and white, pyjama-like *calzones*. He slipped his blackened, calloused feet into heavy huaraches cut from an old rubber tire. A sparse, untrimmed mustache covered his upper lip and he almost always looked unshaven. On Saturdays when he bathed and changed into clean clothes or on the days he went to town or to Mexico City, Pedro wore a pair of dark store-bought trousers and looked more sophisticated. He usually wore his straw sombrero tilted down over his eyes, a rather cocky angle for a man of fifty-nine.

Felipe, Martin, and Ricardo all looked like their father and until recently had dressed as he did. Now they wore factory-made shirts which they had demanded, but none of them owned dark trousers. The youngest son and the grandson wore old-style, homemade white *calzones* and shirts, used small sombreros, and always went barefoot.

Esperanza began to serve the men cinnamon tea, *tortillas,* chile, and salt, while Machrina filled four hemp shoulder bags with the same food for their midday meal. She added a handful of acacia pods to each bag and poured tea into four gourds. The men ate quickly, without conversation. Speaking in Nahuatl, Esperanza asked Pedro to bring home some squash for the evening meal. When Ricardo coughed over his food she warned him to wrap himself well in his blanket when they passed by the stream, the abode of *los aires*, the spirits of the air.

The Martínez family had good reason to avoid these malign spirits; some years before Esperanza had become ill with a fever and had suffered a partial paralysis of the legs after having washed clothes in the stream. *Los aires,* as everyone in her village knew, could sometimes take the shape of winds, sometimes spirits, sometimes little malign people who could cause sores, pimples, paralysis, and other illnesses. One had to be on one's guard against offending them near anthills, stream beds, ravines, in stagnant pools, and atop the highest hills. Sometimes it helped to ask their permission in Nahuatl before taking water from a stream, but in any case it was safest not to venture too near them without being well wrapped up. Many men took a morning drink of alcohol to protect them from *los aires* before they started out to the fields, but Pedro preferred to take his when he came home at night.

By five-thirty the men were ready to leave. Each slung a bag and a serape over his shoulder. Pedro called to his dog in Nahuatl, "Now let's go." He used the old tongue with his wife and his dog, but he spoke to the children in Spanish except when he was angry. When Martin, on the other hand, said, "We're going, mamá," it was in Spanish.

The men set off in silence. Pedro walked with his dog a few paces behind the boys. When neighbors saw them walking along in this formation they would say that Pedro looked like a veritable *patrón* striding behind his peons. Yet there were mornings when Pedro talked to the boys in the course of their two-hour walk to the fields, giving advice or telling what work had to be done. The boys, however, spoke only in answer to a question. Out of their father's earshot they would joke about their sweethearts or visits to the saloons of Cuahnahuac. But this morning they moved silently down the road.

It was still barely light. All around them, just beyond the far edges of the fields, the blue-green slopes of the pine-covered mountains rose through the morning mist. Pedro and Ricardo were headed for the mountain slope cornfield which they had cleared the year before. This was communal land belonging to the municipality which consisted of seven villages; anyone could work it. New clearings had to be made every two or three years, for heavy rains washed the topsoil away. To acquire new fields Pedro and his sons burned the brush and weeds, cut down young trees, and built new stone fences. The boys worked well; they had the largest mountain clearing in Azteca. But the crops could supply enough corn and beans for only three or four months. So Pedro had to try other means of earning a living as well—making rope from maguey fiber, selling plums, hiring out his sons as farmhands. One thing he would not do to earn money was to make charcoal for sale, as so many of his neighbors did. This practice, he knew, was wasteful of the precious oak and pine forests and ultimately ruined the land. He had been one of the leaders in the struggle for the preservation of the communal forest lands. So he made charcoal only once a year and only for the use of his family.

Felipe and Martin were on their way to Don Porfirio's fields where they were working as peons. These fields, located on fairly level ground, were cultivated by plow rather than by the ancient *coa* or hoe which Pedro used on his mountain strip. The land was easier to work than the mountain clearing and Don Porfirio was less of a taskmaster than Pedro. So the boys were glad of a chance to work for Don Porfirio and to earn some cash for the family. Pedro could be expected to give them something later on—a new shirt or a sombrero or some pocket money.

When they got to Don Porfirio's field the two older boys left the road. Pedro nodded in parting and walked on in silence with Ricardo, absorbed in his own thoughts. He had sold a mule to Don Gonzalo the day before in order to pay off his debt to Doña Conde, and it infuriated him to think that he had had to sell it for only 300 pesos when it was easily worth 450. And now he had only one mule left. This meant that the boys could bring only half the usual amount of wood down from the mountains and that there would be little left to sell after Esperanza took what she needed. Besides, during the plum season the boys could earn only half of what they had made the year before hauling crates of fruit to the railway station. And at harvest twice as many trips would have to be made to bring the corn down from the fields.

Pedro couldn't remember a time when he hadn't been in debt. Early this past year, after he had come out of the hospital where he had had surgery, he had borrowed 300 pesos from the widow Isabel to pay medical bills. Then, finding his indebtedness to her irksome because she expected free "legal" advice from him, he had borrowed 150 pesos from a wealthy politico to help pay her back, and 300 pesos from Asunción to pay other bills. And all this time he was paying back, at eight per cent monthly interest, a loan of 200 pesos from the previous year. At times it seemed as if he were walking forever in a treadmill of old obligations. "The debt remains; only the creditors change."

For Pedro as for most of the inhabitants of Azteca, getting enough money for food and clothing from one harvest to another was the all-absorbing, never-solved problem. At best Pedro, with the assistance of his wife and sons, earned 2,400 pesos a year ($300 at the 1948 rate of exchange). The boys earned about half of this by hiring out as peons and by gathering and selling firewood. Another third came from plums, rope-making, and corn. A small amount, hardly more than 60 pesos, came from fees the villagers paid to Pedro for going with them to see a lawyer or to attend a court session in Cuahnahuac. Pedro had learned something about legal matters during his years of political activity and had gained the reputation of being "half a lawyer." However, his income from "legal" advice was no greater than that from Esperanza's occasional small sales. Pedro could have doubled his income if he and the boys had worked as peons throughout the year at the local rate of four pesos a day, but he refused to work or permit his sons to work on haciendas which were still a symbol of oppression to him. Steady, year-round work was not available in the village, and in any case Pedro preferred to work as an independent peasant.

It was to become an independent peasant with a parcel of land of his own that Pedro had fought with Zapata in the Revolution. Pedro had worked for others since he was eight years old, first tending cattle for his Uncle Agustín who often beat him, then from age ten until after his marriage as a servant and peon on haciendas where he also had been beaten. Even during the brief, happy period when his mother had brought him and his sister to live with her and their stepfather in the large town of Tepetate and he had entered a public school, Pedro had had to defend himself from his "superiors." At that time he spoke only Nahuatl, the language of the Aztecs, and he would get into fights because his schoolmates called him "Indian," in an insulting manner.

"I did not know how to speak Spanish, but I knew how to fight. Then they would go crying to the teacher and he would come out and give me more strokes. I had a lot of trouble but I really liked school. One day when it was almost time to go home at noon the teacher was out of the room and the boys began to say to me in low voices, "Indian, Indian." I just raised my elbow up a little and hit one of them right where it hurt. Uy! He began to yell and the teacher came running, saying, 'What's going on here?'

"Well, all of them told on me and he hit me twelve times with a stick. Zas! Poor me! He even pushed me around on the floor. He threw me around until I urinated. Then, since it was time to go and the doors were being closed, he took me and made me kneel on a table with my arms stretched out and a stone on each hand. I tell you I was scared. They were leaving me a prisoner! But just as the last teacher was leaving I jumped off that table and began to yell and ran all the way to my house. I told my mother and stepfather what had happened. My mother said, 'Well, you may be ignorant, but you *did* stand up for yourself.' "

Pedro did not finish the first grade and barely learned to read because his stepfather took him out of school to begin to earn eighteen centavos a day at a nearby hacienda. When the Revolution came Pedro was already married and the father of a child; it was natural for him to sympathize with Zapata and he joined the fight. Later, he worked for the improvement of his own village, taking part in the rebuilding, in the new elections, in the local government, in the fight for the conservation of the forests, and in the construction of the road. And old abuses had been ended. The village regained the right to use its communal hillside land and some fortunate peasants received *ejido* land reclaimed from the haciendas. Indebtedness and acute poverty were lessened, the pawning of children as servants was abolished, school attendance increased, and there was more personal freedom. But for Pedro the Revolution was a failure. He believed that he did not live much better than he had under the pre-Revolutionary government of Porfirio Díaz. High prices and the increasing need for cash made life difficult. "What good is it to have freedom if we don't have enough to eat? Before it was the hacienda owners who exploited us, now it's the government and the bankers. It's all the same."

Yes, Pedro felt defeated. For him the Revolution had ended with the death of Zapata. His twenty-five years as a politico had gained him little more than prestige. His laborious effort to teach himself to read and write and to educate his eldest daughter had not "raised up" the family as he had hoped. Even his conversion, fifteen years ago, from Catholicism to Seventh-Day Adventism had left him dissatisfied. Pedro's life had been a search for ideals and causes rather than a struggle for personal aggrandizement. He did not understand the changing times, the money economy, or the business values of post-Revolutionary Mexico. He knew only that he was still a poor, landless peasant who depended heavily upon the labor of his sons to make ends meet.

Pedro was worried because his two older sons had begun to resist his plans for them. Felipe complained that too hard work was ruining his health. He wanted to learn a trade! Martin wanted to become a baker. When he had turned eighteen his godmother had offered to take him as an apprentice in her bakery and he had been eager to accept. Pedro had firmly forbidden it. He needed his sons to work in the fields. But as soon as Martin became of age he apprenticed himself to the godmother without consulting anyone. He had worked for six months without wages, and Pedro had scolded him until Martin wept in desperation. Whenever Martin missed a meal at home Pedro became enraged and shouted, "I don't want you to work for that piece of *tortilla* they give you." He ordered Martin to refuse all food at the bakery and to take his meals in his father's house. When the planting season started Martin returned to work in the fields, but Pedro feared that he intended to go back to the bakery when the harvest was over.

Pedro had different plans for his youngest son, Moisés, who was too delicate to bear up under the life of a peasant. With God's permission and the help of his older sons, Pedro hoped to educate Moisés to be a teacher "or perhaps even a lawyer." Pedro would be happy if one of his children could have a "career." It would benefit the whole family.

The path was lighter now and Pedro came out of his reverie to realize that the walk to his field was nearly over. He caught up with Ricardo and began to tell him just where to begin the weeding for the day.

When the men had gone Esperanza took stock of the day's food supply. There was only a little corn dough left, barely enough for the two boys still asleep, and some chile, cinnamon, sugar, and salt. There was no money because Pedro had used the mule money to buy huaraches for Felipe, a sombrero for himself, and a machete for Ricardo—all badly needed for work in the fields. The rest of the money had gone to the hateful Doña Conde. Where could she borrow now? What small thing could she sell?

These were the questions that faced Esperanza nearly every day. Yesterday's money was usually gone by the next morning except when she put away a small sum in one of her hiding places around the house. Even when Pedro gave her larger sums it would usually be spent quickly, either to repay debts or to buy something they urgently needed. But the really bad times were when there was a serious illness in the family. Then they had to sell nearly everything, sometimes all their young turkeys or a grinding stone, sometimes a mule.

Esperanza wondered from whom she could borrow. She could not ask her cousin Maria for a loan, for she had not paid back the ten pesos borrowed a few days ago. Nor could she approach her Aunt Gloria: she had herself stopped by yesterday to ask for a small loan. There were her neighbors to the right but they had spoken badly about Pedro ever since he had become a politico. Why they were so resentful Esperanza could not see, for his political activity had certainly not made the family "even a little rich." No one else nearby ever had enough money to lend, and Esperanza did not want to borrow a small sum at interest from those who had plenty. It was better to sell the turkey even though it would be a long time before she would be able to buy another baby turkey to raise. Esperanza drank her cinnamon tea and went to look for the bird. It was seven when she put on her shawl, hiding her turkey under it (why should her neighbors know her business?) and left for the barrio of San Martín where she knew of several houses where they ate well.

Machrina went out to the back of the orchard. The younger boys were still asleep and there was no danger that they would spy on her through the bushes as they sometimes did. Like most of the villagers, the Martínez had no toilet and no outhouse. When she came back Machrina washed her hands before she knelt at the grinding stone to begin making *tortillas*. She called sharply to Moisés and Herman and told them to wash. She generally adopted a scolding tone toward the younger boys, particularly to Herman, her special charge. She had taken care of him ever since her sister Conchita had come home from school and given birth to the fatherless boy. Even during the six months when Conchita was nursing him and still stayed at home, it was Machrina (then ten years old) who had carried Herman about, bathed him every three days, swaddled him carefully so that he would grow up to be quiet and well-mannered, and washed his soiled clothes. But during the past few years Machrina had gradually stopped playing with him and picking him up and had begun to scold him often. When he misbehaved she spanked him. It didn't trouble Machrina that Herman now avoided her and seemed to prefer Moisés' company to hers; it was right that he should keep his distance and respect her.

The boys had finished eating and were playing in the patio when Esperanza returned an hour later, still carrying the turkey. While she ate the two *tortillas* Machrina had made for her, she told her daughter she had been offered only two and a half pesos for the turkey. There was nothing to do now but go to Señor Don Porfirio and ask for an advance on the boys' wages.

Before she left again Esperanza reminded Moisés to bring water from the fountain and then to go to school. She sent Herman to her cousin's house to bring back the scissors she had borrowed. Machrina knew her work and needed no instructions. Ever since Esperanza's illness of the year before Machrina had shown that she could be depended upon. To show her family, particularly her father, that she could be depended on seemed in fact to be Machrina's only goal nowadays. She had gone to the local school through the fifth grade and had wanted to become a teacher, or at least a seamstress. But suddenly Pedro took her out of school to help her mother and no one dared say a word in protest. It was true that Esperanza had not been well and that looking after so many men and her little grandson seemed to be too much for her.

Alone now, Machrina folded the blankets on the two beds, then picked up the twig broom and began to sweep the dirt floor. She swept unhurriedly, taking special pains with the corners, for her father noticed whether or not the work was well done. She had often heard him speak, half jokingly, half scornfully, of how ignorant her mother had been when he had married her: "She didn't know how to sew, nor sweep, nor iron, nor wash clothes. She hardly knew how to grind corn or make *tortillas*." Pedro had showed Esperanza how to do much of the housework; he had taught her even how to sweep because at first she always missed the corners. When she had tried to make him his first pair of *calzones* she had had to call in her mother to help. Actually, as Pedro himself knew, this was not Esperanza's fault. Formerly parents did not teach their daughters many domestic skills because girls married very young and the mother-in-law was obliged to teach the daughter-in-law. Esperanza was about fourteen when she married and her mother-in-law was dead.

Machrina went to clean the room where her brothers slept. She folded the blanket and straightened the straw mat on the *otate* shared by Martin and Moisés. The other boys had taken their blankets with them. The blankets were almost the most expensive things in the house; each one had cost about fifty pesos. She then piled up the rough plum crates which served as a bed for Ricardo. For a while he had shared the cot with Felipe, but Felipe had wanted it all to himself and had quarreled and complained so much every time Ricardo lay down on it that he had finally rigged up eight plum crates, two across and four down, to make a bed of his own. With a straw mat and a rag-stuffed pillow under him, and a blanket, this new bed was only a little more uncomfortable than the cot. But the crates were heavy and made more work for Machrina; they had to be piled one upon the other during the day because they took up too much space.

The adobe walls, papered here and there with old newspapers, religious posters, and calendars, had nails jutting out to hold extra clothes and sombreros. The room had little furniture and did not take long to clean. Machrina dusted the wooden chest where her father kept his most prized religious books, a copy of the Constitution of Mexico, and the Civil Code of Morelos that he referred to when neighbors consulted him about legal problems. Here too were kept important papers and a few pieces of good clothing. Machrina lined up against the wall seven stools and two reed chairs that her father had bought in the past few years. Formerly the family had used the plum crates as chairs. She also arranged three small benches that Martin had made when he studied carpentry in a class held by a recent government cultural mission.

Machrina dusted the remaining piece of furniture, a wooden table that had served as an altar when the family was Catholic. It now held small piles of old, worn school texts that Conchita had used when she taught school, some religious pamphlets, and a little frivolous reading matter which Pedro hardly approved of: several sheets of popular songs, the comic books "Chamaco" and "Paquín," and three paper-covered novels which the older children had read and reread. This was more reading matter than could be found in most Aztecan homes. In addition, there was a special pile of six Bibles, one for each member of the family who could read. Machrina carefully dusted these and when she lifted Felipe's copy a folded paper, a note from the widow, fell to the floor. "Widows are bold," she thought as she put back the note. "With no man at home to tell them what to do they can have lovers and go to all the fiestas."

Machrina went back into the kitchen, wiped the low table where Pedro and the three oldest boys ate, and picked up some plum pits from the floor. From force of habit she looked into the table drawer to see if there was a little money there that Esperanza could use for food. There was nothing, not even Pedro's toothpicks or the aspirins that Esperanza took for her headaches.

At half past nine Esperanza returned empty-handed. Don Porfirio had gone to the courthouse and would not be back until about ten. It would have been humiliating to wait for him so Esperanza returned home, sat and talked with her daughter for fifteen minutes, and then climbed the steep hill once more to Don Porfirio's house. At ten-thirty she was back again, this time with four pesos in cash and twelve *cuartillos* of corn which Don Porfirio had given her. Tired from having walked so much, she lay down to rest for half an hour.

Esperanza had noticed that she tired more easily than she used to. Maybe she was getting old, but in truth she could not say what her real age was since her mother had never told her just when she was born. Or perhaps she drank too much alcohol, as her Aunt Gloria thought she did. The tiredness had grown upon her since her long illness of the year before. Perhaps she was being bewitched by some enemy of hers or Pedro's. Pedro, who studied the Bible, had taught her not to believe in that sort of thing unless it was an absolutely clear case of sorcery. She always tried to please her husband, but if it were sorcery should she not go to a *curandero* before it was too late?

While her mother rested Machrina washed the few breakfast dishes, cleaned the grinding stone, and prepared half of the corn by soaking it in water and lime. She revived the fire with a straw fan and placed two iron bars across the hearth to hold the tin can in which the corn would be boiled.

At eleven Esperanza got up and left for the plaza to do the day's marketing. She hurried down the hill, turned left, and walked along an unpaved street heedless of the mud and deep puddles of water left by the daily heavy rains. In fact the water felt good to her bare feet for it was almost noon and the ground was getting hot. At the end of this long street she turned right onto a steep, stone-paved street that was lined with houses, several of which had windows and were smoothly plastered and whitewashed and much finer than any in her barrio. She was now in the larger barrio of San Martín where some well-to-do peasants lived.

Esperanza quickened her step, pulled her shawl more tightly around her shoulders, and, as any good Aztecan wife would, kept her eyes to the ground except for an occasional swift glance when she passed a house or looked up to see who was coming her way. The street was quiet and empty except for a few pigs and chickens. Two women, still in the distance, were returning from the plaza. Esperanza could hear the slapping of *tortillas* in the houses and regretted that she had made such a late start. Her head ached, she was thirsty; and for the first time in a long while she felt that she wanted a drink of alcohol.

Actually, things at home had been peaceful for a time. Pedro had not scolded her since he had taken the widow Eulalia of the barrio of Santo Domingo to the fair two weeks ago. Esperanza had been resentful when Pedro told her to prepare food for the widow and she couldn't hide how she felt when she was serving him his dinner. Pedro had picked up the plate and thrown it at her, food and all, scattering beans and *tortillas* on the floor. And the flow of ugly words that followed! He had said that she was ignorant and he didn't know how he had come to marry her. He needed a woman who could read and write and who was able to earn money—like Eulalia! He said that he was a man and had the right to do what he pleased, that she, being a woman and a very stupid one, would have to bear anything he did or said to her, even if he should decide to bring the widow to live in the same house. Better yet, he would go away with the widow who also knew how to cook and serve him and who would be of more help to him because she was clever. Then Pedro had forced Esperanza to scrape up the beans and eat them while he sat and watched her. After he left she cried and took out her bottle and drank. The children didn't like to see her drink alcohol but sometimes she had to. Three days later Pedro returned and ever since he had been quiet and had not lost his temper. He had brought home some sweet chile, dried cod, salt, and sugar, and everyone had been pleased.

Esperanza knew her husband was hot-tempered and sometimes treated her and the children unjustly. But he was kind too, and she knew he loved her. When they were young he used to console her after he had made her cry by taking her in his arms and saying, "Come on, don't get mad." Yes, she had had a better life with him than with her mother and elder half brother.

"In my house my brother scolded me and my mother hit me and I never talked back. Once I said, 'You hit me so much that I would rather go to my godmother.' My *madrina* liked me a lot and gave me many things. Then my mother hit me more, hard with a rope. I ran out into the street to look for my *madrina's* house. My mother followed me and threw a stone at me. Possibly she just wanted to frighten me for it fell to one side. Later my brother came and defended me. 'Why do you hit her so much?' he said to my mother. I had no liberty whatsoever then. In truth I never went anywhere. Many times people wanted to hire me to watch their children but my brother never wanted me to. He never wanted me even to go to school."

Esperanza had never learned to read or write and could not defend herself when Pedro accused her of being ignorant and stupid. But she would say, "Didn't you know what I was when you sent your mother to ask for me?" Indeed, when Pedro had looked about for a wife he had decided that the young Esperanza, who was virtuous and innocent and poorer than he, was the ideal girl for him. Esperanza had not wanted to marry him or anyone else, but when his mother died and he was left an orphan with no one to make his *tortillas,* she took pity on him and consented.

A few days before the marriage her mother had given her advice: "Now that you are going to marry you must have a different character. Here you have one character but there you must have the character of your husband. If he scolds you, do not answer. If he beats you, bear it because if not your husband is going to say, 'What kind of upbringing did we give?'" Esperanza had followed her mother's advice. "And I was always that way," she thought. "When Pedro hit me I only sat down and cried."

The marriage took place in the village church in 1910. Pedro gave Esperanza the first dress she had ever had (before that she had always worn a blouse and long skirt). He gave her a fifty-centavo piece to spend. He took her to live with him and his aunt in his one-room house.

"I remember the night we married. I was terribly afraid. Pedro still bothers me sometimes when he says jokingly, 'Why were you so frightened that night?' In reality I do not know what it was that troubled me. Chills came over me. I was terribly afraid, for never, never had we spoken to one another. After we ate dinner Pedro's aunt went to bed and so did he. He had gone to bed with his clothes on. He has always done that. I also always go to bed with my clothes on. The aunt told me that for this I had got married and that I should go to bed. I was very afraid and ashamed. Pedro covered me with the blanket and then began to embrace me and touch my breasts. Then he went on top of me. I didn't know what the men did to one, and I said to myself, 'Maybe it's like this.' I felt like crying or going to my mother, but I remembered that they had married me and then I said, 'If I die, I'll die. I have to go through it here even though he kills me.' And I closed my eyes and waited for the worst. Pedro already knew how these things were done because he had even had a daughter by a married woman. I don't remember that I bled, but I know that it hurt a lot, and I didn't cry because there was someone else there and it would make me ashamed if she heard.

"Two weeks later I was still afraid. Little by little one picks up confidence. I didn't even tell anything to my mother. I only told a cousin of my husband. I said: 'Men only play with one. Why do they have to get married?' Then she said, 'That's the way they are and you have to let him.' After about two months I was feeling pleasure and then I began to love my husband."

Esperanza hurried down the street and without slackening her pace said *"Buenos dias"* to two women whom she passed. One of the women was her former *comadre,* the godmother of her little dead son Angel, the last of her children to have been baptized in the Catholic faith. When Pedro turned Protestant all their Catholic *compadres* had broken off the relationship with them. Esperanza had become Protestant because of Pedro's insistence and because "no one recognizes me any more anyway." That had been eighteen years before but it still upset Esperanza to meet her former *comadres* and *compadres*.

Why Pedro, when he was forty years old, had decided to abandon his old faith and incur the wrath of the village, Esperanza had never clearly understood. She was only dimly aware that he had been disillusioned with the Mexican Revolution and that his defeats in the post-Revolutionary political struggles in Azteca had been hard for him to bear. Then several things had happened all at once which led to his conversion. He was given a Bible which seemed to him the great revelation of his life. He treated it "like a saint," and when a Protestant missionary came to the village he was ready to listen to him. One night at a wake he denounced priests and Catholicism to his Uncle Agustín who was a devout Catholic and who, moreover, had treated Pedro cruelly as a child. When Agustín berated Pedro for his anti-Catholicism and taunted him about his ignorance, Pedro vowed to make a serious study of one of the Evangelical faiths. After a year the two met again for a debate which lasted throughout a night, and Pedro argued down this uncle who had once been such an authoritarian figure to him. He told his wife, "I really gave it to him good. I showed him all the lies. I fought my uncle with his own books. I showed him that the dead don't return, that Sunday isn't the day of rest, that baptism is done by immersion, that confession and communion are useful but not if done to another human being, that purgatory and hell are lies, all lies. The saints, too, these pictures before which they cross themselves, it's all a lie." He was so hard on his uncle that "the poor old man even cried."

Then Esperanza, Pedro, and a daughter Rufina fell ill. The villagers interpreted these calamities as his punishment from God and Pedro grew angry. "Now that people are talking so much," he had said, "I'm going to become a Protestant so that they will be speaking the truth. I'm going to take down all the religious pictures and saints we have. In this way once and for all we'll die or we'll be saved."

*41*

Rumor of Pedro's intention to "burn the saints" traveled through the village. Friends and relatives came to protest; other people stopped speaking to the family. This was the beginning of several years of ostracism. The Martínez boys had to sell their firewood in Tepetate; Esperanza went to more distant parts of the village to sell her chickens and eggs. Pedro was once stoned, and when Rufina died her godfather refused to make her coffin. At school the children were shunned or tormented. Conchita's classmates once dragged her by her hair toward the church to force her to kiss the priest's hand, and two boys nearly strangled her with her own braids because, they said, she had been trying to convert them. One rumor which persisted for many years was that Pedro had been seen kneeling before his eldest daughter who stood on a table "like a saint" surrounded by flowers.

Although Esperanza was greatly disturbed when she realized that her husband was approaching conversion, she felt helpless to prevent it. She did nothing but weep and avoid people. Her relatives came and warned her not to leave the religion of their fathers. "Protestantism has just come out," they told her. "It is something new. Besides, Protestants don't believe in God." Pedro's sister urged her to leave Pedro. "It's awful, what he has done," she said, "to remove the saints and have those devils meeting in my mother's house. Leave him and his children and then you'll see how he will leave the Seventh-Day Adventists." But Esperanza had answered, "What can I do? He's the boss."

It had been more difficult for Esperanza to adjust to the change of religion than it had been for Pedro. He had always been ardently interested in religion and as a Catholic had been a prayer-maker and twice a *mayordomo* of the barrio. He was used to going to church often, especially on all the feast days. He had prayed all night on Good Fridays, fasted during Holy Week, and confessed and took communion once a year. When he became an Adventist, he threw himself into it just as passionately, reading and joining a study group, converting others, and conducting services in their home. He even seemed to enjoy standing up against the whole village!

*42*

Esperanza, who believed in a vague mixture of Catholic and pagan concepts, had never been deeply involved in the Christian religion. Once when she needed firewood in a hurry she had burned a cross which Pedro had set up in their patio to protect the house! She actually saw little difference between the new and old Christian faiths and even after her conversion she did not make a clear separation between them. Once, on the Day of the Dead, she "felt sorry for our dead little ones" and put a candle and flowers in the barrio chapel for them. Another time she went to the chapel of San José "to pray to God to give me peace in my home because Pedro was insupportable. And he really did calm down after that." On the whole the conversion brought Esperanza only confusion, inconvenience, and ostracism, and made it less possible for her to find comfort in her old folk beliefs.

The family did benefit, however, from a spiritual change in Pedro and for this reason was able to accept his conversion in spite of the severe social disapproval. Pedro dropped out of politics, stopped drinking, and turned to work and religion. As part of his faith he tried to control his temper and speak humbly in the face of provocation. "If we fight, everyone criticizes us." The family began to eat better and to have a more peaceful domestic life. In fact, at no time was the family so united and contented as during this period when Pedro devoted himself to their physical and spiritual well-being. For his part he was repaid for his efforts by the support and admiration of his children and, to some extent, of his wife.

In recent years Esperanza had been aware that Pedro was slowly but unmistakably drifting back toward Catholicism. He had become disillusioned, little by little, by the behavior of some of his co-religionists. He had hoped that the high moral principles of the Adventists and their emphasis upon brotherhood would give him the trust and love he wanted. The first jolt came when the man who had converted him attempted to seduce his daughter, Conchita, while he was a guest of the family for a night. Pedro also had been hurt by being treated as an inferior by some of the Protestant ministers. One incident had been crucial and stood out as a turning point.

Conchita wanted to study in Mexico City and Pedro had taken her to the city to the home of a Protestant pastor who had promised to give her room and board in exchange for work.

"Conchita had malaria at the time," Pedro said, "but she was so enthusiastic about studying that she wanted to go anyway. So I brought her. It was a two-story house. It was beautiful, like heaven. I only saw it from a distance, like Moses when he went to . . . just from a distance, that's as much as I saw of it. Yes, the house was pretty but they took me into the kitchen and I never got any further than that. That so-and-so treated me like dirt. My poor daughter started right in helping his wife even though she was very sick. I said to her, 'Come on, let's go. I don't like this man's character and you're sick. I can tell he's very harsh and his two children are even worse.' She answered, 'I'm not leaving even though I die here.' Hmmm, what could I do? The pastor invited us to the evening service and said I could sleep there that night. They gave me a cup of coffee and when it was time to go to bed they took Conchita upstairs to sleep on a dirty carpet in their daughter's room. The pastor told me to make myself comfortable in the kitchen. But how could I make myself comfortable? They didn't give me anything, not even an old rug did they throw at me. The floor was made of cement and was still wet from being washed. It was very cold. I thought, 'Caray! Are these people Christians?' That's how I began to lose faith.

"So I said to myself, 'This isn't right but what can I do? I'll stay this once. After all, it means her future.' Well, I suffered through it. I didn't sleep the whole night long. I just sat down on my pack and leaned against the edge of the charcoal burner. As bad luck would have it I had to go to the toilet but I couldn't find a place to go. There was a great big dog outside the kitchen door in the patio and as soon as I opened the door a bit he would start to growl. He was an enormous dog and angry. That was worse. Now I was a prisoner! The animals there were just as bad as their master. God was punishing me, I was really in a fix.

"At about four-thirty in the morning the mother came downstairs to sweep the street. She was so much of an Indian that the children treated her like a servant. Just imagine! The children and the hus-hand sleeping and the poor mother out in the street sprinkling and sweeping. And these people were Christians! The son came into the kitchen at night and didn't even speak to me. Just walked past me. What kind of upbringing do these people have? At five o'clock my daughter came down. She saw me sitting there and said, 'Papá, let's go.' I said, 'Yes, these bourgeois! the kind who won't work!'

"That was the way they treated me. It entered like a big thorn and hurt a lot. That man a Christian? A lie! That man a brother? A lie! I hated him. May God forgive me but I still hate him. I wrote him a strong letter saying, 'You are not a Christian, you are a king bee who doesn't work. You are nourished by the health of the faithful. You are even worse than the priests.'"

After that Pedro participated less in the affairs of the Adventist church, although he continued to attend Saturday services fairly reg‐ ularly. In 1943 he stopped contributing tithes (one-tenth of his crop) to the church. He prayed but no longer underwent penitential fasting. He drifted back into politics and because of politics began to drink again. Also "because of politics," he began to attend wakes and fiestas with his Catholic supporters. He grew more tolerant of Catholicism and in fact took pleasure at being accepted again by the Catholic community. Yet he believed at the same time that his Protestant faith and his high standard of morality had gained him more respect from the villagers than they had had for him before.

But it was too late for Esperanza. She was too far withdrawn from social and community life to pick it up where she had left it eighteen years before. She was unprepared to build anything new. Her con‐ version had been one more traumatic experience in a lifetime of traumas. She would be content, so long as God gave her life, to keep on working for her family, accepting whatever fate brought her and asking for nothing.

From the paved road Esperanza made another left turn and walked quickly past a few more houses, past the park, and across the plaza to the archway where the women waited in the shade to sell their little piles of food. From them Esperanza carefully made her small purchases—one-fourth of a kilo of rice at thirty-five centavos, ten centavos' worth of coffee, fifteen centavos' worth of lard, fifteen centavos for tomatoes, and twenty for chile. The rice and lard were wrapped in little cones of paper which Esperanza placed along with the other articles in the basket which she carried under her shawl. She then went into one of the small dark stores under the archway and bought one-tenth of a liter of drinking alcohol and twenty centavos' worth of kerosene for the lamp. On the way home she stopped at the drugstore for two aspirin.

The noon church bells were ringing when she reached home after the long climb up the hill. Without sitting down to rest she gave the basket of food to Machrina, took up the can of boiled corn, and hurried back to the plaza, this time to the corn mill. The corn was still too hot to be ground but it was already late, and even though the dough would be tough and rubbery it was needed for the noon meal for those at home. Machrina had put aside some corn to cool for the evening meal. It meant another trip to the mill but that was better than giving the men inferior *tortillas*. Like all men, they had bad tempers and had to be served properly.

Esperanza looked expectantly at the mill entrance to see who was waiting there. She enjoyed standing in the long queue; it was one of her few chances to chat with the women she knew. But at this hour the mill was empty and the miller put her corn through the noisy machine without delay.

Machrina was preparing the rice when Moisés came home from school. Without greeting his sister he sought out Herman, who had been playing quietly in the patio all morning. Herman's face lit up when he saw Moisés, but he did not move away from the little pile of stones he had gathered. When Esperanza came in she called to Moisés to take the mule to pasture. This was one of his daily chores. He also brought some water from the fountain every morning, picked fruit for his mother, ran errands, and every afternoon after school he went back to the plaza with a small can of corn for the mill. During school vacations he had more responsible jobs, selling a little corn or wood, cleaning the maguey fiber, and helping his brothers make rope.

Herman also had regular chores since everyone was expected to work. He had to make five daily trips to the fountain with two small water pails, bring in firewood as it was needed, and run errands for Machrina or his grandmother. Herman liked to go with Moisés to pasture the mule and asked Machrina to let him go. She said no because it looked like rain. Herman then appealed to Esperanza, who said yes. Since the food was not quite ready, the boys were sent to pick a few hog plums to stay everyone's hunger. Then, after a lunch of rice, *tortillas*, and coffee, the boys set out with the mule. Machrina shouted to them from the door not to loiter because if they came home wet she was going to hit them.

At one o'clock the two women sat down to eat. Esperanza was too tired to talk about the people she had seen in the plaza and fell asleep, still seated on the low bench. Machrina washed the few dishes and then took a can to fill at the fountain. The men of the barrio had built a new fountain near the house. Machrina was proud of it because it was largely due to her father's efforts that the fountain had been built. He was the only man in the barrio who wanted to advance and who could get things done. It had taken him more than a year to persuade his neighbors to form a *cuatequitl* (a cooperative work party) to build the fountain. Pedro might be poor, but he was a man of importance not only in his own barrio but in the village. Machrina had often heard her father call men who did not take part in politics "stones," "balls of flesh with eyes," or simply "women!" and she judged her neighbors by his standards.

Machrina was too young to remember how the family had suffered because of Pedro's political activity. He had been jailed three times and twice he had had to flee the village for his life. When he worked during elections he forgot his family entirely and left them to shift for themselves. He drank with his friends, had love affairs, and got into debt. That was why Esperanza said that, "Politics only grinds one into dust."

Down the street Machrina saw Elena, the daughter of the widow Gloria, sweeping her patio. Elena put down her twig broom and leaned over the stone wall. "I have something to show you," she said. She pulled a folded letter from her blouse. "A little girl ran over and gave me this letter at the mill this morning. It's a love letter." Love letters were very much prized by the young people in Azteca and severely frowned upon by the adults. This form of courtship, indeed courtship itself, was a recent phenomenon.

"Who sent it?"

"Who knows? There is no name."

Machrina read the letter carefully:

*Most Beautiful Señorita:*

*It is impossible to see you and not to love you and that is what has happened to me. Your beautiful image is engraved on my heart, so deeply do I see you everywhere and, in the same way, I hear your sweet harmonious voice which shatters my whole being. If I contemplate the countryside, it appears to resemble you, so beautiful is it; its odor carries a memory of a divine vision. Upon looking straight at the sun, my eyes become wounded; so do your beautiful eyes equally wound me. When I hear the song of the birds, it seems that I hear your divine voice. I beg only one word of you to indicate that you are not indifferent to the sensations of my heart; tell me this word which will make me think of myself as the happiest man on earth and which will make me fall upon my knees at your feet. If you are utterly disinterested, then I will die little by little as a flower dies on being plucked. But in my agony I shall always say I love you, I adore you.*

"He must be very cultured," Machrina said.

"*Que va?* He probably copied it out of a book." Elena, who was eighteen, had a reputation of being *loca*, crazy about men. The year before she had gone to Cuahnahuac to be a servant in a doctor's house, but it was not long before the doctor's wife had managed to send her back home.

Machrina went on to the fountain to fill her water can. She thought about the letter and wondered whether she would ever receive one like it. And would she ever marry? Machrina was not sure. Where would she meet a young man who was not a Catholic? She would be glad to marry a Protestant and be able to keep her father's religion. If she married a Catholic she would have to become a Catholic and go to church to confess. She didn't want to do that. Better to stay at home with her parents.

When Machrina came home her mother was asleep in bed. Machrina poured the water into the water jug and sat down to read the Bible. The conversation with Elena had somehow disturbed her and reading the Bible made her feel better. She dozed off; with a start she heard the village clock strike three. She got up to sweep the patio and was watering the plants when Esperanza joined her, yawning and combing her hair. Esperanza said there was some mending to do. Without a word Machrina went into the kitchen for needle and thread and brought out the clothes. She always sewed under a tree in the patio because it was too dark to sew in the house. From the patio she could also see what was going on in the street.

Esperanza left to visit Conchita, her oldest daughter. During the morning she had twice passed Conchita's house on the way to the plaza, but she hadn't gone in because Juan, her son-in-law, might still have been home. He had forbidden Conchita to see her family, and Pedro had forbidden anyone in the family to visit Conchita. So Esperanza had to choose her hours carefully.

Conchita's troubles had begun eight years before when she left home to study to become a teacher. She had attended the State Normal School and a lot of money had gone into her education—for books, clothing, and transportation. For three years her father had given up planting and worked as a peon to earn cash for her expenses. Of course the neighbors had been critical from the very beginning. They had warned Pedro that he was striving too high for a poor man. They said that a girl could not be trusted away from home and least of all Conchita, who was "hot-blooded." Pedro ignored them. He had faith in his favorite daughter. Conchita had been born after the first children had died, and for five years she was an only child. Both Esperanza and Pedro had babied her, played with her, and enjoyed her more than they did any of their later children. Pedro gladly spent the money on her schooling in the hope that when she became a teacher she would help raise the economic and social standing of the entire family. Then she had had to come home from her very first position even before she had begun to earn any money. The school principal had made her pregnant.

It was a terrible blow to Pedro. He gave Conchita a merciless beating and did not speak to her for months. But he let her stay home and have her baby. After Herman was born Pedro ignored his presence; even now he seldom spoke to his grandson. Conchita went off to teach again when she was well, and sent home thirty pesos a month to help with expenses. She also brought little gifts from time to time, and everyone liked her for that. Pedro had begun to forgive her too. She had her father's temperament, he said; she couldn't help herself.

About a year before Conchita had first gone away to study, Pedro had met a young man named Juan who was an orphan born out of wedlock and unrecognized by the relatives of both his dead parents. At twenty-two Juan was still a bachelor with no home of his own. Pedro took a liking to the young man and invited him to live with the family for a year. Conchita was fourteen then and soon became Juan's secret sweetheart. The following year Conchita left the village, but for the next ten years she and Juan managed to be together whenever she returned home. Meanwhile he had other sweethearts and began to have children by several women. Conchita too had other sweethearts at school, but she liked Juan best. When her high status as a teacher was diminished by the appearance of Herman, Juan felt that he could ask her to marry him. She agreed, and her father quickly accepted. After a civil marriage ceremony the couple went to live with Juan's married half sister, leaving Herman with his grandparents.

But things had not gone well. Conchita could not adjust herself to being the wife of a peasant and there were many quarrels. When Conchita became pregnant she felt that Juan did not take proper care of her. He refused to hire a servant when the baby was born and she was not able to rest for the traditional forty days. The baby was only a month old when Conchita asked her father to take her home because Juan was neglecting her. Pedro took her home and because of his experience with legal matters he had his son-in-law brought to court on a charge of neglect. All this, of course, caused antagonism between the two men. Conchita later returned to her husband, but he began to get drunk frequently and to beat her. Just before the birth of their second baby he beat her so badly that Pedro took her home again. Pedro said, "While I live, your husband won't abuse you." Again there was a reconciliation and again Conchita became pregnant. Now her husband was even more violent and she went back to her father's house. This time Pedro demanded that Juan pay for the children's maintenance. Juan refused. Pedro had him arrested. Juan charged Conchita with abandonment.

Conchita gave birth to a healthy looking girl who died in a few days. The midwife accused Esperanza of having killed the baby through carelessness—she had attended a wake and then had sat in the kitchen near the baby without first having washed and changed clothing. Juan heard the accusation and refused to go to the child's funeral or to contribute to the expense.

Pedro wanted his daughter to stay home for good, and she seemed to agree. Actually she was not happy in her parents' home. Pedro made her work all the time and sometimes struck her in her children's presence. Conchita got in touch with her husband and he consented to take her back provided she would never again speak to her family. When Pedro came in from the fields one day and found that Conchita and her children were gone, he disowned her in a rage and forbade the rest of the family ever to see her again.

That was why Esperanza had to make secret visits to her daughter nowadays. And not only she: Machrina and the boys visited her too, for everyone missed Conchita at home. She had helped with the housework, had sympathized with her brothers, and had given each of them gifts. From Conchita, Esperanza had received her first silk dress, Machrina her first pair of shoes, Felipe a mirror, Martin a flashlight, Ricardo a pocket comb, Moisés his first toy. And Conchita had never come without a present for her son Herman.

When the dogs announced Esperanza's arrival, Conchita came out of her dark little one-room house with her sons beside her. Her long hair was uncombed, her clothes looked old and torn, and she limped from an infection in her foot. Partly because of her husband's jeal-

51

ousy and partly from pride, Conchita seldom left the house. She preferred to grind corn on her own grinding stone rather than walk to the mill.

"Come, greet your little grandmother," Conchita said to her sons.

With no change in expression each boy walked up to Esperanza, pressed his lips to her outstretched hand, then ran off to the rear of the patio to play among the chickens. Esperanza wiped the back of her hand with her shawl and, still standing, said, "Just imagine, I could not sell the turkey today. They offered only two and a half pesos for it." Conchita went into the house and came out a moment later with a sardine tin full of beans. Esperanza dropped the beans into her shawl and returned the measuring tin. They exchanged a few words, Esperanza said, "Thanks, little daughter," and quickly left.

It was five o'clock, not much time to prepare the beans for the men. At home Esperanza found that Machrina had stirred up the fire and put on the large bean pot full of water. Esperanza picked over the beans, washed them, and dropped them into the boiling water. Machrina went on mending clothes.

At five-thirty Moisés and Herman came back with the mule. Moisés was sent off at once to the mill with the can of boiled corn which this time was properly cooled. Herman went back to play with his pile of stones in the patio. Esperanza put up water for coffee, stirred the beans, added some *epazote* leaves and salt for taste, and prepared a sauce of onion, tomato, and chile to be eaten with the *tortillas*. Then she sat beside her daughter to mend an old shirt. They talked about Conchita, the evening meal, and what new clothing each might receive at harvest time.

When Moisés came back with the ground corn an hour later it was Machrina's turn to get up and make the *tortillas*. She complained that Moisés had taken so long she wouldn't have the *tortillas* ready in time. To make matters worse the corn was poorly ground and would have to be reground by hand. Esperanza went on calmly sewing. "Don't upset yourself, little daughter," she said. "There's no help for it. That's how it is."

Machrina was still grinding corn when her father and three

brothers walked in at seven o'clock. Obviously tired, they went to lie down. Esperanza went to sit on a plum crate beside Pedro's bed, to recount to him her efforts to get money for the day's food. Pedro nodded approvingly when she told him that she had refused to let the turkey go at the low price offered and that she had succeeded in getting an advance on the boys' wages from Don Porfirio. She said nothing about her visit to Conchita and the gift of beans. She complained that her head ached and Pedro told her to go to bed early to avoid getting ill. She got out the alcohol and gave her husband his evening drink; this was to guard him from the ill effects of the winds which had blown against him as he had walked home hot and tired. She too took a short drink and then joined her daughter.

Machrina was kneeling at the grinding stone, working quickly now because the men did not like to be kept waiting long for their meal. She already had a little pile of *tortillas* which she kept warm in a napkin near the hearth. For each *tortilla* Machrina rolled a ball of corn dough between her hands, then slapped it out flat with a quick pat-a-cake movement. She was justly proud of her ability to make fine *tortillas*. When she was only eleven she had made them better than her older sister, and now her father and brothers said that she made them better than her mother.

Esperanza examined the young squash her husband had brought home from the field and prepared it for cooking. By eight o'clock it was done, and by then also Machrina had a large pile of toasted *tortillas*. Esperanza called out, "Pedro, come to eat!" More affectionately she said to the boys, "Come, little fathers, it's ready." Pedro and his sons washed, then straggled into the kitchen one by one, still drying their hands on their shirttails. The four men sat down on low benches on either side of the small table. Esperanza placed a pile of *tortillas* in the center of the table and handed each one a plate of beans. The boys waited for their father to take a *tortilla* before they took one, rolled it, and expertly scooped up mouthfuls of beans with it. The only sounds in the kitchen for some time were the noises of chewing, the slap of Machrina's hands making more hot *tortillas*, the crackle of the fire, and Moisés and Herman laughing in the patio. The older boys had talked and joked with each other in their bedroom, but now they sat eating soberly, as though wrapped in their private thoughts.

Pedro gave full attention to his food but he took everything in with his alert, small eyes. He noticed the pile of unmended clothes, the swept floor, the marketing basket with its little rolled paper packages, the basket of corn from Don Porfirio, and he mentally checked these things with Esperanza's tale of the day. He saw the Bible still opened on Machrina's bed in the corner and for a brief moment he permitted himself to glance affectionately at his youngest daughter. She was a good girl and a serious one, he reflected. She accepted wholeheartedly her father's new religion. She worked hard and was obedient. She might not be as intelligent or well educated as her sister but at least she would stay out of trouble and behave as a woman should. "Little daughter, how good these *tortillas* are!" Pedro said.

Machrina smiled. The boys nodded assent. Esperanza added some hot *tortillas* to the pile. Everyone was at ease for Pedro was in a good mood. There would be no ugly words tonight. Esperanza gave a dish of rice to Pedro, then one to her eldest son. Felipe was annoyed if she served any of his brothers before him. For Martin, her favorite, she spooned out a little more rice. Little was said. While the men drank their coffee Esperanza called to Moisés and Herman to come in, wash their hands, and be quiet. Before eating the two boys greeted Pedro silently, brushing their lips against his outstretched hand. They ate their beans, rice, and squash sitting on the floor near the hearth where Esperanza also sat.

The three older boys left the kitchen as soon as they had finished eating and went to lie down on their cots. They lay talking and laughing together. Moisés and Herman soon followed them. Martin and Felipe took out little bags of candy which they had bought on their way home from work. Machrina, who ate last since she had to keep providing hot *tortillas* for the others, hurried through her meal in order to join them before all the candy was gone. Soon Esperanza and Pedro were left alone in the kitchen. They listened to their children, who were now singing songs from the song sheet that Machrina had borrowed from her friend Elena. Pedro made a move of displeasure.

"Let them sing," Esperanza said. "It makes me feel a little happy." But Pedro went to the boys' room. As soon as his children saw him in the doorway the singing stopped. "There is always High Mass among my poor children when he appears," Esperanza thought.

"Be quiet," Pedro said sternly. "The people will think we are a house of crazy ones. If you want to sing, sing a hymn. Let them see that we take our religion seriously." But when Pedro left there was no more singing. Herman came out and went to bed. Machrina helped her mother with the dishes. Felipe said that he was going out for a walk. Now that he was twenty-three years old he no longer asked his father for permission to go out. Nor did either of his parents demand to know where he was going as they had formerly done. Pedro merely called after him not to stay out late. Felipe did not reply.

At about nine o'clock Machrina climbed into bed and settled herself next to Herman, who was already asleep. She covered her face with the blanket and lay quietly on her back with her legs demurely stretched out before her as her mother had taught her to do when she was a little girl. Pedro and Esperanza sat near the fire occasionally saying something in a low voice. "Do you have money for tomorrow?" asked Pedro. "Who knows if it will be enough?" Esperanza said. They heard the sound of coughing in the other room. "Ricardo has a cough," said Esperanza. "I'll rub his chest with alcohol." She took the bottle and went into the boys' room. A few minutes later she came out. "He says that his lungs hurt. His body is hot. I think the spirits have hit him." Esperanza was worried; for her illness in the family was always a serious matter. She had given birth to twelve children and only six were alive. Their first child had died at eight "of the stomach," the second at eight months of smallpox, the third at two of a scorpion bite. Later two more children, aged seven and three, died "of the stomach." The last child, a daughter born in 1940, had died at ten months of "bronchitis."

Pedro was impatient with his wife. "It's a little thing. Don't make a woman out of him. Just give him some lemon tea and he will be better by tomorrow."

Esperanza stirred up the dying fire and put on the water to boil. She took a candle out with her into the garden and after groping about for a moment came back with a few blades of lemon grass which she dropped into the water. When the tea was ready she added some drinking alcohol and took it to her son. "That will cure him," Pedro said when she returned. But Esperanza said, "He has chills now. Let him stay in bed tomorrow. He is barely eighteen and still but a boy." Pedro looked at her with annoyance. "Be quiet!" he said. "What do you know, woman? When I was ten, I was working like a man, supporting my mother and my sister. He must learn what it means to be a man."

At nine-thirty Felipe walked in. His father said, "Now you are here." Felipe nodded and went to bed. He had never been one to talk much but for the past two weeks he hadn't addressed a word to his father. "He is angry again," observed Esperanza. "Who knows why?" Pedro knew why. It was because of the girl in Mexico City whom Felipe had decided he wanted to marry. He had met the girl only once for a few moments when he and his father had gone to the city to arrange for a sale of plums. She was an Aztecan girl but she had gone to school in Mexico City and was now a "lady of fashion." She wore shoes and stockings all the time and had cut off her braids. But she had smiled at Felipe and although he was a poor country boy he had dared to hope that she liked him. Felipe did not sleep well for a whole week after he had seen her. Finally he had asked his father to arrange the marriage with the girl's family.

Pedro had been against it from the start. "Think well," he had argued. "She lives in the city and we don't know her habits. She might even be a street woman and we wouldn't know." Pedro had really been taken aback by Felipe's request. Nowadays young people arranged their own marriages in secret before their parents were called in to carry out the traditional steps. If the parents objected the young couple usually eloped and made peace with their families later. But Felipe, who had never been fortunate with girls, did not smooth out the path for his father, and Pedro, although he had agreed to ask for the girl's hand, kept putting it off. Sometimes he growled at Felipe, "Do you still want to marry that girl in Mexico City?" He succeeded in turning the whole thing into a joke and Felipe was furious. So now the boy wouldn't speak to his father at all. Pedro did not mind. The financial burden of the wedding, the gifts to the bride and her family, the support of his daughter-in-law while Felipe lived with them—all this would be more than he could manage. In the old days a son might live on with his father and more than repay these expenses by working for him, but nowadays young couples generally moved away after a year, leaving the parents with all their debts. The worst blow of all would be to lose a good worker. So Pedro kept his sons under close watch and saw to it that they worked hard and did not spend much time in the streets with the other young men. He discouraged them from thinking of having a good time or spending money on clothes, diversions, or other vanities. He also discouraged Machrina's attempts to look smart and pretty. Actually, marriage was the last thing he wanted for his children. Esperanza had much the same attitude. If she had needed a daughter-in-law to help take care of the menfolk, it might have been different. But she had a good worker in Machrina.

At ten o'clock Esperanza and Pedro got up from the low kitchen benches and went to bed, carrying a lighted candle. Pedro adjusted the wooden board which served as a door at night to keep out the animals. Without removing their clothes they got into bed and were soon asleep.

*The Casa Grande:*

## THE GOMEZ FAMILY

CAST OF CHARACTERS

| | |
|---|---|
| Agustín Gómez, age 42 | *the father* |
| Rosa Hernández, age 39 | *Agustín's wife* |
| Alberto Gómez, age 20 | *the eldest son* |
| Hector Gómez, age 19 | *the second son* |
| Ester Gómez, age 14 | *the only daughter* |
| Juanito Gómez, age 6 | *the youngest son* |
| Señor Gallardo | *the landlord* |
| Leticia | |
| Carmen | |
| Elena | *friends of Ester* |
| Luz | |

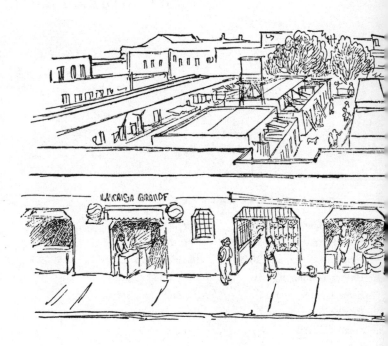

# THE GOMEZ FAMILY

BETWEEN the Street of the Barbers and the Street of the Tinsmiths, only a short distance from the Thieves' Market, stands the Casa Grande. This is a giant *vecindad* or one-story tenement which houses over seven hundred people. Spread out over an entire square block, the Casa Grande is a little world of its own, enclosed by high cement walls on the north and south, and by rows of shops which face the streets on the other two sides. These shops—food stores, a dry cleaner, a glazier, a carpenter, a beauty parlor, together with the neighborhood market and public baths—supply the basic needs of the *vecin-*

*dad* so that many of the tenants, particularly those who come from rural areas, seldom leave the immediate neighborhood and are almost strangers to the rest of Mexico City. This section of the city was once the home of the underworld, and even today people fear to walk in it late at night. But most of the criminal element has moved away and the majority of the residents are poor tradesmen, artisans, and workers.

Two narrow, inconspicuous entrances, each with a high gate, open during the day but locked every night at ten o'clock, lead into the *vecindad* on the east and west sides. Anyone coming or going after hours must ring for the janitor and pay to have the gate opened. The *vecindad* is also protected by its two patron saints, the Virgin of Guadalupe and the Virgin of Zapopan, whose statues stand in glass cases, one at each entrance. Offerings of flowers and candles surround the images and on their skirts are fastened small shiny medals, each a testimonial of a miracle performed for someone in the *vecindad.* Few residents pass the Virgins without some gesture of recognition, be it only a glance or a hurried sign of the Cross.

Within the *vecindad* stretch four long, cement-paved patios, or courtyards, about fifteen feet wide. These are formed by wide rectangular cement buildings divided into 157 one-room apartments, each with a barn-red door which opens onto the patios at regular intervals of about twelve feet. In the daytime, rough wooden ladders stand beside most of the doors, leading to low flat roofs over the kitchen portion of each apartment. These roofs serve many uses and are crowded with lines of laundry, chicken coops, dovecotes, pots of flowers or medicinal herbs, tanks of gas for cooking, and an occasional TV antenna. A few feet back, a higher roof that is less accessible and usually bare rises over the main room.

In the daytime the patios are crowded with people and animals, dogs, turkeys, chickens, and an occasional pig. Children play here because it is safer than the streets. Women queue up for water or shout to each other as they hang up clothes, and street-vendors come in to sell their wares. Every morning a garbageman wheels a large can through the patios to collect each family's refuse. In the afternoons gangs of older boys often take over a patio to play a rough game of soccer. On Sunday nights there is usually an outdoor dance. Within the west entrance is the public bathhouse and a small garden whose few trees and patch of grass serve as a meeting place for young people and a relatively quiet spot where the older men sit and talk or read newspapers. Here also is a one-room shack marked "administration office" where a bulletin lists the names of families who are delinquent in paying their rent.

The tenants of the Casa Grande come from twenty-four of the thirty-two states of the Mexican nation. Some come from as far south as Oaxaca and Yucatan and some from the northern states of Chihuahua and Sinaloa. Most of the families have lived in the *vecindad* for from fifteen to twenty years, some as long as thirty years. Over a third of the households have blood relatives within the *vecindad* and about a fourth are related by marriage and *compadrazgo*. These ties, plus the low, fixed rental and the housing shortage in the city, make for stability. Some families with higher incomes, their small apartments jammed with good furniture and electrical equipment, are waiting for a chance to move to better quarters, but the majority are contented with, indeed proud of, living in the Casa Grande. The sense of community is strong, particularly among the young people who belong to the same gangs, form lifelong friendships, attend the same schools, meet at the same dances held in the patios and frequently marry within the *vecindad*. Adults also have friends whom they visit, go out with, and borrow from. Groups of neighbors organize raffles and *tandas* (informal mutual savings and credit plans), participate in religious pilgrimages together, and together celebrate the festivals of the *vecindad* patron saints, the Christmas *Posadas*, and other holidays.

But these group efforts are occasional; for the most part adults "mind their own business" and try to maintain family privacy. Most doors are kept shut and it is customary to knock and wait for permission to enter when visiting. Some people visit only relatives or *compadres* and actually have entered very few of the apartments. It is not common to invite friends or neighbors in to eat except on formal occasions such as birthday or religious celebrations. Although some neighborly help occurs, especially during emergencies, it is kept at a minimum. Quarrels between families over the mischief of children, street fights between gangs, and personal feuds between boys are not uncommon in the Casa Grande.

The people of the Casa Grande earn their living in a large miscellany of occupations, some of which are carried on within the *vecindad*. Women take in washing or sewing, men are shoemakers, hat cleaners, or vendors of fruit and candy. Others go outside to work in factories or shops or as chauffeurs and small tradesmen. Living standards are low but by no means the lowest in Mexico City, and the people of the neighborhood look upon the Casa Grande as an elegant place.

Number 60, the one-room home of the Gómez family, was the last in the long row in the third courtyard. The latch on the battered door was broken, and the door was held shut at night by placing the ladder against it on the inside. During the day, when the ladder was kept in the patio, the door was usually half-open; Rosa didn't believe in locks because they were "an invitation to thieves."

Inside the dark, windowless room, crowded with furniture, the Gómez family slept huddled under thin covers on a cold January morning. The smells of unwashed feet, sweat, shoe leather, and fried food pervaded the room. Agustín Gómez and his wife Rosa slept on a narrow cot against the right wall, she at the head and he at the foot. Alberto, the eldest son, aged twenty, Ester, the daughter, aged fourteen, and Juanito, the youngest son, aged six, all slept in the big bed which jutted out from the left wall across half the small room. When Agustín and Rosa quarreled, he would leave the narrow cot and exchange places with little Juanito, so that sometimes Ester would awaken in the morning to find that she had been sleeping between her father and her older brother. Rosa was the only one who lamented the crowded sleeping arrangements. She frequently scolded her husband for not building a *tapanco* or balcony, as some of the neighbors had done, so that the boys could sleep "upstairs."

The crowding had been even worse when Hector, their second son, had been at home. But Agustín had thrown him out of the house almost a year ago, and now Hector slept in a tiny room with an old couple in a poorer *vecindad* a few blocks away. Agustín had forbidden his son to come to the house but Rosa had been adamant. "He is my son, not my lover, and he has a right to come here." After that Hector came home for meals and a change of clothing, but Rosa could not count on it because his habits were erratic. If Hector happened to come home when his father was there, they didn't speak to one another.

The kitchen, just inside the front door, formed a passageway to the bedroom. This area had not been roofed when the *vecindad* was built and each tenant had to provide his own roof. Agustín had solved the problem by attaching two sheets of corrugated tar paper to a stick laid across the center, forming a low peak. The front portion was left open to allow smoke from the stove to escape. But it also permitted rain to enter, and during the rainy season the kitchen floor was often wet and sometimes the table had to be moved into the bedroom to keep the food dry. Hanging from the roof as a good luck charm was an infant's shoe that Alberto had found in his bus. On the wall was a calendar with a picture of Marilyn Monroe.

The short left wall of the kitchen was entirely taken up by a gray cement washtub and the toilet. The toilet enclosure, with its half-shutter swinging door, was barely large enough to contain the low, rust-stained stool. It was a flush toilet but the chain had been broken for more than a year and Rosa had not troubled to fix it because there was rarely water in the tank. A pail of water, kept under the washtub, was used to flush the stool a few times a day, and a pile of torn-up newspaper tucked behind the water pipe served as toilet paper. The space was crowded with a collection of rags, cans, brushes, boxes, and bottles piled in a corner. More articles of the same kind, as well as the garbage tin, were stored under the kitchen washtub. Recently, following the example of other tenants, Hector had hung a pink flowered nylon shower curtain to hide the toilet area.

The other side of the kitchen contained the family's most valuable possessions, a new American-made gas range, a white metal cabinet, and a breakfast set consisting of a table and four chairs. Hector and Alberto had presented Rosa with the stove and cabinet on the last

Mother's Day, promising to pay monthly installments of one hundred and twenty-nine pesos for two years. Alberto also undertook to pay for the breakfast set at sixty-four pesos a month. The new furnishings created no small problem in the tiny kitchen. Rosa could not open the oven door without moving the table, which then blocked the front door. But since she used the oven only to store pots and pans and empty soda bottles, it was not too inconvenient. However, there was not enough room to permit the family to eat together.

At four in the morning the alarm clock rang noisily. It was Agustín's turn for the early morning shift on the bus line. He had been a bus driver since he and Rosa had come to the city seventeen years before. They both had been born and raised in the little village of Azteca and Agustín had farmed his widowed mother's land, working occasionally on a nearby sugar plantation. Rosa had hated her mother-in-law, however, and Agustín had found the work of a peasant difficult and unrewarding. Both of them believed that life would be easier in the city and that their children would get a better education. So they had moved to the Casa Grande and Agustín had found a job with one of the private bus lines that serviced the city. Now Alberto too was a driver on the same route.

Agustín let the clock ring itself out, hoping it would wake Rosa. He wanted her to get up and make some hot coffee to wash away the taste of the bitter herb mixture he drank each morning for his diabetes. Rosa did not move. He sat up, roughly pulling the cotton bedspread which covered them. She muttered something angrily, covered herself, and went back to sleep. He sighed. It had been different in Azteca; there a wife knew how to care for her husband.

Agustín groped for his shoes under the bed and stood up. He was fully dressed, for he had come home late and hadn't troubled to remove his clothes. But he had not slept well. During the night he had felt a corpse or a ghost lying on top of him, not permitting him to move. It had been oppressive and had filled him with anxiety. He had been able to move only his arm and with this he had weakly nudged his wife. She didn't wake up and he had to wait until the sensation had passed. Now he stood unshaven, stoop-shouldered, and desperately tired, not wanting to begin the day. His pale face was lined and his light blue eyes, which had always made him popular with the women, were watery and dull. In the morning Agustín felt particularly weak, empty, and unable to carry on. It wasn't until after breakfast, when he was among the other bus drivers in the crowded streets, that he began to feel more alive.

Agustín's poor health had begun five years before when he had been severely burned in a bus accident. His recovery was slow and he had never regained his former strength. His stammer had become worse and he had developed diabetes. But the worst blow, one which often made him want to die, was his sexual impotence. Since the accident Agustín had not once been able to satisfy his wife and she had become ill-tempered and aggressive toward him, accusing him of rejecting her for another woman and tormenting him daily for one thing or another. Agustín believed that low blood pressure, caused by a loss of blood in the accident, had brought about his impotence. Rosa was convinced that another woman had bewitched him.

As a matter of fact, Agustín *had* found another woman, a young girl named Alicia, whose gentle patience and affection were a great comfort to him. He usually visited her twice a week but came home to sleep. Two years before he had managed to impregnate her and he was very pleased with their little son. He had been with Alicia last evening and wondered anxiously if she were satisfied with him. He would try to give her more money for expenses, come what may at home.

Agustín crossed the narrow space between the cot and the foot of the big bed and entered the kitchen, turning on a bare electric light that glared through the open doorway into the bedroom. Ordinarily he used a flashlight; today he wanted to annoy his wife. But the sleepers, their faces covered by blankets, did not stir. Agustín poured a glassful of dark green liquid from a pot on the stove and drank it down, grimacing as he did so. A street curer had prescribed it along with a pint of pulque, and Agustín had faithfully taken both every day for the past six months.

He used the toilet, then looked for a comb on the cluttered back ledge of the washtub that served as kitchen sink. The sink was full of water, for Rosa used it to save water when the landlord turned it on briefly several times a day. Not finding a comb, he dipped his hand in the water and plastered down his hair with his fingers. He rinsed his mouth with clean water from a jug and washed his hands gingerly, drying them on a corner of the tablecloth. He then picked his way through the crowded bedroom to the altar Rosa had improvised in a back corner.

Religious pictures of various sizes were tacked to the pink plaster wall above the altar. A large glass-framed image of the Virgin of Guadalupe hanging in the center was the most imposing. On a shelf beneath it a small red electric light bulb, intended to illuminate the holy pictures, had long since burned out. A short, thick votive candle in a glass jar stood beside it and Agustín noted with annoyance that Rosa had forgotten to light it the night before. She tended to be careless about Catholic ritual, particularly if it involved spending centavos. Agustín was of the opinion that Rosa was more backward and "Indian" than he in religious matters. Like the women in her village she rarely went to confession or took communion. She grumbled about the time her daughter "wasted" attending Mass every Sunday and confessing once a month, and she laughed at little Juanito for kissing the hand of the priest as he had learned in catechism class.

Agustín criticized his wife for not encouraging the children to respect the priest. "That is why our children do not respect us," he told her. "How can they respect their father if they do not even respect the priest?" Rosa disagreed. Besides, she considered herself the more religious of the two for *he* was "the bigger sinner." She too was devoted to the Virgin of Guadalupe and had twice gone barefoot to her shrine. But Rosa's particular devotion was to the Sacred Heart. She kept a picture postcard of the Sacred Heart in her purse and had presented several silver medals to its image in thanks for help in overcoming her terrible jealousy at the infidelities of her husband.

Now Agustín crossed himself before the kindly face of the Virgin of Guadalupe. He had bought this picture himself, paying ten pesos down and five pesos a week. It had been blessed by the priest before he hung it on the wall. Agustín was the only one who prayed before it every day. Hector had once said, jokingly, that the picture of the Virgin was his father's only contribution to the household. Recalling his words, Agustín thought of his son with anger. That bastard! People were calling him a homosexual because of the way he walked and talked. To have an effeminate son was a deep blow to Agustín and he could hardly bear the sight of the boy. And to make matters worse Hector squandered his money. Things would be easier if he contributed to the household expenses as Alberto did. Agustín decided that if Hector would stop interfering in his affairs, ask his forgiveness, and show him some respect, he would allow him to return home.

Wearily, Agustín put on his necktie, wiped the corners of his eyes with his handkerchief, and picked up his leather windbreaker from the kitchen chair. Moving the ladder to one side, he turned out the light, opened the door, and stepped into the patio. He fumbled in his pocket for a twenty-centavo piece as he rang the bell to summon the gatekeeper. While waiting he dropped a centavo piece in the alms box next to the Virgin of Zapopan and crossed himself. The doorkeeper's old wife came to unlock the gate to the street, and with scarcely a greeting Agustín gave her the coin and went out.

The street was dark and Agustín wished that Alberto were with him. When he walked to work alone at this hour, he followed the bus route for security and would gladly have taken the bus for the few blocks if one had come along. He kept to the center of the street, away from the shadowy doorways, and was alert to every sound, looking back nervously over his shoulder from time to time.

Agustín hated his job. The hours were irregular, and the bus he drove was a battered one that frequently needed repairs and caused him to lose many work days every month. Also, the hectic traffic of the capital had begun to frighten him. He didn't react as quickly as he once had and he lived in dread of another accident. He had looked for a different job and was waiting now to hear about getting a position driving a CEIMSA truck. CEIMSA was the government food distribution system and Agustín was confident he would be accepted because he had had a letter of recommendation from a senator who happened to be Rosa's cousin and a native of Azteca.

Agustín had already informed the bus line that he was planning to leave and had put in a claim for the 1,800 pesos they owed him. This money had been deducted from his wages, supposedly to repay a loan from the company. Agustín had had to sign a receipt for the "loan" in order to get the bus job in the first place. He had been willing because they had promised that the money would be returned in full when he left the company. With the money he planned to have his teeth fixed (they needed to be capped with gold), to buy himself a complete suit of clothes with matching jacket and pants for the first time in his life, and perhaps buy something for Alicia and the baby. But now the bus line would give him only 500 pesos, and he was determined to sue them when he got the CEIMSA job. He would hire a lawyer and sue them for all he could get. He had even selected the lawyer, a man from his own village whom he could trust, for were they not both godsons of the same man and therefore spiritual brothers?

A bus approached noisily. As it slowed down, Agustín jumped on the running board, glancing anxiously at the few passengers to see whether any thieves were aboard. Almost every bus carried one or two. They often worked in pairs, and if their pickings were poor, they would turn on the employees of the bus line. The drivers did little about it because they believed the thieves paid the police along the route for protection. Agustín greeted the driver and chatted with him until they reached the terminal where both went into a *café* for coffee.

Back in No. 60 no one stirred until six, when Alberto uncovered his face and sat up. He looked at the clock and jumped out of bed. He was supposed to have his first bus out by six-fifteen. He pulled on his gray cotton work pants and shoes and socks. His driver's uniform was dirty and wrinkled but Rosa hadn't washed his other one. Taking out a pocket comb, he dipped it into the kitchen sink and

*The Gómez Family*

combed his long black hair before a broken mirror on the back of the
door. In the dim light that filtered in from the open spaces in the
roof Alberto peered unhappily at his plump round face. It was covered with pimples that filled him with despair, even though he was
popular with the girls in spite of them. Alberto had been to see two
doctors but the acne had not been helped.

Rosa roused herself. "Son, shall I make coffee?"

"No, mamá, I am late. Bring my breakfast to the terminal, eh?"

"Yes, son, never fear."

Alberto put on his jacket and went out. He didn't bother to shut
the door behind him and waited impatiently for the doorman to unlock the gate. He too tossed the keeper a coin as he left, for the gate
was not opened to free passage until seven.

At seven the crowing of the roosters and a blast of the bathhouse
whistle awakened Ester. She was in the sixth and last grade of the
neighborhood public primary school and had to be there by seven-
thirty. She slipped out of the big bed, leaving only Juanito lost among
the blankets. Ester was looking forward to her graduation and the
long lazy days when she could sleep late. She also hoped to go to
commercial school and learn to be a stenographer so that she could
wear silk stockings and pretty dresses, but her father made no promises. It would cost fifteen pesos a month, plus uniforms, books, and
bus fare, and where would the money come from? Her brothers
would not help her for they both had many other uses for their
money. Rosa had declared she would go back to work in order to give
her daughter two years of "Commercial" but Ester did not place
much hope in that. She was afraid her father would never let Rosa
do it.

Ester put on her school uniform, a blue cotton skirt and a white
blouse, washed her hands and face at the kitchen sink, combed her
hair, and put on a sweater. She had already worn the uniform three
days, but she had no other and her mother washed only once a week.
The sweater was quite new; her mother had bought it on time, paying ten pesos a week. Ester, too, examined her face in the mirror.
She resembled her brother Alberto, even to the acne. Were it not
for her skin condition she would have been quite pretty; her com-

71

plexion was not too dark, her hair was wavy, and she had a nice easy smile. She was fourteen and found it an exciting age.

Her mother had promised her a pink dress of transparent cloth for her graduation and had even hinted at a fifteenth birthday party, with chamberlains and a birthday cake—the dream of all young girls in the *vecindad*. Ester knew it would be too much to expect a dance band or *mariachi* singers; she would be content with a rented record player. She imagined for the twentieth time how she would look dancing the first dance with her father. Her fifteenth birthday would be a turning point in her life for after that she would be a "señorita."

She wondered if her parents would let her dance with boys at the *vecindad* dances on Saturday nights after she had turned fifteen. They were so strict about her seeing boys that one would think they still lived in Azteca! The last time her mother had caught her with a boy friend had been disastrous. Ester had been standing in a doorway with him when she saw her mother hurrying toward them with a group of neighbors. Panic-stricken, she had run toward home while the boy tried to block her mother's way. But Rosa had hit the boy hard and pushed him aside. At home Ester had been promptly beaten by her father who knew from the way she dashed in that something was amiss and did not wait to find out just what. When her mother arrived, she had stopped the beating, saying that Ester had been at Pablo's, a neighbor who was giving a party. Rosa always protected her children from their father even if it meant telling lies. But later, when the women were alone, she had scolded Ester and told her to beware of men, because they "were only good for laying women and then leaving them."

Ester's daydreaming ended abruptly. If she were late she would miss the good breakfast they served at school and would be hungry for the rest of the morning. Two sandwiches, a glass of milk, an egg, a banana, and a chocolate bar were given to the students for only twenty centavos. She hurried out of the house, looking around eagerly to see if any of her friends were in the patio.

It was not until eight-thirty that Rosa sat up and swung her feet to the cold cement floor, feeling for her old black shoes under the bed. Adjusting the wrinkled cotton slip she had slept in, she got

72

behind the wardrobe door to dress. She began to wind a long strip of cloth cut from a flour bag tightly around her hips and protruding abdomen. This binding was one of the few village customs of dress which Rosa still followed. She hoped someday to buy a "real girdle," as well as a fitted brassière instead of the flat one that she now put on. She slipped into a red cotton skirt and a pink nylon blouse, over which she threw a yellow wool *rebozo* or shawl to keep herself warm. Smoothing her hair with her hands she entered the kitchen.

Rosa was a sturdy woman with strong features and a deep, hearty laugh, who moved and spoke with energy and directness. She looked older than her thirty-nine years. Fat shoulders and arms, a short neck, and heavy bulging breasts made her look powerful. She was dark-skinned, with dark brown hair and almost black circles under her eyes. The rest of her face was covered with freckles and pockmarks. She was usually very talkative and she dominated her whole family even though she claimed that she could no longer control her sons and was afraid of her husband's temper. Her main complaint was that the men of the family gave her too little money to run the house and gave it irregularly. As a result she often threatened to go back to work. She had worked as a waitress for two years when Agustín was burned and knew that she could get her old job back.

Rosa set the heavy ladder outside the front door. The patio was still deserted except for the janitress who was sweeping in the distance and some ducks waddling about. Here and there a door opened along the courtyard to let out a dog or a cat. Rosa kept no pets, not even a bird, because they were "a trouble and an expense." But she did keep pots of herbs on the roof—mint, *santa maria*, rosemary, and camomile—which she used for cooking and curing.

Returning to the kitchen, Rosa tied on an apron and automatically began piling up the dirty dishes left from the night before. She washed them with a pad of straw fiber and a bar of cheap soap, rinsing them in the sink. No water came when she turned on the faucet. One could never tell what time of day the water would be turned on, and Rosa often kept the faucet open in order not to miss it. She did not consider this a hardship for in Azteca no one, at the time she had lived there, had a kitchen sink or a faucet and every drop of water had to be hauled from a street fountain. Here in the Casa Grande she had her own sink and there was an outside faucet in the next patio where she and Ester could easily get clean water for drinking and cooking.

The dishes and pots washed and the table cleared, Rosa took the aluminum pot that contained Agustín's medicinal herbs and drained the tea into a clay jug. "*Hijo,* how fast this medicine goes! I have to keep making it," she said to herself. "And to think that I have to carry it to him." Whenever she spoke of her husband, a note of contempt crept into her voice. She washed the pot and emptied yesterday's leftover coffee into it. Adding more water, she set the coffee on to boil. There was still plenty of time to make breakfast; Juanito did not leave for school until the afternoon session at one.

Rosa decided to comb her hair before going for the milk. "If I don't comb my hair now I have no time later." She went to the bed where Juanito was sleeping and tried to draw from under his head a heavy blue cloth that protected the pillow from brilliantine. "Lift your head just a bit, son." She pulled the cloth out and put it on her shoulders. At the kitchen sink she wet her hair and dried it on the blue cloth, then painstakingly undid all the curls of her permanent wave. As she combed them into place again, she fastened each one down with a bobby pin. Finally, she rubbed her face with the cloth and put on lipstick, smoothing it out with her little finger and rubbing some of it on her cheeks.

While doing all this, Rosa had kept walking back and forth between bedroom and kitchen, now looking into the pot on the stove, now putting some cups in the cupboard, now hanging up the clothing scattered on chairs and beds. When she was ready she turned off the flame under the coffeepot, took up her lavender plastic purse and a clay jar for the milk, and left for the store.

The patio had become more lively. Doors were open, bird cages had been hung outside on nails, and women could be seen here and there combing their hair or shaking a blanket. Rosa could hear the slapping of *tortillas* into shape for some women still made them at home. For her part she was "through with slavery" and bought ready-made ones despite the protests of her husband and sons. On

74

the two-block walk to the store she met and greeted several neighbors out on similar errands. The women walked unhurriedly, some dragging a sleepy child by the arm, others carrying infants under their shawls. Rosa did not pause to chat for unlike many women in the *vecindad* she kept to herself. She liked sociability and gossip as much as anyone but she was convinced that it always led to trouble. In Azteca village, she had learned to mind her own business and keep her affairs within the family. For this reason she did not have many friends, and in all the time they had lived in the Casa Grande not one of the tenants had invited her and Agustín to become their *compadres*.

But in spite of herself Rosa got into quarrels with neighbors because of her children whom she always defended whether they were at fault or not. Just last week she had had trouble with the "butcher women." Eutikia, one of the butcher's wives, had started the trouble because her daughter had allowed Ester to hold her gold chain and Ester had lost it. Rosa could not see why she should pay for the chain. Was it not Eutikia's daughter's mistake to have entrusted such a valuable thing to Ester? But Eutikia and her two sisters, who were also married to butchers, were dangerous to tangle with! They had dirty mouths and were quick to use their hands. Everyone was afraid of them—they were known to fight with knives! Now Eutikia and her sisters were calling Rosa and Ester thieves. There had been many accusations and vulgar words, and it had almost come to blows. The butcher women also accused Rosa of pampering Juanito and of letting him take other children's toys. "They are envious because he has a few toys! If a boy finds a toy once in a while is that a reason to call him a thief?" Rosa bristled at the memory of this argument, but she was afraid of the butcher women just the same. These women were tough and they had it in for her.

At the store Rosa bought a liter of milk which the storekeeper poured into her jar. She then moved on to a stand near the entrance of the Casa Grande where she bought a quarter pound of freshly ground coffee. The family preferred coffee from their village but she had used up her supply and would not get more until the end of the month when they went to Azteca for the carnival. She was about to leave when a woman seated on the sidewalk near the coffee stand called, "Don't you want *tortillas?*" "Ah, yes, I almost forgot." Rosa asked for two dozen and both women counted carefully as the vendor picked up the *tortillas* from the large basket beside her on the walk.

Hurrying back to the *vecindad*, Rosa pushed open her door to find Juanito sitting on the floor putting on his shoes. He had already pulled on his worn cotton pants and buttoned his blue shirt. Rosa put her purchases on the table and Juanito came running, a shoe in one hand and a sock in the other, to see what she had bought. Ignoring him, she lit the stove, set the jar of milk to boil, and began to heat the coffee again. Juanito lost interest and sat down on a chair to get into his sock and shoe, then wandered out to the patio, untied shoelaces dangling. Rosa added a spoonful of fresh coffee to the pot and began to grind some leftover chile. In the midst of her grinding she left the stone mortar to go to the sink and wash the rag she used to clean the stove. Meanwhile Juanito had found the patio empty of friends and had returned to sit down at the table. Resting his chin on his hands, he watched his mother.

At nine-twenty the door opened quickly and in walked Hector, his jacket carelessly draped over his shoulders. Rosa turned to greet him, "Look at you!" Hector smiled and walked toward the wardrobe. "Mamá, do I have a clean shirt?" he called, searching in the closet. Rosa answered, "I don't know, son," and wiped the top of the stove. She kept bumping into Juanito as she walked back and forth from stove to sink and finally she pushed him aside. "Move over, son, we can't all fit here." Juanito obeyed and went to stand close to Hector who was putting on a black-striped shirt in front of the mirror. "Look, mamá, I come up to his armpit," Juanito said. Rosa laughed, "Listen to him— Oh, I thought he said, 'I smell his armpits.'" She went on laughing as she carried clean plates from the sink to the table.

Hector went into the toilet, pulling the curtain and closing the shutter door after him. Juanito grinned when he heard his brother urinating but stopped at a frown from his mother. She had tried to teach her children to ignore the sounds from the toilet and was angry when they joked about them even though she sometimes did herself. The presence of a toilet inside their home had seemed strange to the family at first and even indecent. In the village the custom had been to relieve oneself at a distance from the house, usually at the back of the orchard. But having a toilet at all was the source of much pride; in Azteca even the wealthiest had neither toilet nor outhouse. Rosa's sense of decency made her forbid anyone to use the toilet while the family was eating, but this was a rule she found difficult to enforce. Everyone seemed to eat at different times and urgent needs could not be postponed. But if there were visitors in the house, the family preferred to wait, if possible, or to use a neighbor's toilet.

Delicacy did not prevent Rosa, however, from conversing with Hector through the flimsy door. "Yesterday," she said, "Leticia of No. 29 came in and said to me, 'Señora, may I use your toilet?' I let her and when she came out she said, 'It's a joy to go in there, it's so clean.'" Rosa laughed. "She's a cute little thing. That's why I tell Ester to wash it every day. That's how it stays clean. It won't embarrass people who go in, don't you think?"

Hector made no comment. He came out buttoning his pants and went to stand in the front doorway, watching Juanito playing in the patio with a kite he had made.

"Why didn't you come yesterday, disheveled one?" Rosa demanded.

"I couldn't."

"Good God! You couldn't, you couldn't! You and your dates, eh?" Her arms crossed in characteristic fashion, Rosa looked affectionately at her son. He was nineteen, of medium height, and darkskinned, with rather fine, small features. His face had a bright, alert, impudent expression, he talked quickly in a high voice, and walked girlishly. Lately a small, dark line of hair had appeared above his upper lip and he referred to it as his "mustache." His dark hair was brushed straight back and kept in place with heavy applications of brilliantine. Meticulously clean, he wore neatly pressed wool trousers, fresh shirts, and well-polished shoes. His fastidiousness contributed to his reputation for effeminacy which so disturbed his father.

His parents denied the rumors that Hector was a homosexual but they did believe that his testicles had been damaged when he was thirteen by a severe kick during a street fight. Hector cared little what was said about him and devoted himself to dancing, fine clothes, and gaiety. As a matter of fact, he regularly had sexual relations with women, but not more than once or twice a month because he "didn't want to use himself up." He was also afraid of contracting a venereal disease and chose his women carefully. The one he preferred was a woman five years his senior whom he had known a long time. It was she who had initiated him to sex when he was fourteen.

Hector made friends easily and was often invited to parties, dances, and movies. He went only to first-class movie houses and liked to have coffee and *churros* in elegant restaurants on the Reforma. His schooling had ended with the fifth grade but somehow he had made friends among the students at the *Politécnico* College and was proud that they invited him to their homes. He made a conscious effort to improve his speech and vocabulary and sometimes used "big" words incorrectly. He loved to impress his friends in the *vecindad* and also new acquaintances with the importance of his connections. He boasted that his employers invited him to eat with them, that he had a friend who owned a car and another who was a lawyer, that he had a charge account at a large department store, that he had been to Acapulco, and so on. He had, in fact, taken many trips and excursions with friends and had spent two weeks vacationing in Acapulco. Periodically he would save up a sum of money, leave his job, and go off somewhere until his money was spent.

In contrast to his outer appearance and behavior, Hector lived in squalor with the old couple who had befriended him. Their home was a tiny, cavelike room in one of the poorest *vecindades* of the neighborhood. They gave Hector their bed and slept on the floor, but he had to cover himself with a dirty, torn blanket and sleep without sheets. For a pillow he used a rolled-up coat. He did not mind, but he would not have dreamed of inviting his fine friends to visit him there or even at his family's home. Despite the kindness of the old couple and his promise to pay the monthly electric bill in lieu of rent, he had not done so, not even once. Señora Guadalupe complained to Rosa about this and also said that Hector was ruining her mattress. She wanted him to leave but lacked the courage to order him to go.

Rosa "minded her own business" and made no attempt to make Hector fulfill his obligations. As usual, she covered up his blunders and bad manners. Nor did she try to change his condescending attitude toward his brothers and sister or his lack of respect for his father. Though she admitted he was a rascal, he was her favorite because he was "so nice and affectionate" to her. When Hector lost his temper with Rosa he always made up for it with a gift. It was he who bought all of her clothes and whatever little conveniences she had. Once Agustín found a pair of new high-heeled shoes in a box in the wardrobe and accused her of having a lover who "gave her things." She had a good laugh when her "lover" turned out to be Hector, though Agustín suspected that the two of them were in league to deceive him. More than once Hector had defended his mother from his father's blows. This interference so enraged Agustín that once he had beaten Hector with a stick and once he had called in the police and accused his son of attacking him. But Hector's protection did act as a deterrent to Agustín, and for this Rosa was grateful. "Yes," she often thought, "in my family Hector loves me the most. If only he weren't such a stubborn mule!"

Now Hector turned to his mother. "No, mamá, I couldn't come yesterday because I went downtown to buy a shirt. I was in God-knows-what lousy rich street, and they showed me some lovely shirts—but guess how much? One hundred eighty pesos! How was I going to give them so much? And they were no better than that one there." Hector pointed to a shirt hanging on the back of a chair.

"I too went shopping yesterday," Rosa announced, sitting down. "I took Angélica from No. 21 to buy a dress. She asked me to go with her. First we went to all the cheapest stores, around Tacuba, but she didn't like anything so I took her to the Palace." Rosa began to laugh. "We went all through the store and even went on that big caterpillar. That's the thing you just have to put your feet on and it carries you up. I didn't want to at first. Imagine! Angélica didn't know what to do." Rosa laughed heartily.

"Oh, mother, always being ridiculous."

"But I wasn't. It wasn't only me. Another lady didn't want to go up either." She laughed again. "The other lady said, 'I won't go on that, it looks awful.' And I didn't want to go on it either. So what?" This time Hector laughed along with his mother.

"Listen," Rosa went on, "do you know Angélica doesn't even know how to get around the streets as well as I? I had to keep saying, 'Now, let's go here. Now, let's go there.' Angélica just said, 'Where do we go now?' Well, she said she wanted a good dress and they showed her a very expensive one—five hundred pesos. We offered one hundred and forty pesos. That was all we had with us but they didn't want it. No, things cost a fortune in that store. They're crazy if they think I'm going to spend so much for a rag to put on. Never, not a chance. But Angélica—she said she wanted a good dress."

"And finally she didn't buy it?" asked Hector.

"How in the world, if they're so expensive?" Rosa stood up, saying, "Come on, boy, let's have some breakfast." Hector sat down at the table and Rosa started to serve him some leftover *huazontles* (the flower of a wild green which Rosa fried with cheese in egg batter).

"Ay, no! How horrible. Don't give me that! Give it to some Indian, not to me."

"Well, then, delicate one, what shall I give you?" Rosa said good-humoredly. "Would you like a little rice?"

"Yes, that's more like it. But not much, my little stomach is delicate."

Juanito rushed in and Hector stood up to let him pass. The boy rummaged in his box of toys under the bed for a moment and then pushed his way by his older brother once more. Hector sat on the bed to avoid being disturbed, and his mother gave him a plate of rice and a cup of coffee with milk. She had put the rice on the plate which had held the *huazontles* and Hector made a face.

"Ay. So you won't have to dirty another one of your filthy plates!"

Rosa laughed. "Well, didn't you say you eat little? Then why use many plates?" She picked up an almost empty jar and showed it to her son.

"Let's see if you will bring me a kilo of sugar because I have no more."

"Yes, yes, just see, there is no more," Hector said, mimicking his mother. He looked at the clock and jumped up. "It's nine-thirty already and I am still here. Oh, mother of mine, I am going." But he went instead to the stove where his mother was toasting some *tortillas* and helped himself to one.

"I have to bring breakfast to both of them today." Rosa did not like to carry meals to her husband and son at the bus terminal, especially when she had to wait for them to come in from their routes.

Juanito ran in to eat, but Hector asked him to go to a friend's house for a jacket Hector had lent him. "Tell them I said to give it to you because I need it." Rosa told Juanito to put something on because it was cold but he paid no attention and ran out. Hector asked for more coffee and *tortillas*.

Rosa began to take jars and dishes out of the closet. She was searching for the cover for the casserole. She found it finally inside the oven and covered the *huazontles* which she had reheated in chile sauce. Juanito came back with the jacket.

"Mamá, mamá, I saw papá," he said. "He was over there by the Social Security building."

"Ah! the hell!" Rosa said disgustedly. "Did you yell to him?"

"No, because he was in a big hurry and if I call him he always scolds me."

Rosa decided to eat before her husband came home and served herself a plate of *huazontles* and a cup of coffee. She stood near the stove toasting *tortillas* while she ate.

"Look how this house is in the morning," she said to Hector. "I get up like crazy to clean. There are things to do all day. You should see how Rufelia in No. 70 spends her mornings. If you happen to walk in there you don't know where to begin, diapers here, diapers there. When I had diapers I couldn't stand to leave them around. I had a special box where I used to throw them."

Hector stood up. "I'm going now. God knows what time I'll get there." He smiled at his mother and walked out.

Juanito asked him for ten centavos but Hector refused. Juanito then came in and asked his mother for the money. She gave it to him, saying, "Buy yourself some bread." But he rushed out and came back with a little jar of paint. "Look, mamá, for my soldiers," he said, and disappeared under the bed. When he reappeared to sit at the kitchen table where his mother was now eating, he asked for coffee and objected when his mother gave him rice.

"You went and spent ten centavos. Now eat." Rosa was annoyed because Juanito had spent his money on paint instead of food and was now punishing him by forcing him to eat.

Rosa bit into a strong, green chile and helped herself to rice. She ate unhurriedly, half-listening to what her son was saying about the film he had seen on television the week before. Every Friday evening and sometimes on Saturday and Sunday he and Ester went to one of the neighbors to watch television. They paid from twenty to fifty centavos for this privilege and stayed until the stations stopped broadcasting at about midnight. Competition for customers was keen among owners of TV sets. At one time there had been only a few sets in the *vecindad;* people had flocked to watch them and the owners sometimes earned enough to meet their monthly payment on the set or to pay the electric light bill. Now that there were many sets, some owners offered customers free potato chips or candy and let them remain as long as they liked. Rosa always sent her children to the house that offered the most.

Their favorite programs were "El teatro Nescafé," "El programa de Max Factor," "Pedro Vargas," and "El conde de Monte Cristo." Juanito liked the cartoons, "El cluk Indito" and "Boston Blackie." Rosa could not watch TV often because she had to be home to serve the men and guard the house. She envied those who had a set and often mentioned that half of them were three months behind in rent. Nevertheless she believed it well worth going into debt for. If she could see the dramas, the new hair and dress styles, and the way other people lived she would not feel so shut in. She also believed that TV had a beneficial and educational effect on the children. And it might even keep her husband at home more. Rosa had noticed that men with sets spent long hours at home watching games and boxing matches.

Rosa was aware of the way life in the *vecindad* had changed in recent years. Since the coming of television people stayed up later. Previously, children and young girls had not been allowed out after dark and most families went to bed at about ten o'clock. Now people no longer listened to their radios as much or went to the movies as often; children spent more time indoors. Girls dressed more in style and more things were bought on the installment plan as a result of television advertising. People also had new ideas—a neighbor's daughter wanted to become a ballet dancer after she had seen a dance group on TV.

The electric record player too had brought changes. Now every Sunday night and also on special occasions dances were held in the *vecindad* courtyards, and boys and girls danced to American, Cuban, and Mexican records until one or two in the morning! Hector liked to organize dances and as a result many of them were held outside the Gómez house where Rosa could sit and watch. Agustín did not permit her to dance. Ester was allowed to dance only with other girls but lately Rosa had caught her dancing with boys. Ester was growing up and Rosa would have to keep a sharper eye on her. She did not want her daughter to have a sweetheart like the other shameless girls of the *vecindad,* many of whom became pregnant and never married.

"Mamá, is it t-t-true that Jorge Negrete ha-ha-had many w-w-w-wives?" Juanito was stammering badly because he had talked so much. "That's enough chatter now," Rosa said. "You still haven't finished eating. Go on, you're just staring at your plate."

"Mamá, I'm not hungry."

"Oh, yes? Why did you waste your money? Now you eat!"

Like his father, Juanito stammered. He had done this from babyhood and Rosa believed that it was because a tragedy had occurred while she was pregnant with him. She and Agustín had had another daughter, Conchita, younger than Ester. When Conchita was seven, she was run down by a car on her way home from school. She hadn't seemed to be badly hurt but in the weeks that followed she became "very thin and sad." Rosa took her to the Children's Hospital, but the doctors could not say what was wrong. After a few months Conchita died. Rosa could not get over the loss and had cried for a long time. She had wanted to bury the child in her home village but it was too expensive.

Every year on November 1, the Day of the Dead for Children, Rosa prepared a special meal for her dead daughter. This year she had felt particularly sad as she got together Conchita's offering. She had been unable to buy the food in advance because Alberto had not received his wages in time and Agustín had come home drunk without a centavo in his pocket. He had sat at the kitchen table all morning asleep with his head in his hands. By ten o'clock Rosa had only a few of the things she needed; finally she borrowed money from her *comadre* and hurried to the market, for the dead were said to arrive at three o'clock. She was satisfied when the offering was completed even though it was not as elaborate as the ones she had made in Azteca.

On a white cloth on the dresser she placed a votive candle in a new plate (all utensils had to be new), two little pink and white skulls made of sugar "since the dead are skulls too," sweet bread and candy, and two cups of hot milk and rice. She stood the picture of the Virgin of Guadalupe on the sewing machine and surrounded it with bananas, a *jicama,* bread and *tortillas,* a plate of limes, glasses of milk and water, flowers, and candles. Under the dresser there was some copal incense burning in a bowl of charcoal. The flowers were *zempazuchitl,* the traditional yellow flowers of the dead, the water and milk were to quench the thirst of the dead soul, and the two candles were to light the way back to heaven. Otherwise the child would have to use her own finger as a taper.

After she had arranged the offering Hector had come in noisily to say he was going to a dance in the next patio. Rosa had been angry. If he had to dance on the Day of the Dead, he ought to do it somewhere else, not in the Casa Grande, because the dead ones would be visiting and would not like to hear the music. "For them the rosary would be better on this day. They are saints and not sinners like us," she had told her son. But he had just laughed at her and had run off to the dance. He didn't share her "beliefs." Ester had spent the day in the streets with her friends, Alberto was driving

his bus, and Agustín had gone off somewhere. Only Juanito had been
with his mother when she stood before the altar and said, "Here is
your offering, daughter Conchita."

It gave Rosa some satisfaction that at least Juanito had respect
for the dead. She had often described to him how the Day was cele-
brated in her village "where it was nicer because everybody believed
the same way." And she had taught him from the time he could understand that he must not touch the offering "because it burned"
and was pleased that he was still afraid to touch it. The day after
the Dead had visited and had taken the "essence" of the food, the
family was permitted to eat the offerings which, they said, tasted
sweeter than usual. But Rosa had to reassure Juanito that it would
no longer burn him.

The second day of November was the Day of the Dead for Adults.
Rosa set out a simpler offering for her father and father-in-law—only
candles, a glass of water, and candy skulls—because these ghosts
went first to their homes in Azteca where a big offering was prepared for them. This year Rosa had gone alone by bus in the afternoon to lay the *zempazuchitl* flowers on her daughter's grave. At
night there had been another dance in the courtyard of the Casa
Grande and a noisy carnival in the street. It showed a lack of respect for the dead that worried Rosa, especially when her own
children were among the scoffers and sinners.

While his mother was thinking about these matters, Juanito had
climbed up on a chair to reach the broken mirror on the door. Rosa
noticed him. "Go on, break it! Break it!" Juanito put it back and
went to the table again. Rosa was finishing her coffee. "Good! That
was a fine breakfast!" she said. From a paper bag in the cabinet
she took a few small pieces of clay and put one in her mouth. "These
are the blessed ones I bought at the Villa," she said to Juanito. Rosa
had a taste for chewing clay and often had a piece in her mouth.
Now she began to prepare a basket of food for her husband and son.
"How am I going to take that coffee? It'll probably spill." She
washed her hands, rinsed an empty soda bottle, and filled it with
sweetened coffee and milk. She wrapped a dozen hot *tortillas* in
two cloth napkins and placed them at the bottom of the basket with

two spoons, two dishes, a small casserole of *huazontles,* and the bottle of coffee. As she changed into a pair of red shoes and replaced her *rebozo* with a gold-colored sweater, she gave Juanito a stream of instructions.

"Finish your breakfast . . . don't go out . . . guard the house. Your father won't come anymore but if Beto comes and asks for breakfast, tell him I'm taking it over and he mustn't go without leaving me some money. He can't give it to me if he spends it. Show him the purse so he will believe you." Juanito nodded to everything his mother said. At ten twenty-five she left for the bus terminal.


Rosa did not return until almost twelve o'clock. Throwing her sweater on the cot and placing the straw basket on the table, she quickly moved the dirty dishes to the sink. "This housework is a nuisance," she said aloud as she headed for the patio to get a pail of water. Juanito was playing on the roof and she called, "Come on down, Shorty." When he didn't answer, she put the pail down. "What's that boy doing up there?" She went back in the house to change into her old shoes. "Ay! My God! Just seeing this mess gives me the chills."

Forgetting about the water, she removed the faded, purple flowered spread from the big bed, shook the sheets, and made the bed, then carefully placed two embroidered cushions on top of the pillows. Ester had made the cushions for Mother's Day when she was in the fifth grade and Rosa prized them highly and allowed no one to sleep on them. Both had the same design: flowers and fruit and a bluebird in flight holding in its beak a ribbon on which was inscribed "Amor Mio." Rosa patted the cushions, then pulled at the bedding on the cot, shaking her head in exasperation at the holes in the mattress where cotton stuffing was falling out. She took a needle and thread to sew up the tears but new holes kept appearing and she realized the mattress was beyond repair.

She had asked Agustín and her sons to buy a new cot and mattress, but they had said they did not have the money. Rosa knew that her sons were carrying a heavy burden of debt. In addition to the kitchen furniture, Hector was paying forty eight pesos a month for the radio, which was now in the pawnshop, and he had promised to buy a television set as soon as the radio was paid for. Rosa could not blame her sons. If it had not been for them she would still be keeping house with the run-down furniture she had scraped together when they first came to the Casa Grande. Just last year she was still cooking on a kerosene stove and had no aluminum pots—only clay or enamelware. No, she thought, it was her husband who was to blame. He earned between six hundred and six hundred and fifty pesos a month, the same as Alberto, but the only installment he paid was forty-five pesos a month for some sweaters. And he gave her no more than Alberto—only one hundred and eighty pesos a month for food, rent, light, and gas. Hector contributed thirty pesos a month toward the household expenses now.

Rosa wrapped the offending mattress in a blanket and made up the bed. She swept the floor before pushing the cot into place and noticed how worn the broom was. "Soon we will need a new broom —damned money! I don't know where Agustín spends his money. He must have a woman somewhere. If he weren't neglecting the household so much I wouldn't care. I'm here for my children. This is my place for I am his true wife."

Rosa's eyes filled with tears. She had been a good woman and had never deceived her husband. Not that there hadn't been opportunities when she had worked in the restaurant! But that had not been what she wanted and besides she had been afraid of her husband's jealousy. Before his illness he was furious if he came home from work and found her out of the house. Once he tried to beat her but she pushed him down and kicked him in a tender place. He had not tried that again! But in those days he had been "more of a man" and she had generally respected his wishes. She remembered how "greedy" he had been. "He was always on top of me, sometimes nine times a night. He would even surprise me in the middle of the day when he would give the children money to walk around the block a few times so we could be alone. How he has changed!" He had never fulfilled all his obligations at home, but now he was completely useless as a husband. Rosa no longer felt that he deserved her loyalty and sometimes thought of taking a lover, "like other women do," who would give her money and the affection she needed.

Rosa's cousin in Azteca had a husband who had became impotent and she had taken him to a *curandero* to be treated for sorcery. The *curandero* had told him to look near the hearth of a woman who was a family friend and there, sure enough, he had found a package of dried chiles which he. destroyed in the fire. After that he was able to have sexual relations with his wife again. Rosa believed that Agustín too was the victim of sorcery and that her marriage would not improve until she discovered what was bewitching him. She wanted him to go to Azteca where the curers "understood such things," but Agustín refused.

Rosa's suspicions and jealousy had become an obsession. She remembered with great embarrassment how she had once suspected Fulgencia, who had since become her *comadre,* of being Agustín's sweetheart. Fulgencia was not married at the time and when she told Agustín about a possible job for Hector, Rosa decided Agustín was her lover. In order to spy on them Rosa became friendly with Fulgencia and invited her to go with the family to Azteca for the barrio fiesta. During the celebration Rosa and Agustín quarreled and he returned to Mexico City alone. When Rosa learned that Fulgencia too had left, she believed their departure had been prearranged between them. She imagined them making love in her house and she determined to surprise them there. With Alberto she took the next bus for the city.

They arrived home at midnight and Rosa made Alberto climb in through the kitchen roof to catch the lovers unaware. But no one was there and she went immediately to Fulgencia's house where she banged on the door. When Fulgencia opened it, Rosa pushed her aside roughly and searched feverishly for Agustín. She looked under the bed, in the wardrobe, and behind chairs, shouting his name. Fulgencia and Alberto, both frightened, looked on in silence. Finally Rosa realized her error. She was profoundly ashamed and did not know what to say to the innocent Fulgencia. Not until weeks later did she laughingly explain her behavior, and then the two women became good friends. "I was foolish," thought Rosa, "but it was Agustín's fault. If it hadn't been for his deceits I would have been less anxious."

Agustín had always been a woman-chaser, especially in his village days. He was good-looking and liked nothing better than to go about with the young men serenading and playing the guitar on street corners and at fiestas. His father was well-to-do and it was easy for Agustín to win over women; he had dishonored and deserted many a girl. Rosa knew all this when she married him, but she loved him and hoped he would change. He tried to sleep with her during their three years of secret courtship, but she would never yield. She thought now that this was the only reason he had married her— because she was a virgin and he knew that he could trust her.

Both of their mothers had been opposed to the marriage. Agustín's mother had wanted her only son to marry the daughter of a well-to-do peasant. During the marriage arrangements she had refused to present Rosa with the traditional flowers and gifts. At the church she made loud, critical remarks about the bride. Rosa's family had feared that life in the mother-in-law's house would not be happy for their daughter and they were right. After two years of suffering Rosa persuaded Agustín to leave his father's home and to strike out for himself in a distant town where her family had lent them a plot of land. She was happier there, but Agustín was neither a hard worker nor a good provider. Rosa had to help him in the rice fields and raise chickens and pigs to meet their household expenses. To make matters worse, he continued to run after women and to spend his money on them. Often he became ill and went back to his mother to be cured. He would have liked to remain with her in Azteca but Rosa would not hear of it.

When they moved to the Casa Grande in Mexico City and Agustín got a steady job on the bus line, Rosa thought her troubles were over. They now had electricity, they bought their first bed, they wore shoes all the time, and they sent their children to school. Rosa cut off her braids and had a permanent wave. They visited Azteca a few times a year to attend the festivals, and friends, relatives, or *compadres* from the village could always find a place to sleep on their floor. Life was good then, but after a while Agustín "went to see his mother" in Azteca and did not return. Rosa and the children were destitute. She had to sell *tortas* on the street and take the boys out of school to work in the bathhouse. When she heard that Agustín was ill, however, she was concerned about him and sent clean laundry for him every week. It was not until much later that she discovered he had been living with a young girl at his mother's house. The girl died after giving birth to twins. One of the babies was stillborn and the other did not live long. Rosa cursed her mother-in-law when she learned this, called her a procuress for her son, and forbade the old woman to see her children or to enter her house.

Agustín made no attempt to defend his mother and took Rosa's insults meekly. She never really forgave him and their relationship deteriorated after that although later when Augustín was burned Rosa showed herself to be a devoted wife. She not only supported the family but she had Agustín moved to a private sanitarium when he complained of neglect at the Social Security Hospital. She made a special trip to the shrine of Our Lord of Ixcatepec, to whom Aztecans had a special devotion, and left an offering of thanks that Agustín's life had been spared. When he was able to travel, she accompanied him on three pilgrimages to the shrine at Chalma because he had vowed to go there every year if he recovered. Rosa's family had urged her to leave Agustín when he could no longer support her, but she could not do it. It was partly out of pity for him that she stayed and partly out of pride. She did not want to give the people of her village anything to gossip about. No matter how she suffered, she would still "bring honor" to her children's home, she said.

These memories angered Rosa and she swept vigorously until she noticed how much dust she was raising. It was almost one o'clock now, and she went to the door to call Juanito. He came finally, clutching his toy soldiers in his dirty hands. "Look! I painted them all! And they look good!" Happily he put the soldiers away under the bed and washed for school as he was told. He wet down the hair above his thin little face, took his books down from the top of the wardrobe, and checked to see if he had a pencil. When he was ready he said, "Ester isn't here yet. Shall I go alone?"

Rosa hesitated. She did not want him to miss the school lunch, but she was afraid to let him cross the busy street alone even though all his friends did.

"No, wait for a while. She'll be back soon and there's still time."

Ester arrived at one o'clock. "I'm back, mom." She was hungry and fried some *tortillas,* gulping them down with half a bottle of Pepsi-Cola her mother had saved for her.

"Why do you eat standing?" Rosa asked.

"Because more falls into my stomach that way." Ester winked at Juanito and he laughed. He waited patiently until his sister had wiped her hands on a rag and was ready to go.

Rosa went back to her cleaning. She took the vase of paper roses off the dresser and put it on the bed. Then, lifting the other articles one by one, she dusted the top of the dresser. There were on the dresser: a glass ash tray filled with marbles, a box of Revlon face powder, a lipstick, a milk bottle of alcohol, a jar of hand cream, a small jewelry box decorated with snail shells, a framed snapshot of Alberto in a flowered sport shirt, a wedding picture of Rosa and Agustín, and the alarm clock. She also dusted the dressing table, first collecting the bobby pins strewn across it. After wiping the big mirror she put the matching stool and the four kitchen chairs up on the bed. The family was proud of the bedroom set. They had acquired it shortly before Agustín's accident and had had to struggle to meet the installments while paying twenty-five pesos a day to the hospital. They might have lost the furniture if Agustín's mother had not given him five hundred pesos as a part of his inheritance. Rosa also received additional help from her mother and sisters, and she and her sons were able to meet all the payments.

Rosa had picked up the straw *petate* and rubber mats and was sprinkling the floor when Ester returned. She decided to let her daughter finish sweeping. "Hurry up, Ester! It's almost one-thirty already. I'm going to the market. Don't change your uniform because I'm going to wash it tomorrow. Sweep the room. I already sprinkled here but you better throw some water in the kitchen. Take the pot off and put on another with some clean water. Just watch out that I don't come back and find it dirty here!"

As she spoke Rosa took her lavender purse out of a dresser drawer, put an empty bottle in her basket, and checked her money. "I have just five pesos. I'm only going to get dinner for Beto—noodles, and I'll have to see what else. I won't be long, eh? You'll be sorry if you aren't finished when I come back."

When she had gone her daughter muttered, "Sure, sure, you just give orders." Ester looked around at the kitchen floor, littered with trash, and at the dirty dishes. "I don't know how I'll ever finish here." She picked up a large aluminum pot and went out for water, making two trips to the faucet before she began to sweep.

"Is Ester there?"

A girl of six and her two younger brothers stood in the doorway. They were the children of a couple from Azteca who lived in the *vecindad*. The girl was wearing a new hair ribbon and new black shoes and Ester said, "Oh, aren't you dressed up." The child laughed and hid her face in her hands. The children began playing in the patio, but in a few moments the two older ones came running in to hide from Jorge, the baby. Ester joined the game, telling them to hide under the bed. "Pull in your legs, stupid," she warned as little Jorge ran in looking worried. He searched frantically for them while Ester laughed at him. On the point of crying he ran back to the patio, but now Ester chased his brother and sister after him so that she could finish sweeping. Just then Ester's friend Leticia put her head in, calling, "Ester, are you in?" When she spied Ester bending to sweep under the bed, she said, "What are you doing?"

"Nothing. What's it to you?"

"Don't be like that!" said Leticia. "Stupid me, asking for you." They both laughed. Leticia, barefoot, was carrying an aluminum pot filled with large red tomatoes. "My mother is waiting for the tomatoes and here I am," she exclaimed, laughing again as she ran out.

Ester bent again to sweep among the boxes under the bed. Her hair kept falling in her face and she pushed it back. "What dust here!" she said aloud. She picked up a rose-colored belt and dusted it off. "So that's where you were all this time!" She hunted for a bobby pin and tried to arrange her hair. "I wonder if I should get a permanent with that coupon I have. With it I can get a forty-peso permanent for fourteen pesos. But who will give me fourteen pesos?"

She removed the boxes piled high on the treadle of Rosa's sewing machine, dusted them, and swept underneath, then dusted the small table that for lack of space was kept on top of the machine.

She was sweeping the pile of dust and trash into the kitchen when an old woman poked her head in. The woman lived alone two doors away. She was carrying a small radio and wanted to test it to see if it worked. Her own electricity had been shut off because she had been unable to pay the bill for three months. Now she had the money and she wanted to know if her radio would play when the electricity came on again. Ester obligingly put the radio on a chair in the kitchen and connected it to a plug beside the light bulb. "The lights work, then why doesn't it play?" she asked.

"Just as I feared," the woman answered. "It's broken. It has to be checked up. Just think, I haven't even finished the payments on it and it's already broken." She disconnected it, thanked Ester, and left with it under her arm.

Ester stood at the door looking out for a moment. Reluctantly she turned back to the kitchen. She removed the newspaper that lined the cupboard shelf and rearranged the spice tins, wiping them one by one with a wet rag. They were red and white ones that Hector had given his mother. Ester worked slowly, dreamily. She was startled when her mother walked in.

"Did I take long? Just look what time it is! I was away an hour and I didn't buy much."

Rosa put the basket on the table and sat down, taking out her purchases—a small bottle of oil, one egg, three large tomatoes, and a kilo of boiled pigs' feet. "This will be enough for Beto and us too. He liked the *huazontles* fried in batter and I'll cook the meat the same way. Can you imagine? Beto's only given me fifteen pesos in the last ten days and five pesos for today. That's only twenty pesos and of course I don't have anything left."

Ester was cleaning the stove. She moved the table and opened the oven to wipe the broiler racks. To see inside she lit a match.

"It's dangerous to light matches near the stove, Ester," her mother said. "It has a pilot light but just the same it's better not to take any risks." Rosa stood up to examine the top of the stove more closely.

"No, Ester, this isn't what you call clean. Scrape this yellow, it'll come off." Rosa reached in the cupboard for a bag of steel wool and handed a piece to her daughter. Then she went to the sink to wash the dishes. "Hasn't the water come on since I left?"

"When you left it came on a little bit. Mamá, look, the yellow came off with the fiber."

Rosa was looking out of the front door. "Holy Mother! Just look at that trash." She dried her hands, picked up the broom, and went out to sweep.

Soon Ester heard her mother laughing outside. "As soon as my mother sees that someone is helping her she goes outside to chat. Now she's getting chummy with the neighbor. It's a good thing it's not me because she would say, 'You're no help to me! Have you finished your housework? When are you ever going to finish?' And now she's the one who's talking like a parrot." Ester smiled as she shook the table-cloth.

Rosa came back in. "I couldn't bear my hooves any longer they were so cold. Angélica's doorstep is good and hot and you know I need to warm my feet before I start to work." She laughed and went back to the sink to finish the dishes.

"Ma, we don't have to wash the kitchen floor, do we? It's clean. Last night I cleaned it. I will just sweep it." Rosa did not answer and Ester swept the floor, moving the chairs from one place to an-other. As they squeezed past each other in the tiny kitchen the two women would frequently bump into each other but neither seemed to mind.

Finally Rosa looked up and beckoned her daughter to come closer. "Do you know," she almost whispered, "Angélica's face is all black and blue on one side. She told me a drunk beat her up, do you be-lieve that? I think she got into trouble. I think her sweetheart beat her up."

"Does Angélica have another man?"

"Yes, but her husband doesn't know it. The other day when Beto came by for his girl, you know how late that was, he said he saw Angélica arm-in-arm with another man. Your papá saw them too. He says he saw them walking down the street hugging and kissing.

But you know you can't say anything about these things." Ester said nothing but listened eagerly.

"That's why," Rosa went on, "yesterday when I went with her to buy the dress my heart was beating so fast. I didn't want your papá to see us and say I was an *alcahuete* [a go-between]."

Rosa stopped speaking when Señora Felicia from No. 15 came in.

"Have you given anything to Alfredo for the twelfth, Rosa?"

"No, I haven't. Why?"

"Well, Alfredo is going to crown the Virgin. It's a yearly obligation. You know, Leocadio hasn't taken very good care of the little Virgin."

"Well," Rosa said, "we'll see. When my husband gets home I'll tell him."

Leticia had accompanied Señora Felicia and was recording the names of those who contributed to the fiesta. "Oh, come on, Señora!" she said. "Give to Alfredo. Tell Leocadio that you're not giving to him because you've already given to Alfredo, eh?"

Rosa made no move to give them money and the two went on to the next door. A girl, the daughter of a neighbor, came and stood in the doorway a moment, then left without saying a word. Rosa and Ester were working and paid no attention to her. They could hear women talking in the patio. "Ay! I don't know how these women find time to chatter. I can't do it," Rosa said. "You see how I'm always coming and going. How can I find time?" She looked out at the door and yelled, "What are you praying about, huh?" and laughed.

The dishes finished, Rosa began to collect dirty clothes to be washed. She took three pairs of pants from a box at the foot of the bed. "This white one is very dirty. I'll soap it and put it in the sun today and wash it tomorrow. These others I'll wash once and for all." On her way to the sink she saw Beto's dirty shirt on the toilet door and threw it into the tub along with the tablecloth. Just then the landlord, Señor Gallardo, greeted her from the open doorway. She dried her hands and stood still in the middle of the kitchen without inviting him in.

"Señora, isn't Señor Gómez at home?"

"No, sir, he isn't." Rosa's voice was not friendly.

"Well, you know why I've come. Tell me if I should send your contract to you because the rent is going up to fifty pesos. There will be an increase of twenty pesos."

"Well, we'll see once my husband gets here. We'll see what he says."

"Please tell him, Señora, that I have a hundred and twenty contracts signed, so you can see that the majority have accepted. There are only a few who are unwilling and they will just have to take up the matter with my lawyers. You understand that I can't continue to support myself with the same income I had twenty or thirty years ago." Señor Gallardo was becoming excited. "Prices have gone up, you know that, and besides I'm not being unfair. I only want to balance the expenses I've had here—fixing the floors, painting the doors, changing the beams on the roof, whitewashing and, well, small expenses that I haven't been able to cover. I'm trying to speak as a friend because this house is supposed to be torn down and I'm trying to negotiate an agreement with the government so that it won't happen." He paused a moment. "If you all help me I will be very glad to try to keep this house standing. As you see, even though the *vecindad* is poor it isn't like others that make one ashamed to live in them. You are witnesses that I am trying to keep it decent. This house is unprofitable for me now so, as I say, I don't think it's too much to raise only twenty pesos."

Rosa had stood listening to all this with her arms crossed. Now she blurted out, "Another raise? Five years ago we had one and I suppose in five more there will be another."

Señor Gallardo protested, "No. Five years ago it was done by mutual agreement also. But I don't know why they are so unwilling. I tell you the majority have accepted with the exception of eight who have treated me with insults. But I'm ready to turn their cases over to my lawyers. And another thing. I am coming in person so that you will be able to say, 'Señor Gallardo in person came to the house,' so that you will have a pleasant memory of the matter, isn't that so? Because I haven't sent out only a notice or told you all to come to my offices. I come personally, knocking on all the doors and trying to make arrangements with all of you. It's impossible for me to continue this way. Things aren't eternal, Señora!"

Rosa laughed, "That should prove to you, Señor Gallardo, that if you who has money can't make ends meet, now tell me if we can!"

"That's just why, Señora. You know yourself, when I ordered a new floor laid down for you, you saw how you didn't give me one cent for it even though you had agreed to pay a certain amount."

"Yes," Rosa challenged him, "we didn't give you anything because we didn't have anything and it's the same way now. If you who have so much can't make out we can do even less, isn't that true? The more you have the more you spend, so since we have little we spend little and even then we can't make out. Now the beams you ordered put in, well, I don't know why, the old ones were better than these filthy dry sticks they came to put in."

"That's right, Señora. Up to now not one person has said, 'Señor Gallardo, thank you very much for this thing or the other.' That's what one gets. I tell you up to this minute I haven't met a single person who has thanked me. On the contrary, many have gotten angry."

He stopped speaking and the two were silent, looking at each other. Then the landlord said, "And the little dances, Señora, how have they been coming along?"

"They continue, Señor Gallardo."

"Yes, they've told me that your son is the one who gets them up."

"That's not true! People just say that. Let's see, the dance on Monday that ended in fighting was a birthday or a baptism. Hector didn't get up that dance. The one on Sunday was a fifteenth birthday party and Hector had nothing to do with that either."

"Well, I have heard that your son is the one who organizes them and where there's dancing there's drinking and then all sorts of disorderliness. Señor Gallardo is only a farce around here. Nobody ever asks my permission to hold dances. You're always holding dances and Señor Gallardo is conspicuous by his absence. But I'm going to do away with all this."

"Well, just as you say, but I think it's impossible to keep a whole raft of people in order."

"Perhaps you are right, Señora, but where the law enters nothing is impossible. It wouldn't cost me anything to throw all the people here out in the street and rent the rooms for more money."

"Señor, if you throw everyone out don't expect people from the Lomas to come live here. Some other tramps will come, God only knows who, and they may be worse than the ones you have here now."

"All right. As I say that's exactly what I don't want to happen. People from the Lomas may not come but at least these houses will rent for more." Señor Gallardo prepared to leave. "Then you will ask your husband if he will please come to see me because you have only until the thirty-first."

"Yes, Señor Gallardo, when he comes home I'll tell him." Rosa watched him go. She made an impudent gesture, striking one hand against the other with one finger bent between. "Take that!" she said, turning to Ester. "I won't give him anything! I won't give that lousy old *gachupín* [derogatory term for Spaniard] one centavo more. Why should I? Wasn't he trying to make a fool out of me?"

Ester looked confused. "A fool? But how?"

"He meant that if I pleaded with your papá the dances could continue. Now isn't that making a fool of me? He talks crazy and that's why I didn't give him any hope. He says there are only eight who didn't come to an agreement, but just look at all the people along this side. Maria says she won't give. They all say they won't and I'm not going to give either." Rosa stood up abruptly because she had happened to notice the clock. "Ay, Dios! Just look! I was going to make the dinner but I didn't because of that man."

She hurriedly wrung out the white pants and climbed to the roof to hang them out. A red cloth was on the line; she folded it on her way back to the kitchen and put it away before returning to her washing. A little after three Alberto walked in.

With a smile for his mother, he said, "Mamá, I'm very hungry, get going. I'm in a hurry."

Rosa did not stop what she was doing. "Oh, you always have very important things to do. Come on, give me the money. I didn't have enough. Come on. I don't know and I don't care."

Alberto had washed his hands at the sink. He held out some money. "Take this. That's all I have until borrow day." Four days before pay day the bus drivers were permitted to borrow an advance on their wages.

Rosa did not want to wait. "This is all? You've only given me twenty pesos in the last ten days. I'm missing forty pesos. This is not enough!" She did not take the money.

"You don't want it? Then I'm going to a movie or I'll get drunk and that will be the end of it," Alberto laughed.

"No, no. What an idea! Come on, give me the money."

Alberto explained that he was short of money because the company was discounting more than usual from his pay.

"That's why sometimes there isn't any food," his mother retorted, "because I have to beg you for money."

Alberto shrugged his shoulders and stood looking out of the door. Ester had finished her work and was sitting in the sun crocheting. "Lazy girl, come and wash the dishes," Alberto said. His sister did not answer. Rosa called to her, "Come and beat the egg for me," and without a word she went inside. Alberto turned to his mother, "Come on. Give me my dinner. I have to leave."

Rosa looked annoyed. "What? What? You know, Señor Gallardo came to waste my time."

"What does he want? What did he say?" Alberto was interested.

"He wants to raise the rent, what do you think of that? He reminded me of the hundred pesos for the floor."

"What did you say to him?"

"I said to him, 'Ah! And why do you think we don't give it? Because we have the money or because we don't have it?' The old goat made fun of me. He said that if we accept the raise we can keep on with the dances. *Cabrón!*" Rosa laughed.

Alberto caught sight of his brother's shirt in the sink. "Hector got this shirt all dirty. It's disgusting!" he said. "Well, am I going to get something to eat?" he added impatiently.

"Well, there's only beans. I didn't get dinner because I didn't have any money."

"All right. Heat them up for me then."

"Oh! What a bother you are! Can't you see I'm busy? Heat them up yourself." Alberto went to the stove and took out a clay dish of beans from the oven. Ester took it from him and began to heat it. Alberto went to the mirror to comb his hair.

"Mamá, where is the vaseline? I need some."

"There isn't any left."

"What do you mean there isn't any left! You just want to hide it from me." He began to look for it and found it behind the stove. "You see there is some after all," he said in triumph. "You just hide it from me because I use it up fast."

Rosa, unperturbed, watched him take a large dab. "Was it there? I didn't even know."

Ester had been stirring the beans. "Mamá, what about the *tortillas*?" she asked.

"Why, of course, go and buy some quickly." Rosa gave her money for a kilo and a half, and Ester took a small cotton napkin and went out to the *tortillería*. On the way her good friend Elena joined her.

Alberto had finished combing his hair. "All right, mamá, just give me a *taco* and that's all. I won't ask you for food again until tomorrow morning."

"That's all I have to do!" Rosa was still scrubbing the clothes.

"Just give me a raw egg, that's all."

"What egg? What egg? I'd like to have one!"

Alberto was becoming annoyed. "Look, mamá, I want to eat and leave before my papá comes. I don't want to see him because this morning he said to me at the terminal [he began to imitate his father's voice], 'You, boy, wait for me because I want to speak very seriously with you.'" Alberto laughed. "But I'm not going to wait. I want to go before he comes."

Rosa left the clothes in the pail to soak, dried her hands on her apron, and went to the stove. "Look, I'm going to make pigs' feet in batter for you."

"Give it to me the way it is. Is it already cooked?"

"Yes, but wait a minute." Alberto insisted and Rosa served him the cold meat with salt and chiles which he ate with his fingers.

"Your hair is going to fall out just like your father's with all that vaseline you put on," she said. She began to grind some onion, garlic, and tomatoes in the stone mortar.

"When I saw papá this morning he wanted me to relieve him. He said, 'Here boy, you, Beto, take a trip for me.' I said, 'Who me? I can't.' When have I ever asked him to help me? Never. I've never asked him for help."

"That's because you're strong," his mother answered. "He's old now."

"Not that old, ma, don't exaggerate."

"Besides he's working a double shift."

"But why? They don't make me!"

"Ox! It was his fault because he told them he was going to look for another job. And you give me my money, eh?"

"Oh! Are you going to begin that again, mamá!"

"The man you bought the breakfast set from says he wants you to pay up. Didn't Hector tell you? No?"

"All right. I'll pay him next pay day."

Ester came in. "I got there just in time. The woman told me, 'Yes, there are still some for you.'"

"That's right, because you're a regular buyer. They take care of you because we gobble up three kilos every day."

Ester grinned. "Here, let me beat the egg for you," she said. She broke open the egg onto a flat platter and took up a fork. "Aren't you going to take papá his dinner?"

"Yes," Rosa said, looking at the clock. "He's working a double shift. Ah! Well, the more trips he makes the more money he gets."

"I won't work a double shift for my bosses," Alberto said. "Why should I fatten their pockets any more?"

"What a fool you are, Beto." Alberto was about to reply angrily but his mother stopped him. "Shut up. Your father is driving right now. Something might happen to him." She added, "When your papá does the same thing about you, 'Your son is this, your son is that,' I tell him, 'Shut up! He's driving right now. After he stops work you can say what you want to him!' You know when they're driving you can't curse them out because something might happen to them."

Rosa was rolling the pigs' feet in flour, dipping them in the beaten

**101**

egg, and placing them one by one into hot fat in the frying pan. The
hot oil spattered her and she yelled, "Ay! Son-of-a-bitch!" Ester sat
down to crochet. When she saw Alberto was leaving Ester said,
"Come on, give me enough to buy a pineapple with." Alberto answered, "Yes, yes," and she stretched out her hand, smiling. But he
didn't give her anything and walked out without saying good-by.
Ester turned to her mother to complain, but Rosa was talking. "You
see how thrifty I am? This one egg was plenty."

Carmen, a friend of Ester's, came in for a moment, slapped Ester
on the back and ran out, saying she had to do an errand for her
mother "but I'll come back, eh?" Rosa finished cooking the dinner
and began to prepare her husband's meal. She heated some *tortillas*
and wrapped them well, then placed them in her basket along with
a small covered aluminum pan which held meat and tomato sauce,
some beans, a spoon, and finally a half liter of pulque. "Well, daughter, it's four o'clock. I'll be back soon. Take care of everything, eh?"
Ester nodded and her mother went out.

Ester moved her chair outside the front door. In the bedroom
when it was quiet the mice came out of their holes. The last time she
had been alone there reading a comic book a mouse ran right across
her foot.

A young man came by and asked for Alberto. Some children gathered around Ester to watch her crochet but soon moved on to play a
few doors away. In the next patio a gang of boys was noisily playing
soccer. Ester was tempted to go and see if her boy friend was among
them, but her friend Carmen came over with a newspaper and sat
down on the pavement, leaning her back against the warm wall of
the house. Carmen read aloud slowly, "Technical Training Institute."

"What's that?" Ester asked.

Carmen jabbed her with an elbow. "Shut up, I'm trying to read."

Ester leaned over and the two girls read aloud together, stumbling
over unfamiliar words. When one of them made a mistake the other
slapped her or pushed her and then they both laughed.

"What is this?" Ester said. "S.U.T.D.D.F. Oh, 'Sindicato Unico de
Trabajadores del Distrito Federal! [The One Labor Union of the

Workers of the Federal District]'" Ester tried to memorize the initials. "Now I know it. I have a good memory."

"Yes, yes, my friend, no one doubts it," giggled Carmen. Then she said, "Now I'll go home and get my needle and help you." In a few moments she was back with her crochet needle and Ester tried to teach Carmen the stitch she was using.

"Listen, Ester, why are mine so big?"

"Because that is the way they should look, you big fool," yelled Ester.

"All right, why don't you hit me?" Carmen was offended. "You're no good as a teacher. You need an awful lot of patience." Ester laughed. "Look, this one looks like your papá." They both laughed this time.

"Ay! How you talk, Ester. You're getting real crazy."

"Yes, my friend, but not over you, over a man, and what a man!"

"Do you mean *El Divino?*" Carmen was referring to a tall, handsome boy with light eyes who lived in the *vecindad*. All the girls in Ester's gang had a "crush" on him and spent hours discussing him. Carmen went on, "Ay! My *Divino,* so beautiful, *Divino,* my dumb *Divino!*"

Ester laughed. "Do you call that a man? I mean my boy friend!" She began to sing softly. "Ay! Look at me, dear, kiss me. Ay! Look at me dear, you must kiss me."

The girls crocheted silently for a moment. Then Ester said, "Listen, I shaved under my arms the other day."

"You're a bloody liar. What did you want to do that for?"

The two girls were sitting at the kitchen table, still talking and giggling when Rosa rushed in at a quarter past five.

"Just look at what time I'm getting back! Is it fair all the times I've had to wait to eat?" she said good-humoredly. "It's almost time to go for Juanito." She put down her basket and washed her hands at the sink. "It's cold in here."

"Cold," scoffed Ester. "Only cats are cold."

Rosa squeezed past the girls, between their chairs and the wall. "Look out, don't get in the way of the meat market," she quipped.

The girls left their crocheting and went out to the patio. Rosa helped herself to a plateful of cold food and sat down at the table. "Imagine," she called to Ester, "your papá had just left when I arrived and so I had to wait."

Rosa ate with relish, scooping up the meat and sauce with small pieces of *tortilla*. "Those girls do nothing but laugh," she said. She began looking at the newspaper spread on the table. "Dresses are so expensive now and so ugly." She finished eating and leaned back, one hand on her stomach, the other over her mouth. She took a gulp of water and reached over to the closet for the bag of clay, noticing that Ester had cleaned the cabinet and rearranged the tins. "Holy Mother! If Ester weren't here to halfway do things, everything would be in a mess." She smiled as she chewed a piece of clay, her "dessert," and went to lie down on the cot, kicking off her shoes and covering herself with a jacket. It was dark in the bedroom now and Rosa's eyes were closing when Ester put her head in the door.

"Hector is coming. It's five-thirty and I'm going to get Juanito."

"Run along," Rosa said, sitting up, "but don't take as long as you did the other day when your father came home and blamed me because you weren't here. That was going a little too far. Juanito came home alone and you weren't to be found anywhere."

Ester withdrew hurriedly. Rosa got up to clear the table and was washing the dishes when Hector came in with a popular magazine he bought each month and gave to his family when he was finished with it. He smiled and patted his mother's arm. "Just give me some coffee, mamá. I am going to eat with my friends." When his mother looked displeased he added, "You should see how nice they are, how nice they dress. They are students at the *Politécnico*. If we didn't live in such a hole I would bring them around for you to see."

Hector had dreamed for a long time of moving his family from the Casa Grande to an apartment. An apartment! How he loved the sound of the word. He had found an apartment in a "decent" building for three hundred pesos a month and had tried to persuade his parents and brother to take it. He believed they could manage it if he and Alberto each contributed one hundred pesos per month, his father sixty, and if his mother saved forty pesos out of the household money. The apartment had two bedrooms, a living room, a kitchen, a bathroom with a bathtub, windows in every room, and it was freshly painted. How much better their furniture would show up, he thought. He planned to hang up pictures and buy pretty flowerpots, and little by little they would acquire more furniture. Also Hector meant to insist that the family eat with forks and knives instead of with only spoons and their fingers. Then he could invite his friends to his home without shame and give parties there. Hector vowed that so long as they continued to live "like pigs" he would not live at home.

Even though he explained the plan to his family, Hector knew it would not work out. His father was afraid to take on additional expense and besides he liked the Casa Grande and didn't want to leave it. Alberto did not think it important one way or another for he planned to have his own home soon. Rosa might be won over but she, too, was afraid of the expense and she preferred to spend the money to send Ester to commercial school. So Hector had dropped the matter, realizing that if he wanted to get ahead in the world he would have to do it alone. Now he spent almost all his money on himself.

He sat down at the table while his mother heated his coffee.

"What about my papá, has he given you money already?"

"Yes, but you see he gives me hardly anything, only fifty pesos."

"Well, you shouldn't have taken them. Now he'll come for lunch and dinner every day and you know how he expects meat all the time. If you don't give him a good sparerib he's not happy. Better have him eat at the restaurant. He eats up all the money he gives you."

For a month Agustín had not eaten at home because when he didn't give her enough money Rosa stopped preparing his meals. They had quarreled over that but he found that eating out was very expensive and also made him ill. Then he had offered to give her more money. Rosa began to give him meals again but he was not keeping his part of the bargain.

"What do you want me to do, son? He's your father. I do it because, like my *compadre* says, Juanito and Ester can't be without a father. You are already grown but they. . . ."

"What good has he ever been to us?" Hector cried. "When we were little he never took us to the movies. And how many times did he leave us? You've already forgotten the time he went to his mother's place with that woman he made pregnant and left us with nothing to eat? When you were in the hospital for a week he didn't go once to visit you. It was as though you didn't have a husband. You could have died and we wouldn't even have known. He's no good for anything, not even as a man! He can't even have any more children, but he still runs around with women."

Hector warmed to his subject, "When he got mad and threw me out in the middle of the night, it was because I told you the truth about that dame at the workshop, the one he told I wasn't his son! Do you think he threw me out because I went to Taxco without telling him? How come he didn't throw me out when I went to Acapulco without permission? That time I stayed two weeks and was much younger." Hector was angry now and wouldn't let his mother interrupt. "That's why I changed my name. If he denies me as a son, I will deny him as a father." Hector had been using his mother's name, Hernandez, for the past year. Once Agustín saw a letter addressed to him by that name and tore it up. In retaliation Hector tore up one of his father's letters.

Hector jumped up and walked about the room nervously. "I cannot look at him and I'm not ashamed to say so!" he burst out. "He brought it on himself because he was always bad to us and never gave us money when he should. I really hate him."

Now Hector wanted to leave the house as quickly as he could. "I'm going, mamá. Don't expect me later because I am going to bed early. I'll be here tomorrow to bring back my shirts from the cleaners."

He walked out and Rosa looked after him anxiously. In Azteca if a son spoke that way, his father would all but kill him! Even though Rosa believed Hector's complaints were justified it disturbed her to hear him say them openly.

Outside Juanito was calling to Hector. He ran after his brother, clutching his pants leg and asking for money. Hector laughed and finally gave him a coin. Juanito came into the house showing the coin to his mother and sister. He threw his books on the bed and shouted, "Where is my papá? I want to show him what I did in school." He held up a drawing of a dog. "Look, mamá." Rosa made no comment. "Look, mamá. . . . I saved the sandwich from my lunch. Can I eat it now?" Without waiting for an answer he unwrapped it and began to eat.

Rosa was saying, "What day is today? Friday? I'm just thinking, wondering how many more days until the end of this ten-day period. Five more to go and the money almost gone! I wish I was somebody else. I get so mortified about food." She crossed her arms and bowed her head as she sat down at the table. "Today I didn't spend much because I already had beans cooked." Rosa cooked a whole kilo of beans every three or four days to economize on gas. A tank of gas cost twenty-five pesos and if she were careful she could make it last a month. Kerosene and charcoal were less expensive but only the poorest families in the *vecindad* used them.

"Fulgencia owes me ten pesos. She said she'd be here today but she hasn't come. I'll wait until Sunday. Hmm. It's already dark. It seems a lie that when your papá put me on the bus it was still early."

Someone knocked on the door, which Rosa had closed because it was getting cold. "Who is it?" A boy's voice answered, "Me, Nacho." Rosa opened the door. It was Ignacio from No. 10. "Hasn't Hector come?"

"No," Rosa lied, looking him over.

"Please, Señora, when he comes tell him I need him. Please, because he told me he'd bring my pants today and I really need them."

"Yes, of course, when he comes I'll tell him." The boy left and Rosa began to take the dirty dishes from her basket. "Ay! I have to bring some water. I was forgetting." She emptied a pail of water into the toilet and gave it to Ester to refill at the outside faucet. "We will need three pails for the tub. I have to have water for your papá when he gets home." Rosa moved the garbage tin under the sink and swept the floor around it. When Ester came back Rosa asked, "Did you wash the toilet?"

"I washed inside the bowl, not outside." Ester went out again, bumping into Juanito who was coming in.

"Mamá, ask me my catechism." Juanito gave his mother a small book. Rosa leaned against the stove and read the first question. "Where is God?"

"God is in Heaven and Earth and in all places." Juanito recited standing stiffly at attention with his arms at his sides. He answered the next two questions correctly but made an error in the following one and his mother said impatiently, "Here, study it, you don't know it yet. Son, you're wasting my time."

Juanito had recently entered a catechism class which was held at Doña Aurelia's house, No. 14, under the direction of the parish priest. Rosa had not wanted to send Juanito to it because she didn't like Aurelia. She thought the woman was a religious fanatic. Aurelia accused people, Rosa included, of being heretics when they did not go regularly to Mass and confession, and did not always make the sign of the cross as they passed the two Virgins in the entranceways of the *vecindad*. Doña Aurelia also tried to combat the apathy of her neighbors toward the few Protestant families in the Casa Grande. She wanted them driven out but the other Catholics refused to become aroused. Rosa dismissed Aurelia as a "hypocrite" and a "church rat."

Ester ran in banging the door after her. Carmen followed almost immediately. "Don't be afraid of her, Ester," she said. Rosa, at first annoyed, then interested, asked,

"Who? Why?"

"Because Candelaria hit Ester."

"Yes, on the tail." Ester laughed, rubbing her back. "She's very rough. She hit me while I was getting water."

"Why did you let her, you dumb girls! I'd never let her. I'd grab her and pull her ears to cure her. You're fools to let her."

"Come on, Ester, let's go after her."

The two girls ran out but soon were back again. They were laughing loudly.

"Don't you girls know any other way to play?" Rosa said in irritation. "*Pendejas*, pair of fools!"

"Oh, brother, that bump hurt." Carmen rubbed her forehead.

*108*

"If it hurts so much with a hand we'll try it next time with a rolling pin," laughed Ester.

Candelaria poked her head in at the door. "It didn't hurt, did it?" Carmen nodded. "What a coward!" Candelaria said. All three girls laughed gaily.

A little girl holding a candle stopped at the open door. "Aren't you going to confession?" she asked Ester. "The Señorita and I are going right now." Before Ester could answer Rosa said, "What do *you* confess for? Only those who eat saints and excrete devils should confess!"

"Ay! But today is the first Friday," the child answered.

The sound of firecrackers could be heard in the courtyard. "Listen to the procession," Rosa said, impressed. "Just listen, they even have music."

Juanito rushed in. "Mamá, I'm going to confession, eh?" he asked excitedly.

"No, no, no! A child can't confess until he has made his First Communion and you aren't going to make it until your father buys you the clothes."

"But mamá," said Juanito, "you can go just as you are with any old clothes."

"No. No, sir! You just want to go for the excitement, like a crazy fool. Just because you see others going you want to go along too. You don't know what confession is. No, sir, you're not going."

"Mamá, I want to go. Doña Aurelia is going and the Señorita too." Juanito was almost crying.

"I said no. I'm the one who gives orders here not that old Doña Aurelia. Starting you out with your great big sins! No, sir. You can't go with those rags. You have to wear a blue suit at least. Confession isn't just anything."

Ester, who had run out with Carmen to see the procession, came in. "Mamá, imagine! At the very end they carried—what's her name?" She turned to Carmen. "The one who gave water to God, Our Saviour? What's her name? Mary Magdalen? No, the other one, the Samaritan!"

Juanito appealed to his sister, "Ester, isn't it true that you can go with any kind of clothes?"

"Yes, lots are going that way. He can go too."

Rosa was angry now. "No, sir, you don't know the meaning of it." She raised a threatening hand to her son. "Go on, do you want to get it? What if others are going?"

Outside the group was ready to march to the church. "They're going," said Juanito desperately, the tears rolling down his face. He ran out to the patio where he covered his face and cried.

"Look at him, he's crying," Ester said.

"Let him, he won't cry blood," said his mother. "If he's a good boy he'll go to confession next year. Then if he wants to spend all day in church he can."

After a while Juanito came in with another boy. He was calmer now. "Mamá, can I make my First Communion on December twelfth?"

"Well, yes. By then your father will have the clothes. Don't you see how broke we are now? What would people say if I let you go dressed like this? It looks bad when your father has enough money. Yes, he has enough money but he won't even buy you a pair of pants. But he is living with us and earning money and you don't have to go in rags."

The water suddenly began to run from the kitchen faucet. "*Vaya!*" Rosa said. "I hope it will at least fill the tank." She stood watching the water fall into the empty tub. The pail of clothes was still under the sink. "Tomorrow I'll wash them and hang them out early. That way I can iron in the afternoon." Desultorily, she began to tidy the kitchen, putting away the bottle of cooking oil, the clean, dry plates and spoons, the *tortilla* basket. "You see?" she said to Juanito, who was sitting on the bed looking at a comic book, "the tank is already full." When the water stopped she turned off the faucet.

She went out to the patio to fill the coffeepot with clean tap water. Previously she had poured the leftover coffee into a clay jug to be reheated for supper. Rosa never threw out any coffee and sometimes reheated it three or four times during the day, adding water when it became too bitter. She picked up the pot which held her hus-

The Gómez Family

band's herb tea. "Look at what's left! I took it to him this morning. Every other day, every other day, it has to be boiled." She began impatiently to look for something. "I've lost the strainer. I don't see it. I have to strain that man's medicine." Finding it on the sink, she strained the liquid into a bottle.

Rosa sat down on the bed. "One can't get any rest here." She was speaking to Juanito who was not listening. "You see how I have to take him his breakfast and his dinner. Just like a peasant woman! This is the only time I can rest for a moment. When I send Ester with the food at least I have time to wash the clothes. Otherwise I can't with all this coming and going."

Two girls knocked. "Good evening, Señora, is Ester here?" Rosa said no and one of the girls handed her a folded piece of velvet to give to Ester. When they had gone Rosa examined the yard of cloth. "Those girls, coming all that way just to leave this." She put it on the dressing table and went back to sit on the bed.

"Who knows where Hector is now? That boy is the one who worries me." Several days before Hector had witnessed the killing of a neighborhood boy, "the Cat," who was a known thief. The police had been tipped off as to his whereabouts and had shot him down as he tried to escape. Later a man from the Cat's gang had collared Hector, giving him some candles, and had ordered him to leave them at the Cat's house where the wake was in progress. The man said, "Look, tell them these candles are from me and leave them there. We'll see if they are real friends or just a bunch of bastard informers." Hector had recounted the story to his mother. "And I was there with all of them. Ay! Mamá! I was so afraid my heart was beating like mad. There were a lot of men there who are always spoiling for a fight." Hector had heard the Cat's mother crying and saying, "If they were men they would have spoken to my son's face and not to his back."

"But," Rosa thought, "her sons were real bad. They attacked people and robbed them. They say the Cat's wife was the one who informed on him because he threatened to kill her. They say he chased her plenty of times with a gun. The other day I saw his mother. She looked so old! Since they killed her son she's gotten very thin. I say poor mother because really we're the ones who suffer. Anyhow the others in the gang made those poor boys do it. If they didn't want to they'd kill them. Hector is such a crazy one that he worries me."

Rosa rested her chin in her hand. Yes, there was danger all around them. The *vecindad* gang was always fighting, among themselves and with different gangs. Sometimes they fought with razors and knives. A family in the next patio had three sons, all pickpockets. The eldest, "the Chicken," was now in jail, and the two younger ones had been questioned by the police about snatching a woman's purse at the market. Alberto and Agustín often told her of the thieves who "worked" the buses and of killings that occurred. Thank God her sons had never been mixed up in anything.

"Mamá, give me the ink. I'm going to do my homework." Juanito had finished the comic book. Rosa lifted down the small table from the sewing machine, set the table next to the cot for her son to work on, and took down the ink from the top of the wardrobe. Juanito began to copy some lines from a book. Ester came in, still holding her crocheting, and stretched out on the big bed. Rosa lay down on the cot, covering her feet with a jacket. She had been waiting to talk to Ester and began immediately, ignoring Juanito's presence.

"Last night Beto told me that a collector on the Tzotzil line was murdered. They got him when he went to check in. This guy couldn't keep quiet and when he saw someone about to take a man's wallet he said, 'Watch out for thieves.' They didn't try anything more but just looked at him mad-like and that night on the last run this guy got down off the bus to check in and the other guy, without making any noise, hit him on the head with a piece of iron and whistled like the collectors do and the driver started off. Later they found him lying there, all covered with blood."

"Who was it?" asked Ester.

"Well, who knows? That's why Beto says, 'Not me, mamá. I keep quiet. That's why I've never had any trouble with anybody. Let the one who has the money watch out for it. Why should I?' And that's true. They can't speak up because they'll get it too. Beto says he knows who a lot of them are but he doesn't say anything because they're real bad guys. He told me, 'Sometimes they even give me

two or three pesos when I give them a ticket or when they are leaving.'
I used to scold him for that but he said, 'What do you want me to do,
mamá? I couldn't do anything because they would catch up with
me.' And it's true, too."

Rosa fell silent. She was lying on her side, her cheek pressed
against the palm of her hand. She remembered the ill omen that had
occurred shortly before Alberto's birth and that still sometimes made
her feel anxious about him. She had been washing clothes at the
stream when she saw a rainbow. This terrified her because it was extremely dangerous for a pregnant woman to see a rainbow. She ran
home but the rainbow followed her into the house and did not disappear until her mother-in-law had thrown a pail of water over it.
Rosa had worried about the unborn child but now she believed that
the rainbow's only effect had been to extend her pregnancy to ten
months.

Alberto was big and strong at birth and without defect. He had
nursed for two years and three months, even after his brother was
born. "He sucked what was Hector's." When Rosa weaned Alberto,
he became *chipil*, ill from jealousy, and had to be cured with the
cooked flesh of an iguana. Later Rosa's father-in-law cured Beto of
severe temper tantrums by forcing tobacco into his mouth during an
attack. After that he never gave his parents any trouble. He was a
steady worker and a "good" boy, although his mother thought he
was too reserved.

Suddenly Rosa realized that it was eight o'clock. "Ay! I haven't
gone to get that man's milk." She stood up and put on her shoes.
But Ester said, "I want a gelatine. Give me the money, ma, and
I'll go."

"All right. Go ahead." Rosa counted out the money, then went into
the kitchen to set the jug of coffee on to heat. Carmen and another
friend, Irela, came in. "Ester, your boy friend 'Half-Pint' is out there."
Ester laughed, "Half-Pint? Kill him!"

"They say that boy's mother is living with a man in a village now,"
Rosa said. "He was one of her husband's workmen and she took off
with him. That marriage dissolved just like water. She was the one
who was unfaithful and that's why the family broke up. What a

stupid woman I tell you. Not me, ay, no! May God not will it. These women don't think about their children. The boy now sleeps here and there and seems kind of sick-like."

The girls were listening. Giggling, Ester said, "Mamá, tell them what happened yesterday."

"Ah, well, Ester and I were hauling water and there was another woman and two more girls there. Half-Pint was sitting where they sell candy. You know, it's almost in front of the water tap. We looked at him and there he was sitting with his legs apart and his whole fly open." The girls began to shriek with laughter, holding their hands over their mouths. Encouraged, Rosa went on. "Everything was outside his pants, ugly, like a turkey's crest, like this [she drooped one finger], all limp."

"He was ventilating himself," laughed Ester, blushing.

Rosa was speaking with zest as she always did when criticizing the opposite sex. "He had the ugliest balls, all hanging down like those bags they sell sometimes. They were red, as red as tomatoes. Ay! I was horrified." Rosa laughed. "The other woman spoke to him, 'Listen, brother, cover yourself up. It's all right to feel the heat but you don't need to cool off that much. Stop —— around.' Half-Pint pulled his feet together and grabbed his pants and got red, red."

The girls laughed loudly, pushing each other and getting red themselves. Juanito had been listening from the bedroom with a perplexed smile. The girls went out for the milk and Rosa turned off the burner under the coffee which was just beginning to boil. She got back into bed and closed her eyes. Juanito had begun to do his arithmetic homework; the room was quiet. Ester came in with the milk and set it to boil on another burner.

"Tell me, Sis, if I have twelve left over below and have eight above, what do I do?"

"Let's see . . . don't be silly, the lower number has to be smaller than the other. You have to get more . . . look, this way."

"Oh, yes. Let me do it now. I'll show it to you later."

Rosa listened to the children with interest. She had always liked school and she had completed the fourth grade, then the highest grade in her village school. She was lucky to have gone to school at

all for her father had died when she was an infant and her mother
had had to struggle to support her three daughters by renting out
her husband's land and by taking in washing. Rosa would be more
than satisfied if Ester and Juanito could learn a trade and have a
better future than their brothers. It pleased her to see them doing
schoolwork together. It was more usual for them to quarrel, for
Ester had always been jealous of her younger brother.

When Ester sat on the bed again to crochet, her mother said,
"Some women are fools. Just look at Half-Pint's mother. Her husband
was lazy, but he was a good guy. It's true she did all the work and
the old man just sat around lording it over her. But she got fed up
with that and took up with another man. Now they say he gives her
a bad time. I don't know why these women don't think. When she
ran off, her husband did the same and the children were left alone.
They say Half-Pint's sister ran away with the blondish fellow who
lived across the patio. She was so disillusioned it was all she could do."

Rosa paused to cover her feet and went on, "Ay, no! You can bet
I wouldn't do that. No matter how late your papá came home, I'd be
doing my housework waiting for him. Then we'd both go to bed.
That way it's very different." The room was very quiet.

Juanito had climbed up on the bed and was lying next to his sister,
"Mamá," he said, "I hear those sounds on the roof!"

Rosa listened and heard what sounded like blows from above. "It's
nothing! They say there are ghosts there but I've never seen one even
though I've stayed up all alone until late at night. I used to stand at
the door alone, with everything dark all around, and look toward the
baths where they say the ghosts are and I never saw anything. When
we first moved in here we heard blows on the water pipe at midnight, as though someone had climbed up and was swinging on it.
But that was because your cousin Salvador was living here. When
he left, we were not afraid anymore."

Salvador was Agustín's nephew. He had come to the city to look
for work and had slept on the floor of the Gómez home for three
months. Several strange events had occurred while he was there.
Agustín had been awakened one night by someone clutching at
his toes but when he turned on the light everyone was fast asleep

including Salvador. They heard unexplained sounds in the patio at night and the pipes made continual noises. Once when Agustín was not at home Rosa was frightened by someone clacking the pots in the kitchen. She thought it must be a thief but could find no one. When she turned out the light, however, the noises began again and continued until Agustín came home. They both searched the house but everything was in order. They believed that Salvador caused these things to happen because he had a devil tattooed on his left breast and two other tattoos, one on his abdomen, the other on his left forearm. When he left their house the noises stopped. Rosa and Agustín were convinced that he was in a pact with the devil and had been learning witchcraft.

"Listen, mamá, somebody is knocking up above," Juanito cried out.

Rosa laughed. "Go on, you crazy one. What's all this about knocking? Don't you hear the radio in the other house?"

"But my papá saw a ghost, didn't he?" Juanito asked.

"In truth he did, but a long time ago." Rosa laughed when she recalled the incident.

It was soon after the family had moved to the Casa Grande. One morning at four o'clock Agustín was going to work with his cousin, the two of them talking about women and "thinking bad thoughts" as Rosa said, when they saw a woman dressed all in white near the baths. She said, "Psst, Psst!" and beckoned to them. Agustín's cousin said, "Go ahead, she's calling you," but Agustín had answered, "No, man, I'd better not because I'll be late for work." They went on to the gate and were about to knock for the janitor when the woman called more loudly. The janitor came out and they told him about her. "*Ave María Purísima,* this isn't good," he had said, and the three of them went to speak to her. But she wasn't there. They said she was really a ghost because she just floated in the air and had no legs. The men had been drinking but that sobered them up.

Rosa stood up heavily and went to the kitchen to prepare supper. Juanito had dozed off. Alberto entered the house and without greeting anyone handed his mother a copy of the newspaper, *Ultimas Noticias.*

116

"I have a complaint to make to you about Juanito," Ester said to him. Alberto waited in the doorway. "Imagine, he fell against the stove with his chair and made a mark."

Rosa said quickly, "It will come off with water. It is nothing. Besides he was going to topple over."

Alberto said nothing and Ester was annoyed. "It would have been a different story if I had done it!" She grumbled, but no one paid any attention to her. Rosa had begun to read the newspaper. "Why didn't you buy the paper with crime in it?" Alberto cuffed his mother lightly on the head, saying, "It's there. It's in there."

"Mamá, give me ten centavos for a crackling," Ester said. When Rosa said she had no money, Ester turned to Alberto. "Give me some money for a *chicharrón*, won't you, Beto?" Before he could answer Luz, a light-haired girl with a new permanent wave, walked in. Ester insisted, "Come on, Beto, give it to me."

Her brother shook his head. "I don't have any money."

"Why?" said Ester.

"Because he's very stingy," Luz interjected. They all laughed except Alberto, who went to the sink to wash his hands. Carmen came in and began to help Ester unravel a ball of thread. Luz noticed the velvet on the dressing table. "What's this, Ester? Is it yours?" Rosa explained, "Ah, yes, Ester, some girls came to leave it for you." Ester said she was going to use it to make a purse as a school sewing project. The girls talked about the purse and then went on to discuss Ester's graduation dress. Alberto was sitting at the table. "I'm hungry, mamá. Give me whatever you have. No, I don't want coffee."

"Right away, son," said Rosa. "It's almost ready."

"All right, then I'll just take a walk and come back, eh? I'll be back at ten." He went out and Rosa began to read the newspaper.

Juanito had awakened and was playing with a cardboard box on the bed. It got in the way of Ester's string and broke it. "Let it alone, let it alone, you idiot!" Ester said and she slapped Juanito. Juanito angrily pulled at the string and a tug-of-war followed which Rosa stopped. Luz and Carmen went out to return in a few minutes with several fried *chicharrones,* which they shared with the others. They watched Ester crochet. She was making baby booties for her godmother who was expecting a child. "You should knit them with two needles," Rosa said. "They turn out better that way."

"My teacher said that first I have to learn to use one needle well." Ester laughed as she remembered something. "Mamá, tell us about when you stuck the needle into a pig."

Rosa laughed heartily and told the girls that when she was little she could not learn to knit and her mother had pricked her hands with the knitting needle "to take the clumsiness out of my fingers." It was a village belief that if a child was punished with the tool he was trying to master or with the pieces of the dish he had broken, it would stop him from repeating his mistakes. Rosa remembered that one afternoon she was trying to knit some lace for her mother and kept making mistakes. This time her mother hit her in the face. Rosa had gone out into the yard where the pigs were kept and angrily stuck the hook into a sow, "as if it were a *banderilla*." Later she felt sorry for the pig and pulled out the hook and fed it some corn. "But," she said, "it proved that I won't take anything from anybody."

"Do you remember, mamá, how you threw the pot of beans at me?"

The girls laughed as Rosa retorted, "Of course, since you were letting them burn and then only laughed."

Rosa warmed up the leftover food from the afternoon meal and when Alberto walked in she was ready to serve him. She gave him a plate of meat with beans, some green chiles, salt, and two hot *tortillas*. Luz and Carmen said good night and left before he began to eat. Juanito asked for coffee. "Just a minute. Just a minute," his mother said as she gave Alberto his coffee. Juanito tried to grab it for himself but Rosa stopped him with a push. "Leave that alone. That's for Beto. Put on your shoes and wash your hands."

"No," Juanito said sulkily.

"Look at him. He wants to have his coffee with no shoes on. Go on, don't tell me no." Juanito sprinkled water on his hands and dried them on a bit of cloth, leaving it very dirty. Rosa told Ester to hurry out for a quarter of a kilo of sugar because she needed it to sweeten Alberto's coffee.

Alberto ate slowly, enjoying his food. "Has my papá been home yet? No?" Alberto laughed. "He should learn to take it easy like me with my bosses. He works too hard and that's why he's always tired. I leave the terminal and then once I'm away who sees me? When I don't want to take a trip, like that terrible *Merced* market route, I just say I don't have any gasoline left and I hang around in some gasoline station and that's that! Who sees me? I just throw them off the scent."

"What an ox! The more trips you make the more money you get," his mother said.

Bus drivers were paid a flat rate of four and a half pesos for each round trip on their route. One of Agustín's complaints was that he was earning no more money than his son despite his many years of service. And according to Agustín, the union to which he had to contribute dues every month was "full of grafters and bribed officials" and did nothing to improve working conditions for its members.

Ester returned with the sugar in a newspaper cone and Rosa put two spoonfuls in her son's coffee. Getting back into bed, Ester continued crocheting. Juanito had tied a string to his box and was swinging it around his head.

"Shall I give you your coffee now, son?" Rosa said to him. "No, not yet," he answered, interested in his box which he whirled closer and closer to his sister.

"Hold still. You're going to hit me with that box," said Ester.

Rosa intervened. "I'm going to wallop you, Juanito. Just keep on and you'll see." Ester teased Juanito and the two began to fight, playfully at first and then in anger. Rosa stopped it by telling Juanito to come for his coffee and *tortilla*. He obeyed immediately because he was hungry.

"Mamá," Alberto asked, "did you and papá go to speak to Susana's parents?"

Alberto intended to marry Susana and for some time he had been urging his parents to ask for Susana's hand formally. They were already engaged and had stood up together as godparents for Fulgencia's child. Alberto was annoyed with his mother for trying to put off the marriage. Neither Rosa nor Agustín approved of Susana, not only because she was a few years older than Alberto, but because she was "worldly." She had had an affair with a friend of Alberto's and the two young men had quarreled violently about her. Also Susana's aunt had been involved in a scandal in the *vecindad;* she had been caught with a lover and the two of them had been severely beaten by her husband. Agustín had advised his son to bring Susana to the house and live with her in free union to avoid expenses and formalities, but this only angered Alberto. He was blindly in love and was determined to marry Susana as soon as he paid off his "loan" to the bus company. They said he owed them only 1,500 pesos now.

Rosa was defensive. "If I spoke to them, they might set an early date for the wedding and you wouldn't be able to go through with it because you wouldn't have the money. Better wait until you are ready. Then I will ask."

Rosa kept hoping Alberto would forget about marrying Susana. He had been having sexual relations for some time with another girl and perhaps, Rosa thought, he would become so deeply involved with her that he would not want to marry. Aurora, the girl, had previously worked as a servant for one of the families in the *vecindad.* She was in love with Beto, but he did not take the affair seriously. He had forced her to take another job outside the *vecindad* so that Susana would not find out about the relationship and he planned to break it off when he married. Rosa wanted Alberto to put off the wedding another year at least until the kitchen set and stove were paid for.

Rosa had little hope that her sons would help Ester through "Commercial." It looked as though the only way Ester could go on with her schooling would be for Rosa to take her old job in the restaurant. She had enjoyed the work and being out among people, but she didn't like the man she had worked for. He was always getting drunk and making passes at her. Once he had walked her home and, finding the place empty, had thrown her on the bed and was on top of her before she knew it. Rosa was strong and she had pushed him away just as Ester came in. The two of them had chased him out and afterwards Rosa had discussed the matter with her daughter. Ester had urged her to quit the job but work was scarce and with Agustín in the hospital Rosa really had no choice. She complained to her boss's wife who told her not to pay any attention to the "senile old bag" because he was the same way with all women.

Rosa was confident now that she could take care of herself but the sight of the man disgusted her. Still, they wanted her at the restaurant and she could earn ten pesos a day there, enough to pay all of Ester's expenses. And Ester could be at home until four o'clock in the afternoon, doing the cooking and cleaning and looking after Juanito until her mother returned. She could attend the afternoon shift of classes and study at night. The girl would have to work hard for two years but it would be worth it. Other girls in the *vecindad,* most of whom left school after the fourth or fifth grade, had to take the worst jobs in shops and factories. Ester was the only girl of her group of friends who was graduating from primary school and who might continue her education. It was worth sacrificing for!

Alberto was annoyed with his mother. He finished his meal and went out to the patio. It was quite dark. There was to be a dance the next night in honor of the Virgin of Guadalupe and the committee was putting up extra lights. Alberto intended to take Susana to the dance and wondered if he had clean pants to wear. He saw his father talking to someone at the *vecindad* entrance and ducked around a corner to avoid him.

Rosa had just sat down to drink her coffee when her husband walked in. He had been gone from the house eighteen hours; the time between shifts he had spent at Alicia's. He was grimy and spotted with grease and he sagged with weariness. He had drunk a bottle of soda at the terminal and now he was worried that the sugar might make him ill. Without greeting anyone he went to the stove, looking for his herb medicine. Silently Rosa pointed to it and he poured out a glassful and drank it down. Then he went into the bedroom and sat down on the cot. Juanito joined him and snuggled up to him, lifting his father's inert arm and putting it around his shoulders. His father smiled down at him and patted him on the

head. "W-w-what's new? What d-d-did you do in school?" Juanito
told him some of the things he had done during the day. Agustín
listened with interest until he saw the child was yawning. At his
father's suggestion Juanito went to the toilet and then to bed.

Rosa looked at her husband. "Why so late? Did you meet one of
your lady friends?"

Agustín ignored the insinuation. "My crate broke down again
and I spent hours looking for a Stillson wrench. I finally fixed it and
it didn't cost me anything."

"That damned bus! How much time did you lose?"

"Almost all afternoon. I tell you I must get that government job.
This job is killing me and I don't earn enough with this old bus."

"My cousin, the senator, will get it for you," Rosa said. "He is an
important man. They say he will be the future governor of Morelos."

Agustín smiled. "Then," he said, "I will ask him for the job of
assistant."

"Assistant! In what would you assist him? You cannot even carry
a pistol!" his wife snapped back.

Agustín was quiet. "Is there a bit of coffee for me?" he asked almost timidly. He added, "I can give you the rest of the money on
borrow day . . . on Monday." To his surprise his wife stood up and
poured a cup of coffee and milk for him. She also poured one for
Ester who was almost asleep, her crocheting in her hand. "Come,
daughter, have your coffee and then you can go to sleep." Juanito
was lying on top of the blanket, fast asleep. His mother took off his
trousers, placed him in the center of the bed to separate Ester and
Alberto, covered him up, and turned out the light.

The three of them sat drinking coffee crowded around the table
that stood half in the bedroom, half in the kitchen. They heard firecrackers go off somewhere. "It is for our Virgin of Guadalupe. It is
her Saint's day today," Ester explained. "There was a procession
and music today, papá, and they sang *mañanitas*." Ester wondered
if this were a good time to ask for permission to go to the dance.
She decided it would be better to wait until her father was not at
home. "I'm going to bed," she said with a yawn and went into the
bedroom.

Agustín, too, rose and went to bed, first removing his soiled shirt and trousers. He turned to the wall, covered his face, and was soon asleep. Rosa ate the food remaining in the pot, stacked the dirty dishes and jars, but left them on the kitchen table. Almost always she left the dishes for the next morning so as not to disturb the sleepers. She washed her face and hands, undressed, and lay down at the opposite end of the cot next to her husband. She got up again to light the votive candle to the Virgin of Guadalupe and to turn out the kitchen light. The door was left slightly ajar for Alberto, who was still out. A few minutes later, at a quarter past eleven, she heard him come in. When he had slipped out of his clothes and had arranged himself under the covers, Rosa closed her eyes and fell asleep.

# THE GUTIERREZ FAMILY

## CAST OF CHARACTERS

| | |
|---|---|
| Guillermo Gutiérrez, age 34 | *the father* |
| Julia Rojas, age 46 | *Guillermo's wife in free union* |
| Lola, age 14 | *children of Guillermo and his first common-law wife, Esmeralda* |
| Maria, age 11 | |
| Herminio, age 9 | |
| Yolanda, age 27 | *Julia's daughter by her first husband* |
| Rafael, age 30 | *Yolanda's husband* |
| Catarina, age 11 | *children of Yolanda and Rafael* |
| Galván, age 9 | |
| Ema, age 7 | |
| Tomás, age 4 | |
| Maclovio, age 31 | *Julia's son by her first husband* |
| Panchita, age 21 | *Maclovio's wife* |
| Inés, age 44 | *Julia's sister* |
| Alfredo, age 30 | *Inés' husband* |
| Rufelia, age 66 | *mother of Julia and Inés* |
| Anita, age 35 | *Guillermo's sister-in-law* |
| Guadalupe | |
| Ignacio | |
| Don Chucho | |
| Ana | |
| The King | *neighbors and visitors* |
| Don Quintero | |
| Comadre Chole | |
| Melín | |
| Others | |

# THE GUTIERREZ FAMILY

On a bare lot between two brick buildings at No. 33, Street of the Bakers, the Panaderos *vecindad* lay exposed to the full view of pass-ers-by. It was a small *vecindad* and one of the poorest in Mexico City—only a row of twelve small, windowless one-room apartments that housed fifty-four people. The apartments, built of adobe brick, were joined by a common cement roof and extended as a single, narrow structure down the left side of the lot. Each apartment had a small, low-ceilinged entranceway which also served as a kitchen. The kitchen roofs were flimsily put together of scraps of tar paper, tin, and corrugated metal, and were held in place by heavy stones. Firewood heaped in piles and covered with old gunny sacks and pieces of cardboard were stored on the roofs. The doors to the apartments were so low that one had to stoop to enter. In front of some of them the artisan-tenants had built makeshift sheds or lean-tos to provide themselves a dry, shady place to work.

A walk of rough stone slabs laid by the tenants in front of their apartments led to the street and helped combat the mud. Scattered along the walk were large laundry tubs, lying flat or standing on end like big wheels, pails, low benches, chamberpots, and other articles set out to dry in the sun. Untidy piles of equipment—tin sheets, bundles of scrap steel strips, wire, nails, and tools—cluttered the space under the sheds. Hanging from the outside walls or set on rickety tables were plants growing in pots and cans of all types, shapes, and sizes. Some families had a wooden bird cage on a nail outside their door, one tenant kept pigeons, another chickens, and almost everyone had a dog or a cat. They loved animals and also needed them as protection from rats and thieves.

Toward the rear of the lot a cement water trough served the women for washing dishes and laundry and for bathing their children. Two dilapidated toilets of crumbling adobe, curtained by pieces of torn burlap, were used by all the tenants. The earth was strewn with rocks, and forked poles held up the clotheslines that crisscrossed the yard. Here and there a hole dug by the children or an unexpected sewer opening, covered by a rock, made walking hazardous. In the daytime the lot was filled with children, in ragged clothing and ill-fitting shoes, or barefoot, playing marbles or running between the lines of laundry, heedless of the warning shouts of the women. Children barely able to walk and still untrained sat and crawled in the dirt, often half-naked, while their mothers watched them from where they were working.

The Panaderos *vecindad* formed a little community. Nine of the twelve households were related by ties of blood and marriage, and all were related by *compadrazgo*. Borrowing was frequent, and the tenants drifted easily in and out of each others' rooms. However, there was less organization than in some of the larger *vecindades*.

There was no enclosing gate, no patron saint, no committee, no weekly dance, and no organized gang of boys and girls.

The heads of families of the Panaderos *vecindad* came from six of the central states of Mexico—Guanajuato, Querétaro, México, Hidalgo, Aguascalientes, and Morelos. Four were born in small rural villages, seven in urban centers outside of Mexico City, and ten in Mexico City. The average length of residence in the capital was 26.2 years. They worked at various jobs: two of them made tin pails, another made toys from scrap metal, and another, Guillermo Gutiérrez, made miniature stands for toy water bottles and repaired bicycles. Two worked in shoe factories, one in a belt factory, and Señor Ignacio sold newspapers. Because most of the incomes were very small and much of it was spent on drink, all the wives and many of the children also worked. Three of the families had no man at the head and were supported by the mothers. Some of the younger women worked in shops and others were ambulant peddlers, but most of them preferred to work at home, making sweets or cooked food to sell in the street nearby, dealing in old clothes, and taking in washing and ironing. The clotheslines were almost always hung with the laundry of others, providing a multicolored curtain behind which life in the *vecindad* could be conducted with some sense of privacy and dignity. After dark the clothes flapped ghostlike in the night breeze or *sereno* which, it was believed, helped remove the dirt.

On the sixteenth day of July, at five-forty in the morning, the little *vecindad* was quiet and all the doors were shut tight. The saloon where the men drank pulque and where the children were sent to buy the even cheaper *chinchol* was still closed. The bathhouse across the street had not yet opened for early customers. Now and then the silence was broken by a rickety bus or by a dog barking at a passing stranger. The first door to open was that of Señora Guadalupe, the wife of Ignacio the news-vendor. A rag wrapped about her neck and a twig broom in her hand, she came out to sweep the walk and the yard or patio. She was paid ten pesos a month by Ana, the janitress, to do this chore every morning. Before she began to sweep, the old woman paused for a moment, bending her gray head, to murmur her simple, daily prayer, "Oh, Lord, help me, help me!"

The door of No. 5, the "Casa Gutiérrez," as Guillermo had it printed on his business cards, opened noisily and his wife, Señora Julia Rojas, a short, stocky woman of forty-six, stepped out over the high ledge. She adjusted her wool shawl over her shoulders and smoothed her wrinkled black cotton dress. Seeing Guadalupe, she said, "Good morning, *comadrita*. At it already?" Guadalupe was Julia's sister-in-law by her second husband and godmother of "the blessed ribbons of Chalma" to each of Guillermo's children.

"Yes, yes. Going for the milk now?"

"Yes. Let's see if they'll give me enough. Having a ticket doesn't mean a thing. They are a bunch of mules!"

Every morning before six Julia went to the nearby government CEIMSA store to queue up for the milk sold there at half-price. Rumor said it was diluted with water and vegetable fat, but Julia paid no attention to that for she needed four quarts a day to feed the many people who depended upon her. She went early to be sure the milk would not be sold out and to queue up twice, since she could obtain only two quarts at a time. She was late this morning and hurried, clutching her shawl around her against the cold. She had bronchitis and her chest hurt, but if she did not go for the milk no one else would and her stepchildren and grandchildren would have to go without.

Julia felt put upon: she thought her married daughter, Yolanda, or her stepdaughter, Lola, should properly go for the milk when she herself was ill. But Yolanda, who lived two doors down in No. 7, was lazy and besides had recently given birth to her fifth child. Lola was only fourteen and was not permitted by her father to go out so early. Panchita, the wife of Julia's son, Maclovio, who lived in No. 9, could not be expected to go because she worked and her husband paid Julia fifty pesos a month to cook for them and their two children. The only other woman available was Julia's mother, Rufelia, who lived in a tiny room in a nearby *vecindad*, but she was old and no longer in her right mind. No matter how Julia fumed and complained about her heavy responsibilities, she continued to provide food for these people, sixteen in all, because she knew that they depended upon her. Julia had been the eldest of twelve children and was accustomed to assuming the burdens of others.

It was six-thirty when Julia returned to the *vecindad*. Guadalupe was still sweeping.

"You back already? Did they sell you all you wanted?"

"Same as always, little sister. My ticket wasn't worth a damn."

Julia was cross because she had been able to buy only two quarts of milk. She entered her house, shut the door with a bang, and went back to bed.

While the Gutiérrez family slept, the *vecindad* slowly came to life. Señora Maria of No. 12, Julia's *comadre* of the *Santísima Virgen*, came out to clean a bird cage at the washstand.

"You got up mighty early to get your sweeping done, didn't you, *comadre*?" she said to Guadalupe.

"Yes, *comadrita*, I couldn't sleep last night. I don't know why I couldn't sleep anymore. I got to thinking about not having the house rent."

"Ay, *comadre*! Sometimes I can't sleep either. Sometimes because I'm thinking and other times on account of bedbugs! How they can bother a person, eh, *comadre*?"

Ana, the stout janitress, carrying a pile of dirty clothes, joined the two women at the washing place. "If I don't do it now I won't get it done. When those old women start washing there is no room for anyone!" During the rainy season the women competed with each other to wash and dry their clothes while the sun was shining. Some had to finish their scrubbing out in the rain and hang the wet things in their crowded rooms. Ana knelt at the water trough and poured water over her clothes. Guadalupe went over to her, dragging her broom, and said, "Do you love me a lot, *comadre*?" This was the way the *vecindad* people asked to borrow money. Ana shook her head regretfully. "No, I don't love you today, *comadrita*." Without another word Guadalupe went on sweeping. From another house

Señor Juan came out with his wife and mother and young daughter. The girl had been ill and her sunken eyes still had dark circles around them. Guadalupe stopped sweeping for a minute.

"Good morning. Are you going to the Villa?"

"Yes," answered the mother, Lucha. "We are going to thank the little Virgin because Amelia is better now." The family hurried off to catch the bus.

Guadalupe said to the other women, "I'll bet you anything that this time *Comadre* Lucha will get drunk." The women laughed and agreed. Ignacio came out to wash his face and go for the bundle of morning newspapers that he hawked in the street. More doors opened as women came out for a jug of water or to go to the toilet. The buses that drove by were full of people going to work. The sun rose higher, and the birds in their cages began to sing.

Inside the "Casa Gutiérrez" the family still slept. The small windowless room had a foul smell. The bedclothes, the torn blankets, and the lumpy mattresses were damp and musty from lack of sun. The bedroom and the kitchen passageway were so cluttered that even after Julia "cleaned" they looked messy. The passageway, six feet wide and three feet long, was just inside the front door. The right-hand side, a space of only two by three feet, was used by Guillermo as an indoor workshop. Here on a high worktable were his precious tools: a screw driver, a hammer, a file, scissors, pincers, and a vise. "These are like my eyes," Guillermo said of his tools, "for without them I am blind." The top of the worktable was gouged from blows of his hammer, spattered with paint, and strewn with screws, rivets, empty soda bottles, an oilcan, boxes, and jars. Above the table, on a shelf supported by two wires, was a battered radio which Guillermo kept tuned to its one station while he worked. The shelf also held a small rusty scale, a light socket, some nails, and pieces of metal. On top of the radio was a bottle of aluminum paint and Guillermo's dirty blue apron. On the wall under the shelf two large calendars had been nailed up: one was a portrait of the boxer, Ratón Macias, the other of the Virgin of Fátima. Two installment tickets and a rent receipt were impaled on another nail.

Underneath the worktable there were more soda bottles, a twenty-liter tin can holding old iron bars, a jug of gasoline, a pair of old shoes, and a caved-in rubber ball. Every inch of the remaining space, from the floor to the ceiling, was filled with a large pile of scrap metal strip, new, but showing signs of rust and hopelessly tangled. A piece of limp red garden hose draped over this pile, like a decoration, and a pair of child's yellow sandals hung from a protruding strip. On a wide board supported by a chair, one hundred and twenty-four newly painted metal frames for the toy bottles had been set to dry.

The kitchen side of the passage was more orderly. The earth floor was swept, clay and enamel pots and two frying pans hung on nails hammered into the adobe brick wall, and a few chipped plates and mugs stood on shelves over the stove. The rest of the dishes and mugs and three glasses, still dirty from last night's supper, were stacked on the little table beside the three-burner stove. The stove rested on a cement charcoal brazier, now unused.

At the back of the brazier, leaning against the wall, were a stained tray and a huge clay casserole that Julia used when she prepared *mole* or other food to sell in the street. On the floor were a pail of charcoal and a portable brazier with a clay griddle on which Julia made *tortillas*. On the lowest shelf over the stove Julia kept foodstuffs—salt in a glass shaker, powdered chile in a broken cup, a paper package of flour in the bowl of a soup ladle, a piece of bread in a covered pot, an empty oil bottle. A clay jar held four or five bent spoons, two kitchen knives, and a wire egg beater in the shape of a flower. On a stool near the door a glass-covered tray held chocolates, marshmallows, and other cheap candies which Guillermo sold to the people of the *vecindad*. This "candy store" was one of his more recent business enterprises.

The inner room was reached by stepping down one step through a second doorway. A votive light burning on a shelf in the rear lighted up twelve pictures, large and small, of various virgins and saints. The two largest pictures, and the only ones in frames and covered with glass, were of the Virgin of Guadalupe and San Martín Caballero, the patron saint of merchants. The shelf, draped with an orange-colored cloth, held a bunch of paper flowers in a jar and a wooden box with a glass door through which could be seen the Sacred Heart of Jesus and a tiny wooden crucifix. Streamers of colored crepe paper hung from the ceiling beams above the holy pictures.

The eight-foot square room was almost completely filled with furniture; only a narrow aisle, about a foot wide, had been left free for walking. On the left was a narrow blue metal bedstead which Guillermo and Julia, his common-law wife, shared. A small table and a wooden wardrobe, both cluttered with boxes and other objects, took up the rest of this side of the room. On the right a high shelf or half-balcony, about four and a half feet from the floor and four feet wide, jutted out from the wall. On this an old bedspring and a cotton mattress provided a sleeping place for Guillermo's three children—Lola, age fourteen, Maria, age eleven, and Herminio, age nine. The unused metal headboard and foot of the bed were stored on the shelf along with twelve bicycle rims, twelve used tires, and a pailful of scrap iron. Several enamelware pots, the largest of which contained ground chile, sesame seeds, and peanuts for *mole*, also were piled up on the shelf.

Underneath the shelf five old bicycles leaned against a pile of boxes which were filled with empty soda bottles. In one corner near the door a broken-down Pepsi-Cola bottle cooler, now used to hold empty bottles, was piled high with rags and clothes. In the opposite corner, on the far side of the bicycles, stood a steel barrel full of bicycle parts, and a hemp bag holding empty bottles lay on top of it. Behind the door, which was usually kept open, two small painted chairs were stacked one on top of the other beside a cornstalk broom and a heap of dirty clothes.

The rear wall from the parents' bed to well under the sleeping platform was occupied by a large, new, combination radio, record-player, and television set. It was shiny and truly resplendent in the midst of all the junk around it, the one unscratched, unmarred piece of furniture in the house. Still protected on the top and sides by its original paper carton, only the family photos and the alarm clock were allowed to be placed on it. Guillermo had warned his family, when the set had been delivered, that they had to take good care of it, "better than we do of ourselves."

He had bought it on the installment plan, using his first set as down payment and paying one hundred pesos a month. The total cost was seventy-five hundred pesos or six hundred dollars, but to Guillermo it was an investment, even a form of savings, for he calculated that while he was making the payments it would bring in one or two pesos a day from the children who came to see the programs and when the last installment was paid he would re-crate it "as good as new" and sell it. He was counting on the possibility that prices would continue to rise, as they had for the past several years, and on finding a customer whom he could convince that the machine was factory-new. With the money he would make he planned to buy a plot of land in an undeveloped area where land was still cheap. Later it would be worth a great deal more, for the city was growing and land values were going up. This was Guillermo's scheme for starting up the ladder to success. "That's why I take more care of the TV set than of my children," he said. "I'm even buying records for it so I can sell it for more."

The day the set had arrived had been memorable for everyone in the *vecindad* but especially for Guillermo. He had stood there among his neighbors and listened elatedly to their exclamations of wonder at the size and quality of the machine. His brother-in-law had said, "Huuuy, you will soon be a rich man, Guillermo." He had answered calmly, "Yes, one must hustle. One must *do* something to *be* something." He had been happy that day, feeling that he was making progress in the world. He did not expect to run into difficulties, and he had paid no attention to the *indirectas* and criticisms made by some of the women.

Ana had said, "A washing machine would bring in more money." Señora Chole of No. 3 had said, "What do bean-eaters living like that want with it? Better wait until they have a parlor with armchairs to watch in comfort from." Old Guadalupe had said, "It is just pure ambition! He won't part with five centavos for a piece of garlic and Julia has to come borrowing from me!" Still another neighbor remarked, "They are so presumptuous that they will lose every-thing. It would be better to buy a piece of land. If someone digs a hole in that, you can fill it up with a little earth, but if someone puts a hole in this machine what will they do?" Guillermo dismissed it all as natural envy and was pleased when his neighbors came every evening to watch the programs for twenty centavos apiece.

At seven-thirty Julia yawned, stretched her arms, and pushed aside the dirty quilt for the second time that day. Guillermo, plump, light-skinned, twelve years her junior, slept on. Julia made the sign of the cross, said a brief prayer, and got out of bed to look for her cloth, hemp-soled slippers. She was mumbling to herself, ". . . one hour in line to get milk." She noticed that Lola, her light brown hair in curlers, was awake and watching her from the shelf. The girl smiled at her stepmother, who said, "Didn't you say you were going to get up early? Just look at what time it is."

Lola placed one foot on the table for support, jumped down from the shelf, smoothed the ragged brown silk dress she had slept in, and bent down to pull out her shoes from under her father's bed. Lola had finished the third grade in school and now worked in a little shoeshop in the *Lagunilla* market. Every ten days she gave her father fifty pesos out of which he allowed her money for bus fare, lunches, and baths. Lola claimed the fifty pesos were all she earned but Guillermo was not convinced. "I don't know," he would say, "what child tells the truth about that! None! Who is going to say, 'Well, I earn so much.' I believe they pay her more."

"I am going to wash an apron before I go to work," Lola told her stepmother. She searched for something under the wardrobe. "Where's the soap, Julia?"

"Well, I don't know where you put things."

"Here it is. I found it." Lola put the soap into a small pail and went out.

Julia, who was sitting on the bed and holding a corner of the quilt over her arms, noticed that now Herminio was bending over the platform to look at her.

"Mamá," he said, "I'm not going to work today."

"Well, what's the reason now?"

"I just don't want to. I want to go to Melín's birthday party to-night. How much do the little candles for the cake cost? I'm going to buy some."

Julia nudged her husband. "Do you hear what your son says? He's going to buy candles for my god-daughter's birthday cake!"

Guillermo grumbled, pulling the quilt over his head. "I don't know anything about it. I am ignorant of life." He tried to go to sleep, but Lola came in and asked Herminio to hand her the soiled apron from under the mattress on the shelf. He refused and the two began to argue. Julia called to Maria to get the apron and Herminio shook Maria vigorously but the younger girl pretended to be sleeping.

Julia turned impatiently to Lola. "The idea, coming down from the shelf and not taking your things with you! You give me a pain. And the rest of you lazy kids! You want everything to be handed to you. I'm really fed up with you."

Herminio finally chucked the apron at Lola who picked it up and left for the washing place. Julia sat scratching her head and shaking the short tight black curls of her new permanent wave. Guillermo, awake now, asked, "You have to leave early today, don't you?"

"Yes, I'm getting out of here right away. That lousy rain! I wasn't able to sell a thing yesterday. Maybe today I can bring home fifty pesos."

Julia began to cough and said her chest hurt. Guillermo suggested that she take kerosene with sugar to cure it. When she made a face at the idea he said, "Not with salt, that sours it, but with plenty of sugar it will do you good."

Julia got up to take a pile of towels from the wardrobe. "I told Lola not to use these towels in the wardrobe but she won't listen. What a bloody nuisance!"

Guillermo laughed and slapped her on the arm. "You damned runt, they're always giving you a rough time."

Julia smiled but said, "You be quiet or you'll be sorry, eh? You'll start complaining that I'm too rough. You won't be able to stand it."

Guillermo slapped her again, and she took off one of her slippers and whacked him with it on his bare shoulder.

"Quit that, old gal!" he said. "That hurts! I just slap you easy." He slapped her once more and again she hit him hard on the shoulder.

"Ay, *mamacita linda*, don't be so mean. I hit you only twice and you hit me five times. Can't you see that my poor hide hurts? I'm delicate I want you to know."

"Oh, sure, sure." They both laughed.

In the meantime Herminio had pulled on his pants, jumped down from the shelf, and gone out. Julia began to arrange the towels according to size, placing them in piles on the bed.

Guillermo continued playfully: "What's the matter, old girl? When are you going to marry me?"

"I guess being poor isn't enough. You're also crazy."

"What about it, old woman, how much do your curls cost?"

"Oh, quit bothering me, you jackass," replied Julia as her husband burst into loud guffaws. Julia saw that Maria was trying to jump down from the shelf.

"Go on, get down. Stop fooling around."

"But Julia, I might get hurt if I jump." Julia went to lift Maria down. The child immediately ran out, leaving the door open.

Guillermo sat up to dress. He was wearing a soiled T shirt and shorts made of coarse sacking. Over these he pulled on a pair of thoroughly dirty cotton trousers and then pushed his feet into his old shoes. He never tied his shoelaces, even when he wore his better pair downtown, because he believed his shoes lasted longer this way. "If I tie them they get tight and then when I sit down the shoes bust on me." Sometimes Julia complained of his unshaven, disheveled appearance and ragged clothing, but he would answer that it was better to go about looking poor so that people would repay what they owed him.

Without washing or combing, Guillermo went to his worktable in the passageway, turned on the radio, and sat down to work. A ranchero song was being sung. "When we were sweethearts there were kisses and gifts. Now that we're married there are punches and kicks," Guillermo smiled at his wife. "It's true, isn't it? When we were courting I used to hug and kiss you."

Julia nodded and laughed, "You were a skinny bastard then. I could surround you with one arm."

"Really? Don't be a liar."

"Do you remember when you used to take me on the bike I'd hang on with twenty nails? With my teeth and nails and everything! I was afraid because I didn't know you. I thought you were trying to get rid of me."

"Honestly, old girl, I planned to throw you into the canal." They both laughed again.

Lola came in carrying an electric iron and her wet apron. She arranged a towel on a chair, unscrewed the light bulb, plugged the iron into a socket hanging from the electric cord, and stood waiting for the iron to get hot. The apron was too wet to iron so she hung it from the shed roof to dry. Kneeling before the chair, she began to press a blue dress she intended to wear to work. Lola had five dresses, all bought second-hand by Julia, and she always seemed to be washing or ironing one of them just before going out. Julia had often scolded her for leaving such things to the last minute and now, irritation with her stepdaughter mounting, Julia rummaged through the wardrobe pulling out one wrinkled dress after another.

"You're going to have to spend a little time ironing these," she said.

"Sure I will, Julia, but not now. I've got to go to work."

"And why did you leave those rags behind the door? They belong in the box. You don't like to do anything! You're as lazy as they make them. Just because your father never tells you anything you take advantage. I started to work when I was a tiny kid. You sly brat! You'll see how you make out when you get married. You are just like your mother! You can't do a thing. I'm going to hit you even though your father makes me pay for it!"

Guillermo and Lola were silent at Julia's outburst. In the past Guillermo had attempted to defend his favorite daughter's distaste for housework, but Julia had always argued him down. When he said that Lola worked in a shop all day and had a right to rest when she was at home, Julia retorted, with justice, that she too peddled towels all day and then came home to cook and clean for everyone. When Guillermo protested that Lola was still young, Julia pointed to the many fifteen-year-old girls in the neighborhood who already had babies. "She will be hitching up with a man soon and she still doesn't know how to work properly." Guillermo had no answers; all he could do was slip his daughter money once in a while. He had to keep peace with Julia, for without her he would be lost.

Guillermo had prospered in the seven years he had been with Julia, and he was still grateful to his friend Canuto for advising him to join up with a woman much older than himself. That was after his first wife, Esmeralda, had deserted him for a jewelry-worker. Penniless because he had spent all his money getting his three children back from their mother, he began looking for someone who could take care of them. He had seen Julia selling *enchiladas* outside the bathhouse where he went every Saturday and recognized her as a neighbor whose son he had played with when he was a child. Since Julia did not remember him, he never mentioned this to her or to Maclovio, her son. She had seemed to him a likely candidate for marriage and he made a point of buying something from her and talking with her every time he saw her.

Julia, too, had been willing to talk and she told him all about herself. Her father had been a miner in Guanajuato but had abandoned his wife and children. He came to Mexico City where he fell in love with Rufelia, Julia's mother, who was many years his junior, and lived with her in free union for thirty-five contented years. In this marriage he was kind and good but always very poor.

Julia helped her mother bring up a large family; she went to work in a factory at the age of nine, after a year in school. At fourteen she ran off with "the father of her children" with whom she lived in free union, and a year later Maclovio was born, followed by Yolanda and then a baby who died. Her husband did not support her and beat her when he was drunk. She earned her lodging by being a janitress; on the day Yolanda was born Julia had to keep getting out of bed to unlock the door for the tenants. She finally left her husband, returned to her parents' home, and from then on worked to support her children. In time Yolanda and Maclovio both married, and she began to live with another man who also drank heavily and did not support her. He had died a few years before and her mother came to live with her in her little room. Despite this and the fact that she had three brothers and a sister, all married and with children, an aunt on her mother's side, and many friends and *compadres,* Julia declared that she was lonely.

Guillermo had thought Julia dark and unattractive compared with his first wife, who had light eyes and hair like Lola's. Julia spoke and laughed too loudly, she used coarse language, and often she smelled of alcohol. Sometimes when Guillermo met her she was suffering from a hangover. But he had needed help and he told her his story, making it clear that he was looking for a wife who could no longer have children. Julia, whose womb had turned "cold" after several miscarriages, assured him that she could not become pregnant.

On her part Julia was pleased with Guillermo's youth, fair skin, and mild manner and impressed by the fact that he neither smoked nor drank. When he invited her to go bicycle riding she accepted, and after one or two walks together in the Villa they agreed to join in free union. Guillermo and his three children, the youngest then aged two, thereupon moved into Julia's room. She had hoped to be able to stay home and keep house, but she soon found that she would have to hustle if the children were not to go hungry. She also learned that her husband's placid nature had a drawback; at night he slept peacefully by her side and only rarely showed sexual interest in her. He said that he was afraid the children would notice and that this inhibited him. But he never lost his temper or beat her and she enjoyed his good-humored joking. She became fond of him and the children, even though she realized that in this relationship she would have to give more than she received.

When Guillermo saw that he had married a good worker whom he could depend on, he tried to realize his dream of going into business for himself. He started a bicycle business with his ex-foreman. The two men invested all their money in fifty unclaimed, damaged, or stolen bicycles. Guillermo did the repair work, and his partner changed the registration numbers "to make it all legal." They rented out and sold the bicycles, doing very well despite the fact that competitors stole bikes from them. Later they expanded operations by dealing in second-hand clothing. It was Guillermo's job to make a weekly collection round for clothing sold on the installment plan. Every time he returned, his partner would inform him that a bicycle had been stolen. This went on until their stock was down to ten bicycles. Guillermo then became discouraged, took his share of the bikes, and dissolved the partnership. A short time later his ex-partner opened up his own renting agency with a stock of about fifty bicycles, and Guillermo at last realized that the man had been stealing them from their joint stock.

After this setback Julia had to sell her furniture to support the family and they were turned out of her room for not paying the rent. Julia's *comadre,* who lived at No. 5 in the Panaderos *vecindad,* permitted them to sleep on the floor of her kitchen until they could find another room. Eventually the *comadre* moved out, and they took over her place for a hundred pesos. With Julia's earnings they bought second-hand furniture and once more had a home. Julia provided the food and clothing because Guillermo could be persuaded to take responsibility only for the rent and the electric bill.

One day Guillermo saw miniature water bottles in metal stands on sale at a toy market. He figured out how to produce them inexpensively and went into business again. He bought the bottles at a glass factory, trading in broken glass to bring down the price. The other necessary equipment—the metal strips, rivets, chains, corks, labels, wax paper, wire, and aluminum paint—he bought in quantity at a cost of about twenty-three centavos a toy. He kept no record of how many bottles he produced and sold but he had the impression that at the beginning he made from one hundred and fifty to two hundred a day. "I worked without stopping from morning till night. I was working like an animal. You know, I was sort of going crazy. People talked to me and suddenly I answered with something else, like that, without noticing it. I was losing my reason from all the work. I tell you, I never left this table, just worked and worked."

With his earnings from the bottles, he again bought stolen bicycles and began to rent them out. He also got hold of an old bottle cooler, stocked it with ice and bottles of soda, and went into the soda-dispensing business. To build up his bicycle agency he gave a free bottle of pop to each person who rented a bike. When, however, police inspectors began to investigate all bicycle agencies in an attempt to cut down widespread thefts, Guillermo hastily sold at cost all of his "hot" bicycles except five dilapidated ones. His bicycle agency gone, he also stopped selling soda pop.

To make up for the loss of income he stocked a tray with candies to sell to the neighborhood children and continued to service bicycles for the few customers who came to him. Besides this he collected empty bottles and broken glass and gathered and bought up scrapwood. A friendly watchman at a nearby government warehouse gave him small quantities of wood and sawdust on the condition that he would not sell it. But he did secretly sell it and once or twice a week he also exchanged a large bag of sawdust for a few pounds of meat from a local butcher.

Another of Guillermo's money-making schemes had been to supply electric current to four of his closest neighbors by running extension cords from his light socket to theirs through the walls. His neighbors paid him a fixed monthly sum well under the minimum of the electric company, and he made a profit because of the reduced rates on higher consumption of power. That is, it worked out for Guillermo so long as the neighbors used one weak light bulb and were sparing in their use of electrical appliances. To protect his interests Guillermo had to become overseer; this led to quarrels and finally to the discontinuance of the scheme.

In his spare time Guillermo worked on various inventions. He was most hopeful about a hand-operated apparatus he had made out of various pieces of scrap (a typewriter roller, a crank, a corset stay) to speed up pasting labels on a child's lottery game. Above the roller Guillermo fixed a perforated tin can containing glue. The glue dripped onto the roller, making it possible for him to paste labels rapidly and to produce the games in some quantity at his workshop. But he did not have the money to go into business nor had he yet looked for an outlet to market the product.

He also had worked out a design for a modern house of prostitution, a problem that had come to his attention when the newspapers had publicized the appalling condition of houses of ill-fame on near-by Tintero Street. He had constructed a cardboard model of a building in the hope of selling the plan to the mayor who had declared he meant to improve the city. The building, roofed in glass, had no windows in the walls and only two narrow entrances, one at the front and another at the back of a long central hallway. On both sides of the hall were rows of little rooms with curtained doorways. Each room was to be equipped with two cement beds (to avoid bedbugs), with mattresses, a washstand, and two cement chairs. All the prostitutes were to wear identical blue smocks and to wait for customers in the chairs rather than to solicit them stark naked as they sometimes did. The reason for the back exit was to enable a client to leave without embarrassment if he changed his mind, as Guillermo often had in the past.

"I've thought of everything," Guillermo said. "The idea is to put all these women on Tintero Street in this one big house and charge them less rent than they are paying now. Since it is all enclosed, people from the outside can't look in, right? So anybody who walks in knows what he's coming for. Now suppose he doesn't like it inside, why he just walks out through that little door. And these curtains are better than doors so there won't be all this opening and closing. With two women to a room the building will be paid off in one year. When I've got it all finished I'm going to see Mayor Uruchurtu and have him buy the idea from me. I'll let him have it for one or two thousand pesos. That'll be enough for me because that way I'll be able to get a bicycle agency going again. With that, well, I'll be on my way up again. Don't you think?"

Guillermo was aware that his neighbors and in-laws criticized him. "I know what they say, that I'm a fool, that I'm sick in the head. But I know I'm not so why should I worry? I know what I want. I think I'm smarter than anyone else here because they are worse fools. No one else here has television or bicycles or a bottle refrigerator. And you know, it makes them mad that I'm getting along better. As if it was hurting them! That's why at times I would rather not do anything so that they would leave me alone. But I do my little inventions because I have to. Not everyone can do them."

*144*

Guillermo had continued making water bottles but his business began to fall off when a *compadre* in the *vecindad* copied his product and undersold him. Now he made only two hundred a week, selling them at a profit of about seventy-five pesos. He began to invest his money in unclaimed articles from pawnshops as well as in stolen goods, reselling them at a profit. At one time he had in his home three radios, a gold wristwatch, gold cuff links, and a ring with a precious stone. His chief handicap was lack of capital; he often had to beg loans from his wife or borrow from a moneylender at the exorbitant interest of twenty per cent every twenty-four days.

To remedy this situation, Guillermo organized a sort of mutual credit society that he called, simply, the "savings box." Members bought one or more tickets or shares at five pesos a week and were thereby entitled to borrow up to one hundred pesos on each share at an interest charge of three per cent a week. At the end of a year the fund was to be divided up among the shareholders. Guillermo, who kept the savings box in his home, dipped into it in small emergencies, repaying his loans without interest. He considered this his privilege since he was the administrator of the fund. He kept notebooks full of names, addresses, and figures, he gave receipts, he went personally to collect the weekly contributions from forgetful members, and he had the responsibility of guarding the money. He kept it in a cigar box—on his worktable during the day and under his bed at night. "It's just like a bank, see? I'm like a bank manager and take the deposits. It's like a cooperative society. It's like the Russians do, you see, when they build a house. It doesn't belong to one person but to many. That's what I'd like to do with this money, see if we can build us a little house. I mean all of us together and then we divide it up. This is a good thing, for instead of wasting their money on movies, they save it. That's how it grows big. Later we'll lend on things, instead of them going to the pawnshops where they give anything they feel like. God willing it will keep on growing!"

Guillermo stopped hammering and opened the savings box to count the money. After that he looked in a notebook to see who still owed money and calculated how much he would have in the box by the end of the day. He did this several times a day to relax and also because he felt the responsibility of his position.

Lola was still ironing, kneeling on the floor. Julia stood at the front door looking at the sky.

"Ay, what a hard rain we had last night!" she said to her husband. "It's a good thing you fixed the floor or we would have had water up to the mattress like that other time."

Guillermo nodded. "Yes, old girl, they say it rained hard but I didn't even know it for I was at the movies."

Going to the movies was Guillermo's one passion. Before he bought the TV set he had gone almost every night. Now he went two or three times a week because, he said, he did his best thinking there and got new ideas, especially from the American films. He often prayed for luck in the movies, reciting the same prayer over and over. Even when he fell asleep Guillermo did not consider it time wasted because he prayed in his dreams. Julia had been annoyed at first—he never took her with him and it cost money—but she later realized that somehow it helped him and she stopped complaining.

When Julia again complimented her husband on keeping their little house from being flooded, Guillermo smiled but said nothing. He had been especially pleased with this scheme for he had earned money with it. He had placed a high slab of stone on the doorsill to keep out the water and then he had raised the floor of the kitchen by covering it with three truckloads of gravel that he had obtained free from the overseer of a construction project. When the neighbors in the *vecindad* saw the improvement, they wanted to do the same. He had told them, "Good, if you want to fill in like I'm doing, I'll sell you gravel at ten pesos a load." He then arranged to give the overseer three pesos for each free load of gravel and made a profit of seven pesos a load. He was proud of his shrewdness. "It was good business, no? You have to be smart to make money here and there. I made more than one hundred pesos just from that. They benefited because if they had had to hire a truck it would have cost them more. Well, that's how we defend ourselves."

*146*

He had not told Julia that he had made a profit because she would have insisted that he help her *compadres* and children without charge, or she might even have made him spend the money on his children. Instead, at an auction at the government pawnshop he bought another gold watch which he planned to have cleaned and then sell for about two hundred pesos. Meanwhile he had pawned it because he was short of money for the monthly installment on the TV set.

In the kitchen Julia had turned on the kerosene stove after a short battle with the blackened wick. She turned the blue flames low and set the jug of milk on one burner and a pot of water for coffee on the other. She scratched her head as she talked with Guillermo about visitors they had had the night before.

"Don Quintero and *Comadre* Chole were here while it rained and we drank three beers. They drank theirs all right but his sister-in-law hardly touched hers. She's awful! I don't like such strait-laced people. She kept refusing it even though she wanted it. Why, that big old so-and-so!" Julia turned to watch Lola. "Isn't that iron awfully hot, Lola? We've had that iron only a year and it's got to last us."

Lola stood up to disconnect the cord and shake out the damp apron.

Her father said teasingly, "And what do you want an apron for? You never wear one."

"Ay, papá what do you mean, I never wear one?" Lola kneeled again to iron one of the dresses Julia had thrown to her earlier.

Julia began to work in the kitchen, turning her back on Guillermo who was within arm's distance. "Did Agueda give you some money?" she asked.

"Ay, she hasn't given me a thing, not a cursed thing. But after a while I'm going to see her to collect."

Julia went for water. A few seconds later Guillermo heard a voice outside calling, "Don't you have any firewood today?"

"Yes, just a minute, I'm coming right away," Guillermo shouted back. "My hat, where's my hat?" he asked Lola. He found his old black felt hat on the Pepsi-Cola cooler and put it on, saying, "Let's give the poor señora some wood. She comes from so far away." As he went out, he picked up a chair and took it with him. A bent old woman was outside. Guillermo stood on the chair and began pulling down sticks of firewood from the roof. The old woman put them one by one into her shawl and then counted out a few centavos into Guillermo's hand. He called to Maria, gave her one of the coins, and sent her to buy a votive candle. He almost always bought a candle for San Martín with the first money earned each day. "It is a matter of faith," he said. "If I do this I win God's favor and all goes well."

Guillermo returned to his worktable and began to hammer down pieces of bent metal strips. But he noticed two new account books lying on top of a pile of articles on the kitchen table and, irritated, he said to Lola, "Didn't I tell you to put those books away? Don't you understand that a book is very important? If it gets blotched or lost, what will I do then? I'll lose my records and then I won't know whom I owe or who owes me. When you see my books scattered around like that, pick them up." His daughter said nothing and went on ironing.

Julia re-entered the room, shouting to Maria to get the oil bottle and go for oil. She then began to rummage through the wardrobe for a dress to wear, finding a wrinkled white one which she tossed out for Lola to iron.

Guillermo shuddered in an exaggerated manner. "Hand me my jacket, old girl, I'm cold." Julia found a faded maroon jacket and threw it at him.

Lola had been examining the white dress. "Look, Julia," she said, "it's all ripped at the hem. Do you have a needle?"

"I don't know. The way you put things away I can never find one." Julia and Lola both searched in boxes and cans until they found a needle. Lola kneeled on the floor and began to sew.

Galván, Yolanda's nine-year-old son, came by to go to work with Herminio. He respectfully kissed his grandmother's hand and then Guillermo's. Galván and Herminio worked as mechanic's helpers at a nearby garage instead of going to school. Neither Guillermo nor Julia was eager to send the children to school for they were not convinced that two or three years of schooling, which was the most they could hope for for the children, would really help them get better jobs. For that, one needed a certificate of graduation from the sixth grade. Julia, who was illiterate, said that she could earn more money than many who knew how to read and write. This year Herminio had been kept home because he had had a serious illness. His parents did not consider him strong enough for school, but he was permitted to work full-time for two pesos a week.

While Herminio was looking for his cap and jacket, Hector Gómez, the young man who slept in old Guadalupe's house, came to ask for change for a ten-peso bill. Guillermo shook his head. "We're dead broke. I would be glad to change it, really I would, but we don't have any money." Hector thanked him and left. Herminio found his clothes at last and the two boys left.

Julia started to make her bed. She took off the yellow quilt. A dirty sheet underneath, too small for the bed, had rolled up to the head during the night revealing an old mattress covered with jute sacks. It, too, was too short for the bed, and a long narrow pillow laid across the foot served as a piece of extra mattress. Without wasting time Julia made the bed and covered it with an old bedspread. She then picked up the things scattered over the floor—empty soda bottles, rags, shoes, and papers. While she was working her granddaughter Ema, two years younger than Galván, came in and stood watching Guillermo work. She was barefoot, her dirty dress hung down in the back, long uncombed dark hair fell over her face, and her nose was running.

Guillermo smiled at her. "Well, here's the little witch! What do you say? How are things?" The little girl smiled but said nothing.

Lola, hurrying with the sewing, kept looking up at the clock on the TV set. "Julita, look what time it is! It's going to get late on me." When Julia did not answer Lola stood up and said, "Here it is, Julia, you'll have to iron it yourself." Julia looked annoyed as Lola hastily removed her curlers and combed her hair. Lola put on her blue dress, hiding behind the wardrobe door and throwing her dirty clothing onto the bed.

Maria came in carrying the oil bottle. Julia looked at her and cried, "Just look at your dress and your paws! Why, they're a disgrace to God! Nobody but those girls at the tavern ever start the day like that."

"But you're just like that yourself," Guillermo said, defending Maria.

"Oh, yes? Why I never go out like that." Julia playfully swung her arm and slapped her husband's face.

"Ay, don't hit me. in the face. Pretty soon my jaws are going to ache."

"Is that so?" said Julia. "Well, I don't care if you ache all over." She took the needle Lola had stuck into the calendar and began to sew on her torn apron strap.

They looked up to see Yolanda in the doorway, holding her baby in her arms. Ignoring Guillermo, whom she disliked, she told her mother that her husband would not let her go out to work that day even though there was no money in the house. Yolanda sat down angrily on a bench under the shed and nursed her child.

A short, slight woman came up the walk and stopped before the "Casa Gutiérrez." It was Anita, Guillermo's sister-in-law. "Good morning," she said to Guillermo, who kept on working. "Don't annoy me any more, man. You keep having me come back and you never give me a thing." Guillermo had owed her money for some time.

"No," he said, "but today I'm going to give it to you. If not this afternoon, then tomorrow at eleven or twelve o'clock."

"Yes, that's what you always tell me. I don't believe you, man. You're just screwing around. Are you going to pay me or not?"

Guillermo, undisturbed, tried to calm her. "Today I'm really going to pay you. But I'm in bad shape. I've got to pay everybody but how can I do it if I don't have the money?" He looked at Julia as though for support.

"Don't get me mixed up in these affairs of yours," Julia said. "I don't know a thing. You said you borrowed it for me but I didn't get a penny of it. The very idea! Don't try to foul me up. You're always using me as a shield to hide behind."

Yolanda's young son, Tomás, came in crying and grabbed his

grandmother's skirt. No one paid any attention to him or to Ema as Guillermo and his sister-in-law continued to talk.

"If you don't intend to pay me, say so, and I won't have to keep coming back."

"Why shouldn't I pay you? If you do me a favor why shouldn't I pay you? But the man came for the rent and he took the few centavos I had. If you had a few cents and the rent collector came, whom would you rather pay? But I'll pay you back, for that's the law."

"All right, am I going to stand or sit while I wait for it?" Noticing Yolanda, Anita interrupted herself to say, "Why don't you sell *atole* or something during the mornings?" She knew that Yolanda's husband spent his wages on drink. Then when Yolanda tried to earn money to feed their children, he was furious because she left the house. If it had not been for her mother's help, Yolanda's situation would have been desperate.

Guillermo said, "If she sells *atole* in the morning what'll she sell at night?" Julia laughed. "You old bastard, what a thing to say!"

"Why, sure. If she's going to sell something in the morning, why not at night, too?"

Anita said seriously, "No, really. It's good business to sell *atole* or *pancita* for those who start the day with a hangover." Turning back to Guillermo she said, "Well, shall I come back this evening or what?"

He picked up one of the books on the table and showed it to her. "Look, all of these people have to bring their money to me. If they don't, I'll go collect it and pay you out of that. The money isn't mine but I know that I'll put it back in the box."

"Yes," Julia said, "all the members pay him five pesos a week whenever they have the money." She added, "I've got to send a carton of beer to Carmela's for her Saint's Day. We're going to have a party here too for Carmelita, *Comadre* Chole's daughter. They're going to make a cake and I don't know what all."

"Well, I don't know whether I'll go or not. I don't have money for such things." Anita said good-by and left.

Guillermo turned to his wife, crossing his arms in a gesture of despair. "Well, how are we going to pay the señora her money?" "Don't get me mixed up in it. That money you borrowed wasn't for me. How do I know it wasn't for some other woman!"

At that Guillermo said in a coaxing tone, "Don't be that way. When a person is having a hard time you have to help him out."

Julia plugged in the iron and knelt to iron the white dress. Lola had put on a green sweater that was torn at the elbow and had tossed her rolled-up dirty clothes behind the door. "Julita, what about my handkerchief?" she asked.

Before Julia could answer Guillermo said, "Yes, it's a good idea to have something to blow your nose with, in case you go into somebody's house and need to. A person runs into different weather and that's why it's a good idea to . . ."

Julia interrupted to ask her stepdaughter why she never knew where her things were. Lola didn't answer. Yolanda stood up to leave, handing her mother a five-peso bill.

"Here, mamá, get the lottery ticket."

"Ay, daughter, get it changed. I don't have a cent." But Yolanda left the money on the chair and went out, her young son following her. Ema stayed on, watching her grandmother iron. Lola, without a handkerchief, was ready to go to work. It was just eight-thirty. As she went out she said, "I wonder how much the little figures and the candles are going to cost."

A woman brushed by Lola in the doorway and went straight to Julia who said, "Good morning, Carmelita." Julia took some money out of her apron pocket and handed it to the woman, saying, "Thank you, *comadrita*. You know how much it was needed." Carmela, who had become Julia's *comadre* six years before when she had brought a priest to bless the "Casa Gutiérrez," murmured something and left hurriedly. Julia sighed with relief. "Well, I'm even with Carmela. Now I can speak to her again. Ay, I didn't owe her so very much, just three pesos."

Julia stood up stiffly, put the iron under the table, the folded towel on the bed, and the freshly ironed dress over the back of the chair. She turned around to see her sister Inés and her brother-in-law Alfredo at the door. Alfredo, who was much younger than his wife, stuck in his head, sniffed mischievously, and said, "Let's leave, old girl, they're not going to give us anything here."

Julia laughed. "Just a minute. We'll have coffee in just a minute. I've already started making it." She hastily dusted off two chairs and the visitors sat down.

Inés, a very stout woman of forty-four, was out of breath. "We've got to go," she said to her sister. "We were just passing by."

Alfredo took out his purse. "Look here, I've gotten so thrifty that I've been carrying around a five-peso bill for two weeks without spending it." He handed the bill to Guillermo who put it in the cashbox and made an entry in one of the notebooks. Alfredo went on, "Well, I think I'm going to leave Mexico City and get me a job somewhere else."

"Yes," Julia said, "business on the street is awfully poor. Yesterday I didn't sell a thing. It was the rain." She was thoughtful for a moment. "If it isn't the rain, it's those dratted police. They took away Yolanda's merchandise the other day and said she could get it back for thirty pesos. But the fine was more than the towels so she left them there. They won't let us peddle any more. We'll all die of hunger."

They were all silent. Government pressure, an ever-present threat to street vendors, had been increasing. Twice in the past year Julia had been picked up by police cars and taken to spend a day in jail. Both times she had had to pay a fine to reclaim her stock of confiscated towels. She had also been caught selling in a market by a government collector who had demanded three pesos for a permit. Julia didn't have the money and he tried to push her out of the market, knocking her up against a vegetable stand. Angrily she had grabbed some tomatoes and threw them at him, whereupon he took out his pistol and threatened to shoot her. A crowd gathered, jeering at him for abusing her and warning him not to shoot. But he shook and pushed her so roughly that he tore her dress to shreds. Julia fought back and finally got away.

After that Julia avoided the markets and the downtown center where the police demanded bribes from the vendors. She walked great distances and sold her towels to mechanics in shops and garages, to drunkards in saloons, to men in warehouses, and to passersby. She had to work harder than before but she usually managed to sell one hundred and twenty pesos' worth of stock whenever she went out. Guillermo boasted that she was the champion vendor in the city and could sell anything to anyone. When she couldn't get money she exchanged towels for bananas or meat. Her prices were flexible, depending upon what she thought her customer would give. "I tell you," said Guillermo, "no one can beat Julia and her brothers. They're very well known here, that's why. They're famous all over the country because of their ability."

But Julia worried about the future. The mayor was determined to clean up the city for the American tourists. He was tearing down all the old markets and building new ones. Beggars were no longer allowed in the streets and now he was out to get the peddlers. Julia felt persecuted and hated the police and the administration. When she voted for the first time, signing with her thumbprint, she did it only because it was rumored that women who did not exercise their new right would be put in jail. She often said that it was better before the Revolution under Porfirio Díaz because then there was more freedom and everything was cheaper.

"Before," she said, "the poor were allowed to make a living. Now it's money for a license here and a fine there. Then you could buy two or three of anything for one centavo. We eat worse now and at more of a sacrifice." While she talked, Julia had cleared a corner of the table, pushing aside the dirty dishes and wiping the table with a rag.

Alfredo spoke up, "That's right. A person can't do anything. I don't know what we're going to do."

Inés asked her sister if she had bought a lottery ticket. Julia shook her head. "Not yet. But I have two tickets with this fellow here," she indicated Guillermo, "and I have a ticket in another *tanda*. That's all I can do for now." The four continued to chat until they were interrupted by a woman who came in carrying a child in her shawl. "Good morning, Don Guillermo. Here, this is for you." She held out ten pesos which Guillermo put into the savings box. He gave her two receipts and wrote her name, Agueda Carlos, in his book. Inés urged Agueda to buy a ticket in their *tanda*.

Agueda shook her head. "No, I can't right now, especially since my little girl is sick. It's her stomach. She has *empacho pegado*, some food got stuck in her stomach. I wish Yolanda would give her a treatment. People tell me she can cure the sick." Julia said that Yolanda had gone to look for work but that Inés knew how to cure too. Inés agreed to work a cure, and Agueda began to undress the child.

Yolanda's younger son came in. "My grandmother wants to talk to you," he said to Inés.

Julia made an impatient gesture. "Mamá must want her dress."

"Ay, I keep forgetting," exclaimed Inés. "The other day I was going to take it back to her and I forgot." She went out to speak to her mother. When she returned she placed the crying baby face down across her lap and began to massage the child's legs while everyone watched. She turned the child over and rubbed her arms, legs, hands, and stomach. "Just give her corn gruel with cornstarch," she said to Agueda. Turning the baby over again, Inés tapped up and down the child's back by bringing her fist down lightly on her outspread hand. Then she pulled sharply at the skin so that it snapped back.

"Just listen to the way her skin crackles, just like chewing gum," Julia said. She and all the others had complete confidence in this cure for it was an ancient one that they understood. The winter before, when Herminio had been ill, Guillermo had insisted on taking him to the Children's Hospital for "scientific" care. But when he saw how the doctors frightened the child with injections, drains up his nostrils, and transfusions, he grew alarmed and brought him home. He called in a healer instead, and Herminio recovered. Guillermo was convinced that his son would have died in the hospital because the doctor's treatment was "too strong" for a small child.

"Now just give her an enema with a spoon of glycerin or a senna leaf." Inés handed the child to Agueda who began to dress her. Julia had gone out to wash her hands at the water tap. She came back in time to hear Agueda say, "All right, we are going now. Thanks, señora. I'm afraid we've been a bother to you."

Maria stuck her head in at the door to ask Julia if she needed kerosene; she was going to buy some for *Comadre* Chole. Julia gave Maria money and a container, then took a chipped enamel pot and went out to buy bread cuttings. These were crusts and crumbs which cost about half as much as a loaf of bread. Julia usually bought a potful, or about two pounds, a day.

Alone with the guests, Guillermo said with a smile, "She's a worthless little devil, isn't she? A real no-good."

"Who, Julia?" asked Inés.

"Well, Julia is, too, but I was talking about Maria. The other day she was taking a bath and I said to Julia, 'She'll stop up the drain. Man alive, she hasn't had a bath in about a year.'" Inés and Alfredo laughed.

After a few moments Guillermo went on, "Well, if you stay until evening we'll do things up right. Just stay and you won't be able to stand up on your own feet."

"No, sir," answered Alfredo. "Who's going to feel like drinking cold beer with the nights so cold?"

"Are you still going to buy Julia a kitchen stove?" Inés asked.

"Well, I don't know. I've been wanting to buy her a stove but I can't make up my mind whether to get the bicycles or her stove. They use an awful lot of gas, don't they?"

"Oh, not much," Inés said, "except when you cook beans or something like that. It doesn't take much money to run. And say, a friend of mine wants you to lend her fifteen hundred pesos at an interest of three hundred pesos. She would sign a note."

"We used to lend her money," Alfredo said, "but if she knows it is our money she won't pay us back. We could have pawned the sewing machine but why should we if she won't pay us back? But for you it's a safe investment."

"Well," said Guillermo, "if I had it, I'd lend it to her. But where am I going to get the money?"

Panchita, Julia's daughter-in-law, passed by the "Casa Gutiérrez" and said good morning. She was visibly pregnant and Alfredo shouted after her, "It'd better be a boy or we'll send it back." He added, "That's the way women ought to be, not like some silly ladies

*156*

who try to hide it when they are sick [pregnant]. There was this woman who went around all bound up. Finally one day I asked her if she was pregnant and she said, 'Ay, no! God forbid!' About three days later they had to take her away because her time had come."

Julia came in and put the pot of bread on the table. "Carmela just told me she's going to get married next month," she said.

"We thought it wasn't until September," Alfredo said. "She must have changed her plans."

"Or," said Inés slyly, "maybe it was some other reason."

"I'll bet it's nothing but a dodge," added Alfredo.

Inés continued. "That's what I say. All they're trying to do is fool people. She's already carrying her advance under her belt and she still plans to be married in white."

Guillermo saw the warehouse watchman, who had been nicknamed the King, coming up the walk and said to Julia, "Here comes the King. That means some wood for us. When Maria comes send her for it." Rufelia, Julia's mother, arrived at the doorway at the same time as the King but the old woman stood quietly behind him while he greeted the others.

Julia pushed by both of them to wash a pan at the faucet outside. "I'll be right with you," she said to the King. "Just wait till Maria comes back to help me with the wood."

Inés stood up to lean against the door frame. Alfredo examined a roll of copper wire the King was holding, and the men began discussing the cost of the wire. Then Inés made a move to leave. Her husband signaled to her to wait and Guillermo, too, noticed her impatience.

"You ought to make a sauce to give them, even if it is made only with chile," he called to Julia.

"Yes, right away. I'm going to make it right away." Julia bustled in past her mother, who was still standing in the doorway. "Yes, King, we'll eat soon."

"Yes," Guillermo said sarcastically, "at about one o'clock." He turned to Alfredo, "At times we eat breakfast at twelve, would you believe it?" Alfredo winked at him.

"Go on, you gossip," Julia said.

Alfredo boasted, "I eat breakfast at eight. At one I eat lunch and at six my supper."

"Really?" exclaimed Julia in disbelief. She was accustomed to serving only two meals a day and those at whatever hour was convenient for her. By serving a late breakfast the family could do without lunch; this saved money on food and gave Julia time to earn money for supper. But things were better for her sister. Alfredo was a good peddler and Inés did not have to work except when she needed extra money. Besides, she earned a few pesos as a medium in the Temple of Light. With good reason they could enjoy three regular meals a day!

Julia put a chile on the griddle to toast and hurriedly peeled the garlic. Inés sat down again. Julia's mother had wandered off to the toilet and was slowly making her way back to her daughter's house in the hope of getting something to eat. The King, who was watching Julia, smiled and said, "Why, I won't scorn the Queen's *taco*." Julia felt hungry eyes on her and moved more quickly. She did not want her sister to leave without having eaten. She and Guillermo had great respect for Inés because of her spiritual powers and also they were grateful to her for having helped them. She had once cured a bad skin condition for Guillermo and a few months before when Julia had had an attack of appendicitis, she had performed "spiritual surgery" and had removed the pain. When Guillermo had opened his bicycle business he had prayed to his special saint, Martín Caballero, for good luck, but it wasn't until Inés brought him certain white flowers and mint in a jar of water that his luck improved. He took the very first money he earned, dipped it into the water, and sprinkled it over the entrance of the house so that he would not lack customers. "I had to stop taking the flowers because I got more work than I could do," Guillermo said admiringly.

Inés and Alfredo conducted a spiritualist center in their two-room home on Tuesdays and Fridays, the days traditionally associated with witches' sorcery. The Temple of Light was a combination of Catholic, evangelical, and folk beliefs which continued to attract Catholics of the lower class even though it was denounced by the priests. Guillermo explained how he reconciled his belonging to both the Catholic church and the Temple of Light in the following way, "Both religions are spiritual. The Temple of Light does only good. You have everything there that you find in a Catholic church except that it is in Spanish, not Latin. The Catholic priests use Latin because they benefit by it. At Mass they tell the story of Christ in Latin. I don't understand anything and I keep going to Mass. If they told it in Spanish I could learn it. After that what's the sense of going to Mass any more? And don't believe that the priests tell their secrets. When did you ever see a priest leave the Christ [crucifix] in the Church? Never! With that they defend themselves. It is like a deputy who doesn't leave his gun. Why? Because it is his weapon, his defense. Yes, the priests keep their secrets.

"In the Temple they help people in trouble. They cure sickness and fight black magic with white. Here in Mexico City there is even more witchcraft than in the villages. When we are sick we can't afford expensive doctors. If we go to Social Security they rob us in the drugstores. In the Temple they cure you and give you the medicine too. That is why people keep going."

Inés' reputation as a medium had earned her a large "parcel" of followers and she devoted a good deal of time to the center. She had furnished the room and kept it clean and provided the flowers and candles. Against one wall of the room stood a green staircase of seven steps, each with a thick candle and a vase of flowers. The top step held a crucifix and four votive candles arranged in the form of a cross. Tacked on the wall above was a triangular picture of a woman's eye from which rays emanated. In a corner of the room a large armchair was draped with a red and white cloth that matched the red and white curtains at the windows. These colors honored the Sacred Heart. Other saints were honored by different colored materials. During the rites Inés sat in the chair, leaning back with closed eyes, her feet resting on a small carpet, and went into a trance. As Julia said, "She contributes her material being as a medium for receiving the orders from the Almighty and transmitting them to the people."

Opposite her chair were two small chairs topped with white cushions as headrests. Inés' special assistants, who wore white robes, sat in these. Bottles of oil and a small barrel of "balsam" or holy water on the table were used in the cures. People who came to be cured were expected to leave one or two pesos for expenses. The rest of the room was filled with benches for those who came to witness the cures and to pray. Special services were given by Inés, Alfredo, and other "brothers" and "sisters" on the first, the ninth, and the thirteenth day of each month.

Julia was a "sister" in the Temple of Light and faithfully attended meetings. She was "marked" as a potential medium because, like Inés, she sometimes had visions of herself or of others walking among the clouds. But she had neither the time nor the wish to develop her powers and was content to be a disciple. Guillermo had faith in Inés but he no longer went to the Temple because it had an ill effect on him. "Every time I go I get a feeling as if somebody inside me grabs hold of me. Then I feel I've got some sort of spell inside of me and I get chills and flushes. I practically feel sick. I shake all over. When I walk under the crucifix, I get worse."

Guillermo believed that he had certain spiritual powers which conflicted with those of Inés. He saw visions of saints walking on the walls and faces in the clouds or on anything he looked at. He had also divined certain events, among them the crash of an airplane and the death of Jorge Negrete. Once as he watched two men approaching each other on bicycles he told Julia they were going to bump and a few moments later they did. At times he felt that his spirit was so strong that it was dangerous to others, and he was convinced that he had inadvertently caused the death of Maclovio's ailing son because he had carried him to be baptized, and of his brother's child by holding him in his arms a day before he died. Guillermo no longer caressed or carried children, including his own, for fear he would kill them.

When he was about ten years old Guillermo had worked as a priest's helper and had acquired a strong taste for the life of an ecclesiast. The priest had encouraged him to enter a monastery and Guillermo was tempted, but he had been too mischievous a boy to be accepted. He rang the churchbells at the wrong hour, stuffed himself with holy wafers, got drunk on holy wine, deliberately misplaced the priest's bookmark, turned the Bible upside down just before Mass, and finally was caught parading about in the priest's robes. Even now Guillermo thought he would like to enter a monastery or to become a *Padre* or Father of the Church but Julia did not approve. When he mentioned it she cut him short, saying, "It would be enough to be a father to your children!"

Guillermo began hammering out some metal strips on the worktable. Julia called to Maria who was dawdling up the walk. "Come on. Run to the store for thirty centavos' worth of coffee. We're waiting." As the girl ran off, Julia yelled, "And get a half-peso of aged cheese. And hurry it up!"

Alfredo meanwhile was talking to Guillermo about the party to be held that night. "Well, do you expect to walk away on your own feet the way you did the other night?"

Julia turned to look at her husband and laughed. "You were awfully drunk, brother. You go too far."

"You can't take it," Alfredo added. "Just a few beers and you fall flat. You can't hold your liquor like a man."

"Yes, stewed through and through. But don't think this lousy old bum lost his senses. He was just pretending to sleep because he had such a hangover. Don Chucho was there, remember? All the time Chucho was there he didn't sleep. He was spying, watching Don Chucho. Because," Julia said, turning to Guillermo, "you said, 'This guy isn't going to screw me!'"

Guillermo smiled sheepishly. "Oh, is that so! Well, I'm telling you that you can't leave things unguarded. I was just taking care of things. You know, you can't trust the devil after all."

"Yes," Julia said, "after Don Chucho left, this mule fell on the bed like a post." They all laughed.

Rufelia, who was sitting on a bench outside the door, spoke up, "But he isn't a fighter the way others are. No sooner do they drink when right away . . ."

"Why should I fight?" Guillermo said. "Anyway when you live next door to a person, well, what for? I see him every day."

Alfredo slapped Guillermo's back. "Really, what a hangover you had!"

Julia shook her head. "I like people who like to drink and can hold it. I can't stand tight people. For Guillermo's saint's day we are going to have a party and blow the roof."

"Like the one I gave last time, eh, old one?" Inés said, nudging her husband. "Nobody on the block can make it the way I can."

"That's true," Julia said. "Here, too, when it comes to a poor man's party no one in the *vecindad* can make one like us, isn't that right, old boy? When I took these three kids to First Communion I spent five hundred pesos, but it was a pleasure. I like to stuff people with food—a pot of *mole,* some good chocolate, a few beers. I had enough for everyone!"

"Let's make one like that for Alfredo's saint's day, too. You'll see, let the wine flow on that day!" Inés exclaimed.

"We'll have Cubas and punch for the invited guests and pulque for the others." Julia began to laugh again. "And we'll play a trick on the janitress. We'll have the old woman going this way and that."

Old Ignacio came in to deliver the newspaper *El Universal.* He handed Guillermo five pesos, took his receipt, and left without a word. Guillermo made a notation in his book.

"That fellow," he said, "is the poorest one of all and he is the best payer. He never asks to borrow anything. Those who don't borrow are going to be the big winners. You know, they pay a little bit at a time and don't miss it that way but when they get it back in a lump sum, that's pretty nice, eh?"

Maria hurried in and gave Julia the cheese and coffee. Julia handed the little girl a yellow basin to fill with water. When she returned, Julia sent her on another errand. "Hurry, child, go get a kilo of *tortillas,*" she said and gave Maria seventy-five centavos and a napkin. Julia began to grind the cheese into the chile sauce. Little Ema was still leaning against the kitchen table, shifting her position when Julia passed by. Alfredo asked Guillermo about the gas stove for Julia.

"Yes, I think I'll buy her one," Guillermo answered. "And I want to put on a new roof there." He pointed to the low roof over the kitchen. "I wonder how much it would cost?"

Alfredo took a pencil stub from his pocket and began to figure on a piece of paper. "Let's see. Are you going to buy the beams?"

"Those don't cost me anything. The King gives them to me." Guillermo looked around for the King but he had unobtrusively left.

"Forty-two pesos is what it will come to," Alfredo said. "At most about one hundred pesos. That's not much and it will make it a lot better for you. Then you can put a stove in there."

Julia had been listening. "Ha!" she said. "Then these old women around here are sure going to lynch me. Why, if you buy me a gas stove, they're going to kick me out. You know, all the women here are *cabronas*. They are envious." She went out to wash some cups and dishes. Inés kept looking at the clock on the TV set. It was a quarter to ten.

Guillermo yelled to his wife, "Get going there, old girl!"

Julia was already on her way back with the clean cups. "Oh, stop bothering me all the time," she said. She stirred the leftover beans that were heating on the stove, then asked Inés to take the coffeepot off the fire while she went to wash the spoons. Inés stood up unwillingly and waddled toward the stove.

"Ay, but I'm going to get soot all over me. Damn this thing! Just look how dirty it is!" With the ends of her apron she moved the hot pot. She noticed little Tomás standing in the doorway and went up to him to examine his swollen neck. When Julia came back she said, "This child is really in a bad way. If he isn't cured now he will stay this way even when he is grown up."

Guillermo said quickly, "If it weren't for his grandmother he wouldn't even eat. For instance today Yolanda ambled off without knowing whether or not they would eat. That's the way she leaves them. Isn't that true, Catarina?" he asked of Yolanda's oldest daughter who had come to the door. The girl left without answering. Guillermo went on, "And sometimes they don't eat until Julia comes back from selling, at six or seven, sometimes at eight o'clock."

"But it's not Yolanda's fault," Alfredo said. "It's her husband who is to blame. After all if I am so proud that I don't want my wife to work I'll bring her and the kids food and that settles it. What is so

*163*

hard about it? If she is stubborn, I get rough with her and she remains at home. If not, she would be the one to wear the pants. I am fussy about that."

"Yes, but he spends all his time drinking and never has any money. He's a real drunkard, poor thing." According to Guillermo's standards, Yolanda was more at fault than her husband in neglecting their children. She was in control of herself whereas he was not and therefore could not be blamed.

Maria came in with the *tortillas*. At five of ten Herminio came back from work.

"Didn't they pay you?" Guillermo at once asked him.

"Yes, three-fifty for each of us but not until later." Herminio threw his jacket and cap on the pile of bicycles in the bedroom. "Mamá, I don't want milk," he said. "Better give me black coffee." Alfredo had left his chair, and Herminio hurriedly sat down on it, only to be pushed off a moment later.

"Here, what are you doing? You saw that I was sitting there, didn't you, joker?" Herminio shifted to the bed, receiving an affectionate pat on his thigh from Inés as he passed her.

"You skinny brat," she said, "why do you get grease all over clear to your tail?"

Herminio looked at his hands. "Well, I'm a garage worker."

Alfredo teasingly asked the boy to give the names of some auto parts. When Herminio made an error everyone laughed, and Herminio hid behind Julia's skirt. "Well, then what *do* you call it?" He asked Julia for another pair of pants to wear to the party.

"Another pair of pants, boy?" Guillermo said. "And whose saint's day is it now?"

Julia answered impatiently, "Look, don't you understand what your boy keeps saying? He told Melín that he would play the record for her party and that he and Lola were going to buy the candles and the little figure for the cake because we're the godparents."

"But we're supplying the record-player and the electricity. Isn't that enough?" Guillermo protested.

Julia was ready to serve a mug of coffee and a plate of beans to her sister and brother-in-law. Guillermo set up an empty cardboard box in front of them. "Here you are, use it for a table." Guillermo ate his breakfast at the worktable.

Yolanda came in. "Give me something to eat, mamá." Julia gave her three mugs of coffee with milk and Yolanda went out again, trailed by her children. Julia gave coffee and beans to Maria who sat down on the doorstep to eat. Herminio ate sitting on the bed. Julia put the stone mortar with the ground chile and cheese on the worktable and everyone helped himself to the spicy sauce. The *tortillas* were rapidly disappearing and Julia told Maria to go for more. Rufelia came in, received her coffee, beans, and sauce and sat down in the doorway. Guillermo was contentedly eating his *taco* of beans rolled in a *tortilla*.

"Which one of your brothers-in-law do you like best?" he asked his wife jokingly.

Julia looked Alfredo over. "Which one of the *cabrones* do I like most? None of them. They're all cut out with the same pair of scissors."

"Well, we're even, little sister," Alfredo said. "Whenever I meet you at night you scare me, I swear to God."

Señora Rufelia nodded. "I think that's right. With that pack of fat she carries behind her she looks like an elephant. She'd scare anybody. I don't know why Guillermo doesn't get scared."

"No, with him it's just the opposite, eh, brother-in-law?" Alfredo said. Guillermo went on eating placidly.

"Those two like each other," Rufelia went on. "The one because she's fat, the other because he's not. That's the way they get along and they'll go on being like that."

Yolanda came in for a *taco* which she ate standing under the shed.

Alfredo began singing, "Chile in the morning, chile in the evening, chile in the. . . ." He didn't finish because his wife had slapped him.

"Shut up, snouty. Don't be so foul-mouthed."

"What's the matter? Isn't that right, sister-in-law? Don't you eat chiles all day long? Whenever I come here, no matter what time of the day, you give me chile?" Julia and Guillermo laughed.

"I'm going to work, mamá. I'm leaving, papá." Herminio left with Galván who had been sitting on the ground outside eating. Yolanda's other children, Catarina, Tomás, and Ema also were sitting on the ground, eating rolled-up *tortillas* and drinking coffee.

"Shall I throw you some more beans?" Julia asked Inés.

"Don't *throw* them, *serve* them!" corrected Alfredo. Inés looked reproachfully at her husband.

"Why sure," he said, "wouldn't it be better to *serve* the beans? What's all this stuff about throwing them!"

Julia was half-annoyed, half-amused. "Oh, quit bothering me! Every person talks the way he takes a notion to, brother. You understood me, didn't you?"

"Why sure, but the way you said it was incorrect."

Julia laughed. "*Cabrón!* You mule, you! Damn you, *compadre*, don't you be frigging me! I'll talk anyway I please." Julia turned to Maria and asked, "Shall I toss you some beans?"

"Throw them, throw them," Alfredo said, making everyone laugh.

Inés was finished eating and handed Julia her plate. "Thanks. May God give you more than thanks for that's all I have." Alfredo, too, thanked Julia and gave her his empty plate.

Yolanda came to the doorway. She blocked her grandmother's view into the house and the old woman said sharply, "Just look at that one! What is she doing standing here? The whore is just standing!"

"Ay, where can I go? Where do you want me to stand?"

"Ay, *mamacita*, shut up!" Julia said to her mother. "Where can Yolanda go when every place is occupied?" Yolanda went home, but Julia continued, "You know, mamá, the other day you hit at Yolanda with a pan and if I hadn't blocked the blow you would have split her face open. And you even hit me once with the handle of the skillet and made me see stars for nothing at all. Let her stand where she pleases. There is no room to pass in here." Everyone was quiet until Rufelia muttered sullenly, "Well, why are you all so rude to me?"

"Ay, mamá! Whoever does anything to you? All your life you've said the same thing and we've never done anything to you."

Maclovio's little daughter came in asking for food and Julia fixed a *taco* for the child, then playfully offered Alfredo some more chile.

He nodded and again began to sing, "Chile in the daytime, chile at night . . .," only to receive another slap from his wife.

Julia laughed. "Now keep still or people will be saying that this place is a saloon!"

Guillermo, who had been quietly working for some time, looked up. "Really, they are closing up all the saloons and whorehouses on Tintero Street. They took them all away, didn't they?"

Alfredo nodded and was about to speak but Inés stood up and said, "Come on, old one, let's go." She discovered a hole in the back of her husband's trousers when he stood up. Embarrassed, Alfredo first covered his bottom with his hands and then took off his jacket and tied it around his waist.

"No!" Inés said, "don't make yourself look ridiculous. No one can see anything. It doesn't show at all and you are making it worse."

"Well," he said, "that makes me feel better. I don't want it to happen to me again the way it did once. Nobody told me a thing and there I was with my pants all ripped down the back and when I got off the bus my underclothes were showing." Everyone laughed. Inés and Alfredo said goodbye and left.

Julia sat down to eat her breakfast but she was interrupted by Yolanda who gave her mother the baby to hold while she filled a soda bottle with coffee and milk. She then sat down to give the baby the bottle, at the same time searching through the classified ads of Guillermo's newspaper for a job. Julia went back to her breakfast, only nodding when her mother said, "Well, I'm going and thanks. We'll see. God will help us." Panchita came in and at a nod from her mother-in-law took the jug of beans and the remaining coffee to her own house.

Guillermo called to Maria. "It's late. Hurry up and get me the sack so I can make my deliveries." The girl searched through the wardrobe but could not find the sack. Finally she gave up and complained to Julia that her head ached. Guillermo said, "You're sick, eh, daughter? Then don't go to school. It will make you worse."

Maria shook her head. "No, papá, I'll go. It won't hurt me."

"Here comes the King again," Guillermo said. "Hurry up, Maria, you and Catarina go and get the wood."

**167**

Julia was piling up the dirty dishes. "Ay, and just look, here I am busy." When the King stood in the doorway, she said, "Well, look, you got here too late. We're all through. But I'm going to give you some chile." The King smiled, "Go right ahead, Queen." Julia put some chile sauce betweeen two *tortillas* and handed them to him on a plate. He picked them up from the plate, thanked her, and went off eating.

Julia noticed her husband looking through his notebook and she shouted, "Hurry up, go on and go if you're going. It's getting late."

"Didn't I tell you to give me the sack and a handkerchief?" Guillermo said. He patted his book as he put it away. "Just look, a while ago I didn't have five centavos and now the wool has arrived. But some *canijas* still haven't paid me. I'm going to collect from them. Darn that Agueda! She finally paid that ten pesos."

Julia went to the wardrobe and found the sack at once. She muttered in disgust that the girls could never find anything. Guillermo caught the sack when she threw it and then put on his hat. "Well, I'm leaving. First I'm going to get the TV volume control and then I'm going to collect and I'll be back right away."

Julia called after him. "Don't be too long or the rain will catch me the way it did yesterday and I didn't make even five pesos."

Guillermo turned around and came back with his hand outstretched. "Pay me, because I have to buy chain for the bottles." Julia said she had already given him ten pesos. They talked back and forth and finally decided that she owed him four pesos aside from her total debt to him of one hundred and thirty pesos. She was still paying back the money she had borrowed from him for the Communion party. She agreed to give him the four pesos later, and at a quarter of eleven he left, his sack over his shoulder. But in a few minutes he came back up the walk.

"Ay, Guillermo, you dirty cur! How come you decided to come back? Just see what time it is getting to be."

"All right then, shall I buy the chain?"

Julia, disgusted, almost screamed at him. "No! Go on! Now!" He ducked before her fury and hurried away.

Julia looked after him, shaking her head. "I don't know what is happening to that man," she said to Yolanda. "Someone must have put a hex on him! Instead of making money, he's just going downhill, downhill. He's got everything pawned right now and is feeling the lash. When I go out to sell I bring home my few centavos, but he doesn't. He can't. I'm fed up with him. I've got him catalogued as half a fool or something like that."

Julia started to play with the baby and almost at once was gay. She held her grandson high over her head. "Ay, you *cabrón*, you cute little son, you little father!" She kissed him loudly and set him down on the earth floor. Another night watchman who took care of several houses on the street came by and Julia searched in her apron pocket for some coins for his weekly tip. After that Señor Quintero who lived in No. 11 paused to greet her as he passed by on his way to the street.

Julia again spoke to Yolanda about Guillermo. "I promised to help him with twenty-five pesos every week. Now that the TV will be on again, our little sweets and chocolates will sell. Even if not much money comes in, still it is something." Julia shook her head sadly. "Yes, that man would go under without me."

In the first years of their marriage Julia had been impressed by Guillermo's intelligence and by his certainty that the future had something better in store for him. But his repeated failures to live up to his rosy promises had disillusioned her. She had long since concluded that his desire to improve, what she called his "excessive ambition," was ruining his chances of earning a simple living. She did not ask to live in comfort. "I was born in poverty and I'll die in poverty," she often said. Julia wanted only to be relieved of the burden of supporting the family. She was working too hard and she feared for her stepchildren and grandchildren when she could no longer go on. When she didn't peddle towels, she not only cooked, cleaned, washed, and ironed; she also prepared huge casseroles of chicken *mole*, rice, and beans, and made eight kilos of *tortillas* to sell in the street. Even with the help of Lola, Maria, Catarina, a niece, and one of her *comadres* who prepared the many ingredients for the complicated *mole* sauce, it was too much for her.

Julia went out to fill a pan with water for her bath. Yolanda went home with her children. As Julia set the pan on the stove to heat, Maria and Catarina returned, carrying between them a heavy sack full of lumber scraps. They set it outside the door and ran off to play, but Julia called them back. The three of them began to throw the wood up onto the shed roof. Panchita came by. "More wood, Julita?" "Yes, I've already got quite a bit but they say that one oughtn't to look at the teeth of a gift horse, isn't that right? We'll find some use for it. We ought not to refuse anything." Turning to Maria she said, "Get me the broom, quick." Julia swept the trash into a heap and Catarina scooped it up with a metal street sign. A quarrel arose among some children playing near the washing place and little Tomás accidentally received a blow. He began to howl and Julia shouted to Yolanda to take better care of her children. Yolanda picked up her son. "Ay, *chata*, I wonder what sort of a woman you are," Julia said.

Yolanda did not answer but rocked her son for a while, then set him down and went back to washing clothes, stepping aside for her grandmother who was coming toward the house carrying a box of buttons. Rufelia sat down on a stone and began to separate the buttons according to size and color. Although she depended on her children for support, she earned two or three pesos a day by selling buttons, pins, and small bottles. Sometimes she sold them on the street from a tray suspended around her neck but usually she went to the *Merced* market where she sat on the sidewalk and spread her wares out on a newspaper.

"I won't go out to sell today," she said to Julia. "It's an awful day. It's the moon that brings all this water."

"Well, awful or not, I'm selling today. I go around in worn-out shoes and our quilt is falling apart, but Guillermo doesn't trouble himself in the least about anything around here, so I must. I'm going to take a bath over at Yolanda's. Imagine, Lola goes to the bath-house for one peso fifty every other day but I never do. Well, if he wants to give his children the life of the rich, let him. But it isn't right, is it?"

Julia was more sad than indignant. Guillermo's exploitation and neglect of her and his obvious preference for Lola hurt her deeply.

She was hurt too by the fact that Lola gave the greater part of her earnings to her father and only once in a while slipped five or ten pesos to her. But she loved her stepchildren and believed they loved her "more than they do their papá." It was because they needed her that Julia continued her union with Guillermo. And she was afraid that if she lived alone she would again begin to spend her days drinking with her many *comadres*.

"Well," Rufelia said, "she gave him forty-five pesos just today. It's only right that he gives her spending money."

"But don't I keep lending him money? Just the other day I gave him a hundred pesos I won in the *tanda* to get a watch out of hock. He paid seven hundred pesos for that watch and there he was in danger of losing it. Then we had a terrible fight because he wouldn't pay me back." Julia went on. "I like to have a pretty house with flowerpots and plenty of pails and dishes. In order to serve meals I have to be up all the time. I don't like to go around borrowing from the neighbor women. I say he ought to do his share." She paused, then said vehemently, "My whole life I've never had enough to get along. I've had to work all my life. Sometimes, mamá, I feel all tired out. I feel sick but I tell myself, 'Well, I've got to go on working. Maybe I'll drop dead someday.'"

Maria came out of the bedroom with Julia's clean dress, her petticoat and drawers made of sacking, and a towel. Julia nodded approvingly and went to Yolanda's house where she bathed behind a burlap curtain. Just before eleven Guillermo returned with the TV control in his sack.

"Seems that the people from the light company are coming to re-stretch the wires," he said to Julia who was combing her wet hair in the sun. He started to leave again. "I'll be right back. I want to see the men from the light company about why the bill is still so high."

"No, no," Julia shouted impatiently. "I can't wait any longer. You're not going anywhere. I'm sorry, brother." She rubbed brilliantine on her hair and cold-creamed her face.

Don Quintero came by and handed Guillermo fifteen pesos. "There are still seventy more to go, *compadre*," Guillermo said. Quintero nodded and waited for his receipts, then left. Julia looked

up at the dull sky. Rufelia said, "He isn't going to let you go." Julia
snorted. "What do I care whether I have my husband's permission
or not? What difference does it make to me?" To that Guillermo
smiled and showed a fist. "I'll hit you and knock you flat on your
back," he said.

Rufelia laughed. "Sure, man, so easy. Just throw a little water on
him and he's dying."

But Guillermo spoke seriously to his wife. "One of two things.
Either I leave and you stay or you stay and I leave. The house can't
be shut because we may get customers. Because even if we don't
sell anything it is a sort of a shop."

Julia ignored him. She threw her pack of towels over her shoulder,
found her purse, and was ready to leave. Her mother asked her to
pick up her dress at Inés' house but Julia shook her head. "No, I'm
going the other way, mamá." Guillermo told her not to tire herself
and asked if she would give him a payment when she came back.
Julia shrugged. "Who knows what kind of luck I'll have. It all de-
pends if God helps me." Julia went down the path, greeting neighbors who were working under their sheds or in the courtyard.

Guillermo watched Julia go. He was painfully aware of his lack
of control over his wife. When they first began to live together he
had been able to put a stop to the drinking sprees she indulged in
away from home and to keep her drunken friends out of the house.
"What was the good of her making twenty or fifty pesos a day if
she threw it away on beer? And it was a bad thing for the children
to see." She had more or less obeyed him then and never went anywhere without his permission. Her family had credited him with
having improved her. But things changed. "I lost command here,
see?" Guillermo told a friend. "Because she just had to tell me 'I'm
going out selling' and, well, what could I say to that? It was my fault
because if I hadn't let her go out selling I would still be giving
orders. But now, well, she doesn't pay attention to me.

"I think I'll give orders again when I can move out of here because
then her family won't interfere in our affairs. Now if I fight with her,
her children right away come and butt in. Just Yolanda has to butt
in and then there are two women against me and why should I

*172*

have to fight both? That's why I say that if we move it will take away some of Julia's forces. Then she won't have anyone to back her up and I think she knows it and that's why she doesn't want to move. Her family goes around saying I'm lazy and helpless but they don't notice that we are in a hole because we help them. If they all didn't come here to eat we wouldn't have to work so hard. They just notice what suits them. Julia's brothers came here once and shouted at me that I was taking advantage of her and why did I have the TV and the bicycles in my name? They said I wanted her to help pay for them and then I would leave her. They don't realize that I *had* to give my signature and that she doesn't know a thing about bicycles. In case I were to leave here, do they think I would take the things? Do they think my children would go with me? They love her more than me!"

Rufelia struggled to stand up. She repeated to Guillermo that she was not going to work.

"Particularly because it is Carmela's saint's day and there will be something to eat," he said in reply.

"Why, yes," the old woman said. "You know that every year I go to give her an embrace." She left slowly for her granddaughter's house.

Guillermo connected the TV control to the set and soon had the machine working. Maria came in and they both watched it silently for a few minutes, then he turned it off. "It uses too much electricity," he said and went back to his worktable.

Maria climbed up on the shelf to make the bed. She gathered up some clothing and put it in one corner. Jumping down, she began to put empty soda bottles into the boxes next to the bicycles. From the wardrobe she took out a dress of coarse cotton and a worn sweater and laid them on the bed; from a box under the wardrobe she took three notebooks and a school textbook. She smiled at herself in the mirror, combing her fingers through her hair. She looked contented and seemed oblivious of her torn clothes and unkempt appearance. All she wanted was to go to school a few more years for she was good at her studies and her teacher had encouraged her. Once the principal had questioned Guillermo about Maria's irregular attendance and he had lied, saying the girl was weak and always getting ill. Maria was fighting a losing battle for education; no one in the *vecindad* thought it important.

Maria went into the kitchen, piled the dirty dishes onto a board on the table, and looked for a fiber pad with which to clean the stove. "Papá, give me money for soap."

"What? Isn't there any around?" Reluctantly Guillermo gave Maria twenty centavos.

Yolanda came in and took the kerosene can. Guillermo looked after her in annoyance. "They take anything they want out of here." A little girl came in to buy marshmallows. He handed her two and she gravely gave him a ten-centavo piece which he dropped into his pocket. When Maria returned, he said, "I expect the policeman to come today. Are you sure he didn't come while I was away?" Maria shook her head. "When he comes to pay his five pesos I always have to give him an accounting. I have to keep up to date or all the members will be down on me."

Maria wiped the stove, then hurried to wash the dishes. She made several trips back and forth between the washing place and the kitchen, straining under the weight of large clay pots, piles of plates, and the heavy stone mortar. She hung the deep vessels on nails and made a quick attempt at sweeping. Her father talked to her now and then as she worked.

"Well, I studied this out real good. This way they can't catch me by surprise. I can't screw them and no one can screw me. . . . That cop didn't come, after all!"

A woman came in with a large leather bag full of empty bottles. "Won't you buy them, Don Guillermo?" He agreed to take them at two pesos. "Put them under the table, Maria."

The woman said to Guillermo in a low voice, "Just don't tell anybody. You know how they are around here. They'll say that now I don't even have the price of beans." Guillermo shook his head. "No, this is just between the two of us."

A bell was heard ringing in the street. Maria jumped up and grabbed the can of garbage. "It's the garbage truck, papá. I have to hurry." Women and girls were coming out of all the doors, car-

*174*

rying cans and paper bags filled with garbage. Maria waited her turn and then ran back with the empty can.

"Papá," she said, "give me the peso to buy beans."

"The peso? What peso? What beans?"

"Oh, papá, the peso Julita left for the beans."

Guillermo slowly reached in his pocket for the money. Maria asked him to light the stove, handing him a small packet of matches, and went out to the store. Guillermo hit a match with the hammer but it did not light. "Before I used to light it with one tap," he grumbled. "Not now. Now everything is going to pot. Things aren't like they used to be."

When Maria came back the stove was not lighted.

"Ay, papá, you didn't light the stove. I'm going to be late for school."

"Not if you aren't going to school."

"But I *am* going, papá," the girl said frowning.

"And what are you in such a hurry for? Huuuy, yes, you're going to see your boy friend and that's why you want to go."

Maria stood on the bed and put a rolled-up newspaper to the votive candle. With this she lighted the stove, then went for water to cook the beans.

"I *am* going. I don't want to be absent. You'll see, papá. I *am* going."

Guillermo was silent for a moment. "All right. But don't leave the stove on because I have to go out to collect and I don't want to come back and find the TV set burned into cracklings." Guillermo watched his daughter clean the beans. "Why you little runt, you're better than Lola. You sure are clever, eh daughter?" Then he added, "So what does Quintero have to say to you, eh?"

"Ay, papá. I can't talk now. I'm late already."

Catarina came in and leaned on the kitchen table. "Are you going to buy the chain?" she asked Guillermo.

"Yes, come on, I'll take you along. I'll buy you a *taco*. What do you say?" The girl smiled but shook her head.

"Come on, I'll buy you ice cream. Please!"

The girl was stubborn. "Don't be promising me because afterward you don't even take me," she said. "You just say so but it's not even true."

"Ay, Catarina, don't be like that." Guillermo put on his black hat, hitched up his pants, said good-bye, and left.

Maria sat at the worktable to do her homework. It was one o'clock and she was not due at school for another half-hour. Catarina helped herself to some bread and went out. Tomás wandered in and stretched out on the floor. A few minutes later Yolanda came in. She wanted the baby watched while she did someone's laundry. Yolanda was happy to be able to earn some money without leaving the *vecindad*.

Maria agreed to watch the baby. "My papá doesn't want me to go to school anyway because he needs help with the water bottles." When the baby began to cry Catarina came in, filled a spoon with sugar, and fed it to him. Maria was irritated but said nothing. She too resented the fact that Yolanda and her children took things without asking permission or saying thank you.

"Why are you so lazy, Catarina?" she asked. "You haven't done any work since you got up. No wonder your mother yells and yells." Catarina was unperturbed. She clapped her hands and made a sign to Maria to throw her the ball. Maria threw it and then grabbed a stick that was poking out of a hole in the roof and ran out to the courtyard. "Come on, let's play 'outs.'" They played for a few minutes, then Yolanda reminded them to watch the baby. Catarina picked up the baby and tried to go on playing with him in her arms.

Panchita's daughter came out into the yard carrying a big ball that she had received on the Day of Epiphany. "That was all she got from the Three Kings," Yolanda said to the girls. "Everything is so expensive on that day! Panchita and I saw some big dolls, real beauties, but what they cost! You don't even feel like asking the price. All we could buy was a ball for each one." Little Tomás tugged at Maria. "The Kings are the parents, aren't they?" When Maria nodded he said indignantly, "Not true. They are Melchor, Gaspar, and Baltasar." His mother and the girls laughed at him and he ran off.

Yolanda was nursing the baby now. "So you are not going to

school today," she said to Maria. "But at least you like to go. Not Catarina, she doesn't care for school at all. She's almost twelve years old and still in the second grade. Galván likes school but he has to help me. My mamá tells me I ought to put Catarina in a house somewhere to work as a little servant, but I don't want to. I don't want my daughter to have to go through that. In some houses they are real mean. No, it is better for her to be here at home. At least she helps me take care of these kids while I wash or whatever." Yolanda nuzzled her baby affectionately.

Maria went into the house, turned on the radio, and lay down on the bed to listen to the popular music. It was half past two when Guillermo returned, his sack bulging with bottles. "Ah, how I suffer!" he joked as his daughter helped him lower the heavy sack. "Didn't you go to school?"

"You wanted me to stay home to help, didn't you?" Maria answered rather tartly.

Guillermo emptied the sack. "Get me a tub and fill it with water. Count off fifty bottles and I'll wash them." The girl emptied an old metal tub that held nails, boxes, and a folded raincoat and went out for water. The tub was heavy and the water sloshed over her dress and sandals when she set it down on the floor. She began numbering off the bottles. Her father dipped the bottles into the tub of water, swished them around, and set them to drain on a newspaper. He told Maria to begin pasting labels on the clean bottles. "And hand me the pliers, daughter."

A man rode up on a bicycle and wanted some repair work done. Guillermo told him to come back later because he was too busy.

"But I've got to have it done right away, *maestro*," the man said. "See, the brakes stick."

Guillermo got up to take a look. "It needs some new spokes and bars. I can't go out to buy them because I've got to finish all this work. Come back next Wednesday and I'll fix it for you." Maria had all the while been looking for the pair of pliers, finding them at last on the bed shelf. Guillermo continued to wash the bottles. "I'll finish washing these and we're out of the woods, right? We'll be finished right away."

Maria took a can of glue out of the wardrobe. She made a face. "Boy, it really stinks. It even makes me dizzy."

"Yes, but it sticks."

The two worked in silence. They could hear dishes rattling in other kitchens. Smoke was coming out of most of the doorways; some women were making *tortillas* over charcoal fires in the yard. Guillermo raised his head and smiled at his daughter. "You'll see, the old lady is going to be back right away. It doesn't take her long to get rid of a pack of towels."

"Ay, *papacito*, I hope so. I'm getting hungry."

Guillermo looked roguishly at Maria. "So what did Don Quintero have to say, eh?"

"Oh, papá, I don't remember."

"Tell me. Don't be ashamed."

"Oh, papá, don't talk to me anymore." Maria was blushing.

After a while Guillermo said, "Fetch me the soap." When Maria could find only a small piece he asked for more. "Look, this is all used up." Maria went to the washtubs where Yolanda was washing clothes, found their new bar of soap which Yolanda had taken, and brought it back to her father. "Now get me something to wipe myself with." She handed him a piece of towel.

Maria emptied the tub of dirty water into the courtyard, brought in clean water, and began filling the little bottles up to the neck. Guillermo took a paper bag of corks from the sack and corked each filled bottle. In the wardrobe he found a roll of thin wire and a pile of small rounds of thin wax paper. He placed a paper circle on the top of each corked bottle, pressing the paper down and bound it tightly with a strip of wire. He did this in imitation of the seals on the large bottles of purified drinking water sold throughout the city.

Maria was thinking of the coming party. "When Melín was two years old they made her a cake. Now again. Swell for us, eh, papá?"

Her father answered, "So what *did* Don Quintero have to say, eh?"

Maria grew serious. "Ay, papá! I don't know. I can't say and you keep asking and asking. Don't talk to me anymore."

Rufelia came to the door. A pail was lying on the ground near the washing place and she wanted to know whose it was. Maria said it was hers, and the old woman became angry. "Then go pick it up. Don't be such a bad girl. You see someone's things lying around and you don't pick them up. Sons of bitches! Just wait till someone tries to borrow it next time!" Maria didn't answer and Rufelia shuffled over to pick up her pail.

A little after three Herminio came running in to take a handful of bread from the pot. "They haven't paid you yet, have they?" Guillermo asked him. "No, not till Saturday." Herminio took some money from his father's jacket on the bed. He said he wanted to buy a hot *taco* from a street vendor.

"Don't take so much," Guillermo said. "I know how much I've got." While Herminio was counting the coins, his father quietly put a piece of wire between his ankles, and when the boy tried to take a step he fell flat on his face. Guillermo laughed loudly. He enjoyed his joke all the more because Herminio thought he had become entangled in the wire through his own carelessness. When the boy had gone Guillermo told Maria what he had done.

"I'm a mean one, all right. Didn't I ever do anything mean to you?"

"To me? Yes. Once when Catarina and I were wearing the same dresses you hit me on the head. You thought it was she and hit me real hard!"

Guillermo laughed heartily. "Ah! I didn't see that you were my own daughter and I hit you by accident. But I am mean, don't you think?"

As they worked, Maria and Guillermo listened to the radio. A program called "The Police Are Always on Guard," was being broadcast. Catarina had come in quietly and after a while Don Chucho, the baker, came in. One of Chucho's legs was badly crippled and much shorter than the other, forcing him to walk with a deep dip. He was a young, rather good-looking man, with a small black mustache and an affable expression. He had once planned to be a student at the *Politécnico,* for his father had been a bakery shop owner, but after he graduated from secondary school a series of costly operations on his leg had impoverished the family. Chucho often rode over on his bicycle at about this time for a talk with Guillermo and now he asked Guillermo to turn off the radio.

"No, no," Guillermo said. "This is a marvelous program because it shows you how to protect yourself from thieves."

Guillermo went on to explain how a thief could be recognized: He wore a loose-fitting jacket and well-shined gum-soled shoes. His fingernails were well-trimmed except for the thumb and index finger of the right hand because he used these fingers for lifting pocket-books. Guillermo admired the skill of thieves and also studied their habits to avoid being one of their victims. As a young man he had known many thieves and when he had had his bicycle agency a well-known pickpocket named Silk Hands had used it as his unofficial headquarters. Guillermo was proud of his friendship with this member of the underworld.

"He was a very fine fellow. If somebody would come into the shop and tell us his troubles, Silk Hands would just ask where he lived. Many would come and tell us they had a sick child and didn't have money for medicine. Silk Hands would listen. Then he'd go off and return in a little while with ten or two hundred pesos which he'd send over to the people who needed money. He was a fine fellow except that he used dope. He'd come to our place and smoke mari-huana. He needed it so much he even planted some under the floor-ing of the shop."

Guillermo's acquaintance with Silk Hands and with other thieves had stood him in good stead more than once when at the end of a day's peddling or collecting and with his pockets full of money, he would find himself surrounded by a gang of attackers. One of the gang would always happen to be a friend of his and he would be spared.

Chucho said he was thirsty. "Say, Maria, I left some change from a beer here last night, no? It was fifty centavos, wasn't it? Now give me a lemon soda." Guillermo told his daughter to take some empty deposit bottles and to bring back three lemon sodas, or *Lulus* as they were called. Catarina took Maria's place at the table and began pasting labels.

"What time did you get back from the movies last night?" Chucho asked.

"Early."

'There you are. You have no money but you are always at the movies."

"Yes, but all I spend is one little peso. That's not very much, is it?" Guillermo had often had to defend his spending money on movies, but Chucho was easily won over.

"Well," he said, "everybody is free to do what he likes, isn't he?"

"That's it. That is what I say."

Chucho offered to help Catarina paste labels. "You smear on the glue and I'll paste them. You'll go faster that way." Catarina refused. "Don't be like that, shorty. Here I am dying of love for you and you ignore me because I am poor!"

Catarina looked at Guillermo and smiled. A radio program on which victims of robberies or accidents were being interviewed by the police came on the air. Guillermo asked Chucho to turn the radio up louder and they all listened closely, sipping the sodas Maria had brought. Maria pushed Catarina aside to take her place at the table again, and Catarina went home. When all the labels had been glued on, Maria retouched bare spots on the painted frames. Guillermo asked Maria to get him a rag for drying some bottles. This time she impatiently pointed to the wardrobe. "Ay, papá! Get one from over there!" He insisted and she got up to get it.

It was about four when Herminio came home again from work. "I'm back, papá. I want to eat."

Guillermo had been intent on cutting the wire for the corks and started at the sound of the boy's voice.

"Isn't there a sweet roll, papá?"

"I don't know," Guillermo answered unconcernedly.

"Tell Maria to go for thirty centavos' worth of rolls. I have the money but my hands are full of grease. Give her twenty centavos for cheese, papá. No, better bring me a twenty-centavo roll and forty centavos of cheese." He went to the kitchen shelf to hunt for something to eat while Maria was gone. He found some bread and asked his father to turn on the TV but Guillermo refused.

"Papá, the *maestro* saw you this morning and asked me why you don't come to work in the garage. I told him you were sick but that now you are all right."

Guillermo nodded. The foreman of the garage had offered him a job as an unskilled mechanic but he did not want it. He believed he could earn more money when he was not tied down to a time-consuming, low-paid job. Moreover, it irked him to pay dues to a union and to have the government deduct "taxes," that is, social security, from his wages. Guillermo was not resigned to poverty and he dreamed of getting ahead. Unlike his wife and neighbors, he did not squander his resources on drink, parties, godchildren, the church, or even on food, clothes, and schooling for his children. He used his money, cunning, and thrift to put his ideas to work and to further his business schemes. He was an entrepreneur and a gambler with an elastic sense of morality and a chronic need for capital.

Guillermo's family had been poor but his father, Leon, had been an intelligent, resourceful man. The son of a certified teacher and the grandson of an industrious Spaniard, Leon had taught school, made furniture and toys, and had owned some land. At twenty-five he formally married Guillermo's mother, an Indian girl of thirteen, and the marriage was a peaceful one. Guillermo never saw his father scold or beat his mother even though he often came home drunk. Leon was strict with his sons, even beating the older ones, but he was also affectionate with them. He refused to take part in the Revolution because he was against killing. After the war he got a job in a silver mine in which he worked for twenty-eight years, first as a laborer, then as manager. And the American owner gave him special jobs and favors.

Guillermo was the last of eleven children, but five of his brothers and sisters had died before he was born and by the time he was six only two brothers, Everardo and Juan were left. Both of them refused to work in the silver mine and went off to Mexico City. Thus Guillermo was brought up almost as an only child and was lonely. His father had become a chronic "drunk" and his mother pined for Juan, her favorite son. Guillermo believed that he himself resembled his mother rather than his father, but he felt that his mother had rejected him. All his life, it seemed to him, he had been unappreciated.

His mother had been given to frequent illnesses and could not take full care of him. Once she became paralyzed and was treated for sorcery. Guillermo remembered that she had been carried ten miles on a chair to an Indian curer who drew pins and maguey thorns from her mouth and head and knees. For a month she went to him on Tuesdays and Fridays, the witches' days, until finally she was cured. The curer said she had been bewitched by an envious neighbor. Guillermo, almost seven at the time, had had the fixed notion ever since that his family had been singled out as a target for witchcraft.

At the same age he was often sent alone into the hills for three days at a time to guard the turkeys and sheep. During the daytime he was not afraid and provided for his meals by shooting birds with a slingshot and cooking them over a fire. But at night he was kept awake by his intense fear of the dark in which he thought witches and ghosts were roaming. When he was eight he was lost in the woods for almost a week before he was found by a search party. After that his father began to talk of selling the animals, abandoning the land, and going to the city to join Everardo and Juan. In the end, however, it was sorcery that settled the matter. At night the hearth began to light itself, and the family believed that a ghost came after dark to look for money that was rumored to be buried there. Guillermo's father was afraid of money "that belonged to the dead" and he moved his family to the city.

It took them a week to walk to the city, a trip that now takes five hours by car. They arrived barefoot, in peasants' dress, carrying everything they owned on their backs. Everardo gave Guillermo his first pair of huaraches, then shoes, and little by little other city clothes. Guillermo entered the first grade and was so quick at learning that before the year was over he was advanced to the third grade. He was often kept out of school, however, to help his father sell mangos and to make toy wooden carts out of scraps of wood that Juan stole from the factory where he worked. His brothers married and lived in their own homes. His father had three jobs and earned five pesos a day, but he spent most of it on drink. Yet food was cheap in the 1930's and they ate better than Guillermo's family did now, always having three meals a day.

Guillermo got a job with a bicycle agency and learned how to make repairs. When he was fourteen he was knocked off a bicycle by a car, landed on his head, and was unconscious for twelve hours. His family was informed that he was dead and Juan came to the hospital with a coffin. Guillermo recovered but for a month he suffered severe headaches and he was left permanently deaf in one ear. He continued to work for his father and brother but he wanted more money and took additional jobs. At one time he held seven jobs: he delivered newspapers at four in the morning, worked in a bicycle factory until two in the afternoon, delivered mail and telegrams for the rest of the afternoon, made toys and repaired bicycles at home in the evening, and during the night was a night watchman. He considered the job in the bicycle factory his best because there he could also earn money "on the side."

"We got three pesos for each bicycle we assembled but that wasn't where we made our money. What the foreman and I did was to report that certain parts were missing from the crates received from England and since such accidents did happen from time to time, they believed us. Then we'd put the stuff under our clothes and take it out and sell it to the stores. We had more customers than we could satisfy. We sold it like hotcakes because it was brand new and cheap. We gave them a good buy for their money because I've always been a stickler for honest dealings."

Guillermo did well, sometimes earning as much as thirty pesos a day, but he gambled and spent money on drink and clothes. When he saw how his money was disappearing he became alarmed and decided to join a neighborhood organization called the "Monks." This was a fraternity made up of fifty youths led by a puritanical old man whom they called Father. The Father advised them not to smoke, drink, or go with women. He said, according to Guillermo, "The flesh is weak. If you give in to your body's demands it is bad for your health. If you don't go with women, you will live much longer, you will get strong and fat." These teachings impressed Guillermo, particularly since they said nothing about gambling which had become a passion with him. The Monks was "like a religion, like a sect, to protect ourselves. Anyone who broke the rules was dead as far as we were concerned. The girls used to chase us because we had no sweethearts. Since we paid no attention to them they said we were fairies. But we just laughed."

The Monks also caught the attention of a group of homosexuals, who showered them with attention: they took them to the movies, lent them money without asking for repayment, served them delicious meals, and so on. Guillermo took advantage of them as much as he could without submitting to their advances. Once the group of homosexuals gave a lavish party in one of the union halls with three dance orchestras, food, drinks, flowers, and decorations. The homosexuals themselves dressed as movie actresses. "It was a fine party, not a thing was missing. There was a jail where you paid fines and there was a house where you could get married to any one of the boys. The next day the police came and took them all off to prison. If they had come the day before they would have picked me up too." Guillermo had sympathy for these men, although he did not fall in with their practices. He believed they became as they were because they had had too many women.

Guillermo went on gambling and became involved in big card and dice games with professional gamblers, criminals, and dope "pushers." His older brother Juan grew worried and exercised his authority to force Guillermo to give up his jobs and work with him in a paper factory. Juan also tried to interest his brother in the union. But Guillermo would not be reformed. Instead he taught his fellow workers how to gamble and organized his own games. "I taught them how to play cards for big money. There were times when we bet one hundred pesos or a whole week's wages. Why, we'd bet the whole thing on one hand and gamble away a week's work. There was a cooperative store where we could buy shoes and things on credit. Well, we gambled with those too. I got into the worst company. I had no hope of keeping my job at the end of the probationary period because they knew me for a gambler."

Guillermo mentioned his fear of losing his job to a girl named Esmeralda, the daughter of a woman who owned a bicycle agency, and the girl gave him a bottle of bewitched water to sprinkle on the doorsill of the factory manager's office. A week later he was given a permanent job at thirty-five pesos a day. Guillermo believed that from then on the manager was bewitched in his favor.

"That's the way it was. They didn't believe I was the bad one. Once the manager was coming down the corridor to inspect the machinery while we were having some fun with an oil-soaked rag. It was rolled into a ball and we were tossing it to each other. Someone tossed it to me when they yelled 'Holy Water!' That's what we said when the gringo, the manager, came around. Just the same I threw the rag over some crates and it fell right on top of him. Wow, what a fuss! They sent for me at the head office. I thought to myself, 'I'm screwed this time.' When I walked in, the union secretary was there. The manager asked me who threw the rag and I said I did. But he said to me, 'No, it wasn't you. Why do you want to take the blame? Tell me who it was. Nothing will happen to you.' I kept saying I did it but they didn't fire me."

At a union meeting Guillermo learned about social security. In cases of illness the workers were paid their full salaries; for operations the union would pay nine hundred pesos, one peso from each member. Guillermo began to experiment. He found that if he rubbed garlic under his arms and put his feet in boiling water, a thermometer placed in the armpit would record a fever and he would be ordered to rest for three days. He did this several times but was not satisfied with such small pickings. He was after the nine hundred pesos. He tried eating twenty popsicles; they gave him a sore throat and made him ill. The doctor recommended a tonsillectomy and Guillermo won the money.

"But I still wasn't satisfied," he said. "I wanted to make another nine hundred pesos. I began to have a slight pain on the left side of my belly so one day I went to see the doctor. I thought it was a hernia and I would need another operation. After the doctor examined me he said there was nothing wrong. 'Nothing wrong? Don't I have a hernia?' Then the doctor explained to me what a hernia was and how you get it. In the factory I began lifting the heaviest crates I could find. But nothing happened except I kept on having the slight pain in my belly. One day I carried a pile of boxes upstairs

*186*

and then I couldn't walk down again. I couldn't move my leg. I was stiff and couldn't move. After the doctor examined me he said, 'If you don't have an operation within two hours I won't be responsible for your life. We have to remove your appendix.' When I heard that I was good and scared because in order to earn some pesos I was now practically on the verge of death. But they operated on me and I got my nine hundred pesos."

When Guillermo learned of the compensations for permanent injury he thought of mutilating himself. "I worked at a press and I had to be very careful when I fed the paper into it, otherwise I could lose my hand. I began to think about how much I'd get for losing a finger. Then I began to wonder which finger I could do without. I wasn't going to lose a hand or an eye but I thought a finger isn't much. I decided I didn't need the middle finger of the left hand and I put it in the machine. It hurt terribly. But some bastard saw me and stopped the machine in time. Then they accused me of putting my finger in the machine intentionally in order to collect compensation."

At eighteen Guillermo took Esmeralda as his common-law wife, the first woman with whom he had had sexual relations. His parents and his brothers disapproved of her because she had the reputation of being "*loca*" or promiscuous and because she insisted on nice clothes and new shoes every month. Guillermo gambled more than ever to keep her satisfied, getting deeply into debt to several workers in the factory. Then his father died and the burden of the funeral expenses fell on Guillermo.

Before he died Guillermo's father had told his wife that over the years he had saved some money to pay for his funeral expenses. At the bottom of a tin box in which Leon had saved cigarette stubs that he rerolled into cigarettes, Guillermo had found a large pile of coins, five hundred and seventy pesos in all. These Guillermo turned over to his brother Juan, who was to arrange the funeral. In addition, each of the sons received five hundred pesos from their unions at their father's death. Juan took the five hundred and seventy pesos and his union money and bought a small lot on which to build a house. Everardo got drunk in a saloon and was robbed of his union money.

This meant Guillermo had to pay for everything and it caused a permanent breach between him and his brothers. He never trusted them again.

Shortly after his father's death Esmeralda ran away with the children. Guillermo gambled and borrowed more and more to pay the police to search for them. He ended up with a debt of three thousand pesos which he realized he could never repay. To escape his creditors he managed to have himself fired from his job at the factory. That was his last job and for two years he was in miserable straits. Then he met Julia and went into business for himself.

Guillermo looked up as a young man rode up on a bicycle. "Ay, Dios mio! I can't work on it right now. Better tomorrow, better next week." The customer rode away. Maria came back with the roll and cheese. Herminio had been waiting impatiently and snatched it from her.

"You see how Herminio is, papá? Wait a minute, man! Give me a little piece."

"I'm the one who is working."

"Yes, but look at me. I work, too, helping my papá." Herminio gave her a tiny piece of cheese.

Don Chucho had fallen asleep on the bench. He awoke to say the radio program was terrible but went back to sleep when Guillermo refused to turn it off. A woman came in to make a payment to Guillermo. Guillermo was hungry and called to Maria, who was watching Catarina and Yolanda wash clothes. "Go see if you can find some of those little candied apples." Maria held out her hand for the money but dawdled at the doorway. "Go get the fruit! I'm telling you, eh?" She made a face and ran down the walk, her father glaring after her.

Señora Guadalupe came to the doorway and asked for Julia. She had been washing laundry almost all day and her hands were red and wrinkled from the water. Guillermo, intent on his work, did not lift his head when she left. Chucho was still napping, his hat over his face, his legs outstretched. Maria came back slowly with the apples in a dish. Herminio dashed up to her and before she

*The Gutiérrez Family*

could stop him grabbed a piece of fruit and ran off, stuffing it into his mouth. Maria complained but Guillermo ignored her and began to eat. He pushed Chucho with his foot.

"Chucho! Chucho! What happened, boss, did you go to sleep?"

"What's that? What? Ah, yes, I did. Last night I threw a real drunk and I went to bed late. And this morning I got up early. I hardly slept at all." Chucho took the fruit Guillermo offered him.

Herminio came up. "What about me, papá?"

"Maria can go get more." But this time Maria said she was tired of running errands all the time and refused to go. Herminio did not make an issue of it and went out to play. Maria went out, too, eating a piece of fruit. A woman stopped at the door to ask for change for a peso. "We don't have any, señora. We're dead broke." Some children came in to buy candy.

Every now and then as he worked Guillermo winced with pain and held his hands. Chucho asked if he were ill. "No," Guillermo answered. "It's just that when I work with the metal strips I get cut and my hands get infected on me. I put some pomade on but it doesn't help. Right now they hurt from the wire which cuts me too." The men were silent for a few minutes. Maria came in to add water to the beans and stir them. She asked her father for money to buy *tortillas*.

"No. Go and get them and Julia will come by to pay for them later."

"But she didn't pay for the ones we got yesterday and they won't let me have them."

"Yes, Julia paid for them."

"No, no. We haven't paid for them. I won't go. They'll make me feel ashamed. They'll scold me." Maria went out angrily. "I'll go get some for my godmother. I won't get the ones for this house and that's that."

Catarina came along and Guillermo sent her for the *tortillas*. Maclovio's little daughter returned an empty soda bottle which Guillermo rolled under the table with his foot. The little girl looked at the candy tray for awhile, then left.

"Well," Guillermo said to Chucho, "it looks as though my old lady is doing some business. She's not home yet. Man, it's getting late! Sometimes she comes home early, sometimes late. If it rains she'll be here right away. When she's not home, you can see how the house is. Sometimes she stays home because Lola is working, Maria goes off to school, and Herminio to his *maestro*. And I, why I come in and go out and the house cannot be alone. But when she's home she steps lively and makes chicken *mole* to sell here. But the people don't pay right away and her family eats it all up and I say in the end we lose out, no?" Guillermo looked out at the darkening sky. "I wish she'd come soon."

Maria walked in with a napkin full of *tortillas*. She had taken them from Catarina. Still annoyed with her father, she put the bundle into a pot and went out without speaking. Catarina came in soon after and took the *tortillas* away to her own house. After that Yolanda carried away the stone mortar and the salt. Guillermo watched all this without saying a word. Chucho was asleep again, and music was now coming from the radio. Guillermo called to Maria, who came in reluctantly. He wanted her to help him insert the finished bottles into their metal frames. Maria ran out, saying, "Pretty soon. I'll help you pretty soon."

Guillermo shook Chucho, who grunted sleepily. Guillermo wanted to talk. "I want to buy Julia a stove," he said, "but it would be just our luck for all of us to get blown up. I tell Julia that if we're careful there's no reason to fear, but she is afraid an accident will happen unexpectedly. The house couldn't be left alone. No, indeed. It would be risky." Chucho didn't answer and Guillermo called to his daughter, "Maria! Maria! Come on, girl, where is the light bulb? I don't know where Lola put it this morning while she ironed. Get it for me!" The bulb was in clear view on top of the TV set but Guillermo wanted to get the girl into the house.

Maria came at once. "Why, here it is!" she said, and she handed it to her father.

"Come on now. Help me put the frames on." Guillermo packed the labels, corks, chain, and wire into a cardboard box and gave it to Maria to put in the wardrobe. Once more he shook Chucho, who this time awakened with a start.

"All through, Don Guillermo?" Chucho stood up and stretched, then took a strip of metal and began to pound it flat with the hammer. Guillermo reached under the bed for a pile of large bulletins marked USSR in big red letters which he put on the table. Maria began handing him the water bottles that were lined up on a board on the bed, and he set each bottle into its small, swinging frame, connecting the chain with a pinch of his pliers. He placed the completed toy on the top of a bulletin and wrapped it carefully, tearing out a page with a quick jerk. He handed the wrapped toy to Maria, who placed it in a large sack, the top of which she had turned down over the back of a chair to keep it open.

"Pack them so that there are no spaces," Guillermo said. "Lola packs them well but you don't yet."

Don Chucho's attention was caught by the wrapping paper. He picked up one of the bulletins and read it aloud, *Information Bulletin of the USSR.* "See here, Guillermo, don't you know this is a communist paper?"

"Yes, yes, my *compadre* who works on the railroad already told me. I saw an advertisement saying they would send it free to anyone who asked for it so I put my name on the list. Just look, it has twenty pages and I can wrap twenty bottles with it. And don't think that is the only thing they send me and, well, I never lack for paper now. I look at the pictures when I have time. Well, it doesn't do any harm because it is registered as second-class mail in the post office and can't carry anything in it against Mexico, can it?" Chucho was reading the bulletin and did not answer.

Guillermo's interest in politics was limited. He voted in the presidential elections but he believed that the outcome was predetermined by the party in power. He read a daily newspaper and listened to the news broadcasts on the radio and TV and that was all. His father had enthusiastically supported Cárdenas. When Mexico's oil reserves were expropriated from foreign control, Leon had given a sewing machine to the government to help buy back the oil. Guillermo had contributed a hen. His father also had worked on a political committee for the *Partido Revolucionario Mexicano* of Cárdenas "in the hope that they would throw him a bone." Guillermo expected little of the government for he saw it as a police force that one had to submit to. "Obey or things will go worse for you." The president he respected most was Alemán because he was strict. It was during Alemán's administration that Guillermo was inducted and did military service every Sunday for a year. Guillermo had been impressed by the fact that he could not bribe his way out of this obligation, at least not with the small sum he could afford. All the other administrations were "bad" because of the rise in the cost of living.

Guillermo was not strongly antigringo and was willing to forget past wars. He thought that the North Americans had "a lot of personality" and that their investments were helping Mexico but he complained about the low-quality arms the United States sold to his country. He also thought the United States was trying to keep out other foreigners, the Japanese and the Australians, who might be helpful to Mexico. "They want to keep us under their yoke alone because they got used to that, no?" He was aware of the effect of the rise in the dollar exchange on the cost of living. "Just think, because aniline dyes come from there [the United States], when the dollar went up the price of towels went up and, well, that's not good."

Guillermo's brother Juan was active in his union and, when Guillermo had worked in the same factory with Juan, he had unexpectedly been elected general secretary. Guillermo's experience in that office taught him to distrust union leaders. "It's all a lie. The union leaders grab the secretary general and get together their gang of four or five men and say, 'The company is ready to pay the wages we want, right? Let's tell them to give less and we'll take fifty per cent of the raise and give the workers twenty per cent.' Yes, the majority of union leaders are thieves, lawyers or government men. Not one is honest. The biggest leaders are the worst thieves. The C.T.M. [Confederation of Mexican Workers] is very powerful. If a boss wants to fire a man for not working or for stealing he can't even kick him out!"

The Soviet bulletins had not influenced Guillermo in favor of communism. "Well, I'm not informed but, according to what people say, it is like a religion that one submits to. Well, the workers have to do forced labor and I don't think that is very good. And what is this about yours being mine and mine yours? Suppose, for example, I make a hundred water bottles a day, why should I let my neighbor take fifty? Why? That señor over there makes his pails. Should I take them away from him? No, that's not good." Guillermo believed that Russia had "pulled down her curtains" because she was preparing for war. But he also thought that wars were started by the capitalists "who made a lot of ships and arms and then had to use them so they wouldn't go to waste and so they could make more." He was against big business because "they don't leave anything for the little businessman."

When the sack was filled Guillermo told Maria to turn off the radio. Chucho, who was still reading a bulletin, looked up. "Did you have to shut it off?"

"Yes, because it's been on since the morning and that's enough."

"All right, I won't say another word!"

"Besides, the plays are over and they are what I like."

"All right, Señor Guillermo, I was just saying. . . . But not a word!" Chucho began toying with the hammer and metal again.

Guillermo sat back and looked at the clock. "Well, I guess your mamá is going to be late. We're not going to have any supper tonight."

"Ay, no, papá. I hope it rains!" Maria said. She got up and added water to the beans. Not having anything else to do she took some dirty socks from a box and went out to wash them. Chucho said he was hungry and said good-by.

At ten minutes to six Julia came home. There were only three towels slung across her shoulder and on her head she carried a bundle tied up in her sweater.

"So you've come home! Do you still love me, old girl?"

Julia just smiled. She let down the bundle and threw the towels over a chair. Sitting on the bed, she began to count the pile of pesos in her purse.

*193*

"Look, you won't believe it but I sold everything except those three pieces." It was difficult to count in the dark room. "Put up the light, Guillermo, I can't see."

The only outlet for electricity was in the kitchen but Guillermo had run an extension cord into the bedroom for the radio and the TV set or for a bulb. He put in a bulb and turned it on.

"Yes, I did real well today, thank God. Look, a hundred and seventeen pesos' worth I sold! At first I didn't sell a thing. Then I met a friend and I guess she brought me luck." Julia jubilantly put the money in an old black coin purse and tucked it into her bosom. From another purse that she carried in her apron pocket she took out some change.

"Go get a tomato," she said to Maria, "the cheaper kind that are a little squashed to cook with the meat I brought." She got up and went into the kitchen. "Did you salt the beans?" She tasted the beans and nodded. "They're all right. They're done so now we can eat."

"Well, hurry up about it!" Guillermo said.

"Ay, my feet hurt from all that walking! How awful those new market places are! There's no shelter for a person. I tried to get out of the rain and do you think I could? The rain hit me from every direction. I got soaked."

"You say it rained, old girl?"

"No, that was the other day." Julia went back into the bedroom and took off her shoes. "Ay, my poor feet! How they hurt!"

Catarina came in. "The baby had a terrible fall and got hit on the head," she said to her grandmother.

"He fell! God's truth?"

Yolanda came in looking worried. "Yes, mamá, off the bed. This girl here wasn't taking care of him."

"Really? Because if you are not telling the truth you'll find out!"

Guillermo spoke up, "They take such good care of that damned kid that he's going to die off."

Yolanda looked at him and laughed. Julia realized that they were joking and reached over and grabbed Catarina by the throat. "Damn you, little one, don't you be playing any tricks on me or one of these days I'm going to choke you!"

At this point little Ema came in and said with a straight face, "The baby fell. Catarina pushed him." Everyone but Julia laughed. "Don't make me hit you," Julia said angrily. "God's truth, no more jokes." But then she too began to laugh. "I was about to beat you all with a club to make you quit fooling me."

Guillermo had put on his hat, lifted the heavy sack of bottles over his shoulder, and was ready to go out. "I'm going to deliver this," he said to his wife, "because if I don't go now then maybe tomorrow she won't want it. You know, a sale can't be made just any time from one minute to another. If this bunch is sold then I can begin to make that lottery game and then you'll see how the money rolls in! Damned if I won't rake in the wool!"

Julia was whispering with Yolanda and didn't answer. Guillermo went a little closer to them and raised his voice, "I told you something. If you don't want to believe me, then don't believe me." The women went on talking and Guillermo tried to hear what they were saying. Galván came in looking for his mother.

"So what? Didn't the *maestro* pay you boys?" Guillermo asked.

"No, I told him we'd wait until Saturday."

Julia looked up. "Ay, that lousy old bastard! He hasn't paid you for three weeks! Some nerve!"

"Yes," Guillermo said, "but it's because he hasn't gotten any repair jobs. Whenever he has work he pays you right away. Right, my boy?" Galván said yes and ran out to play.

Julia and Yolanda resumed their private conversation. Suddenly Julia exclaimed loudly, "No! All I said was that last night we had a little beer right in here. Don't be a liar!"

Guillermo had become very much interested in what was going on. "Is it that your mother's dying, old girl? She's got a pain you-know-where? Is that right?"

Julia turned around and smiled. "Go on, go to the devil! You don't know anything about it."

"Come on now, old girl!" Julia refused to be wheedled and went outside with Yolanda. Guillermo followed them. Herminio came running up the walk waving a bill. He asked his father to change it for him.

"What? Have you been paid so soon?"

"No, well, only half of it, for me and Galván. They'll give us the rest on Saturday."

"I'll bet he paid you and you're not telling us, you devil," Julia said.

Herminio went into the house. He was excited and hopped up and down, shouting, "I'm going to get dressed because I'm going to have chocolate at Melín's party."

When Maria came back with the tomato Julia unwrapped her sweater and took out a paper cone of green chile, another of salt, and a large newspaper package of *suadero*. *Suadero* was the waste cuttings and skin of beef that Julia exchanged for towels in the slaughterhouses. She served it once or twice a week fried like pork cracklings with onion, garlic, and tomato. Guillermo, too hungry to resist, ate a chocolate from his stock, taking care not to be seen, for members of the family were expressly forbidden to eat the candy. Old Rufelia came to the shed with her shawl around her shoulders and complaining of the cold. She gave Catarina a glass and fifty centavos to buy some *chinchol* at the saloon across the street. Don Chucho rode up on his bicycle and said it would be better to get a small bottle now that he was there.

"No, why so much when I just want to warm myself up?"

"And is it all for you, señora?" he asked teasingly.

"Well, for you, too. Just let her go ahead."

When Catarina returned with the drink Rufelia offered it first to Chucho. He took the glass and swallowed some. "Ay, boy! Why this stuff is pure fire! I can feel it burning my stomach!" Rufelia laughed. "Well, aren't you a fine drinker!" She took a sip. "Look, I drank some and it didn't bother me a bit!" Chucho offered it to Guillermo, who refused.

"Ay, what a coward!" Julia said. But she too refused to drink, saying she'd rather drink at night after supper. Yolanda came in with a napkin full of *tortillas*, which she put into a pot, and stayed on to talk with her mother. Guillermo and Chucho were discussing drinks with Rufelia. Catarina was quarreling with her brothers, who had come in to find their mother. Maria came in carrying the baby and singing. Chucho began to tease Catarina, following her around as she tried to avoid him. "Ay, Catarina, I'm crazy about you and you don't pay any attention to me at all." Herminio was looking for clean clothes. He wanted Maria to find them for him but she refused and they began to argue. The place was crowded and noisy. Julia pulled Maria by the ear and ordered her to get Herminio's clothes but Maria handed the baby to Yolanda and ran out. Herminio found a clean shirt and pants and hid behind the wardrobe door to dress. He threw his workclothes under the bed. When he came out of his corner, he bumped into his father.

"Watch out, Minio, damn you. Just bump me and I'll fix you. You'll get your head knocked off!"

Herminio laughed. "No, papá, I didn't do anything to you."

Yolanda went home with her children. Julia was watching the meat cook. "Well, anyway, in this house we're not too poor to eat," she said to her mother.

For a few moments the house was quiet as everyone stood or sat around waiting to eat. At seven o'clock Julia began to serve the food. She gave Maria and Herminio a plate of cracklings, beans, and three *tortillas.* Clearing the worktable she invited Chucho to eat. "Come on, have something even though it is not much." Chucho declined, saying he would eat later, and sent Maria out for a bottle of beer.

Julia served her mother. Guillermo went outside to the toilet. As soon as he had gone, Julia sprang to the sack of waterbottles and took four of them. Carrying them on her shoulder she imitated the call of the water-sellers and everyone laughed; they knew she took a few of the toys on the sly and sold them. She always used that money to buy things for the children. She hid the bottles in the wardrobe and went back to the stove to heat the *tortillas.* Maria came in with the beer. Herminio belched and she slapped him. "Quiet, don't be such an animal!" Only Chucho interfered in the quarrel that followed between the two children. "Leave him alone, Maria," he said. "It's true it's not good manners but there aren't any rules about it."

Catarina came to eat, sitting down next to Rufelia on the doorstep. Julia was eating standing by the stove. When Guillermo appeared, Herminio moved from the table to give his place to his father. Julia served her husband as soon as he was seated and he quickly began to eat. Yolanda, wearing a man's jacket, was standing outside the door watching her husband, Rafael, walk drunkenly up the walk. Señora Guadalupe stopped at the door.

"What do you say? How are you feeling, Chata?" Julia asked her.

The old woman answered sadly, "Ay, if you only knew how my heart hurts me! Since they killed my boy it hurts me so. I don't know why. I've prayed for him every night." Two years before her only son had been stabbed in a quarrel over a girl.

"You know what's happening?" Chucho said. "Autosuggestion. That's the worst thing in the world for a person."

"You've washed too much, woman," Julia said. "Take me now, tired out from so much of it. Ah, yes, Chata, all your life at the scrubboard."

"The trouble is that my little *comadre* is worked out," Rufelia said. "She needs rest."

"Why, yes, but what can a person do about it?" Guadalupe said. She drew back her shoulders complaining that her whole back ached. Julia unobtrusively handed her a plate of food and she went home with it.

Guillermo had cleaned his plate and now stood up to leave. "Hand me my jacket," he said to his wife. "I'm going to deliver these now." Julia tossed him the jacket and he went out with his sack over his shoulder. A few minutes later Chucho stood up to leave. "It is a terrible thing that one so young as I has to work," he said. Julia and Rufelia smiled. Herminio ran in to ask his father to play records for Melín's party. He stood still a moment, disappointed at not finding Guillermo there.

"Just look at him!" Julia said to her mother. "How come the rascal is so generous!" The boy went back to Melín's house to watch the preparations for the party. A moment later Julia heard someone scream. Maria came running in to tell her that Herminio had hit Melín. "Minio! Herminio! Come here," Julia shouted. In a lower voice she said to her mother, "Now we'll see about this *cabrón!*" Herminio did not come and she sent Maria to get him. The two returned quarreling and slapping each other.

"You see, Julita, how Minio is?" Maria said. "He hit me with a stick, the dirty little dog."

Herminio said aggressively, "Why are you butting into this, mamá? Why do you care? She hit me first and you don't think I'm going to let anybody hit me, do you?"

"See here, Minio, you damned little brat! I don't want any trouble with anybody. You'd better get inside!" Julia was angry.

"No, mamá, no! I'd rather stay with Galván." Herminio ran off to Yolanda's house with Maria chasing him. No longer concerned, Julia sat down on the bed and took off her shoes. "My feet hurt from walking. But if a person doesn't work, he doesn't eat. And everything is so expensive, no?" She rocked back and forth, holding her feet. The dirty dishes were still on the table. The floor was littered with paper and beer and soda bottles. Out in the courtyard Julia and Rufelia could hear children running and laughing.

At about half past seven Lola came home. She smiled pleasantly and took a small candy doll out of a paper bag. "Look, Julita, I finally bought it." The women admired the doll. Lola decided to take it over to Melín's house before she ate supper. As she went out Galván came in, shouting at his grandmother, "Mamá, give me something to eat! Hurry up about it because I'm hungry." Julia looked at him without moving. "Why, didn't your mother give you anything?"

"No, she told me that you would. Will you, mamá?" Julia stood up, making a face as she put on her shoes.

"Ay, *chingao!* They won't let a person rest. Let me give this fellow something to eat and then don't keep bothering me, you son of your mother!" She turned on the stove to heat the food and went outside to the faucet to fill the coffeepot, taking along a few dirty dishes to wash. Just as she was serving Galván, Catarina came in and asked for more food. Julia was impatient but she served the child.

"Oh, give me, give me! What a bother you lousy kids are, in God's truth! Don't you have a mother or what?" The children ate quickly and silently.

Rufelia was huddling in the doorway tightly wrapped in her

shawl. "Pretty soon I'm going to bed," she said. "It's getting awfully cold. The cold goes right through you."

Herminio, Ema, and Tomás skipped in, singing, "It's time, it's time!" but Julia chased them out. "Get out of here, you damned kids! We're talking in here."

Lola came back, pleased that Melín had liked the candy doll. "It matched the cake all right. It looks real pretty. I also bought rosettes for the candles." She sat down at the little kitchen table and Julia served her her supper. Herminio came in again, followed by Ema and Tomás, to search in the wardrobe for his sweater. Ema and Tomás watched Lola eat and Ema finally said, a little petulantly, "A fine thing! Don't we get anything to eat?" Julia, who was heating more *tortillas*, answered absently, "Yes, yes, pretty soon." Melín ran in to show her godmother Julia her new shoes.

"Ah, there, aren't they nice!" Julia said. "Now you must take good care of them."

Six children crowded in excitedly after Melín, all talking at once. Lola watched them, smiling. "Just listen to them!" she said to Julia. "They're so anxious." Julia laughed. "Why, yes. They're so young." She told Maria to climb on the shelf and look for some confetti she kept there. "So you can throw it on Melín." Maria found the jar and handed it down to Julia. The children crowded around her clamoring for confetti and Julia was obliged to hold it above her head to keep it from them.

"Stop!" she shouted. "I won't give anything to anybody. It's for Melín. Get out of here!" The children romped out noisily. Julia decided that there wasn't enough confetti and sent Herminio to buy twenty centavos' worth. Maria went with him. Galván walked in combing his hair.

Lola pounced on him. "Ay, look, this kid's got my comb!"

"Your comb! That's not so. I just took it away from Jorge in the courtyard."

"No wonder I looked for it and couldn't find it. I left it on top of the TV yesterday morning."

Galván threw the comb on the table. "There's your filthy old comb!" he said and went out.

Lola picked it up. "I'm going to comb Melín's hair. The mirror there is larger than the one here."

Maria came back alone. She complained of a headache and sat down on the bed. "This child, is she sick?" Rufelia asked. "Yes," Julia answered. "Since yesterday she's been complaining of a headache and yet she wants to go to school. I say in the first place her stomach is overloaded. In the second place she's got worms, and in the third place, she's in her 'development' now. God willing, tomorrow I'll give her a laxative." Maria meanwhile had taken her good shoes out of the wardrobe and had put them on. She went out to the courtyard to join the crowd of children.

Rufelia stood up slowly. "I'm going to bed now, Julia. Ay, please let me have a scrap of blanket. That room is so cold! Man! Toward morning is when I feel it most. Come over later and throw another blanket over me. Don't be so mean, daughter."

"Yes, *mamacita,* I'll send one of the children later." When Rufelia had gone Julia began to pile the dirty dishes into a basin.

"What are you doing, Julia?"

Julia looked up to see Anita standing in the doorway with her young daughter. Julia invited them in, placing a chair next to the bed. Anita sat down and looked at the photos on the TV set. One was a composite photo of Guillermo and Julia; the picture of Julia had been taken when she was in her twenties and she had had a photographer combine it with a recent snapshot of Guillermo. Another was a snapshot of Maclovio, and a third showed all three of Guillermo's children dressed for their First Communion. Anita's daughter was shy and stood next to her mother until two *vecindad* girls invited her out to play.

Catarina walked in. "How are they going to dance with the patio so dirty?" she asked Julia.

"Well, sweep it," Julia retorted. "Throw a bucket of water on it and sweep it. Hurry! So people won't have to walk in the mud." Catarina went for water and sprinkled some on the ground in front of No. 5. Julia nodded approvingly.

Herminio, Galván, and Tomás came back running. "Quick, mamá, here's the red confetti. Mix it with the other so that we'll have a whole lot to throw." Herminio handed his mother a paper cone of confetti. Galván tried to snatch it from her but she slapped his hand quickly. "Stop, *chingado!* Now get out of here! Now I'm not going to give you anything so that you'll learn not to be so impatient!" The boys went out, disgruntled, and Julia put away the confetti.

Panchita came in and quietly began to spoon out meat and beans into two of her own clay casseroles. Julia counted out twelve *tortillas*, wrapped them in a napkin, and handed them to her daughter-in-law, who carried the food home. Panchita and Maclovio usually used their own dishes and ate their meals in their own house. Guillermo came home. "You here?" he said to Anita, putting his empty sack on the sleeping platform.

"Why, yes, I came for the party."

Guillermo turned to his wife. "Didn't the policeman come back?"

"The policeman?" Julia looked alarmed. "Oh, no, he hasn't been here at all."

"I guess he'll come tomorrow. I'm pretty sure of it. In the morning I'll have more money here." Guillermo handed some bills to Anita. "Take this much. I'll give you the rest later on. Just let me get caught up a little."

Anita took the money. "That's all right. After all you don't owe me very much now."

"You see, it's like I tell you, I don't owe just you but many others. And so I have to look ahead, no? If I give everything to one, I can't give anything to anyone else. I can't stand it when they come telling me their troubles and crying for their money. That's my weakness. It hurts me to see them angry or unhappy. That's why they always lend me money—because they know I will pay them back. That's the way I am. No, if I haven't paid you it's because I haven't had it, just like I said." Guillermo took a piece of paper and leaning against the wall began to write down some figures. "Here, I'm going to show you what I have to pay out each week." Anita stood up to look over his shoulder.

Julia took off her shoes and lay down on the bed to ease her aching back. "What, are you going to start that?" she said to her husband. "Go to the devil! It's just like I keep telling you, no? Why do you get so far in debt? You don't spend a centavo on me. You're the only one who knows what you do with the money."

"Now wait a minute, old girl. It's true, like you said, that I don't spend a centavo on you but right now I've got everything hocked so what can I do about it? Right now it's pretty miserable, all suffering. I am losing the game, no? I have only one ace in my hand because if I didn't have that I would be dead. Right now someone else holds the three other lucky aces but tomorrow's another day. Then maybe I'll hold four aces again."

Julia and Anita listened to Guillermo without interrupting him. Lola came in quietly and signalled to Julia behind her father's back. They were waiting to bring over the cake which was to be cut to the music of the *mañanita* or the birthday song. Julia sat up. "Gutiérrez," she said, "I want you to set up the record-player a while for my *comadre*."

Some children crowded into the little room behind Lola. Then Melín's older brother came in carrying the pink birthday cake high over the heads of the children. "Get back!" shouted Julia to the children, springing up and putting on her shoes. "You're not leaving me room to move. Get on outside!" The children obeyed and Julia set the small bedroom table in the center of the aisle and covered it with newspaper.

"All right, put it on this. It's not very nice but we don't have any tablecloth here." The boy set the cake down and the children crowded in again. Guillermo looked through the records, found the one he wanted, and turned on the record-player. Herminio jumped up and down impatiently. "What's the matter, papá? Put on the record now, no?"

"Pretty soon, just as soon as the *compadres* and the saint's day girl get here."

Melín's mother came in with a clay jug of steaming chocolate. The children, unable to contain themselves, yelled and jumped and squeezed each other in excitement. Melín's younger sister brought the paper plates and napkins and put them on the table. Julia meanwhile had noticed the littered floor and was trying to sweep around the children's legs. Finally irritated by the crowd, she lifted Herminio, Galván, Tomás, and four other children onto the shelf and three others she set on the bed. The remaining nine she allowed to stand around the table. Guillermo took his post at the TV set next to Anita, Lola was in the kitchen, and the other adults were waiting out under the shed. Señora Guadalupe looked in and went on her way, shaking her head. Everyone was impatient for Melín and her father to arrive so that the party might begin. When they appeared at last, there was clapping and shouting.

"The girl of the saint's day! The girl of the saint's day!"

While Guillermo played the birthday song Señora Chole served mugs of hot chocolate. The children waited their turn anxiously, rubbing their hands and smiling at each other. Galván shouted from the platform, "Oh, sure, they're not going to give any to us up here. Mamá Julia, mamá Julia, give us some!" Julia, who was helping Chole pass the drink, did not hear him in all the hubbub.

"Turn out the light, Gutiérrez, they're going to light the candles on the cake."

With Lola's help Melín lit the candles in the darkness. Everyone reminded the little girl to make a wish. There was a moment of silence and then Melín said, "Now." She had made her wish and immediately the children clamored for her to cut the cake.

The birthday song had come to an end and Guillermo put on a popular song. He looked at his pile of records and grumbled to Anita. "Just look at that! That's what you call 'dead money.' All that money I spent and for what? For nothing."

"Ah, but at least it's fun," Anita said loudly.

Guillermo shook his head. "Well, I'm not saying it isn't but you put out this much money and don't take anything in. Pure money wasted for nothing." It irked him to play the records without charge. He had hoped to rent out the record-player and records for weekly dances as some did in the larger *vecindades*. But it did not work out that way in the Panderos *vecindad*. Thanks to his wife, over half of the twelve families were *compadres* and two were relatives. All these could not be charged. The remaining families were too poor or would think him uncooperative if he had charged them. His own children would call him a miser if he refused to play music at *vecindad* parties. Guillermo looked with distaste at the noisy crowd in his house.

"Shut up! Quit screaming!" he yelled, but no one heard him or paid any attention to him.

Julia told Chucho to get the confetti from the shelf and throw it on the children. Melín cut the first slice of the cake and then moved aside to let her mother finish while they all watched. A thin slice of cake was served on a paper plate to everyone. The boys on the sleeping platform began to fight and Julia cursed them, threatening to put them out. When they had eaten their cake, three of the older children went out into the yard to dance. They shouted that the music could not be heard outside and Guillermo turned up the volume. Julia noticed that Lola had refused the chocolate and cake.

"See how stubborn she is! She won't eat. Then why is she here? She oughtn't to be so rude. As though she were an Indian girl from the hills! You've got to eat something whether you like it or not."

Lola laughed in embarrassment, but Señora Chole too urged her. "Yes, Lola, eat a little bit just to go along with my daughter. After all you are her godmother too." Lola was persuaded and began to eat. Julia checked to see that all the children had been served. Her son-in-law, Rafael, still drunk, reeled up to the door and looked in, blinking his eyes. "*Madre Santísima!* What a crowd of kids!" Yolanda hit him in the ribs with her elbow and he was silenced. Anita and her daughter were ready to go; they were given an extra piece of cake to take home with them. Now children began streaming out into the yard to dance rowdily with each other on the rough ground. Julia began to serve the adults seated under the shed and in the house. There were Señor Avelino and his wife Lupe of No. 2, Julia's *compadres* of the Child Jesus; *comadre* Chita of No. 10 who was godmother at Maria's confirmation; Señor Aurelio and his wife, Alicia, who were godparents at Herminio's confirmation; and several other neighbors. Stout Ana refused the chocolate and asked when beer was going to be served. Chucho made everyone laugh by singing with a record. He stood up as though drawing guns from his pockets and said, "With that music and a pair of pistols, nothing but dead and wounded!" Someone shouted "Man, you've been on mari-huana too long!"

Everyone was gay except Guillermo, who remained in the house to guard the TV set. He read a newspaper while the records were playing. Julia went into the bedroom to tidy up. She collected the paper plates, put the table back in place, and took the chairs outside for the grownups who were watching the young people dance. The floor was covered with confetti but she decided to let the sweeping go until morning. She went out for water, poured it over the dirty dishes in the basin, and set the basin on the floor under the brazier. Then she put on a sweater and joined the group outside. Some of the guests were waiting to take their leave.

"Many thanks. We're grateful for everything."

"Not at all," Julia responded. "Thank you for coming to this poor house."

It was nine-thirty and the children were still dancing with en-thusiasm. "Change your partners!" they would shout as a record was changed. Lola had not joined the dancing but stood watching from the doorway. Chucho urged her to dance but she refused. Yolanda, holding her baby, watched her older son dance. "Just look at that Galván! He certainly can dance! Why they'll even be throwing coins at him for his dancing!"

"Tell him to dance a rock and roll," Lola said. But Guillermo had no rock and roll music. Chucho, unable to contain himself any longer, grabbed one of the women and danced with her. She didn't want to be his partner because of the way he bobbed up and down on his short leg, but the others cheered him on and he would not let go of her. Chucho began to clown to hide his defect and they all laughed heartily at him. "That fellow is going to make us split our sides," someone said.

Julia gathered up empty beer bottles in the bedroom. Then she took some money from the purse in her bosom and went with Chole and another neighbor to buy beer. When they returned it was al-most ten o'clock and only four couples were dancing and four people were sitting outside. Herminio and Maria had climbed onto the sleeping shelf without undressing and had gone to sleep. Lola was dancing with Chucho while Guillermo watched them uneasily from the doorway. His daughter was at a restless and dangerous age, for between the ages of thirteen and eighteen "a girl's flower is in full bloom and she must be watched." He had warned Lola to be careful until she was eighteen; after that she could marry or do what she pleased. "After that age," he reasoned, "the flower dies, goes away, and she will be calmer and more sensible."

Guillermo had been afraid that Lola might turn out to be like her mother but so far she seemed to have his own phlegmatic temperament. He had never understood Esmeralda's wild fits of anger nor why she had left him three times, each time eight months after the birth of a child. "I never did a thing to her. All I did was come home and eat and sleep." Sometimes she threatened to kill him and the children and once she had actually nicked him with a knife and had drawn blood. This had frightened him so much that when she ran away for the third time he was relieved. His only concern then was that she had taken the children with her. But even after he had recovered the children and was living with Julia he was afraid of his first wife. He believed that she was a witch, that she had sorcerized his manager in the factory, that she had bewitched him into marrying her, and that she had cast a spell over him before she left for the last time. He told how it had happened:

"Once I came home drunk. Very tired. It was about eleven o'clock in the morning because then I was working on the night shift in the factory. I said I would take a little nap to fix myself up. There was plenty of time because I didn't go to work until ten o'clock that night. But I couldn't sleep. My wife was walking here and there, back and forth. I heard her say, 'Today I'll fix him. After all today is Tuesday.' That frightened me, right? She was just waiting for me to fall asleep, no? For a long time she had wanted to harm me. Even her sister had told her not to frig me. I said to myself, 'This one thinks I didn't hear but I know what she is up to.' I got up and told her I was going to the doctor at the Social Security and then to work.

"I did go to the doctor and would you believe it? He told me to take the night off and go home to rest. Imagine how things worked out! I went home to take her by surprise. We had two entrances, one into the kitchen and one into the bedroom. I went in the back way and there was no one there, no one. The house was empty. But in the room there were four lighted candles set up in the shape of a square. I just stood there looking at them when someone said, 'Get in.' I even felt someone push my shoulder and I got into the square. Right away I got a headache. It felt like a knife in my head. It didn't go away no matter what I did. I spent money on medicine but nothing helped until I went to a señora who gave me cleansings. Then I got better."

Even after Esmeralda had left him she tried to harm him, Guillermo believed. He noticed that whenever any relative of hers came to visit him, either he or one of the children fell ill. Finally he had had to tell them not to come. Now sometimes toward dawn he would smell Esmeralda's strong perfume and know she was trying to get at him. Later he would get a terrible cramp in his leg or neck, a pain so strong it sent him spinning around. Whenever he became ill he suspected Esmeralda. But he was happy that she didn't bother the children. The two younger ones had only passing illnesses and Lola was in good health.

At a quarter to eleven Guillermo stopped the music. He took a flashlight and went out to the toilet. Then he said good night to the guests and went in. He turned out the light and got into bed in his underwear. A few minutes later Lola entered, half-closed the door to shut out the glare of the kitchen bulb, changed into an old dress, and climbed onto the shelf next to her sleeping brother and sister.

Julia sat under the shed drinking beer and talking with the remaining guests—Don Chucho, *comadre* Chita, Guadalupe, and Ignacio, who had joined them. Julia was saying that next year when Lola was fifteen she would like to give her a big coming-out party. "Do you think, *comadre*, that I can give her a party for five hundred pesos? If that's what I spent on three children it ought to be more than enough. God willing, I'm going to save to give her a little fiesta.

After all, she will be a señorita! I wonder how much a real nice dress will cost?"

The little group discussed prices and drank a toast to the coming party. Guadalupe said, "Money doesn't go anywhere these days but I leave everything to His care and sooner or later everything is paid up. God is slow but He's always there."

"We should have been women, eh, Don Chucho, so that Heaven could support us," Ignacio said. "But being men we have to pay our own way." He and Chucho drank a toast to the ladies. Julia talked again about the things that were worrying her, the difficulty of selling towels, how tired she was of working, the high cost of things. "But," she said, "hope dies last," and went on to plan the party for Guillermo's saint's day. As they drank their beer she and her friends offered one toast after another.

It was about eleven-thirty when the conversation died down and the party broke up. When her guests had gone, Julia picked up the empty beer bottles and put them under the kitchen table, carried in the chairs and the large white chamber pot that had been airing outdoors all day, and closed the inside latch of the front door. Before getting into bed she looked at the sleeping children in the dim light of the votive candle and covered them with their thin blanket.

# On the Edge of Mexico City:

# THE SANCHEZ FAMILY

## CAST OF CHARACTERS

| | |
|---|---|
| Jesús Sánchez, age 48 | *the father and head of the household* |
| Lupita Linares, about 50 | *Jesús' older wife in free union* |
| Isabel, age 35 | *Lupita's daughter by Juan, her first husband in free union* |
| Gabriel | *Isabel's husband* |
| Clotilde, age 8 | |
| Pancho, age 6 | *Children of Isabel* |
| Maria, age 4 | *and Gabriel* |
| Olivia, age 18 mos. | |
| Elida, age 33 | *Lupita's daughter by Juan* |
| Eduardo | *Elida's husband* |
| Antonia (Tonia), age 27 | *Lupita's daughter by Jesús* |
| Francisco | *Antonia's husband in free union* |
| Carmela, age 5 | *Children of Antonia and* |
| Julio, age 11 mos. | *Francisco* |
| Marielena (Malena), age 18 | *Lupita's daughter by Jesús* |
| Elvira | *Lupita's sister* |
| Daniel, age 9 | *Elvira's son* |
| Lenore | *Jesús' first wife in free union (deceased)* |
| Manuel, age 30 | *Jesús' elder son by Lenore* |
| Roberto, age 28 | *Jesús' second son by Lenore* |
| Consuelo, age 23 | *Jesús' elder daughter by Lenore* |
| Marta, age 21 | *Jesús' younger daughter by Lenore* |
| Delila, age 26 | *Jesús' younger wife in free union* |
| Elena | *Jesús' wife in free union (deceased)* |
| Avelino | *hired boy of Jesús* |

# THE SANCHEZ FAMILY

THE El Dorado Colony on the northeast limits of Mexico City was
a new development, only five years old, built on the salty, dried-up
bed of the ancient Lake Texcoco. It was a "proletarian" colony,
with most of the homes privately owned, though some of them were
only shacks. So far there was only one unpaved road and no streets,
and the development lacked water, drainage, and electricity. An
unfinished chapel and two small stores served the neighborhood.
The stores carried a limited stock—bread, soft drinks, fruit, vegetables, candles, kerosene for stoves, and not much more. A bus line

with old and dilapidated buses connected the colony with the near-by Villa de Guadalupe and with the more central sections of the city. The first bus left the colony at 5:00 A.M. During the rest of the day, until midnight, the buses were supposed to run at half-hour intervals, but the interval often stretched to an hour. The people of the colony had complained more than once about the poor service, but so far no improvement had been made.

The Sánchez house stood on the open, treeless flats some distance from the dirt road in a close cluster of five or six houses. It was by far the largest and the most solidly built and was the only house with a short stretch of sidewalk in front of it. From the exterior it looked like a gray, rectangular block, a kind of fortress, the four walls of which presented an unbroken stretch of cement except for the door in the narrow front end of the building. The original plans had provided for windows on the outside, but Jesús Sánchez had finally decided to set windows only in the inside walls that gave onto the enclosed patio. Some day, he thought, he might like to add a second story to the house, and with this in mind he had embedded steel cables in the walls to re-inforce the cement. These cables projected up into the air and made the house look unfinished. Yet even as it was, Jesús' house was much higher than those around it. When he stood on his roof leaning against the parapet which had been formed by extending the walls higher than the roof, he could look down on the roofs of his neighbors and into his own patio where the women might be working. He could also look far out across the flat, dusty wastes to the mountains in the distance.

Inside the front door was the patio, open to the sky and bare except for some water containers and sometimes a few chickens. It was very clean—Jesús demanded that it always be kept clean—and when the sun struck down on the gray cement, it looked brilliantly white. Immediately to the right of the door a rather imposing cement stairway led to the flat cement roof. An open space under the stairway provided the family with a *lavadero* or laundry. Beyond the laundry two rooms for the animals ranged along the right side of the rectangle, first a room for the pigeons, then one for the pigs. At the far end of the patio were a chicken coop, additional space for the pigeons and the dogs, and an enclosed, nonflush toilet. All the animal quarters had been plastered as neatly and carefully as the rooms occupied by the family. The animals, in fact, played an important role in the household, and Lupita sometimes wondered whether Jesús had built the house for them or for the family.

To the left, a stall or enclosure for pigs was flimsily roofed with boards and tin, the only bit of careless building in the whole house. The rest of this side of the rectangle was given over to the family's living quarters, first a kitchen and then two bedrooms. From the kitchen both a door and window opened onto the patio, but the kitchen did not connect interiorly with the bedrooms. Both bedrooms had windows but only one had a door leading to the patio; inside, the rooms were connected by an opening which had no door. The two bedrooms were of about equal size and, unlike the kitchen, had been carefully whitewashed. Both rooms were orderly, even rather stark, with few religious pictures or calendars on the walls and few knickknacks strewn around.

At dawn on the thirty-first day of January, 1957, everything was quiet inside the Sánchez house. Even the two watchdogs Popo and Amapolo, who protected the animals, were silent. Jesús, the father, awoke, reached for his flashlight, and beamed it on the clock on the wall. It was only five-fifteen so he went back to sleep. Sánchez slept alone in a double bed which Consuelo, his eldest daughter by his first wife, had bought for herself with money she had earned as a stenographer. At first she had slept in it, but in time her father had decided she "would get lost in such a big bed" and had taken it for himself. However, on the nights he spent with his younger wife, Delila, at his other home, Consuelo moved from the small cot to which she had been relegated, back to the big bed.

Lupita, Jesús' older wife, slept in the same room on a small cot. She seldom slept with her husband anymore. During school vacations when her sister's son Daniel, a boy of about nine, stayed with her, he shared her bed, and on this particular night, Clotilde, a granddaughter of eight, had also slept with her. Clotilde's family actually lived close by, but the evening before when it was time for her to go home, the child had been so sleepy that Lupita had insisted she stay overnight even though it meant that Lupita had to lie on the very edge of the bed.

In the farther bedroom the rest of the family were sleeping. Lupita's two daughters Marielena and Antonia, and Antonia's two children Carmela and Julio, all slept crosswise on a double bed. Carmela was a girl of five and Julio, a baby boy of eleven months. Lupita's stepdaughter, Consuelo, slept on a cot in the same room.

It was not until six-fifteen that Jesús again woke up. This was late for him, and he quickly started to dress. He put on first a pair of blue denim pants which had deep, strong flannel pockets. In the pockets he often kept large sums of money entrusted to him by his employer who owned a restaurant which catered to the middle class; Jesús had been food buyer and kitchen manager for almost thirty years. Over the blue denim pants he put on gray denim overalls as protection from the thieves and pickpockets who were numerous in the city's markets and streets. For the rest he wore socks, sturdy shoes, a shirt, a wool sweater with a high blue collar, and a denim jacket.

A short man of about five feet, Jesús gave the impression of being stocky because he always wore heavy workclothes regardless of the weather. He did not own a regular suit or any other than work shoes. His quiet face was distinctly Indian, with high cheek bones, straight nose, heavy eyebrows, and rather small eyes. His hair was dark, although his skin was fairly light in color. He was now about forty-eight years old.

At a basin in the laundry Jesús washed his hands and face with cheap bar soap. In the kitchen he rinsed his mouth two or three times with water, dried his face and hands with a large handkerchief, then hurriedly combed his hair and put on his sombrero. Dressing and washing up had taken very little time because he was a quick-moving man, energetic in everything he did.

Jesús was a hard worker. It seemed to him that he had worked all his life and had never had a childhood. He remembered being lonely and sad, for his brothers were all much older than he and his father

216

never gave him toys or allowed him to have friends. His father had been an illiterate mule driver who managed to become the owner of a large grocery store in his village near Vera Cruz. During the Revolution the store had been wiped out, and the oldest son was killed fighting. Another son was killed in an accident, and a third son murdered. When Jesús was eight years old his father left the family, and Jesús, his mother, and another brother were forced to become laborers on a hacienda.

A few years later his mother died and Jesús went back to his father, who had re-established his store, to work there until he was twelve. His father was strict and Jesús grew restless, longing to be independent. He left home to take a job as a sugar-cane cutter in the fields and later as a sugar-mill worker. The work was exhausting and he earned barely enough to subsist. He began to know real hunger, sometimes working from early morning until evening without food. The memory of those years was still so bitter that his eyes filled with tears whenever he spoke of them.

When he was nearing sixteen, Jesús went to Mexico City with a man who had offered him a job. Within a few days he was fired without explanation. Alone and penniless, carrying everything he owned in a small box under his arm, he walked the city streets. "There I was, going hungry again. I didn't have a centavo. Well, as some people say, 'Where everything else is wanting, God comes in.' A man passed by as if he had fallen from the sky and asked me if I wanted a job. He asked me if I had references and I said, 'No, sir. Nobody knows me here.' I was praying to God that he give me work. I needed work. I had to eat."

The man gave Jesús a job in a grocery. "I worked from six in the morning to nine at night without a rest. I ate my breakfast cold, there was no time to warm it. I delivered orders and lugged boxes I could barely lift. Then one day Señor Velazquez brought a boy, barefoot, and said to me, 'Hey, Jesús. This boy is going to take your place here, so you go look for work. Get out tomorrow morning.' That's all there was to it. 'All right, Señor Velazquez.' There was nothing to be said. I had nowhere to go. I was out on the street again."

Finally, half-starved, with his box in his arms, Jesús found a job as kitchen helper at the La Gloria restaurant, where the other employees laughed at him and nicknamed him "Jesusito," little Jesus. At first he worked fifteen hours a day for eighty centavos and his meals, but later he was promoted to kitchen-helper, baker, ice-cream maker and, at last, to food buyer with four boys to help him. Now, some thirty years later, he received the minimum wage of eleven pesos for an eight-hour day, although he also earned money in other ways. He rarely missed a day's work and was considered unusually prompt and reliable by his employers.

Lupita woke up when Jesús was ready to leave. He said to her only, "I will send you some supplies with Avelino." Avelino was a boy of fifteen whom Jesús employed as a kind of general helper and errand runner. Lupita nodded and said nothing, but she got up to go to the outer door with him. On the way Jesús looked into the pigeon coop. He was particularly proud of his fine breeds of pigeons and took excellent care of them. At the door Lupita took the flashlight from him and, when he left, fastened the door securely after him.

Jesús hurried to the bus terminal. He had many responsibilities and was a busy man. He supported three different households which were located in widely separated parts of the city and spent most of his free time after work going by bus from one house to another on daily visits. Ordinarily he went first to the home of his young, favorite wife, Delila, with whom he had been living for the past two years. Here he ate, kept his clothes, and usually slept. Delila, who was twenty-six, was the mother of his youngest daughter, a baby of two months. Delila's household included her son by her first husband, her mother, and the four children of Jesús' eldest son, Manuel, whose wife had died.

After dinner and a short nap Jesús would take the bus to Lupita's house and from there go to visit his daughter Marta, who lived with her children in one room in the Casa Grande *vecindad*. Jesús had established his first home near this same *vecindad* thirty years before when he was eighteen and had taken his first wife, Lenore, in free union. A few years his senior and the unwed mother of a child who had died, Lenore had also worked at the La Gloria. They had two sons, Manuel and Roberto, in quick succession, but Jesús suspected his wife of having relations with other men and left her for a time. He even suspected that their sons might not be his. It was during this period that he had his first brief affair with Lupita, who gave birth to Antonia. Then he returned to Lenore and they had two more children, Consuelo and Marta. Five years after Lenore died, Jesús found a second wife, Elena, who bore him no children but who was a good mother to those he already had. When Elena also died, Jesús tried to raise his four children with the help of a hired woman. He did not establish a home with Lupita because he feared trouble between the half brothers and sisters. His apprehension was not ill-founded, for when Antonia later came to live with his other children in the Casa Grande, her half brother Roberto fell hopelessly in love with her.

Now the house Jesús maintained in the Casa Grande was primarily for Marta, who at only twenty-one was the abandoned mother of three small girls. Unfailingly, Jesús arrived every evening at seven o'clock to bring Marta food and to give her ten pesos daily expense money and one peso each to his granddaughters. Jesús' son Roberto still slept there, although he took care of his own expenses. No one knew where Manuel was living. Consuelo had lived here until she had had a serious quarrel with her father over Delila, and he had turned her out. Consuelo subsequently had run off to Monterey with a young man named Mario, but in a few months she fell ill and wired her father for help. He borrowed seven hundred pesos for expenses and brought her back to Lupita's house where she could recuperate. And all the while Consuelo was ill, Jesús came to the colony house at five o'clock each afternoon and slept there two or three nights a week.

Although the location was not a convenient one for Jesús, he was glad he had decided to buy a plot and build a house in this colony four years before. He had wanted a permanent home for his daughter Antonia, and her children, because her husband could not be depended on to support them. Jesús had also needed a better place to raise the animals he sold to supplement his income. He had been renting a small corral for them on the outskirts of the city and every day, rain or shine, he would take the bus at four o'clock and go out to feed and clean them. Then he would take the bus back during the rush hour and, often as not, would fall asleep on his feet standing in the crowd. It was too much for him, and when he won 2,500 pesos in the national lottery he began to dream of building a place of his own.

One day Isabel, Lupita's daughter by her first husband, told him that a lot with a two-room hut was for sale for 2,500 pesos in the El Dorado Colony where she lived. Jesús had only 1,700 pesos left of his winnings but he owned a valuable stud pig. He immediately went with his pig in a taxi out to the colony and closed the deal on the spot, "all straight, legal, and clean," as he described it. A few days later, he sold another pig, bought some building materials, and began to work on the new house. It was the most ambitious project he had undertaken and it meant a great deal to him, but all he said when he talked about it was, "Should I call it a palace? Well, for a man like me, who never had anything. . . ."

Jesús had long thought of having Lupita take care of his animals for him, thus relieving him of a heavy burden. She was a serious, responsible person and he trusted her, but he had not known how to broach his plan, for she was proud and had always insisted on being independent. In the many years of their union they had rarely lived together under the same roof. As he had hoped, Lupita could not resist his offer of a new home near her daughter Isabel and her beloved grandchildren. Nor did she want to deprive Antonia of a better home for her children. Her daughters' interests were always important to Lupita. For the first time in thirty years, she gave up her job at the La Gloria restaurant and stopped supporting herself. She moved to the colony with her two younger daughters and her two grandchildren while Jesús was still building the new house.

But Lupita was not happy at the colony. At first they had to live in the tiny, dirt-floored hut, animals and all. It was damp and windy on the flat plain, and Lupita suffered from rheumatism for four miserable months. She found the colony depressing even when the house was completed for she had lived the greater part of her life in city *vecindades* surrounded by people, friends, and neighbors. After four years she was still afraid of the silence and isolation of her new home. Her lifelong fear of ghosts troubled her more than ever. She was nervous about opening the front door and at night would go to the roof to see who knocked. The fear of thieves was always with her. "Someday someone will come in and we will be trapped without being able to get help or escape. Jesús is not afraid because he hardly ever sleeps here. But we do, and if it weren't for the dogs and the six men who live next door and the man on the corner who has a rifle, I would not agree to stay." Had she known beforehand that Jesús would take another wife and prefer to sleep in his other house most of the time, Lupita certainly would not have agreed to move to the colony.

When her husband had left, Lupita, too, looked in on the pigeons. She went to the toilet, then returned to the bedroom where she gently patted her nephew, Daniel, and pulled the covers better over him as he slept. The boy was like a son to her for he had lived with her almost from his birth. His mother, Lupita's sister Elvira, had worked as a waitress in a cafe after she was abandoned by her husband and had not been able to take care of him. Two years before Daniel had returned to live with his mother because there was no school in the El Dorado Colony. Now he stayed with Lupita only during school vacations.

Lupita went into the farther room to see if all was well. No one awoke, but the baby began to fuss. Antonia patted him drowsily, saying, "sleep, sleep," and gave him her breast. Soon the house was silent, for Lupita had gone back to bed. It was seven-fifteen when she got up for the day. She straightened out the dress she had slept in and smoothed down her hair. When Jesús was there Lupita never undressed; at other times she changed into old clothes for sleeping. Now she put on a faded maroon sweater and wrapped her everyday *rebozo* around her head and shoulders. She put away her special round pillow in a box at the foot of the bed. She had heart trouble and the pillow, which she had made herself, kept her more erect while she slept and permitted her to breathe more easily.

Lupita was about the same height as Jesús, but she was somewhat heavier in build, and in contrast to his quick, abrupt ways she was slow and awkward in her movements. Her face was attractive, but her body was big-breasted and looked ungainly, and she made no attempt to dress smartly. She never wore make-up, and her dark hair was drawn carelessly back from her face, braided or pinned into a bun. She took care of her appearance only on the rare occasions when she went out. When she was asked her age, Lupita always answered, "I am a child of God. I don't even know how old I am." In the presence of strangers or acquaintances she was quiet and retiring.

Lupita opened the doors of the pigeon cages to let the birds fly free for the day, then went to the laundry where she rinsed her hands before washing a milk container she wanted to have ready for the milk boy. She paid a peso and a half for a liter of milk. In government stores (CEIMSA) it cost only eighty centavos, but the colony didn't have a CEIMSA store. Besides, it was rumored that CEIMSA milk was adulterated and made children ill. Lupita's family had to get along with about three liters of milk a day, which they used usually in coffee and in cooking cereal. Consuelo, because her father had ordered it, drank a large glass of milk every day. Isabel, who nearly always came with her four children for breakfast and to spend the day, sometimes brought milk to add to the supply. When there was little money for milk, the adults drank tea made of cinnamon or lemon or orange leaves.

Lupita began to line up the twenty-liter water cans in the patio so that when the water truck came she would not have to go scurrying around for them. Eight cans were used to carry the water from the truck to the house. The water was then poured into larger containers which stood in the patio and covered with boards to protect it from dust and animals. Each day's supply was used with little to spare, for water was needed for the animals as well as for the family.

The pig, Chacha, and the dogs were frequently bathed, for Jesús insisted that they too be kept clean.

Now it was time for Lupita to go for bread. There were no bread deliveries in the colony and no bakery, but the storekeepers brought bread from the city each morning and late afternoon. Sometimes the bread was sold out or the storekeepers made only one trip, so if Lupita didn't get to the store early, she might have no bread. She paused, however, to watch the patterns the pigeons traced against the morning sky, and to scatter handfuls of wheat for them. The chickens roosting on the higher perches in their coop could not get down without help and today, as every day, she lifted them down. Then she left the house, walking slowly over the loose earth, for her feet were tender and walking was painful.

Lupita attributed her foot trouble to her many years of work as kitchen helper and cook at the La Gloria restaurant. It was at the La Gloria that she had met Jesús. The first two years they worked on different shifts and did not become acquainted. When finally they did meet and had a quick affair, Lupita knew almost nothing about him. It was not until she was pregnant with Antonia that she learned he had a wife and two sons. He was the second man to have deceived her this way and Lupita had been deeply upset. Juan, the father of her two older daughters, Elida and Isabel, had also turned out to have a wife and children. But at least Juan had loved her and had made a home for her and the babies. She could have stayed on with him in Queretaro and let him support her. He was good-looking and she had loved him from the moment he had begun to court her. He had first seen her sitting on the balcony of her aunt's house and had begun to send her love notes. "Or else I would sit by the window and he would ride by on his horse, very tall, very handsome. But he drank a lot. He would get awfully drunk and fire off his gun in front of the house and scare us half to death.

"And he was the kind of a man who would carry off girls by force. He had said once that I was going to be his by fair means or foul. I really did like that man but he was jealous and very suspicious. He never took me out to a movie or anyplace. He always gave the excuse that the air wouldn't be good for our little girl, or that he was too tired. I was from a small town and was very countrified and all the time I lived with him I never pestered him to take me to this place or that. Do you know why he never took me out? For fear somebody would see me with him, because he was a married man. What a good liar he was! I noticed that at times he would come home late but I just kept my mouth shut. They say, 'If a woman has what she needs at home, she has no reason to keep an eye on her husband. A man is free, a man belongs in the street.' And so, like it or not, I'd put up with it all. But when I found out he was married, I said, 'To hell with you, you dirty dog!' And I took my children and went to Mexico City to look for a job."

With Jesús it had been different. He had cooled toward her almost immediately and ignored her pregnancy. He seemed relieved that she made no demands on him. The worst part of it for Lupita was that she had to keep on working at La Gloria where, of course, she saw Jesús frequently. "Oh, I had a hard time of it! That business of having to go on putting up with those girls I worked with. They would call him my man but only I knew how little I saw of him. They would say, 'Your Romeo is on the prowl.' And I would say to them, 'Is that so? Well, then let him keep on.' But a person has to work. And when a woman is pregnant, she has to work up to the very last moment. How nice it would be to rest for forty days after having a baby! But within a week, there I'd be, back at work, carrying heavy loads out in the cold, and never sitting down a minute."

After Antonia was born, life was more difficult than ever for Lupita. "When my daughters were little I suffered horrors. Why, once they put me out into the street because I didn't have money to pay the rent. When I got home from work they had put my things out in the patio. Not that I had very much, just a little table, a chest, some stools, a couple of soap boxes where I kept our clothes, and a straw mat to sleep on. It was raining and I was out there, sitting under the table with my three girls—all of them sick with the measles—crying. I could have looked for Jesús to ask for help but I never did . . . he was nothing to me. That was when I met Bertita. She lived there and called to me, 'Señora, bring your daugh-

ters over to my house to sleep. I'm not doing this for your sake but
for the little girls. Bring them over here and we'll put them to bed.'
I took along the few little pieces of furniture I had and she told me
I could live there for a week or so, until I found a place. Some week!
It turned out to be years. Antonia was her favorite and always
called her grandmother. They adored each other. Even when Bertita
was dying she said that Antonia was the one person she regretted
having to leave. May God reward her. I have to admit how much
I owe her.

"When Antonia came down sick, Bertita said to me, 'Señora, this
child needs her father.' Finally I agreed to tell him and he came
to see her. He came back to the house many times. But don't think
he ever saw me, eh? I would boil the tea and serve him and Bertita
and then go outdoors again. Why, I couldn't stand to look at his
face! He wouldn't speak to me and I wouldn't speak to him. When
he came I would almost always be washing clothes. The place where
we washed was right next to the front door and beyond that was
Bertita's room. Well, Jesús would go into the house right on past
me, as if I weren't anybody at all, and then go out the same way.
He never said a word to me. I would think, 'To hell with that bum.'
But all I did was think it, I never dared say anthing like that to him.
Bertita was the one who talked with him. The two of them would
sit down, she in a chair he bought for her and he in another, and
they would chat. I could see them talking but I never went in. I
couldn't. Then he would come out of the house and go off without
saying good-by to me."

Nevertheless, Jesús was so good to Antonia that when he made
advances, Lupita did not refuse him, and the couple had two more
children, one of whom died. The relationship brought only more
bitterness and hardship to Lupita. "When I would find out that I was
pregnant, ay, ay, all I could do was cry and cry. Bertita would say
to me, 'Señora, you've done the job, haven't you? All right then,
there's nothing left for you but to face up to what's ahead.' I would
tell her, 'Ay, Bertita, it was this way, it was that way.' 'Let's not
have any of those excuses, Señora. We went looking for it, so we'll
bear up under it.' And like it or not, along came one baby girl after

another. The little girl who died was the prettiest of all my girls. She was the image of her father, the same nose, mouth, hair, everything just like him. She had an unusual complexion, sort of a pale pink, very pretty. Her father didn't even see her until she was laid out. He kept saying over and over, 'Why didn't somebody say something? Why didn't they tell me about this? How is a person supposed to find out?' I was too mad to answer. Didn't he know he had a daughter and was responsible for her?

"Then came Malena. I just cried and cried. Bertita, may she rest in peace, said, 'The darkness of the night and the weakness of the flesh,' and I—well, how do you suppose I could answer that? I had the luck of a dancing dog. Poor Malena had a hard time of it too. Jesús did provide for Antonia but Malena and I didn't rate one cent from him, not even a penny. Once he told me, 'I'll give you money for my own daughters, but not for those others. They are not my daughters.' But I told him, 'When I give to one I give something to all of them because all are my daughters. If one has anything to eat, the others will get the same too.' But the day never came when he gave me money for them. I haven't cost him a single penny, and I don't ask him for anything either.

"I remember once, on the Day of the Three Kings, since I never had any presents to give my children, I said to myself, 'I'll take my little girls to the movies, so that they won't notice anything. Well, my Malena was a baby and I walked to the movie with her in my arms and the other three little ones. I was carrying the baby wrapped up in my shawl when a fellow and his girl came along, may God reward them because I can't. They said to me, 'Here Señora, we don't want to offend you but look here, take this box. You will be able to make some use of it. But we don't want you to take offense.' I took it. 'Oh, thank you very much. May God repay your kindness.' The idea that I would be offended! Here was just what I needed, and for nothing! And you know, it had cheese in it, the sticky kind, and salted fish and crackers. We had a feast that time.

"I had to scamper lively to feed those four children. Their fathers never helped me. Whenever I'd see Jesús, I'd always say to myself, hoping that he would help me, 'I wonder if this time he will.' But no, that day never came. He didn't talk much but he never stopped coming to see Antonia and bringing her things.

"And that is the way it's always been, and even afterwards when we were living on Rosario Street, after Bertita died, yes sir, he would just come to the door and stop, and if he saw that there was somebody in the room, he would say, 'I'll come back when you aren't busy.' Then he would leave, and by the time I stuck my head out he was downstairs and away. Just like that, like a flash. I would say, 'Aha, so Jesús was here!' Sometimes I only knew he had been there by the smell he left. And so I wouldn't see his face again for a couple of weeks, a month, three months. And if he came again and found my neighbor there it would be the same; he would throw down whatever he had brought and leave. But after he got to know me better he would run the neighbor woman off. He would say, 'Señora, it is getting pretty late to have visitors.' And she would jump up and leave, carrying her jug of coffee and her cigarette. I would turn away to the stove, unable to keep from laughing. At times, that is. But sometimes it made me angry."

Lupita would not admit, even to herself, that she felt hurt by Jesús' treatment of her. She would say to her daughters that she was accustomed by now to his silence and distance. "If he comes and speaks to me, good. If not, also good." But to herself she added, "When he talks to me it is only to tell me what I have to do for the animals, to change this, to sweep that. Outside of that he says nothing to me." Before Delila, Lupita had still enjoyed joking a little with him when he came to visit. His usual answer then had been, "Go on and make your jokes!" But later he became angry at her most innocent jibe. Once he had come wearing a new pair of shoes and she had said, "Look who is all dressed up." He had brusquely shut her up by saying. "Yes, that is why I work, to buy what I want. If I buy something it is because I have the money. One cannot put on anything without you noticing it. What business is it of yours?"

His visits became briefer and he spoke little to anyone but Antonia and her children. Sometimes he came and went so quickly that Lupita did not know he had been there. He would put food and money on the table and go, leaving by the same bus that had brought him. Then for some time he had stopped coming to visit this household altogether. Avelino brought the food, supplies, and money.

While Lupita went for the bread, the rest of the family still slept. The little girl Clotilde woke briefly, sat up in bed, and began to sing a little song that she had learned from her grandmother, "Mr. Cat was sitting in his golden chair, Meow—" Lupita sang the song when she was in good spirits but it seemed to Clotilde that more often she was sad or upset. Clotilde interrupted herself to call out to her grandmother, "Mamá Pita." When no one answered she went back to sleep.

After a while she awoke again and this time got out of bed. She went to look at herself in the mirror above the dresser but a Christmas manger scene was in her way. She climbed up on a chair to see better and combed her hair with her fingers. Meanwhile she prattled to her stepaunt Consuelo who was now half awake. "Can you imagine? Look how my dress got wrinkled and now I'll probably have to wear it until Sunday. Mamá's like that." Clotilde put on her old red shoes and, dressed for the day, left for her own home.

It was almost eight o'clock when Lupita returned with the bread to find the milk boy waiting at the outside entrance. She hurried into the kitchen, put down her maguey fiber shopping bag, and went to pay the boy and bring in the milk. It was time to prepare breakfast. She lit the kerosene stove and set the milk on to boil, washed some of the dirty dishes left over from the night before—enough for breakfast—and put on water to boil for coffee.

The kitchen in this home was larger than either of the two bedrooms, and for this reason was sometimes used for visitors. The family would also sit or read or sew in the kitchen. It was a bare room and the walls were quite dark, but the four-meter long cement *bracero* or charcoal stove was a deep red and gave the kitchen some color. The family rarely used the charcoal grill any longer, but the *bracero* was a convenient place to keep the kerosene stove and to stack dirty pots and pans and dishes. The kitchen also contained a small table around which the family sat to eat, shelves for dishes and kitchen utensils, and a fairly large tin bathtub, covered with boards, in which clean dishes were placed to protect them from the fine sand dust which was ever-present in the colony.

While she waited for the milk and water to boil, Lupita had some time for herself. Quietly, in order not to awaken the sleeping children, she went to the wardrobe in the far bedroom and began to rummage among papers kept in shoe boxes for a prescription a doctor had given her. She could not find the paper and began talking to herself in a low voice, "Don't tell me, Pita, that you are not going to find it. Will I or won't I? Where did you leave it, Pita?"

She replaced the shoe boxes in the wardrobe and went to the kitchen to look in a can where she kept money, needles, thread, buttons, Daniel's plastic toys, and personal papers. The prescription was not there either and she went back to the bedroom to search through the shoe boxes once more without success. Consuelo was fully awake now and Lupita said to her "*Carajo!* Imagine! I've looked everywhere and I can't find the prescription, I've put it away so well."

"Isn't it in the box where you keep your pillow?"

"I don't know, but just in case I'm going to look."

In the box, in the pocket of an apron, Lupita found a piece of paper. Her face lighted up in relief, but it was not the prescription. "*Caramba,*" she said, "I thought it was the yellow one, but it's only a piece of paper." Still again she returned to the shoe boxes and this time she found the prescription almost immediately. "Look, here it is," she said as she put everything back in place, "Here you were, and I was looking like crazy for you. What a memory!"

She tucked the prescription carefully into her pocket. She had been anxious about finding it because she was going to take it that day to her daughter Elida who would get it filled for her. As she started to leave the bedroom, she winked at Consuelo and said cheerfully. "Listen to your brothers [the chickens]. We are going to eat them. That's why we're raising them. I said last night to your father, 'The reason we bought them is to eat them, Señor.'"

Lupita laughed aloud, remembering her joke at Jesús' expense.

As she well knew, Jesús didn't particularly like jokes of any kind, much less when he was the target of them. This joke referred to a film and a well-known actor, Chato Ortín. "In the movie," Lupita said to Consuelo, "Chato Ortín worked in the house of a rich miser. The rich man came home and said. 'Anything for me, Margarito?' Chato Ortín answered, 'They called us on the telephone to invite us to a fiesta to see if we can go, Señor.' 'You should say they called *me* to see if *I* could go.' 'It's all the same, Señor.' Later the rich man went to his study, opened his cigar box, and asked Margarito where all the cigars were. Margarito is really Chato Ortín, you understand. Chato said, 'We have already smoked them, Señor. That's what we bought them for, wasn't it, Señor?'"

Consuelo laughed too, even though ordinarily she could not tolerate criticism of her father. But the analogy was too apt. Lupita was never the one who bought the chickens or who had anything to say about eating them. Although she and her daughters raised them, they were not free to kill a chicken or even to eat an egg. Once in a while Jesús would take three or four grown birds to his daughter Marta, but if a pigeon should be missing from the coop, he would become angry with Lupita. Consuelo and Marta pitied Lupita but did not dare say anything to their father.

Lupita left Consuelo and went back to the kitchen to prepare breakfast for her. Between this stepdaughter and stepmother there was a friendly relationship which almost never involved friction, not even a slight argument or quarrel. Consuelo felt safe with Lupita. She believed Lupita would never come between her and her father as both Antonia and Delila had done. Lupita was not possessive or demanding; in fact, she took an attitude of proud withdrawal from Jesús which was reassuring to Consuelo. Lupita had accepted Consuelo when Jesús brought her there ill and, following his orders, had fed her better than the rest of the family. Jesús had always worried about Consuelo's health and had nicknamed her Skinny when she was four. Now, although she was twenty-three, he was still concerned about her.

Consuelo's breakfast usually consisted of coffee and milk, any cooked food left over from the day before, and a raw egg. On the days when she went to work, Lupita prepared breakfast for her early, boiling a little of the milk separately. Today, since Consuelo was not feeling well and was staying home, she could wait for all three liters to boil. Neither the milk nor the water for coffee was boiling yet, and Lupita began to chop up some of the lettuce that Jesús sent every day for the chickens. Her nephew Daniel had meanwhile got up and had come into the kitchen. Lupita talked to him almost as though she were talking to herself.

"Elida said to me yesterday, 'Give me the prescription, mamá. I will buy the injection for you. I'll try to get the pills for you today when Eduardo comes!' [Eduardo was Elida's husband.] I will go soon to take the prescription to her. Imagine! The injection costs eleven pesos and the pills the same. Think how expensive medicines are now. It's awful! Before, they didn't cost that much. If things had been as expensive then as now, I would have had to go without food for eight days to buy one injection."

Lupita threw some corn from a sack onto the grinding stone and began to break it up. This feed was for some small chicks that had been hatched under a turkey hen. Clotilde, who had been home and now had come back to her grandmother's house, watched for a while and then said, "Mamá Pita, I'm hungry. Can I have a piece of bread?" Lupita told her to help herself but the child changed her mind. "No, Mamá Pita," she said, "it's better for me to wait. If I don't my mamá will scold me."

In the second bedroom the baby Julio began to cry and woke Antonia, his mother, who sat up on the side of the bed to change his diapers. Julio always cried when his diapers were wet. Marielena and Carmela still slept soundly even though they were in the same bed. It was eight-twenty and time for Antonia to get up. She removed the dress she had slept in and, taking needle and thread from the wardrobe, began to mend her slip which was old and torn. Julio didn't go back to sleep at once but lay cooing. Antonia sat him up in bed, kissed his cheek, and said, "Well, son, we are going to iron because if not, your papá will come and mop up the floor with me."

She kissed the baby again, this time on the nose. "How beautiful my little son is!" she said to Consuelo. "How handsome. Just like his mother, eh?" Consuelo smiled and began to dress.

Her slip mended, Antonia put on a skirt that belonged to her sister Marielena, because her own dress was wrinkled from having been slept in, then an old green sweater with holes in the sleeves. Standing in front of the mirror she combed only the top of her hair and went out to the laundry to wash. The water was cold and she called out, "Ay, pretty little mother, my hand is frozen. Pita, why are you so wicked? You allow my little princess hands to be frozen."

Lupita answered from inside the kitchen, "Yes, my darling, don't you want me to heat the water up so it won't hurt your princess hands? This girl is a dizzy one. Learn from strong and healthy women like me." Lupita and Antonia both laughed.

Antonia, now twenty-seven, was a little taller and more robust than Consuelo. The bridge of her nose was flat and her nose was long; no one would call her pretty. But she had more verve and sparkle than the withdrawn Consuelo. Antonia liked to make jokes both about herself and about other people, and often enough her jokes were ridiculing and aggressive. Like her father she was quick-moving and a hard worker, but she gave the impression of working under tension. She was capable and responsible, and a great many of the household chores devolved upon her. Her dark hair was wavy and she wore it loose, at shoulder length. Her clothing was that of a lower-class housewife—cotton dress, sweater, and *rebozo*. Of all the children it was Consuelo alone who owned some better dresses and a full-length coat, which she had bought after working for several years.

Consuelo appeared in the kitchen and Lupita turned to her to say, "Your father says that because there is a shortage of corn dough, he's going to buy the corn so that we can cook it and grind it ourselves. What do you think of that, eh? Does he want to make work animals out of us?"

Antonia, coming in from the patio, spoke up before Consuelo could answer. "Ay!" she said, "he really will make you spin around like a top," and laughed. Consuelo waited for quiet, then said seriously,

232

"Now I don't want to hear any more," and the subject was dropped.

Antonia had decided she would not wash until the sun came out and warmed the water. In the meantime she put the iron on the stove; she was going to iron Francisco's clothes. "You know how demanding that man it," she said to her mother, imitating a little girl's voice as though to mock her husband. Both she and Lupita laughed. Antonia began to read the newspaper that her father had brought the night before, but soon she said to her mother, "I thought you were going for the corn dough, Pita."

"That's what I've been thinking all morning."

"You should have gone with my papá."

"Yes," Lupita answered, "like that time when Daniel and I went out. It was late and your father went on ahead. When we came to the bus terminal he pretended he didn't see us. Daniel said to me, 'Look mamá, there's my papá.' 'Yes,' I told him, 'but be quiet.' After a while your father came closer to the clock, looked around, and said to me as if he had just seen me, 'What! Are you here?'" Lupita laughed. "He had already been waiting for about a half an hour. I said to him, 'Well, yes, Señor.' He pretended he didn't understand me and asked the dispatcher, 'Today the buses are late, aren't they?'

"Just then the bus came and your papá said to us, 'You get on.' He must have thought the next one would come quickly behind the first, but when it didn't he had to get on the same bus and he paid our fare. I had already given the driver the peso for our fares. When your father sat down he said to me, 'I got the bad end that time.' And that's right because he gave me the change he got back and also my peso and I didn't have to pay a thing.

"Later, at the Villa [the Villa de Guadalupe, where the Virgin of Guadalupe, patron saint of Mexico, has her famous shrine, was also a shopping center and a place to change buses] your papá wanted us to get off the bus. He said, 'Here. You get off. I go on.' I said, 'No, I don't get off here. I don't have anything to do in the Villa.' We stayed in our seats. Then he told me that here I could take the trolley which went right to the corner near Elida's house. But I said, 'No, I'm not getting off here,' and I didn't. He was quiet, but looked annoyed. Finally, I got off at the corner of the movie house. He followed me off and said, 'I'm going to see Chubby [his daughter Marta].'"

As she finished her story, Lupita laughed and Antonia joined in. Both women believed, of course, that Jesús was not going to see Marta but to see Delila and that all his actions on the bus had been to hide his real destination from Lupita.

"He thought I didn't know about Delila, eh? But I did not lack people to tell me. Yes, I know him and his tricks. Now I know that when he begins to pretty himself up and is short-tempered with everyone the old boy is after someone. In that way he is very alert. There is nothing he likes so much as young girls. She is young now, but the time will come when she is old and then she will see! So he thought I didn't know about Delila? One day he couldn't find his jacket and he asked Antonia, 'You, girl, look for my jacket. I left it here.' Antonia said, 'No, papá, it isn't here. I think you left it at the café.' He was confused, eh? He said, 'Ah, yes, yes, at the café.' He was dizzy and almost gave himself away that time. It is years since he left any clothes here. But how time goes. Before that woman came along I washed and ironed for him, but then he said, 'No, I will bring my clothes to Marta because she does nothing all day. Let her do it.' I have never done them since. I don't know what he does with his clothes. He doesn't even have a pair of socks here."

Lupita had never seen Delila, but she knew how the union between Jesús and Delila came about. Two years before, Manuel's wife had died, leaving four small children. This meant four more grandchildren for Jesús to bring up because Manuel was a vagabond and neglected his responsibilities. Delila was the sister of Manuel's wife and Consuelo herself had suggested that Delila would be a good person to raise Manuel's children, little thinking that her father would want her as his wife. Delila was pleased at finding herself a home because she had just left a drunkard husband and had a son to support. She moved into the already crowded room in the Casa Grande, and soon, according to Consuelo, she had "taken over" the place. After a year of quarreling with Consuelo, who hated her, Delila returned to her mother's house, taking with her her son, Manuel's four children, and Jesús. Recently Delila had begun to threaten to leave Jesús if he continued going to Lupita's house and supporting so many people.

Lupita knew all this, and although she tried to hide it, she viewed Delila with not a little hostility. What she feared most was that she would have to die without confession, like Jesús' previous wives, because she had not fulfilled the sacrament of marriage. When his first wife, Lenore, was on the point of death, Jesús had run for a priest to marry them in order "to save her soul," but he had been too late. It seemed unlikely that he would do the same for Lupita now that he had Delila. Lupita had confided to Consuelo that ". . . the day one of us is deathly ill, the priest will not let us confess. Yes, when our time comes he will have to choose, either he marries her or me. But I think it will be her because I am old. Then I will know that I don't count."

Lupita had complained to Jesús of his union with Delila when she had learned of Delila's pregnancy. She spoke angrily to Jesús about having children here and there with so many women. His answer was threatening. "You don't have much right to be high and mighty," he had said. "You have food and a home, which not everyone has. So what if I have children with you. They are old enough to work and take care of themselves now. If you continue to complain about this matter of Delila, you will have to leave this house and support yourself. And I will not give you any help. If you don't want to be here I'll leave this house for one of my children." After this scene Lupita went to bed for two or three months with rheumatism.

At a little after nine o'clock Antonia left the kitchen to see if her children were all right. She was always checking on her children. Carmela had been sickly from birth, and Antonia continually fussed over her, making no attempt to conceal her anxiety about the child's health. She was also excessively careful with her little son and did not permit him to crawl about or remain outdoors for long. He sat quietly on the bed or in a box most of the day and showed great fear of walking. Both children were light-skinned like their father, and Antonia kept them indoors much of the time to prevent their skin growing dark. Lupita was as protective as their mother. She often said to them, "Don't play with cold water. Don't take off your shoes. Don't play in the dirt." She and Antonia put sweaters on the children even in the early afternoon when the sun was still strong.

Consuelo never ceased to admire the devotion that Antonia showed her children. To Consuelo, who had lost her mother when she was four, these. two partially abandoned, penniless children, born out of wedlock, were fortunate beyond measure simply because they had a loving mother. Her father and sister Marta, however, were critical of Antonia's overprotectiveness. Jesús scolded her for pampering the children and for not allowing the boy to exercise, but Antonia would flare up angrily and talk back to him.

Antonia entered the bedroom just as her sister, Marielena, woke up. She went to Marielena's side of the bed, saying, "Move your two big buttocks to the other side and let mé sit down."

"Chatterbox!" Marielena answered sleepily. "I'm not bothering you. They're not so big."

Antonia sat down and began to take off the skirt before Marielena could see her wearing it. Marielena, stretching her arms and legs, accidentally pushed Antonia off the bed onto the floor. "Look, now I'm not going to get up," Antonia said, laughing, then stood up and rubbed her back. Marielena kept on laughing until Antonia gave her a slap on the buttocks. "Get up," Antonia said. "Don't be a fine lady. You'll wake up my daughter. If you don't get up I'll throw you out of bed."

Marielena began to dress, first taking off the cotton robe she used as a nightgown. She wore slips of coarse cotton cloth because her mother believed that lighter material "caused the cold to get you." She put on a cotton blouse, the skirt Antonia had handed her, and shoes. Without jacket or sweater she went outside to the laundry to wash her face and hands in the cold water. Antonia saw her there when she returned to the kitchen and called out, "What are you getting prettied up for, child? Are you going to try to catch a man or something? Is that why you're washing so early?" Joking of this kind almost invariably stung Marielena to anger, for she detested men, she said, and was never going to have anything to do with them. This time she disappointed Antonia and didn't say a word but went back to the bedroom to dry herself with a piece of cotton cloth and to comb her hair.

In the kitchen, Lupita was mixing the black coffee with the milk and Antonia had spread a piece of blanket out on the table for ironing. She planned to have Francisco's clothes ready for him whenever he came to see her. It might be that very day or it might be a long time—she never knew. Just then Isabel came in carrying Olivia, a baby of eighteen months, and followed by Maria, four years old, and Pancho, who was six. Isabel looked to see if the coffee was ready before she said, "I'm going to leave my children with you, mamá, while I go out for bread."

Marielena, who had come to the kitchen, asked Isabel how she was feeling. Isabel was eight months' pregnant and since all her children had been born prematurely, the family was quick to look for signs of distress that might mean the baby was coming.

Antonia had to postpone her ironing because the family needed the table for breakfast. She went to make the beds instead, starting with her father's bed, the only one in the house in good condition. As she shook out the spread she said to Consuelo, "Look how soft my father's bedspread is. It looks pretty, doesn't it?" She handled it carefully because her father valued it highly.

Daniel, who had gone back to sleep, was still in Lupita's bed. "Stand up, you," Antonia said to him. "Get your little ass out of bed. You look like a little worm squirming around." Daniel sat up and put on his threadbare gabardine trousers. Still half asleep he bent over to put on his shoes, forgetting to button his fly. "Button up," Antonia said. "Just look at you, aren't you ashamed?" Consuelo's narrow cot was next. "Hm! This won't take long," Antonia said. "They say that everything looks like its owner." Consuelo laughed easily this time, not minding the reference to her thinness and slight build. When Consuelo laughed her face lighted up and she looked pretty. Antonia thought it a pity that Consuelo couldn't be more gay. She had always taken things too seriously.

The little girl Carmela woke up and Antonia went to pick her up and hug her. The child was apathetic and felt hot and Antonia suspected she had a fever. "What's the matter, my daughter? Do you want a little coffee?" Carmela raised her head and a little blood oozed from her nostrils. Quickly Antonia snatched a diaper from a box where she kept Julio's clothes and held it to the child's nose. There were only a few drops of blood. Worried, Antonia told Consuelo, "The bleeding must be caused by the child's great weakness." The doctors at the Social Security had told her the child was very weak. Three times she had been so ill she had had convulsions. But Antonia didn't know what she could do about it. The money she earned washing for her sister Elida was not enough to buy the food and medicine Carmela needed.

She gently set Carmela back on the bed and went to nurse Julio who had been playing on the floor. Carmela waited until her mother was free to tend to her again: to put on her socks, and to wash her face with a wet cloth. Since the water was so cold Antonia also wiped the child's face with cold cream, then combed her hair.

With Daniel up, Antonia could make her mother's bed. After that, placing both Julio and Carmela on Consuelo's bed, she made her own. This one took more time than the others for on it were an old overcoat, two light coats, a sheet, two blankets, a bedspread, the baby's rubber sheet, a folded blanket that was a covering for the rubber sheet, a piece of smooth cloth used to cover Carmela and to prevent the rough blankets from chafing her skin, two cotton pillows, and three cushions. As she hung the coats in the wardrobe, Antonia said to her son, who held out his arms to her, "Oh, you little devil. You think I'll carry you but I won't." Instead she picked up the baby's wet diapers and carried them to the roof to hang them out. She frequently used the diapers several times before washing them in soap and water, and as a result Julio's skin was sometimes irritated.

From the kitchen Lupita had caught sight of a turkey hen in the patio whose legs had once been injured so severely that they were now permanently knock-kneed. "You're a poor mother," she said to the hen. "Because you walk crooked, you cannot have chicks. What good is it to buy little chicks or eggs and put them under the turkeys? They should lay the eggs themselves and hatch them. That way, yes. To buy them, no. But there's no help for it. Your master says that's what he wants and that it is his money." Lupita shrugged her shoulders and went on washing some clay mugs and a large glass that Consuelo used for her coffee and milk.

Marielena meanwhile had remembered that she had an errand to do and began to hurry. She was to be godmother or *madrina* in the ceremony of *La Candelaria* (the birth celebration of the child Jesus) which took place on February 2, and it was her responsibility to dress the statue. She had broken a finger of the statue, however, and had had to have it repaired. Now it was ready and she planned to get it that day. Marielena was only eighteen, but active in church affairs. The previous December she had taken charge of a benefit dance to raise money for the colony chapel. So far the building had only four walls, half a roof, and part of a concrete floor, and benefits were constantly being given to raise money to complete it.

Marielena cleaned her face with cold cream, washed her feet, put on stockings, and then a jacket which Francisco had given to Antonia. Isabel came into the bedroom and from a window ledge took a shoe box which held gold ornaments and pieces of cloth to dress the statue of the child Jesus. She began to sew and Marielena asked if she should help. "Go ahead," Isabel said, and the sisters sewed a while without speaking.

Isabel's children came running into the bedroom.

"Mamá, Clotilde won't give me my stick," Pancho shouted.

"It's not true. It's not his. Maria gave it to me," Clotilde yelled back.

"I don't know anything about it," Maria said.

Daniel and Olivia sat on a bed laughing at the hubbub. Then Antonia appeared in the doorway. "What's the matter?" she said. "Why are you fighting? Isabel, stop them from making so much noise. Carmela is sick, and the racket won't do her any good."

Isabel had been quietly sewing but now she said, "Pancho, Clotilde, Maria, go play outside. You're too noisy." The children ran to the kitchen to see if Lupita could settle their quarrel.

Antonia was tending her baby when Lupita came to the doorway.

There was a breeze and Antonia said, "Close the door, mamá. I'm going to change him." Lupita patted the baby's head, saying affectionately, "Oh, my little ugly child," then left for the kitchen with Marielena and Isabel. Consuelo stayed on in the bedroom.

"Now I am left without money," Antonia said to Consuelo. "Yesterday I gave Carmela the yolk of an egg, the day before yesterday a chicken leg which cost three and a half pesos. No, that was Monday. Tuesday I bought her a wing for two and a half pesos, and yesterday I gave her chocolate too. Now I'm without money. I want to take her to the Nutrition Hospital, but I know already what the doctors will prescribe. What can I do when I don't have daily expense money? If I did, then I wouldn't worry, but this way—"

Antonia spoke in some anger at her "bad luck." Francisco, who never bothered about the children, was the kind of man who wanted one love affair after another and freedom to have good times with his friends. That's where his money went. But he told Antonia that he earned very little as a taxi driver or as a worker in the Coca Cola plant, and he had to pay for his food, laundry, and Social Security as well as to pay back a loan he had got from his sister. From the beginning, Antonia had accepted his excuses. She had no choice, for she loved him and became ill without him.

Antonia's union with Francisco had begun six years before without her father's knowledge or consent. When Jesús came to know of it it was too late to stop it. Antonia had not feared being punished by her father, for he was afraid of causing one of her attacks. Jesús had beaten her severely because of an earlier affair but he knew that when she quarreled with Francisco or did not see him she stopped eating. He had to yield and consent to their union.

The relationship between Antonia and her father had been particularly close for many years. She was his favorite child, and her love for him approached passion. Antonia had not known her father until she was eight years old because he had practically abandoned her and Lupita. Antonia had been living with her mother and sisters in Bertita's house when she began to realize that, unlike other children, she had no father.

"I began to question my mother and once she took me to the

Inca Plaza in the morning at the hour when my father would pass between the cars on his way to the café. We were hidden so that he could not see us, and my mother said, 'That is your father.' I cannot explain how or why there grew in me such a great love for him because I really didn't know him. But as time passed there came over me a great sadness at not being able to see him or talk to him, at never having felt a single caress from him. My mother told me he had fondled me when I was only a few months old, but how could I remember that, being so young?

"I would become very sad at mealtime when I thought of him. Porfirio [the adopted son of Bertita] would make fun of me, saying, 'Are you going to cry for your father again, eh?' This was enough for me to stop eating and begin crying. I was sad all day. I became exhausted, fell into bed, and could hardly move. My mother bought me medicines but they didn't help. That was when my grandmother [Bertita] began to insist that my mother bring my father to see me. But my mother always refused, saying that he was out of the city or that for all she knew he may already have died. Imagine saying this when they worked in the same café!

"But my mother usually didn't see him because they worked at different hours. Then one day the owner told her to come at a different time and she saw him. He asked about me.

"My mother answered, 'Well, how do you expect her to be? She is dying.'

" 'What! Why doesn't someone let me know?'

"Soon after that he came to visit us. When I saw him I straightened up, shouting, and when he came near my bed I opened my arms to hug him. I said 'Papá, why haven't you come? I've missed you so much. Whenever I saw you, you were always going by in a hurry.'

"He hugged me and said, 'My daughter, don't cry. It's bad for you.' And he gently put me to bed again and he and my grandmother cried along with me. Right away I asked my mother for something to eat, and my grandmother said, 'This is the best medicine for the child.' From then on I improved. In a week I was well.

"My father would come to see me every third day, and from that time until now he never came with empty hands. He didn't seem to get along with my mother at all but to me my father was kind and gentle and I loved him a lot. He was my adoration. I knew that I had other brothers and sisters although I don't remember when I first learned about it. But I wasn't angry since we didn't know each other."

When Antonia was about fourteen Jesús brought her to live with him and his other children in the Casa Grande and she became acquainted with her half brothers and sisters. At first she seemed quite happy and soon dominated the household. She did a large share of the housework, sang, and joked with friends and neighbors. In time she found a sweetheart but he left her to marry a friend of hers. This was when Antonia was about nineteen, at which time she began to show symptoms of a more than ordinary disturbance. She was sleeping then in the same bed with Consuelo who noticed that she was grinding her teeth and scratching the walls, the bed, and the sheets. One day she fell on the floor in a faint. Roberto and Manuel carried her to the bed and saw that she kept scratching while unconscious and that water-like saliva ran from her mouth. They applied alcohol, cigarette smoke, and an onion to her nose hoping to bring her to, but were unsuccessful. She began to bite her tongue, and when Roberto tried to hold her mouth open she bit his hand. When Manuel tried the same thing she bit him too. She also pulled her own hair and seemed to be laughing even though to all appearances she was unconscious. Finally, when the attack had lasted about a half hour, Consuelo put a green chile in Antonia's mouth and she suddenly regained consciousness.

The attacks continued, became more severe and more dangerous. When they began to be directed against other people, her father rented a nearby room in the *vecindad* and locked her up in it. Two doctors were called in but they were ineffectual. Jesús then took Antonia to her mother's house on Rosario Street, but the attacks did not abate. During one of her most severe attacks, four young men were called in to hold her down. One of these men was Francisco. At last Antonia was put in a private sanitarium, and there she grew better, although even after she was released she was still subject to the attacks. When she came home she met Francisco again and began to live with him.

During Antonia's illness Jesús was preoccupied and sad. Whenever news came from the sanitarium that she was worse he would weep, trying to hide his tears from his other children. He did what he could. To the general nurses he took gifts of fruit or vegetables and to the nurses who had more particular charge of Antonia he gave flowers and sometimes even money. He wanted to be sure that his daughter would receive as good or better care than the other patients. He did this even though Antonia's illness was a financial drain on him. When Antonia was pregnant the first time she tried to cause an abortion because Francisco had insisted on it. She didn't succeed but again became seriously ill and again her father called in doctors. It became apparent that Francisco did not intend to assume any responsibility for Antonia and her child, and Jesús bore all the hospital and medical costs. When Carmela fell ill there were still more doctors' bills for the grandfather to pay.

For a long time, Antonia had taken for granted everything her father did for her. If he did not satisfy her whims she would grow angry and shout at him. She wanted better clothes than her sisters, and got them. All her sisters were jealous. According to Marta her father let Antonia have her own way in everything. "He loved her best and he gave her the life of a queen. I think it was because he had once abandoned her. She used her illness to frighten my poor father into giving her everything she wanted. Nobody could do anything with her but Francisco. As soon as he came over to grab her she would calm down. She was a first-class bitch."

After Carmela was born, Antonia grew quieter and was less demanding of her father. She was coming to appreciate what he had done and was doing for her. Moreover, when they moved to the El Dorado Colony, she became active again, took care of the animals, and helped Lupita a great deal with the housework.

Now, in the bedroom of the house, Antonia changed Carmela's dress, putting on some flannel rompers to keep her warm. She told the child she couldn't go outside because she was a little sick.

"All right, mamá," Carmela answered, "but I want my coffee."

"Yes, little one, and let's see what else you'd like."

In the kitchen Lupita was serving breakfast to Isabel's children and to Daniel—coffee with milk, beans left over from the day before, and bread. For Carmela, however, she made a cup of chocolate with the yolk of a raw egg and took it into the bedroom. Antonia sat with the child while she ate, to see that she didn't tip over the chocolate.

"My poor little daughter," Antonia said to Consuelo, "she has suffered so many illnesses and she nearly died three times. The first time I almost went crazy. I screamed, 'Mamá, my baby!' and mamá and papá came running. They were crying too. The baby wasn't even breathing and was stretched out stiff. My father hugged me and said, 'Be brave, girl. I'm going for the doctor.'

"It was the same the other two times, and that's why I'm afraid to go out when she has a cold because she could catch pneumonia in a minute. Now I don't count on her getting well any more, but we'll see. Thank God she's still alive. But now my little girl is going to get better." Antonia turned back to Carmela. "Daughter, now you are going to get well." She stroked the child's hair.

Antonia remembered that she had work to do on Francisco's clothes. "I am going to steal a piece of mamá's cloth to mend the pockets," she said with a laugh and went to a box where Lupita kept scraps of material. She replaced the box quickly because if Lupita happened to come in and catch her she might be really angry.

In the kitchen Antonia and Consuelo found that Isabel, Lupita, and Marielena had had their breakfast. Antonia asked Marielena if she would take Francisco's pants to a neighbor who did mending. Marielena agreed and said to Daniel, "Hurry, son, let's go." Daniel combed his hair with water and brilliantine and scrubbed at his face with a dry rag. He and Marielena were soon back.

Outside there was the sound of a motor and Lupita went to the door. "That car was around here yesterday, too," she said when she came back. "Two boys are selling wool blankets. They were behind in the payments on the car and needed money. That's why they were trying to sell the blankets quickly and at such a low price. But I said I couldn't buy anything because I'm as poor as Cinderella."

Lupita smiled and began throwing alfalfa into the patio for the chickens. Marielena poured herself another cup of coffee and sat down at the table beside Antonia who was eating her breakfast. "Tonia," she said earnestly, "I want to buy the little shoes and paint them gold myself. If I buy them already gilded they will cost twice as much. I'll see how much they cost when I go to pick up the child Jesus, but if you are going to the market, you can look too."

"Yes, Malena, but buy me some chocolates, eh? If you don't, I won't do a thing for you."

Marielena was annoyed. She knew her sister was joking but she didn't like jokes, especially when they concerned something as important to her as the church. Marielena was a serious girl and although at times she was good-humored, her good humor could vanish suddenly and she would withdraw into herself, refusing to speak to anyone. Now she became silent and intent on her sewing while Antonia said laughing, "What! Don't you like me? I alone like me. Ay! but how pretty my little sister is."

Marielena didn't answer. Antonia got out the cotton bag in which she kept clothes to be ironed. Her mother had already put the irons on the stove to heat. After some time in which no one spoke Marielena again started talking with her sister.

"Imagine! The other day we were rehearsing for the play, and Lila, the president of the committee—she's the one I was telling you about who is very presumptuous and who has a braid that stands up like a horse's tail—she said to me, 'Listen, how many sisters do you have?' I asked why and she said, 'Because I saw a girl going into your house the other day and I hadn't ever seen her before. Who is it?' I said, 'Perhaps that's my sister Consuelo.'

"The other day Lila's mother was talking with another girl's mother and Lila's mother said, 'I have to go because Lila is working with a lawyer and I have to get up early so she can get to work on time.' Can you imagine? She wanted to humiliate the other lady who hadn't even asked if Lila worked. She is always boasting that all her daughters have good jobs."

"Yes," Antonia said, "She told me the other day that she works in a very important company and who knows what. But it's a lie. She works in a laundry near here, and it's not even a nice one but one of those where everything is dirty and ugly." Marielena answered, "But didn't you notice she has changed her place of work?"

The sisters were silent until Antonia said, "Ah, how I suffer! And I dream and dream of my ugly old man. Last night I dreamed that I hugged him. Oh, heart, why do you suffer?" This time they both laughed. Lupita, meanwhile, was still finding things to do before she could leave for Elida's house. Daniel, who was going with Lupita, was buttoning up his pants. "Hurry, son," she said, "let it alone now. Come on because the church bells are striking eleven." She took Daniel by the hand and started toward the outer door, saying to Antonia, "Now sweep the patio, put on a pot of water to boil, take care of the pigeons and the little chickens, and change the straw in Chacha's pen."

Antonia answered, "Yes, yes, but go on." But when her mother had gone she crossed her arms and said, "Ay, Ay, Pita! Maybe you think I'm an octopus?" She then grabbed her head and pulled her hair while her sisters laughed.

Antonia went to the bedroom to see about her children. To Consuelo who accompanied her, she said, "I have to iron the clothes but I'll go to the market first because if I don't, Francisco will come and then I'll have to stay with him."

"Is he going to come?" asked Isabel who had also come into the bedroom.

"Yes, he said he'd be here at twelve and now it's eleven. If I don't hurry, he'll find me here."

Antonia reached under her bed, removed the chamber pot which was used by Carmela at night, and emptied it into the toilet at the rear of the patio. She then began to sweep out the bedrooms, under the beds, in the corners, and under the wardrobe which had been a birthday gift to her from her father. She swept the dirt toward the door and out into the patio, humming a song while she worked and turning every little while to smile at her children. Using an old diaper, she dusted the furniture, and finally went for the floor mop, which was a stick with a cloth attached to it. Julio, gurgling and stretching on the bed, accidentally kicked his sister. Antonia took hold of his foot. "How dare you hit your older sister? This, sir, is

not permitted. Remove your foot immediately. If not, I'll eat it."
She tickled the baby. "Ay, what a beautiful son. You resemble your
mother completely. Don't you see my blue eyes and blond hair?"

She went to the kitchen to clear off the table and saw Pancho
sitting in the doorway. "Button up, child," she said. "Can't you see?"
Pancho buttoned up his pants and went on playing, smashing little
stones with a larger one. Antonia had finished her chores and began
to get ready to leave for the market. She rinsed her hands, then put
cold cream on them and on her face. "My cherubim brought this to
me. Yes, even though he may deny it, I live in his little heart." She
combed her hair, more carefully this time, then wet it. "And you,"
she said to Consuelo, "aren't you ever going to work? What an easy
life! Well, I'm going to the plaza. If you want to come with me,
fix yourself up, girl. I won't take you the way you are. We are going
in my limousine."

"What a joker," Consuelo said.

In the kitchen Antonia got out her shopping basket and put a
large glass and an empty pop bottle inside. She went back to the
bedroom and changed her dress. "Listen, can you see through this?"
she asked Consuelo. "No? What a pity!" She combed her hair again
and cleaned her feet with cold cream.

"Hurry if you're coming with me," she said to Consuelo. "I'm
going to the store here to see if I can get some cream and then we'll
go." Antonia went out.

Isabel in the meanwhile was combing her children's hair. "Just
look at this head," she said. "Is it hair or sand? I tell them to comb
themselves, but no. It's because they're lazy they don't pay any attention to me."

Antonia returned from the store without any cream because it
had "looked bad and might have harmed my Carmela." She got out
all Carmela's toys and gave them to her. Carmela was pleased because usually her mother allowed her to play only with the doll.
Antonia had bought rather expensive toys for Epiphany, a doll for
eighty pesos, a tea set for thirty, a wagon for fifteen, so that Carmela
would have as good playthings as the other children in the family.

Antonia put a sweater and cap on the baby, wrapped her green woolen *rebozo* around her shoulders and then around the baby, and was ready to leave. It was eleven forty-five. The two sisters started walking to the bus terminal. They hadn't often gone anywhere together for their present friendship was recent. Antonia had come into Consuelo's life abruptly when Consuelo was eleven and still in primary school. She had been living fairly contentedly with her father and stepmother Elena, her life marred only by quarrels with her brothers and sister. Then Elena fell ill with tuberculosis and Jesús was forced to isolate her in a room in the *vecindad* and to hire an old woman to take care of his children. Some time later Antonia graduated from the sixth grade and began to run wild in the streets while Lupita was at work. It was then that Jesús decided to bring her to the Casa Grande where she would have some supervision.

From the very beginning Consuelo saw Antonia as a threat. "I was asleep the night my father brought her. The next day I found a new face in the house. She was lying next to me in my bed. 'Why don't you greet your sister?' my father said. My brothers talked to her but not I. I just wrapped myself in a woolen jacket and went out into the patio. I didn't say a word to her. I watched from afar. I was extremely jealous. I never before had seen my father with anybody. How was it possible that Antonia existed? But I didn't dare ask my father and he gave me no explanation.

"And when Antonia arrived my father changed completely. That night I refused to eat my supper, thinking that it would bring the results it had on many other occasions. If I refused to eat, my father would lovingly talk to me and ask me what it was I wanted and would send for delicacies. This time it wasn't that way. I went to bed without eating anything and my father paid no attention to me. He began to read the paper to Antonia. I was under the covers holding back my tears. I was ashamed to cry before this new person who was my sister.

"On countless occasions the taste of tears was part of my coffee. 'Stop clowning and eat,' was what my father would say. It no longer mattered to him if I cried. The first time I heard Antonia answer him back I couldn't believe my father's reaction in not saying anything about her ill-mannered behavior. In our case we didn't even raise our eyes when he scolded us, not even Manuel, who was the oldest, while she could shout at him freely. Whenever he bought a dress for Antonia, it always had to be better quality than ours. My father almost always gave things to her to dish out. All this made me feel like I was nobody in the house.

"The continual lying to us also began. In the afternoons when my father came home, Antonia was all dressed up and they would go out. They would say that they were going to the doctor but they went to the movies. I would see my father and Tonia walking across the patio. She would take his arm and the two of them would walk away together. When papá went out with us he always held us tightly by the arm and when we arrived home or when we were going, my arm hurt. As for my brothers, he never even let them come near him. Almost always they walked in front or in back but never next to him.

"Naturally I asked myself a lot of questions. At night my head went round and round and many times I would get lost in the darkness of the room. Sometimes when I would cry, Antonia tried to console me, but I always rejected her. I wouldn't accept her words or her caresses. 'What's wrong, Consuelo? Why are you crying? Did my father scold you?' This last question seemed so cruel to me that if I could I would have slapped her. At night when my sister would try to read us some story or the paper, I didn't like the idea. I thought that she did it only to win over my father more, and so when she began to read, I would turn my back and sometimes make believe I was asleep.

"I couldn't understand that Antonia was older. I only knew that my father loved her more. When we grew up a little more, I began to doubt that I was the legitimate daughter of my father, that is, I thought my father was some other man. That is what I felt when I would see my father's indifference, not only toward me, but toward Marta who used to be his pet and now he even hit her when he got some complaint from Antonia. He never hit me, but the words he said to me were worse than whiplashes. But I never answered anybody back. I couldn't—the words wouldn't come out of my mouth. They only went to my head and made me want to get out of the place and not see anybody."

Consuelo fought for her father's attentions by trying not to annoy him with demands, by studying hard to please him, by going to work and keeping herself well-dressed, but she succeeded only in alienating him with her jealousy and her unhappiness. Then two years ago, when her father took Delila as his wife, Consuelo turned her hatred from Antonia to Delila who even more than Antonia had stolen away her father and her home. Consuelo blamed Jesús for the fact that she had to go away with a man she did not love in order to find peace and a home of her own. But she could not endure it and was brought back by her father in a weak and pitiable state. At Lupita's, Consuelo found temporary security and kindness and was regaining her health. She was grateful to her stepmother and to her two half sisters and tried hard to get along well with them.

Consuelo and Antonia walked along; the sun was already high and strong and not many people were out. Farther up the street, some of the colony residents were setting out their twenty-liter water cans for the daily water delivery. When Antonia saw this she shouted back to Isabel who was standing in the doorway of their house, "Isabel, if mamá comes tell her to take the cans outside for the water. If we don't get some water today, blood will be drawn from me."

The bus was parked at the terminal and Antonia hurried across the street to a store to return the deposit bottle and to pay for *tortillas* which she would pick up later in the day. But she was afraid the bus would leave without her and took time only to pay for the *tortillas*. She ran back across the street, still holding the bottle, climbed into the bus, and paid her fare with money Consuelo had given her. The bus jounced and bumped along for several blocks before Antonia said, referring to her baby, "He surely isn't a trouble-maker, is he? Look, now he's even going to sleep." Antonia looked out of the bus window. "Listen, while we're at it let's go to the

*Merced* market because at the Villa a quarter of a kilo of tomatoes cost eighty centavos and in the *Merced* a whole kilo cost sixty."

After a half-hour's ride the bus arrived at the market. Antonia said to her sister, "Now watch out. Be careful of your pretty little feet because you might have your toes smashed. Really, Consuelo, you hardly ever come to the plaza, do you, because you're so high class." Consuelo only laughed as they started walking down the street toward the market. A man who passed them whispered something to Antonia. She answered him in a loud voice. "Yes, you miserable one, and don't you also want my husband? Stupid!" The man had said, "You have a pretty mouth."

Inside the market Antonia turned toward the stalls where viscera were sold. She decided to buy a kilo of liver for dinner because it was rather late, and liver could be quickly prepared by frying it with onions. Today she had taken some money from Francisco's savings and could buy meat; very often the family ate only fried rice or noodles with beans.

Antonia was tired and tried to stand the baby in front of her while she made her purchase but the child, who was still half-asleep, whimpered and she picked him up again. She bought cream, two kilos of tomatoes, and a kilo of onions. At fruit stalls she bought two slices of pineapple and a kilo and a half of bananas. The family could have fried bananas and cream. They enjoyed this dish and used it often as a substitute for meat. She also bought cooking oil, a half kilo of noodles, and at a toy stall two small toy donkeys, which cost only ten centavos apiece. The last of her shopping was candy for the whole family—forty centavos of chocolates and twenty of toffee. She spent eleven pesos forty centavos in all.

Back at the bus stop the sisters found they would have to wait a few minutes for the bus, and Antonia bought a Coca-Cola. "Ay, mamá," she said. "It's late. It's two o'clock already and it was twelve-forty when we came here. Francisco is probably already there."

Consuelo was looking into a store window. She said, "I would like a crinoline like these."

Antonia nodded and said with enthusiasm, "Have you ever seen such pretty things? Here there is clothing of good quality. Don't believe it's all cheap. Well-dressed people come here to buy clothes. The other day a lady bought a dress for a hundred fifty pesos. God, it was pretty! I wanted to buy a little rose-colored dress for Carmela, but better to buy some warm pants because when it gets cold she hardly has anything to cover herself with."

Julio reached up to pull his mother's hair and Antonia smiled down at him. "My son, how handsome you're going to be when you're grown up. You're going to know how to keep the old girls in line. But, no, you are going to be gentle. The mean, troublesome old woman who tries to pervert my king had better be careful. . . . Ay! The bus isn't coming. If it doesn't come we won't eat."

When she had finished her coke, Antonia bought a large paper bag. Her basket was too small for all the things she had bought and the bananas were about to fall out. "Everything in one bag is too heavy," she said. She looked up at the clock in the tower of the church of La Soledad. "Oh, it's late. It's ten minutes after two." Soon the second-class bus came along and Antonia tightened her hold on the paper sack and on her baby (Consuelo was now carrying the basket), ready to fight her way if necessary through the crowd of people waiting to get on. "Lively, girl, step on it," she said to Consuelo. The sisters were in luck, for the bus stopped directly in front of them and they got on ahead of the crowd.

"Uff!" Antonia said when they were seated, "if we hadn't stepped lively, now, we would have been flat as raisins. I hope the bus goes by way of the Avenida because it goes quickly that way. If it goes around by the Zocalo I'll bump my behind three times on a rock."

A young boy selling magazines for twenty centavos apiece came up to the sisters, and Consuelo bought one of adventure stories. Antonia read it for a while and then exclaimed, "How thick! The hero is always on the point of dying and always gets saved. What a fat lie!"

Again the sisters were in luck because the bus took the fast route. At Avelina Street Antonia pointed to a building they were passing and said to Consuelo, "Do you see that building? Well, that isn't it." When she had finished laughing at her own joke she went on, "Behind that building is Francisco's sister's house. It's a pity she is so mean. I've had my first quarrel with her. Would you believe it? I went to her house to visit her all dressed up and perfumed and so was Carmela, and all so that she could tell me she had expected something better for her brother. Since that day I haven't gone back. What for? I don't want to see her. She has her life and I mine. That day I felt bad because she looked down on my Carmela. I bathed my daughter early, combed her, and put on her best dress. She looked pretty in pink because she is light like her father. And I made myself beautiful and everything so that old woman could say to us, 'Well, I hoped that Francisco would find something better.' It made me so angry, Consuelo, that since then I don't go to her house."

"I would feel the same way," said Consuelo sympathetically.

Antonia continued, "He'd like me to go. After a while he said we should go to his sister's but I didn't want to. What for, just to get angry? He took my baby there, my little Julio, the innocent." Antonia was speaking quietly and seriously now. "He wants us to get married, but I say then he can take away my children. I said to him that we are well off this way, so why marry? He also wants us to have a house, but with what he gives his sister every eight days he hardly has any money left for me. Now he gives me sixty pesos a week to hold for him. Sometimes he gives me more so that when we have enough we can buy furniture and rent a house. I don't know what neighborhood I would like to live in.

"On the one hand I want to live with him and on the other I don't because now he says one thing but if he gets angry he will say another. How can I leave my home just like that? Then they will take away my two children who are not at fault. Poor little things, what fault is it of theirs? At least here in my father's house, it is poor but good. The children eat well every day and have a good place to sleep. If I go with him I don't know whether he will keep his promises or whether they are just lies. I would like to take his word, but it's better not to. Just think, they tell me that he goes from one woman to another, but I don't pay any attention any more. Before, yes, poor him, if I knew he was going with someone! There were quarrels, truly bad quarrels. He told me that he even was afraid of me, but that's the way I loved him. Not now any more. Now I have my children, and if he goes with another, let him go. So long as I don't see it, we get along.

"Once my father offered to rent him one of the empty rooms in our house. I don't think papá meant to make money off him but did it so that I would feel a little better about everything and papá and Pita would too. But Francisco said, 'No, not with your family, not with mine.' And I guess I am really to blame for all of it because once in the beginning when we were still in love, he said he was going to find us a house. He said that his sister would rent him one of her rooms so that I could cook and wash in the same house with her. Then I said no. I said if he wanted to start housekeeping all right, but not with his family or not with mine. And now here I am. If I had grabbed the chance then, I might be better off now, because he would have got used to paying rent on a house and later I would have looked for another house. I'm afraid it's too late now, but who knows? His sister loves him very much. Unhappily she doesn't like me because I didn't want to live in her house. Even so, I think he's going to get me a house in November, if we don't fight before that."

Consuelo had been listening to Antonia without interrupting her. Consuelo had a poor opinion of Francisco, as she did of most men, and thought it better not to speak for fear of making Antonia angry. Antonia had had a number of quarrels with her mother and sisters because they had voiced their disapproval of her husband.

The bus was braked suddenly, and Antonia was almost thrown out of her seat. She said angrily to the driver, "Animal! That's why we have so many accidents. You drivers never look where you're going. I think you're cross-eyed."

The driver answered, "It wasn't my fault, Señora. That driver on the left pulled out in front of me and I didn't have time to get out of his way."

Antonia did not answer but as the bus neared the terminal she spoke up loudly enough for those around her to hear, "Well, at last. The bus did get here pretty fast. We haven't been on the road more than three hours." Some of the passengers laughed, and the bus driver turned around to glare at her. Antonia picked up her baby, arranged her purchases, and said to the driver, "Take it easy. I'm going to get off here. Hurry up, sister. Don't get left behind because the men around here are really rascals."

In the street again, Antonia noticed that the water cans were still lined up outside the houses. Obviously the water truck had not yet come. This meant a delay for her in getting the housework done. Near their house, the sisters met their niece Clotilde who was setting out another water can and an empty bucket.

"Is Mamá Pita home yet, daughter?" Antonia asked.

The child said no, and Antonia hurried toward the house saying, "That's really great. Mamá's having herself a good time. Yesterday she went early and didn't get back until seven, and today you saw at what time she went. Who knows when she will come back!"

"Marta's here," Clotilde called after them, but they said nothing and hurried on. Marta often came with her three little daughters to visit at the colony house. Like the rest of the family she saved dry bread and *tortillas* for La Chacha and had brought a sackful. Besides, she was fond of Lupita who was always hospitable and never let her leave without offering her something to eat, no matter how little there might be in the house, and without giving her the return bus fare. With Antonia she was on more intimate terms than with her other sisters because, as she said, "We're more or less in the same situation, she and I."

Marielena, her dark hair pinned up with bobby pins, was kneeling at the edge of the sidewalk in front of the house, removing stones and rocks which the children had been playing with that morning and had dropped into the small cement drain that led from inside the patio out to the street. Now the foot-wide channel was stopped up.

"Where did you go?" Marielena asked as Antonia went by. "I thought you were never coming back."

"We went down to the *Merced* market, little sister," Antonia answered.

In the patio, Marta's two older daughters were playing with their cousins. Antonia set her bag on the kitchen table and greeted Marta, who was in the kitchen, her baby in her arms. Antonia unfolded Julio's walker, put two diapers across the seat, and placed the baby in it. She then took the chocolate and a toy from the bag and started toward the bedroom, stopping to ask, "Has my daughter cried? Did she go out into the patio?" Isabel, who had been talking with Marta, answered, "No, she's still asleep."

Antonia tiptoed into the bedroom, placed the chocolate and the toy beside Carmela, and tiptoed out again. It was late and she still had work to do, but she always could find a little time to talk with Marta. Consuelo, tired from the trip to the market, went to lie down, and Isabel took her sewing and sat in the patio to watch the children play. Antonia and Marta were left alone in the kitchen.

"Sister," Antonia said, "I can't tell you one way or the other, but I feel something moving."

"Well," Marta answered, "it can't be worms."

"The doctor told me I had the face of a pregnant woman. If it's a boy my stomach will hardly show at all until after four months, but if it's a girl it shows sooner."

"Maybe you are pregnant again."

"I told my old man I felt something moving and he said he didn't want any of my foolishness. Then I asked him why he didn't just leave me alone. Even my papá asked me, 'Are you pregnant again?' "

"My papá notices everything right away."

"Yes, he scared me."

"You might easily be pregnant, and that's why I don't go near my man any more."

Isabel had come to the door of the kitchen and asked, "Marta, are you pregnant again?"

"No, I haven't got a rooster and anyway I've closed down my factory."

"Marta's on strike right now," Antonia laughed. "She's put on the red and the black" [The colors of the flag of the labor union].

"Well," Isabel answered, returning to her sewing, "as soon as Crispín comes along he'll take off the seals and it will begin to work."

Antonia continued their conversation. "Francisco was here on Monday. He wanted to sleep with me but I told him I was just getting over the grippe and I didn't feel like eating, much less like rolling around. Francisco got mad and said to me, "When *you* want to, then we have to do it right away, but when *I* want to touch you, you always put on a long face. When I've got a woman, why should I have to go with the whores in the street and have to pay?'"

"Did he give you any money?"

"That day he said he hadn't been paid and he didn't have any money to give me. He said, 'And I know when I don't give you money, you won't even let me talk to you.' He went away then but two days later he was here again, wanting to sleep with me. He was still without money."

"That's how men are."

"He told me, 'Go ahead, tell your mother you're going out to supper or something. I want to sleep with you and we'll "take a bath" in the hotel.' I asked him how he expected my mother to believe that I was only going to have supper or go for a bath. If it had been still daytime, I could have told her a lie but at night there aren't any baths open. He told me, 'What's your mother got to say about it when you're my wife?' That's why he got angry and didn't give me any money. If I am pregnant, he will be mad too. He doesn't want any more family, the bastard. It's not as if he were taking care of them and taking them around with him wherever he went."

"Your man is like my Crispín. They give something only in return for something."

"You'll see how he'll come back with his tail between his legs."

"You forgive him?"

"What choice do I have? If I get mad he won't give me any money at all for next week."

"Maybe Julio will become *chipil*," Marta said. She was referring again to Antonia's possible pregnancy and to the illness of jealousy a nursing child was believed to contract when another child was conceived.

"I've only been with my old man three or four times since my son was born," Antonia answered, and changed the subject. "Now I go around in such rags and with my hair so messy. I don't even have breasts any more. I'm very skinny. When I was living with my father I had everything I wanted. Francisco dresses me like a beggar. If I go anywhere, I try to go in my best clothes. Otherwise I stay home."

"What happened to the house Francisco was going to get for you?"

"He gave me money to buy a mattress but I spent it on medicine and household expenses and Elida sold me a mattress for sixty pesos. Now I want to buy dishes. I've been looking over the pigeon rooms and calculating whether or not we'd fit in there—the four of us. Don't you want to look at those rooms?"

"No, Antonia, I'd get full of lice."

"I told my man that we should ask my father if he'd fix up the rooms and rent them to us, and my old man said that we'd better get him to give them to us and fix them up ourselves, but do you think it's that cheap to fix up? And I don't feel right about leaving my mother. But if my man says that he's found a room in such and such a place, that will be that. I'll have to go with him."

Marta stood up, saying she could not wait any longer for Lupita. She called her daughters and said good-by. As she walked toward the bus terminal, she thought of how men caused women to suffer. In her own family, Elida had become pregnant before she married and Isabel and Antonia both had had abortions before they were twenty. She suspected that Consuelo's illness in Monterey had been due to a miscarriage. Lupita, who knew nothing of her daughters' early mishaps, had herself been deceived by men. In the case of Antonia, when she became pregnant with Carmela, Francisco left her, saying that he didn't want a family, especially with a crazy woman. Poor Antonia went to pieces after that. She went to work in a cabaret where she was paid for dancing with men and for what she got them to drink. She had told Marta that she had never spent the night with any of them, but several times Marta had seen her at noontime, still asleep and drunk.

After about a year, Francisco saw Antonia drinking in the cabaret with men, and when they left, he went to her and said, "Now, you'll drink with me. I shall pay you too." The sight of him made Antonia cold sober. Francisco got drunk and slapped Antonia when she would not drink. "But," she told Marta, "he had a right to hit me. He was my man." They went to a hotel where they beat each other up, and a few days later Antonia left the cabaret. Then when Julio was born Francisco said the child wasn't his. Marta thought, "Poor Antonia! I don't think Francisco will ever live with her, but she is full of illusions. With reason she is worried about having another baby."

When Marta left, Antonia began to work rapidly because it was so late; she was afraid her father would come before the house was cleaned. She took everything off the charcoal stove and started cleaning the tiles with soap and scouring pad. When she was through, the colors of the mosaic were bright again. Then she put everything back in its place and cleaned the table. She moved the benches up to the table and put away several things that were stored in the kitchen—a screen door, some buckets, and a tin tub in which Lupita kept various articles. She went to the pigeon room to clean it also. She replaced the newspapers in the boxes, took out the pans used for water and feed, swept the floor, gathered up all the trash, and put it in a barrel underneath the stairs. Next she shook the chickens' roosts which Jesús had set up in the toilet and again swept up the trash and put it into the barrel. After that she cleaned the upper cubicle where the best pigeons were kept. In the lower cubicle she shook out the sacks that the dogs slept on and swept the floor. Finally she swept the patio, cleaned out the water and feed dishes which she had taken from the pigeon room, and put them back in place.

She paused a moment, for she felt very hot, and wiped her forehead with her hand. "Chihuahua! And that water man still hasn't come," she said. "What a bad habit they have of keeping one waiting. Think of not being able to give the animals any water all this time and all because we have to wait for that old woman-chaser."

The coming of the *pipa*, the water truck, was an important daily event in the colony, since this section of the city had no other water supply as yet. But the water delivery was irregular and came at inconvenient hours. For some time the truck had come at five o'clock in the morning, and there was nothing to do but get up at that

FIVE FAMILIES

hour to receive it. Cold weather or not, the people came out half-
dressed to get their water. When the water came early in the morning or late at night, Jesús would get up too, if he happened to be
sleeping in the house, to see that no harm came to his daughters
when they brought in the water. One of the girls would stand in line
and watch the cans while the other would carry the full cans to the
front door where Lupita would take them and pour them into the
large containers.

Antonia had swept all the trash together at the patio entrance
and went to get the trash barrel. On her way she saw two pigeons
fighting. "Listen, stop that, you worthless scamps," she shouted. She
added to Isabel, "One can never leave even the pigeons alone because
they begin to fight." She turned to see some chickens on the pile she
had swept together and shouted again, "Get out of there, you good
for nothings. Stop scattering that stuff around! And you, Cariana,
how about some eggs?" She rushed at the chickens with a broom and
frightened them into their coop, but then she had to gather up the
trash again because they had scattered it.

From the kitchen door the baby stretched out his arms to her.
Antonia said, "What is it, son? Let me finish my work and I'll come
to you right away." To Isabel she said, "I'd better take my Julio outside, but he can tip the walker over easily. I'm going to bring a box
to set him in." From the bedroom she got a large wooden box which
she set just outside the kitchen door and in which she placed a
blanket and two pillows. In this she set the baby and gave him a
rattle to play with.

Her next job was to sweep the flat roof as well as the stairs which
led up to it. Then she still had the kitchen floor to sweep. Sweeping
the roof raised such a thick dust that she sprinkled some water on
the floor. She began to hum a tune that Francisco sometimes sang.

Isabel said, "I think the water truck is not going to come. But I
don't know what we'll do if it doesn't. I am very saving of water but
I have only a jarful left."

Antonia answered, "He may come as late as six o'clock, but he
has to come." By now she had finished sweeping the kitchen and
had put all the furniture back in place. She went to the pigpen and

*260*

swept up the straw. She said aloud, "Now what will I wash with in here when I have only this little bit of water left? The worst part of it is that soon my father will come and he'll see everything dirty. But after all it's Avelino's fault, not mine."

She turned to Isabel. "Would you believe it? When Avelino first started to work here, he brought water from the well, took out the garbage, swept out Chacha's pen, and put in fresh straw. But now he is lazy. Anyhow, today I'm going to leave it for him to do. I've done part of it. He can take care of the rest."

Antonia hesitated but finally gave a little water to the animals. Then she went to the kitchen to prepare dinner.

Isabel was ironing in the kitchen. Her daughter Clotilde looked at her and said, "Listen, mamá, why are you so fat? You look very ugly that way. I don't like it at all." Isabel began to answer but Maria and Pancho started to fight. Clotilde yelled at them, "Shut up. What a racket. You never leave anyone in peace." Isabel reprimanded her daughter sharply, saying, "You be quiet. Let them shout. But soon they'll pay for it, those tramps." The three children went outside to play.

Isabel looked down at the dress she was ironing. "How pretty this dress was," she said. "It's a pity about clothes. One can't keep them clean. If it isn't water it's dust. It was so much trouble to make all these clothes and now look at them. Now I don't even want to make any more because the children tear them and dirty them."

"Why don't you let them go naked to save their clothes?" Antonia asked. "Don't be foolish, my daughter." She patted Isabel's head.

Marielena came in holding a small piece of the rock she had been trying to dislodge and looking dejected. "Listen," Antonia said teasingly, "you need more practice so that when you start something you can finish it. You do everything the way you did your shorthand." Marielena flushed with annoyance and went out without speaking. Antonia had referred to the fact that she had quit studying to be a stenographer and then had refused to look for a job. She had said, "Why should I work? My father has the obligation to support me." Marielena believed that an unmarried girl should remain at home where she would not be molested by men. She said she dreaded working in an office among men. Yet she was not happy at home; she wanted a better life, a beautiful home and good clothes.

Antonia went on cooking the rice. Isabel had finished ironing and sat down on the tub near the kitchen door. Julio cried because his diaper was wet, and Antonia changed him. At about three-thirty there was a knock at the door. Isabel moved away the heavy rock set against the post and unbolted the door. Lupita and Daniel came in.

"Ay, Pita, you took a long time," Antonia said. "We were waiting and waiting for you, and you were roaming around holding hands with a man in the streets." She winked at Daniel.

Lupita was too tired to answer. She fell into a chair and fanned herself with her shawl. But after a little she said, "Antonia, did you take care of the pigeons? If you didn't your father will hang us."

Marielena came back into the kitchen. "Daniel, bring me the hammer," she said. "I'll see if I can break up the rock with that. Isabel, do you see why I sometimes hit the children? Those little tramps!"

Isabel knew Marielena was angry with the children but for a moment she didn't speak. Then she said, "Yes, little sister, when they are mischievous it would be better to send them home." Marielena went out with the hammer, saying, "One of us has to win, and if that rock doesn't, I will."

Lupita was still tired and hot. "It's too much. I can't even take off my sweater," she said, "and even if I could my dress is ripped all down the back. I should sew it up, but I can't even take it off yet." Antonia said, "Why don't you take it off in one of the other rooms? No one will see you in there," but Lupita instead went out into the patio to stand under the stairs in the shade and fan herself. Marielena had started hammering at the rock with a broomstick without yet being able to budge it. Antonia said, "Well, mamá, now it's your turn. I'm going to wash the toilet, which is very dirty. See what a mess the chickens make. I didn't want to take water for them but there was no help for it." Since the rice was almost ready, Lupita told her to go ahead.

Antonia carried broom, scrubbing brush, and a bucket of water into the room that housed the toilet. She threw water onto the floor with a small can and scrubbed a section of the floor at a time. In the kitchen, Lupita, now a little cooler, washed her hands, dried them on her apron, and began to remove the things she had bought from her bag. Most of it was feed for the animals, but like Antonia she also had bought rice and tomatoes. "But that's all right," she said, "it's better to have too much than too little."

"Mamá, will you give me this piece of banana?" Isabel asked.

"No, you'd better take one of the others because your father hasn't brought the bananas for the animals yet, and I have to guard each piece. Yesterday he brought rice after fifteen days. Well, I'm not sure how much time, but he didn't send it. He said to me, 'Here are these two kilos of rice.' I told him, 'This will hardly be enough.'"

"Oh, you, how you complain," Isabel said.

Antonia came in to ask her mother if she had looked at the rice. Lupita tasted it and said it was good, then asked Isabel to chop up four heads of lettuce for the chickens. Antonia hurried back to her work, saying to Isabel, "Sister, will you please make the avocado salad for me while I finish my work?" Outside she passed Marielena and gave her a whack on the buttocks. "Hurry, you lazy, troublesome child," she said. Marielena was singing and didn't answer.

Lupita washed the liver Antonia had bought and heated some oil in a casserole. Marielena came in holding up the rock that had stopped up the drain. "Finally I won," she said. "If not, it would have been more powerful than I. Look, it's big, isn't it? Now you see, if I say no, it's no."

Lupita smiled at her, and Marielena went out to wash her hands and feet, using as little water as she could. She dried herself in the bedroom, combed her hair, and cold-creamed her hands, face, and feet.

The child Carmela was still sleeping, and Marielena had taken care not to wake her, but when she came out of the bedroom Antonia asked, "Did you wake up my daughter? She's slept a long time. Maybe I'd better wake her and give her some rice."

"No, better let her sleep," Marielena answered. "If she wakes up she's going to want to come into the kitchen and she'll probably get sick again."

Antonia dropped the matter and finished cleaning the toilet. She washed her hands again, and then went in to stretch out on her father's bed. "What heat!" she said. "But now I'll take off all my clothes to see if I can cool off a little." She removed her dress and slip, but she knew there was a great deal of work still to be done so she put on a thin skirt and blouse, combed her hair, fastening it up with hairpins, and went back to the kitchen. Isabel was making the avocado salad and Lupita was frying the liver. Antonia sat down to nurse her baby.

It was after four o'clock, the water truck had still not come, and everyone was worried. "I don't know what we're going to do without water," Lupita said. "Hurry and get me some from the well, Antonia, since you used the last little bit."

"There's a little bit left," Antonia answered, "enough to wash the dinner dishes."

"Yes," Isabel spoke up, "I can wash them, but what will I rinse them with, earth?"

"Be quiet everybody," Marielena said, "I'll bring some water from the well. Why is there so much talk about it?"

Isabel said, "Sometimes I'd like to punch that old woman-chaser in the nose, but I don't dare to because he's too big."

"Little jokes are all very well," Lupita said, "but what will we do without water? What will we do tomorrow for breakfast and tonight for supper? We can't make complaints because this section of the city isn't even on the official route so it wouldn't do us any good to complain. They'd probably just stop bringing us water, and we'd have to go over to the next colony the way we did before. We are better off now because that other driver was really a mean one. If any of the cans got tipped over, it was just too bad, he wouldn't give any more water. And if he saw anyone try to get water a second time, he would punish all of us and leave us without water for two or three days. Oh, what a time that was. Be glad we have water, even at six o'clock."

"Well, I won't wash any more dishes than what we need for dinner. How many are we?" said Marielena.

"Count them, lazy," Antonia said. "Isabel and her children—five. We are four. That's nine."

"I might as well wash all of them at once," Marielena said then, "but what if I run out of water?"

"Stop being a godmother to everyone," Lupita interrupted. "Let each one wash his own dish."

Antonia and Isabel as well as Daniel and Clotilde immediately protested. "What? After working all day like a slave, do I still have to wash my own plate?" Antonia asked, and Isabel said, "I'm pregnant, I can't." Marielena spoke up, "Nobody can. True? Then I have to be the drudge."

Lupita only smiled at the quarreling. For a while there was silence. Then Lupita said, "Elida bought me the pills today. My poor daughter. I hope the Lord will keep her, because she's helped me so much."

One of the small turkeys had come up behind Isabel and she accidentally stepped back on it. This was a twelve-peso turkey and Lupita was alarmed. "Watch out, for the Sainted God," she said. "Please don't step on the chickens."

There was a quiet knock at the door. Marielena happened to be outside and she opened it to Avelino who took off his straw hat in lieu of any kind of greeting and went straight to the kitchen where he gave Lupita a sackful of things Jesús had sent. Then he started toward the pigpen.

"Avelino, will you go to get water from the well?" Lupita asked. "Imagine, we have no water. But you bring a little. If not, with what will we wash Chacha?"

The boy only nodded. Lupita gave him the shoulder pole and two cans and he went out. Antonia carried her sleeping baby into the bedroom and came back to the kitchen to ask her mother if she could help with anything. When Lupita said there was nothing for her to do, she went to check on the pigeons. Then suddenly she began to skip about in the patio.

Isabel saw her through the window. "And you—what's the matter with you?" she asked.

"I'm getting rid of the fleas," Antonia answered.

"That won't help a bit. You'd better take a bath."

"I'm taking a bath, a sweat bath. When the water truck comes, you'll see how quick I can take a bath."

Marielena was still singing. "Enough, enough, little sister," Antonia said. "Don't make me suffer." Marielena kept on singing, and Antonia went into the kitchen to prepare feed for Chacha. Into a bucket she placed a large lump of corn dough. "And with what will I fix this feed if there isn't a drop of water?" she asked her mother. Isabel offered to go home to get some. "But I'll have to keep a little in case the water truck doesn't come." She left for her house. While she waited Antonia broke some old *tortillas* into the feed bucket and began emptying the sack which Jesús had sent by Avelino. There were bags of wheat and corn for the animals and also provisions for the family: four large heads of lettuce, two bars of soap, sugar, white bread, and a kilo of coffee. Marielena came in, picked up a piece of one of the bananas that Isabel had been chopping up for the chickens, and began eating it.

"Mamá," Antonia shouted, "Marielena is taking a banana."

"Let her be in peace," the mother said, "if Malena eats the banana, it's not important. After all, that is why we bought them, as Chato Ortín says."

When Isabel came back with the water, Antonia put some in the bucket and took the feed to Chacha. She grabbed the sow by the ears saying, "All right, all right, Chacha, big glutton. Here's something good for you." Then she went back to the kitchen to get the bones that her father had sent for the dogs. "Look, this is what is left for them, the poor things, there isn't even a bit of meat on these bones, and they'll have to do for the cat too. Really, he should have bought some skins for the cat."

The meal was ready by a little after four o'clock. Lupita always served breakfast and dinner late so that they would not be hungry for supper. That is the way she had saved money on food for many years. The children were served first to permit the adults to eat later without being interrupted. Lupita began spooning out rice for the children sitting at the table, Daniel, Olivia, and Clotilde on one side, and Maria and Pancho on the other. Clotilde said, "Hurry, mamá Pita, I'm dying of hunger, I'm fainting."

Isabel was sitting in a corner of the room next to the stove. "You can't imagine, mamá," she said, "the things that Clotilde says to me. The other day she said, 'Ay, mamá, knock down a piece of the wall because you can't fit in here any more. Can you imagine? I must look like a whale."

"No, not like a whale, but you do look like a balloon," Lupita said.

Antonia was up on the roof dividing the bones among the dogs. She held the animals back with her feet in order to give each one his share. Lupita stuck her head out of the kitchen and asked her, "How many kilos of *tortillas* did you pay for this morning?"

"Only two tons."

"Joker. I asked how many kilos you paid for, not how many you ate."

"Two kilos, Pita, two."

"You go get the *tortillas*, Malena," her mother said loudly. "If Antonia goes she usually comes home with nothing."

"Do you think I have the trunk of an elephant, Pita? You are very insulting. You will see when papá comes," Antonia yelled back.

"Tell him. Tell him. I'm not afraid of him. After all, we're *compadres*."

Marielena went to the store for the *tortillas*. Avelino returned from the well and began to wash the pig. Antonia came down from the roof because it was too hot. "Mamá, where did you hide Bolo [the cat]?" she asked.

"He should be in the bedroom," Lupita answered. "He doesn't get to go outside much. Poor thing, he helps us so much. You remember when the mice got so bad and your father brought him one day. The mice began to disappear as if by magic."

"That's why I say you should give him a piece of liver," Antonia said.

"And will you eat the cat's bone? Go on, I don't have meat for so many."

It was four-thirty when Marielena returned with the *tortillas*. Lupita placed them on a plate on the table. Since the children had finished eating, Antonia promptly sat down. Lupita eyed her as though in reproof, and Antonia said, "It's because I'm very hungry. Also remember that I have to feed my two little angels."

"Very well, everyone sit down," Lupita said, "because later I won't be serving." Her daughters and Consuelo sat down at once, Isabel with some difficulty. Lupita sat at a corner of the table nearest the stove in order to serve more easily. She passed a plate to Consuelo first and Antonia leaned over to see how much was on it. There was silence for a while as everyone ate. Then Antonia said, "I'm going to give my Carmela her rice. I'm coming back, mamá. Meanwhile serve me."

When Antonia came back to the table, her mother gave her a piece of liver and avocado and lettuce salad. Marielena said, "I have to finish the dress for the statue of the Child Jesus. If not, the day will come, and I'll still not have anything done."

"Yes," said Isabel, "but what about the crown?"

"I'll ask Elida to make one. After all, she knows how to make pretty things."

"Ay, that's true," said Lupita. "Before she was married she dressed the Child year after year, and it came out so well that her friends asked her to dress theirs."

"Let's see how mine comes out. I'm going to take pains with it."

"Yes, little sister, I believe it will come out well," Antonia said, "and now prepare to dust the saints for the rest of your life with your little duster and broom." She was implying that her sister was going to be a spinster.

"Mamá, will you keep Antonia quiet?" Marielena protested while Isabel laughed aloud.

The mother said only, "Patience, child, patience. Don't give up."

Lupita served each of them a portion of beans, but to Consuelo she also gave some bananas with cream. At once Antonia complained. "How is it you don't give me any? Only to her because she's the favorite. Yes, it's true. You keep me as thin as a worm. Now I don't want anything."

Lupita put out her arm as if to take away the plate of beans she had just given Antonia. "What, you don't want anything? Well, give it to me, child of my soul."

"Ah, yes?" Antonia answered back. "What are you saying? I will leave it, but no one will have it."

"What color shall I paint the trimming on the clothes, red or gold?" Marielena asked Isabel.

"Red? Ay, Malena. Everything is supposed to be painted gold."

Antonia said, "Yes, Malena, you are stupid, and your face helps you along," but no one paid any attention to her this time.

"Do you want more salad, Malena?" Lupita asked. "Here's a little left."

"Why not a banana with cream instead?"

"The devil!" said the mother. "What girls! If you want, take. Eat all there is." And she handed the little that was left of the bananas and cream to Marielena.

Antonia spoke up, "Why don't you give some to me?"

"Oh, take it, take it, child! *Caray!*" Marielena said angrily. "Tonia you are like a schoolgirl. Everything is a joke to you, and no one knows when you're serious."

"Oh, you bitter child!" Antonia answered. "What do you know about life?"

Marielena got up from the table abruptly and ran into the bedroom. She put on her coat, combed her hair, and, telling her mother she was going for the Child, left the house.

Antonia did not finish eating until after five-thirty. "Now, yes, I'm going to iron Francisco's pants," she said to her mother.

Lupita had her own concerns. "Your father is not coming now," she said. "He'll probably come as late as eight and leave five minutes later."

"Well, it's good whatever hour my father comes."

Lupita changed the subject. "Did that Avelino throw out the garbage? Or did he leave the full pails outside again?" Antonia went outside to check. Avelino had disposed of the garbage.

"Fine," Lupita said. "That saves Marielena work."

At five forty-five there were three loud knocks on the outside door. Lupita, who was about to eat a little more salad, hurried to open it.

She knew it was Jesús because his knocks were unmistakable, and he didn't like to be kept waiting. Jesús came in rapidly, carrying a cloth sack in his hand. He walked a few steps past Lupita who remained by the door long enough to put the heavy bolt back into place. The father seemed preoccupied. He asked if Consuelo were home, and when his wife answered that she was in the kitchen eating, he went there quickly. He set his bag down on the table and asked Consuelo, "Didn't you work today?"

"No, papá, I didn't go to work at all." Consuelo hoped he would ask her how she felt, but her father just looked at her silently and she dropped her eyes. As usual, she couldn't tell what he was thinking.

Consuelo resembled her father, having his dark hair, small, dark eyes, and high cheekbones, yet Jesús sometimes doubted that she was his daughter. She had the stubborn, headstrong, manipulative ways of her mother and was always interfering in his life. She had almost cost him Delila, the one person he now felt close to and loved. When they had all lived together in the Casa Grande, Delila had complained to him of Consuelo's insolence and jealousy. Consuelo had called Delila a street woman who would sleep with any man and at one time had accused her of having sorcerized Jesús. In retaliation, Delila stopped making meals for Consuelo, and would not permit Manuel's children, whom Consuelo had helped raise, to speak to their aunt. At night when Consuelo returned from work there would be no supper for her, or the door was locked and her knocking brought no one. She had to look for food and a place to sleep at a friend's or neighbor's house. One night Jesús came home to find Consuelo quarreling violently with Delila. He told Consuelo to leave and not come back and she, in a rage, tore his picture from the silver frame she had bought for it, and stamped on it, screaming that if anything bad happened to her it would be his fault. She ran out. Jesús learned later that she had gone to her aunt Guadalupe, who lived in a nearby *vecindad*. Jesús looked down upon Guadalupe and her husband as drunkards who lived in squalor. Later Consuelo appeared at the Casa Grande with her young man, Mario, who wanted to marry her, and asked for her father's blessing on the union. Jesús, still angry, had brushed them both aside. Two months later Consuelo's wire had come from Monterey.

Now Jesús hoped that Consuelo was not getting ill again, for he wanted to appease Delila and spend less time at Lupita's house. "Aren't you feeling well?" he asked, and his voice was cold even though, whenever anyone in his family was ill, he was extremely concerned.

"It is nothing, papá," Consuelo answered. "Tomorrow I will be able to work."

As soon as Antonia heard her father's voice she came into the kitchen, and Jesús at once asked her about Carmela. "She's better today, papá. She doesn't have any fever, but I haven't let her go out yet."

"Well, that's better," Jesús said. "Now I can be calm. But one can never be tranquil. If it's not one thing it's another. When everyone's well, I work without worrying, but when someone's sick, I can't even work." He took a newspaper, *Las Últimas Noticias*, from his bag. Both Isabel and Consuelo immediately offered their chairs to him, but he paid no attention and sat down on the tub near the kitchen door to read. No one spoke because they knew he wanted them to be silent.

Jesús had a way of separating himself from people even when he was surrounded by them, as in the busy restaurant, the markets, and in his three crowded households. He had always been a solitary figure, for he distrusted people and did not understand them. He had never had friends, and had alienated even his few relatives. He did not want his wives or children to have friends either, and he rarely permitted them to have visitors. When his children were small he had kept them behind locked doors in their one-room home; they had to sneak out when he was not at home to play in the patios of the Casa Grande. Jesús blamed many of his children's difficulties on the evil influence of their tenement friends. He said that the best (and only) inheritance he received from his father was a piece of advice: "Don't get mixed up with friends because it leads to no good. It is better to go your own way alone. Whether you are good or bad it is only you that is concerned and nobody else. You don't involve anybody." Jesús would have followed his father's advice to the letter if his own need for a wife and a home had not caused him to become deeply involved indeed.

The dogs came into the kitchen. He patted them and said, "Popo, get out of here. You look fat enough today to make barbecue out of. And I don't think much of you, Amapolo, because you go off playing and leave your brother alone." The dogs lay down at his feet, but Lupita saw that they prevented Jesús from reading in peace and chased them out with a broom.

As soon as Jesús had read the headlines, he stood up in a sudden, swift movement. "Well, I'm going," he said. He picked up his straw hat and climbed to the roof to see if a bus were coming. In a moment he came down again and went into the bedroom to see his grand-daughter.

"How are you, little mother?" he asked Carmela, "I'm going to bring some chocolates soon, eh, daughter?"

He patted the child's head and went on to the pigeon room next to the bedroom. He opened the cubicle where the best pigeons were kept and stood looking at them. Then he closed the door and left the house without saying good-by.

Antonia came into the kitchen with her arms full of clothes to iron.

"Did your father leave?" Lupita asked.

"No, Pita, I think that he's on the roof."

"Ha! I ask because he always lets you know. He doesn't pay attention to me.

"Why does my papá call everybody 'you'?" Antonia wondered.

"He hardly ever calls anyone by name. He always has addressed everyone like that. He's always said 'you' to me and to Malena. He says, 'Listen, you,' 'You, girl,' or 'Do that, you.'" As Lupita talked, she finished eating the beans. "Malena and her father have the same character. She never asked him for things like you did and if she saw he was angry she didn't even speak to him. She inherited his temper, but usually she's nice enough. Poor girl, she's so thin now."

Antonia, who had been listening to her, said, "Yes, mamá, and when Malena is thin her eyes stick out more. Like mine, although mine aren't that way since they gave me shock treatments in the hospital." The two women were silent for a little. Then Antonia smiled. "Mamá, do you think I'm ugly? Is that why my old man was scared away?"

"Your old man? Can't you forget that horrible creature for a minute?" Lupita turned and spoke directly to Consuelo. "He was saying to me the other day, 'Which one of your sons-in-law do you like best?' And I said, 'Well, it's hard to say. They're all so "good." But if you want me to tell you, I will say I don't like any of them. Not you. Not Eduardo. Not Gabriel. All of them have made my daughters suffer. Of course, my daughters too are not saints, but you know it's hard for a mother to see her daughters suffer.'"

Antonia spoke up, "No, Pita, you are wrong. Eduardo is very good to Elida. He gives her twenty-five or thirty pesos a day. He bought her a television set and he takes her wherever she wants to go. Besides, all his childrren have good clothes to wear. About Gabriel, well, it's true that Isabel wants to come here to live, but he can't give her more than he does because he doesn't make anything. He gives her what he can."

"Yes, daughter, say what you want," Lupita answered, "but I don't like any of them. I treat them as well as I can because I want them to be good to my daughters, but in my heart I'm not content with any of them—they're all men!"

"Pita, do you want them all to be women? For my part, I really love my old man."

"Yes, child, but love doesn't bring shoes or food. You can't eat kisses or walk on sighs. I like the one who least mistreats my daughters, but since none of them has a very good record, I keep on trying."

The conversation was ended when Antonia went to the bedroom to see her children. Isabel was about to go home. She usually left at dusk every day. When she opened the door, pushing her children out in front of her, a great deal of noise could be heard in the street. The water truck finally had arrived. From all directions women and children, some member of every household, came carrying cans and buckets. Boys with water carriers ran from one woman to another trying to sell their services; most of them charged fifteen centavos for carrying one can of water. All the activity had raised a great cloud of dust, but no one noticed, for the matter of getting water was urgent.

As soon as Antonia heard that the water truck had come, she dropped everything, picked up two buckets, and ran out of the house. Marielena jumped up shouting, "The water's here. The water's here. Hurry up, Antonia. The cans are already down there." Lupita went out and removed the board covers from the top of the large water containers in the patio.

The water department sent out each truck with just enough water for an exact number of families. If one family managed to obtain more than its share, others received less or had to go without. It was the truckdriver's responsibility to distribute the water accurately and it was a difficult job. He had laid down rules: all cans were to hold twenty liters and to be painted blue and numbered in white, no buckets were to be used, and each family was entitled to eight cans of water and no more. But the people of the colony took delight in deceiving the driver and in getting away with as much water as they could. They even assisted each other in the game although those at the end of the line ran the risk of being left without water.

The driver stood by the water taps surrounded by the water cans which he filled rapidly. As he filled each can he lifted it aside and it was claimed by its owner. The driver's helper walked up and down, watching to see that no one got into line twice. Antonia, standing a little ahead of Isabel and Marielena in the line, was somewhat nervous because she was carrying buckets instead of the prescribed cans. She listened to the driver. "Wait just a minute, you've already gotten your water. . . . Little boy, where is your mother? These mothers that send their children and then cry afterwards that they don't have enough water. . . . You can't bring those buckets here! . . . I'll give you just four days to get the cans painted, and if you don't there won't be any more water."

Antonia decided what to do about the buckets. She called Consuelo over to her and whispered, "Get in line and tell him that you're new here." When Consuelo hesitated Antonia added, "Don't be stupid. We'll get more water that way." Consuelo gave in and took Antonia's place in the line.

When the driver saw her with the buckets, he put his hands to his head and said, "Didn't I already tell you you couldn't bring buckets?"

"Yes, but I'm new here. I didn't know." People standing around supported Consuelo, "Yes, that's right. She just came yesterday. Go on, give her some water. The poor thing didn't know."

The driver looked Consuelo over, standing with his hands on his hips. He saw that she didn't look quite like the other women in the colony, with her page-boy hairdo and her high heels. Finally he said, "And just what are you doing here with all these hogs? Do you really live here? Well, take what you want today but I'll give you only four days to get the blue cans."

Antonia had been watching from a distance. When the buckets were filled she went to help Consuelo carry them. When they were out of the driver's hearing, Antonia told Consuelo to get back in line with the empty buckets and try to get more water. Antonia meanwhile hired some boys to carry the cans which had now been filled. As soon as all the water had been brought to the house, Consuelo took out some change and paid the boys who had helped carry the water.

"Oh, no you don't," said Lupita. "You stay out of this dance. Here, I'll give you back what you paid." She tried to give the money to Consuelo who would not take it. Antonia held out her hands. "Roll it over this way, Pita. I'll catch it."

"Aren't you the hard-used one though."

"Ha, so that's the way you are. I work day and night like Cinderella and you won't give me a centavo. Pita, you don't love me any more."

Mother and daughter laughed loudly as they went into the kitchen. It was almost six-thirty and the kitchen was already dark. Lupita lighted two candles and began to clear the table, stacking the dirty dishes on the charcoal stove. Antonia reheated the irons and began to press Francisco's trousers. The house was quiet, now that Isabel and her children had left.

Consuelo went into the bedroom to stay with Carmela and Julio, for Antonia did not like to leave them alone in the dark. Antonia

had always feared the dark and did not want her children to become afraid. All the women of the house, except Consuelo, believed
in ghosts and apparitions. Lupita used to be frightened by the dead
who came to "haunt" her. She said they used to tickle her ribs when
she stooped over and they threw bread pellets at her at the La Gloria
restaurant when she worked at night. They troubled her even more
when she moved to the El Dorado Colony. Later someone told her
that the dead followed her because she had prayed to the good souls
of her dead instead of cursing them. One should curse at the souls
that were good and pray to the souls of the bad to avoid being
haunted. Lupita said the dead no longer came to the house when
she stopped praying to them. However, she advised Antonia to be
particularly careful not to leave Julio alone because he had not yet
been baptized. When Antonia was forced to leave him for a moment
she always placed a crucifix at his side to protect him.

Lupita came into the bedroom for her shawl, saying to Consuelo,
"I'll be right back. I am going for the bread and milk and candles.
If I don't go now, I won't get any, because the store closes early.
I have to go so far. My God, if you only knew how hard it is for me.
It's not the road so much as my rheumatism. It gets bad at this
time of the day when it's cold. But it's worse when it rains. I think
the reason it rains so hard here is that we're so close to the hills.
You can hear the lightning strike there. It's enough to frighten
anybody."

Antonia came in with the clothes she had ironed. "What's that?
Are you talking about me again? Tell me to my face."

"No, I am telling Consuelo about the rains we have here. Do
you remember?"

"How can I forget? You will see how it is, Consuelo, when the
rainy season starts this year. It even makes me afraid. Sometimes
it rains so hard we begin to pray. We hear only the zoom and it
seems as though the hills were splitting apart."

Carmela interrupted her mother to say, "Mamá, where's the cat?
The poor thing hasn't eaten all day."

"Yes, I gave him something to eat," Antonia answered. As she
said this, Antonia touched the child's forehead.

"Does she still have a fever?" Lupita asked. Antonia said no, and Lupita went on, "I am happy she's over that. It frightens me a little because if she got sick in the middle of the night, where would we get any medicine out here? Around here if you die you just die and that's all. And another thing. Anyone who dies here can't be buried in the cemetery in the Villa de Guadalupe. One has to go as far as the village Ozumba because there isn't any more room here. So it's better not to die at all. If you do die, you'll have to die standing up so you won't take up so much space."

"Don't complain Pita," Antonia said. "After all you have your little house and your little things. The bad part of it is that you don't want to admit it."

"What little things? The house belongs to your father and so do the animals, and the day he wants to he can throw Malena and me out into the street. But you, you don't have to worry because you can go with your 'husband.' Ha, *carajo!* How bad it sounds to say 'my husband' when one is not married. It hurts my soul. *Vaya!*"

"Yes, you say that because you don't love my father," Antonia said.

"Ay, no!" Lupita said.

Marielena came in carrying a cardboard shoe box from which she took the statue of the Child which had been carefully wrapped in tissue paper. "Look, mamá, how well everything came out," she said. But it was too dark to see the image, for the sunlight was almost gone and Antonia got up to light the kerosene lamp hanging next to the window, and the candles on the top of the wardrobe. Then the four women examined the hands of the figure as Marielena held it in her arms.

"How well it came out, didn't it?" Marielena said. "You can't see which finger was broken."

"In truth, which one was it?" Consuelo asked.

"This one. But now I'll have to be very careful with it because if it falls off again it will cost me another five pesos, and I don't think Elida will give me the money again. I'll put it up here, but don't put anything on top of the box. Especially you, Antonia, because you have the habit of putting things anywhere."

"Who broke it anyway?" Antonia asked.

"Well, I did, but—"

"There you are. Then why do you tell me? What happens is that you like to fight with me, you child. You even scold Julio when he touches your things."

"All right, all right. I only said it."

As soon as the statue had been put away, Antonia lay down on the bed with her children to nurse the baby. Marielena went to hang up the jacket she had borrowed from Antonia, and Lupita remembered that she had intended to go to the store. It was difficult for her to stand up; after she had been sitting a long time her feet swelled and pained her when she moved them. Marielena offered to go but her mother stubbornly insisted on doing her chore. She left the house at seven-fifteen saying, "I'm going to leave the door open. You, Antonia, don't go to sleep the way you did the other time."

When her mother had gone, Antonia smiled and said to Consuelo, "Yes, it's true I went to sleep and she couldn't get in. No one could rouse me." A dog was heard barking in the street outside. Antonia sat up in bed. "Listen, some stranger must be walking out there because when a dog barks that way, it means a stranger is there. When I hear dogs bark in the middle of the night, I'm scared. I'm afraid someone is coming to rob us. When I'm by myself I like to sit up on the roof because here inside I imagine I see someone coming in." Antonia stopped speaking. The baby Julio and Carmela were both sleeping, and Antonia, too, fell asleep. Consuelo went into the kitchen where Marielena was working silently under the light of the candle.

"It will look very pretty," remarked Consuelo, adding wistfully, "I wish that I could make things as well as you and Elida can. My papá says that I am good-for-nothing and, in truth, he is right." Consuelo thought of her father's severe face. He had been harsher with her than any of her sisters, except when she was ill, and never gave her a word of praise. She had worked hard to improve herself but when her father noticed her nice clothes and middle-class friends he scolded her and said, "Don't try to get out of your class because you'll get slapped down. Some people think that because they have a few years of schooling they belong to high society. Look in the mirror, then tell me what class you belong to. I've always been a plain simple worker and I'll always be that way and nobody is going to slap me down."

Consuelo was discouraged at all the rebuffs she had received, not only from her own family and neighbors at the Casa Grande, but also from the people above her socially who looked upon her as a social climber. She was confused but she knew that she desperately wanted to leave the crowded, noisy *vecindad* and her brothers and sisters whom she had tried to help without success. As for Mario, she had not loved him but had gone with him to spite her father and because she had no home. Consuelo picked up a nail file and began slowly to file her nails.

Marielena said, comfortingly, "Don't pay attention to my papá. That is the way he is."

Lupita came home after a half hour without having been able to buy any bread. It was sold out at the store. That night they would have to eat the rolls Jesús had brought. She put on a liter of milk to boil for coffee. "*Carajo!* One can't get anything any more," she said. "Either the stores close early or they run out of bread early. My whole walk was for nothing. Well, thank goodness they gave me milk. If not we would only have black coffee."

No one spoke and the house was quiet. Antonia was asleep and it was she who made things lively. The neighborhood was very quiet at eight o'clock. The long twilight was over and night had come. Through the darkness in one direction the distant rotating red light of the Peñon beacon was visible. In another direction the red lights of the airport of Santa Lucia could be seen, particularly the runway lights which stretched toward the north and seemed to touch Elephant Hill and to join with the lights of the main highway to Laredo. Behind the hills and to the south the sky was illuminated by the lights of the city. The small El Dorado Colony seemed darker by comparison.

Lupita broke the silence finally by saying to Marielena, "Listen, are the chickens all roosting or do I have to go fix them?"

"I don't know, but I haven't put them up on the roosts yet."

"Then you watch the milk. I'm going to see if they are all inside."

Lupita took the flashlight and went into the chicken coop. By setting the flashlight down and beaming it toward the birds, she could see to arrange them correctly. The rooster she placed on the highest perch, below him the hens, and on the lowest perches the turkeys, since they were heavy and might kill the chickens if they fell on them. In the pigeon coop she made sure that no birds were missing, no rats were there, and that the water dish still contained water. On her way back to the kitchen she called to Marielena, "Bring a candle. It's so dark you can't see out here." Marielena immediately took a candle out to the patio and placed it on the washstand. She and her mother then went back to the kitchen where the milk had boiled and the water for coffee was ready.

Marielena had finished sewing the hem of the dress for the Child. She thought she had done very well so far, and held up her work for her mother to see. Now the hem needed to be ironed. "Are you going to use the fire, mamá?"

"No, put the iron on until your father comes. He shouldn't be too long now, and if he doesn't come you can leave the iron on the stove all night if you want to."

"No, I only want to iron this little bit, mamá. What would I want to use the iron all night for? You would waste kerosene."

Lupita smiled but didn't say anything. While Marielena waited for the iron to heat she picked up a newspaper and began to read aloud accounts of the fighting in Hungary. A picture of a child badly wounded and bleeding caught her attention, and she took it over to her mother to show it to her. Lupita pushed it aside.

"Ay, no, no, by your life, don't show it to me. I don't want to know anything more about the war. It is horrible. My God! How can so much cruelty exist in the world! God save us from a new war. I think if we have another the whole world will disappear. Listen, I remember when I lived with my aunts in their big house and Mexico was in revolution and I saw too much. My aunts kept the windows shut but you know what curiosity is, and one day I opened the shutters and looked out. I saw bodies hanging from the trees, Carrancistas, Zapatistas, anyone they could get hold of to hang. And I'll never forget the screams of the people and the whistling of the bullets and the shouts, 'Here come the Zapatistas! Here come the Carrancistas! Hide the girls!'

"My aunt didn't worry too much about me because I was so young, but she hid her daughter in the cellar among some sacks and with some old clothes on top of her. When the soldiers came they saw only my old aunts and me.

"How horrible! My God! Wherever you turned, the only thing you saw were bodies swinging in the air. But in those days they fought with more courage than now. Now they can kill you and you don't know where the bullets come from. All these cannons, bombs, and I don't know what, make one disappear in an instant."

"I think that is the way it is in Hungary," Marielena said. "A man without arms can't struggle, like these poor things."

"Enough!" her mother said. "By your life, don't talk to me about it any more or I'll dream about it tonight."

A second time that day they heard three knocks on the front door and again Lupita recognized them and went quickly to open the door without pausing to ask who was there. She slid back the bolt and Jesús walked in.

"Is it cold outside?" she asked.

"No, just a little."

"But it is still foggy?"

"Yes, but it isn't very cold and it isn't really fog. It's really dust from the bus. Close up and get inside."

Lupita said no more but closed the door and locked it. It was just eight-thirty. Jesús went into the first bedroom, but when he saw through the open doorway that Antonia and her children were asleep, he did not go into the room beyond to get his flashlight for inspecting the pigeons. Instead he set his bag and his hat on top of the dresser and sat down on the bed. Lupita followed him to draw a chair close to the bed and to set a kerosene lamp on it. Jesús adjusted the light, took a copy of *Life* from the back pocket of his trousers, spread the magazine on top of the chair, and began to read. Lupita went over to Antonia and shook her gently. "Tonia, don't you want your coffee?"

"Yes, Pita, I'm coming."

"Hurry. Don't go to sleep."

"Go? I'm already there."

Lupita shook her head and went back into the kitchen where Marielena was still ironing. "Malena, take away those things," she said. "We are coming to eat supper."

"Ay, but I haven't finished yet."

"Tomorrow you will do it. We have more time than money."

Without further protest Marielena gathered up her things and sat down at the table. Lupita served her coffee with milk in a glass. To Consuelo she gave coffee with milk in a larger glass. Then she began to heat a pan to fry some beans and to reheat a piece of liver left over from dinner. She set a bread sack on the table, opening it wide so that everyone might help himself.

"Go call Antonia again," she said to Marielena. "She's always complaining that I don't give her anything to eat, but tell her I'm not going to carry it to her." At that moment Antonia walked in. "Are you talking about me again, Pita?" she asked. "Tell it to my face. You're a great bunch. As soon as a person turns his back there is always whispering. Gossips!"

"Ay, you! Nobody threw anything in your direction and you're already talking," Marielena said.

"Do you see, Pita? You should bring your daughters up better. Tell her not to lack respect. I'm the older or should I make her understand with a few slaps?"

Lupita smiled at Antonia as she said, "Yes, man, don't be so nasty with everybody. Well, sit down. If not, I won't serve you later."

Antonia sat down next to her mother and asked, "Pita, do you think my hands are dirty?"

"Wash them. You still are asking me whether they are dirty? You'd better wash them."

"Ay, heat the water for me. I might catch pneumonia and then who would take care of my little angels?"

"Go on, dizzy one. What do you mean, heat the water! If you don't wash, no supper."

Antonia went out to the washstand to wash her hands in cold water. On her way back to the kitchen she went in to ask her father

if he would like some coffee. He nodded, and Antonia said to her
mother, "Hurry, mamá Pita, my papá wants hot coffee." Lupita
looked up, "Really?" and poured some of the prepared coffee into
a small enamel kettle in which it would heat faster. It was not often
that her husband ate with them any more. In a short while she carried a cup of coffee into the bedroom.

Jesús said, "Look, here it says that—" but he was interrupted by
Carmela who had awakened and was asking for her mother. Jesús
went over to the child's bed and touched her on the forehead. "Your
mamá is coming, eh, daughter? Does your little head hurt?" Carmela
didn't answer and Jesús sat down again, saying to Lupita, who had
remained standing by the chair with the cup of coffee in her hand,
"Tell Antonia to come and look at the child." But Antonia was already on her way to her daughter. She soon came back to the
kitchen.

"Did you save a little milk for my Carmela, mamá?" she asked.

"Yes, but only a very little. Take some bread too and the thick
cream from the morning."

While Carmela ate, Antonia talked with her father. "Papá, what
time was it when you came?"

"Eight-thirty."

"Because Isabel told me that if Carmela didn't get better, she
would give her a shot."

"A shot? What kind?"

"Hemastyl, papá. It's what they prescribed for her at the Social
Security. But I don't think there's any need for it now. She stayed
inside all day and she ate well everything I gave her."

"Then why give her a shot?" Jesús said. "If you don't know how
to very well, better not. And a doctor should prescribe the medicine."

"Very well, papá." Antonia fell silent.

In the kitchen Consuelo, Marielena, and Lupita were finishing
their supper. It was after nine o'clock when Isabel came to the house
with a small pan to ask her mother if she would lend her a little
black coffee. Her husband had asked for some, she said, and she
didn't have any left.

"Yes," Lupita said, "take what you want."

Marielena walked home with Isabel. Lupita went into the bedroom to see if Jesús wanted anything more. If not, she meant to turn off the stove and get everyone ready for bed. She went toward the farther bedroom to call Antonia to come finish her supper.

"Were you coming for me, Pita?" Antonia asked. "Even though you say no you probably were, because I'm your favorite."

"Maria! you the favorite? How modest you are."

"Then you don't love me, Pita?"

"Yes, yes, I love you, my beautiful daughter."

Antonia sat down to finish her rice and coffee. She picked up the newspaper Marielena had been reading and looked at the movie section. "Mamá, that picture you wanted to see is at the Sonora, and it's only fifty centavos there."

"Well,. I still can't go," Lupita said. "I never have time. I tried to see that picture four times, and I never had time to see it through."

"But now you can go some night when papá doesn't come home."

"Yes, like the last time Marielena and I went to a movie. We were confident your father would not be here, but when we got home and knocked at the door who should open the door but your dear papá. He said, 'What! Didn't I leave you in the house? This is a fine time to be chasing around.'" Antonia and her mother laughed, and Lupita went on, "So you see one doesn't really know whether he'll be home or not. I think he keeps me uncertain just to make me angry. But you can imagine how we felt when we opened the door and he said that to us. We came in like puppy dogs with our tails between our legs."

"But he didn't get angry, did he, Pita?" Antonia said.

Her mother didn't answer, and Antonia didn't press her. "Ah, my ugly old man," she said after a moment's silence. "He didn't come. Tomorrow I'm going out early so that he won't find me. He's sure to come tomorrow. In the end, he is the one who makes his own trouble, not I."

Lupita had gone for a new candle which she placed in a little tin can. "I hope this one will last," she said, "because the ones you buy here in the colony are very bad. The light they give is like death.

These your father buys are much better. Well, he knows where to
buy them. Over where we used to live, we could run to the stores, to
the drugstore, but here we cannot find anything. *Vaya!* And I mean
nothing."

"No, no. Pita, don't say that! You make me angry," Antonia said.
"You can always go to the Villa." Then she added, "But how you
exaggerate everything, mamá. One would think we live in a desert.
Don't run down my colony. It is true that we are poor, but here
we're away from the noise of buses and autos. We don't have so
much to complain about."

"You can say what you want, but we're too far away from everything."

"Pita, I say you are wrong. Here we don't have trouble with neighbors. In a *vecindad* you can't do anything without others knowing
it right away. Here no one hits my children, and they can run and
jump without anyone's saying anything. Over there they couldn't
go out because everyone was fighting."

"All right. All right. Let's not talk about it any more. It's time to
go to sleep. I think that's why you're talking so much."

"You're right, Pita. I'm very sleepy. How about rocking me to
sleep the way you used to?"

"I hold you? Don't be silly. I can't even lift such a pile." With
that Lupita began to stack the dirty dishes.

In the bedroom Jesús had been reading without saying a word to
anyone or without looking up to see who came in or went out. He
had taken off his overalls and had hung them over the back of his
chair. Finally he laid aside the magazine and went for the locked
box in which he kept his most valuable papers. When he had moved
to Delila's, he had not taken the box with him, for he was not sure
he could trust Delila's family. In Lupita he did have confidence
and felt that the box was safe in her house. He took out two notebooks, in one of which he kept records relating to purchases he
made for the La Gloria restaurant and in the other, notations of
materials and expenses for the new home he was building for Delila.

He searched through his pockets until he found a long pencil,
took out his pocket knife, cut the pencil in half, and sharpened one

of the pieces. He studied the notebooks, took several large sheets of paper from his pocket, and began to transfer figures from these into one of the notebooks. The family was used to seeing him do this, but none of them really knew anything about his financial affairs and would never have had the temerity to question him. Jesús had found it impossible to support his large family on his wages and for many years had been selling pigs, singing birds, and other animals. These now provided the major part of his income. The large quantities of food he brought to each of his three households did not cost him very much because, as food buyer for the La Gloria, he had been able to make some special "arrangements" with the food dealers in the markets. Also, Jesús had been extraordinarily lucky in the National Lottery.

Jesús considered his daily wage of eleven pesos unfair. He had given his employers worthy service for over thirty years but, he thought, they did not appreciate him. "After so many years of service and of getting rich off the sweat of the staff, the bosses feel no responsibility." Jesús had had an operation for a hernia about three months before and the restaurant hadn't given him a centavo. Years ago, the workers had been given a bonus of ten or fifteen pesos at Christmas, but the practice had been discontinued.

Nor, in Jesús' eyes, was the union to which he belonged of much help. "The union? There's nothing to hope for there, no, sir. We haven't had a convention for years. All we get are dues slips, five pesos every month. When somebody kicks the bucket we give five pesos apiece for the family of the dead man. But it looks like people are dying too often here. The money goes right into the pockets of the leaders. Take my union. One of those fellows owns two houses and sixteen taxicabs. That's the way it goes."

Jesús did not care for politics. "There's nothing dirtier than politics. It's pretty rotten and there's been a lot of bloodshed too. How many people die so a man can get into power! Of course, the people have no education, they're ignorant and are like a flock following wherever the shepherd leads them. You should see how they act in the unions when there's a meeting. All those in favor? Everybody votes in favor. They don't even know what they voted in favor of.

They follow any spellbinder who comes along. And if sometimes
you want to show them that what they're voting for is against their
interests, they won't even listen to you. So how can you straighten
things out?"

Jesús believed that life had been better in the days before Cárdenas because people had worked harder and everything was
cheaper. He associated the rise in the cost of living not with World
War II but with the expropriation of Mexican oil "because that's
when the dollar went up." What his country needed most now, he
said, was a good strict government. "All of this freedom is bad for
people. They should close up eighty per cent of the saloons and
places that breed vice; they should build more schools and have
more control over youngsters, rich and poor alike. The Mexican people are going under because there is no leadership and no faith, only
lousy corruption. Why do thousands and thousands of farm hands
leave Mexico to look for work? Because there's no security here, because wages are terribly low, miserable wages which aren't enough
to support any family. The peasant keeps on eating beans out of an
earthenware pot and hot peppers that he mashes on a stone slab.
That's all the peasant eats, and he goes around half-naked all his life.
He doesn't make any progress, he doesn't get ahead, because there's
no help for him, no protection.

"You have to live among our families to see what we suffer from
and how it can be cured. They haven't made a thorough study of
the problem. Those gentlemen who rule over us have expensive cars
and millions in the bank but they don't see what is underneath.
They stay in the center of town and don't even drive to the poor sections to look from their cars. . . . We need different rulers who can
make a better study of Mexico's problems and do something for the
people, the worker and the peasant, because they are the ones who
most need help. Every day they are squeezing us more. . . . In
other countries, if they don't like a president they toss a nice little
bomb and have a different president. Not here. That's what they
should do here. A bit of cyanide, a heart attack, yes, that's what
many of our presidents and governors and police chiefs need. It's
not nice to say so because they are my compatriots, eh? but I've even

gone so far as to say that I'd like to see us have an American president here in Mexico. He'd pull in all the bums, all the tramps. Then we'd see how Mexico would change and make progress!"

In the next bedroom the baby Julio woke up and cried. "Hush, son," Jesús said. "Wait. Your mother's coming. Go back to sleep." When the child still cried, his grandfather picked him up. Antonia came in and watched her father bouncing the baby on his knee and singing to him. The child grabbed the cigarette from his grandfather's mouth, but since it was not lighted, Jesús was unconcerned. Jesús never lighted his cigarettes. All day long he kept an unlit cigarette in his mouth, throwing the old one away and taking a fresh one every five or ten minutes.

Antonia stood in the doorway massaging her hands with cold cream for a moment, then took two diapers from a box and turned to her father. "Give him to me, *papacito*. I'll change him." When she put Julio back in bed she made the sign of the cross over him. Undressing Carmela, Antonia placed her beside the baby.

Marielena came in yawning and stretching her arms. "Look, you," her father said to her, "see if you can add up these expenses. I want them by tomorrow when I come. I've spent so much time on this and I don't trust the results."

"Ho, but I can't. I've done them over and over, and I just can't make them come out. But I'll finish them tomorrow."

"What do you mean, 'can't'?"

"Because there are so many numbers, papá."

Antonia appeared in the doorway between the two bedrooms. "Let Consuelo do it," she said. "She could do it."

"No one's any help. They just complicate matters." Jesús spoke in some anger, for he had been trying for two days without success to obtain a correct total. When Consuelo spoke up, offering to help, he paid no attention to her. To Marielena he said she must have the work done when he came home the next day.

Seeing that their father meant to say nothing more to them, his daughters made no further suggestions, and Jesús returned to his figures. Consuelo left for the kitchen, and Antonia made her bed ready for the night. She set in place a small pillow for her head and covered the posts of the bed with a cloth—a protection against cold drafts. At her younger sister's place in the bed she set two pillows which she had taken from Lupita's box. Marielena had been sitting on the bed where Daniel lay sleeping. She caught sight of a diaper on the floor and picked it up, saying to Antonia in a low voice, "Look! You leave things everywhere, you Tonia. Can't you pick them up?" Antonia did not answer because in Jesús' presence there could be no quarrels.

It was eleven o'clock when Marielena undressed, taking off her dress and shoes and removing the bobby pins from her hair. She put on an old yellow cotton dress and laid her clothes across the bag where the ironing was kept. She then lay down next to Carmela at the foot of the bed. Antonia, meanwhile, had covered the mirror with a cloth because otherwise, she said, she would see visions. When anyone died the mirror was also covered, because the family believed that death is reflected in mirrors. Antonia put out the candle, but left the small votive light burning. She brought the coats from the wardrobe and laid them across the bed and threw a heavy woolen sweater across Marielena's feet.

In his bedroom Jesús gave up the figures, turned out the light, and went to bed. He was still annoyed and could not sleep. When he was disturbed about his children it affected him physically. He had once said, "Sometimes I get so angry at these children of mine that I think half my body is becoming paralyzed." He had been terribly disappointed by his children. "They turned out to be no good. They grew up in the capital where one can study but they didn't want an education." His oldest son Manuel had married at fifteen and now, at thirty, he didn't give a centavo to support his motherless children. Roberto had been in the penitentiary twice. Jesús had hoped that his sons would settle down and stick to their jobs but they hadn't. "My sons are failures because they want to start at the top instead of at the bottom. First they want to have a pile of money and then get a job. How can they succeed that way?" Consuelo, too, was a headstrong girl who hadn't taken his advice. He had wanted her to improve herself a little for her own good but she had become too ambitious. Jesús believed that these three of his children resembled their mother, Lenore, who had been a "strong character," hot-tempered, jealous, and fond of drinking. But even Marta, who took after him, was a problem because she had married an irresponsible man.

His daughters with Lupita were more fortunate because they had had a mother. This, Jesús believed, "was worth all the money in the world," especially because Lupita was a good person, "very straight in her way of doing things." Jesús felt that of all the women he had had, Lupita was most like his own mother and he respected her for that. Yet her daughters, too, had caused him grief. Antonia had been wild and "man crazy" and might have become a prostitute had it not been for him. Her long illness had been very hard on him—it made him cry even to think of it—and now he had to support her and her children too. Marielena had always been tied to her mother's apron strings. Her schooling was wasted because she was afraid to work and she spent all her time in church, urged on by her mother. "How can she have so many sins that she has to be stuck in church all day long?" Although Jesús considered himself a good Catholic he seldom went to church and was critical of those who did. "I don't like to shoot off firecrackers and bring flowers to the Saints and things like that so everybody will know I'm a Catholic. God doesn't want candles, what he wants are more good deeds."

Jesús frequently compared his own life to his children's and wondered what had gone wrong. He thought he had been a good father. He had not abandoned any of his children (except Antonia), had punished them all severely for wrongdoing, and had given them opportunities he had never had. He thought he may actually have done too much for them. "Lots of times you can do more harm to your children, giving them their food and having the table spread for them all the time. They don't worry about doing anything for themselves. Even though I am a person of no education, I do not fail to see my mistakes." But often Jesús blamed his troubles on other things. "My suffering is because of the bad atmosphere my children lived in. But what can I blame? My own bad luck? My lack of experience in life? The absence of a guide? I don't know, but I don't stop. I keep on going like a *burro* with a load on his back." Whenever Jesús spoke of these things tears came to his eyes. He would say, "Humanity is very selfish. Perhaps things are bad because before God the Father used to be in command. Now it is God the Son."

He thought in a kind of stoic bewilderment of the many responsibilities that confronted him—his wives, his children, his children's children—and of how hard he still had to work. He rested only one day a year, May the first; it was a question of how much longer he could keep up the pace. "I know I've got a responsibility toward my family, especially to all of those tiny kids. It is first for God and then for my grandchildren that I'm on my feet, plugging away. When I'm downtown I'm careful about traffic. At my age it isn't myself I have to watch out for, but the kids. I won't be able to give them very much but at least they go on living and growing and I hope God will allow me to be with them until they can earn their own living." In recent years Jesús had become a builder. His major ambition was to leave a place to live for all of his children and grandchildren. That was why he was now building still another house. "Just a modest little place that they can't be thrown out of. I'll put a fence around it and no one will bother them. It will be a protection for them when I fall down and don't get up again."

Lupita's day was not yet over. In the kitchen she was preparing food for the animals. When they had finished eating she shooed Popo and Amapolo up to the roof. Consuelo held the candle while she opened the door of the pigpen and put in the food for the pig.

"Now, let's go to sleep," Lupita said. "Now we've all eaten. Thanks to the Lord that he gave me bread without my deserving it. But the truth is I do deserve it. Is work nothing?" She smiled as she filled a small pan with water and set it on the table.

"Has your father gone to bed?" she asked Consuelo.
"No."

"Are you sure? Because if he hasn't, when we go in he'll give us the stick. Then he says that he can't rest because everywhere there is noise."

Softly Lupita went out into the patio to line up the empty water cans and to put out the candle. She saw that the light in Jesús' bedroom was out. "You said no," she said to Consuelo, "but he has already gone to bed. Hurry, lie down. If not, he is going to scold. I've still got to see to your brother the cat."

Lupita put the cat's rice into a dish and with a candle in her hand went out to the patio again to look for him. She checked the outside door, making sure the bolts were in place, and pushed the rock more securely against the post. Back in the kitchen, she put a cotton cloth over the bird cage, opened the window above the stove, and fastened the kitchen door with a loop over a nail. Then she went into the bedroom, shutting the door behind her.

In the bedrooms everyone was sleeping. Lupita quietly opened the windows a little and put out the candle. She noticed that Antonia was sleeping on top of the blankets and insisted that she undress. Antonia got up, took off her shoes, sweater, and dress, and lay down again beside Julio. Lupita next went to the bed where Daniel was sleeping, removed his pants and shirt, and covered him well with blankets. Daniel had been out playing most of the day and was sleeping soundly. Then she took her pillow out of its box, placed it at the foot of Daniel's and her bed, and sat down to take the combs out of her hair. After that she put a chair against the door and smoothed out the piece of sacking that served as a rug beside Jesús' bed. Last she checked the votive light and put a can of talcum powder in front of it to screen off its light.

She got into bed at a quarter to twelve. The buses had stopped running and the only thing Lupita could hear were the footsteps of the dogs on the roof as they settled down to sleep.

*Lomas de Chapultepec:*

# THE CASTRO FAMILY

**CAST OF CHARACTERS**

| | |
|---|---|
| David Castro, age 47 | *the father* |
| Isabel Ramírez, age 34 | *David's wife in free union* |
| Rolando Castro, age 14 | *the eldest son* |
| Manuel Castro, age 10 | *the second son* |
| Juan Castro, age 9 | *the third son* |
| Lourdes Castro, age 6 | *the only daughter* |
| Juana | *the cook* |
| Concepción | *the cook's daughter* |
| Josefina | *the chambermaid* |
| Eufemia | *the laundress* |
| Elena Ramírez | *Isabel's sister* |

# THE CASTRO FAMILY

THE streets of Lomas de Chapultepec were almost deserted even though it was ten o'clock in the morning and the rest of the city had been busy for hours. Lomas was the wealthiest and most aristocratic residential section of Mexico City, and its people rose late. In the house of the Castro family, the parents and children were still asleep, for it was the beginning of the winter school vacation. Only the servants were up and about, and even they had not been working long.

The Castro family was typical of the *nouveau riche* who had prospered in Mexico since the revolution. David Castro was worth a few million pesos, owned a cement business which was important enough to be advertised over the radio and on TV, owned also two stores and two apartment houses, a cottage in Acapulco, and his home in Lomas. But his family did not live like a Mexican upper-class family. Their home was modest and located in one of the less wealthy sections of Lomas. A high iron gate, kept locked day and night, enclosed the driveway and the ill-kept garden of English grass and flowering plants. The two-story white stone and cement house had a living room, dining room, kitchen, and bath downstairs, and three bedrooms and bath upstairs.

The house furnishings were expensive and some pieces were in good taste, some were not. There were no paintings on the walls save for a large print of the Virgin of Guadalupe in the front hallway. Nor was there any reading matter, with the exception of some popular magazines and copies of the *Reader's Digest* scattered about the living room. The novels that Isabel, the wife, was in the habit of reading were borrowed either from her sister or from a library and were stacked on a table beside her bed.

The family kept three servants, a cook, a chambermaid, and a laundress, all of whom lived in servants' quarters on the roof. Josefina, the chambermaid, was cleaning the downstairs rooms before the family appeared for breakfast. She moved the furniture aside, vacuumed the wall-to-wall carpeting that covered both the living- and dining-room floors, and carefully set each piece of furniture back in place. The television set and the tape recorder that David had bought for his children she did not touch, however, for if the children noticed anything different about them they would grow abusive. She dusted the bric-a-brac and the pieces of cut crystal that decorated the living room and cleaned the keys of the small piano on which no one in the family played. Then she lighted the gas heater, disguised as a pile of logs inside the stone fireplace, to take the chill out of the rooms. The bottles of cognac, whiskey, and liqueurs, kept in plain view of visitors on top of a mahogany cabinet, also had to be dusted. Finally she covered the glass-topped dining-room table with a tablecloth of damask linen and set six places with the second-best set of silver. The best set, sterling and marked with the initials D C, was kept locked up and brought out only on special occasions. Some time before burglars had broken into the house and had almost made off with it. A glass of orange juice at each place and a vase of gladioli in the center completed the table arrangements.

When she had finished in the dining room Josefina went out to wipe off the latest model yellow and black Lincoln convertible which belonged to the Señor. She took particular care with this job, for the car meant a great deal to David Castro. At one time Isabel also had had a car of her own in which to drive the children to school, but her husband had sold it because he said it made it too easy for her to leave her home.

In the kitchen Juana, the cook, was talking with her daughter Concepción, who was cutting a papaya into small cubes and popping a piece into her mouth from time to time. The girl, a dark-skinned child of twelve, had been promoted in school and the mother was pleased. "I'm glad, daughter," she said, "and now soon you will be working at something else and we won't have to put up any longer with these people who think that just because they have money they can yell at us all they want. I'm sick of the children, those little devils. If I had a few hundred pesos I wouldn't stand them one minute longer. Soon they will come down screeching, but don't let them act high and mighty with you." Juana prepared the pancake batter and placed the griddle on the white enamel gas stove to heat it up in time for breakfast. She took butter and maple syrup from the refrigerator, a jar of marmalade from the cupboard, and gave them to Concepción to put on the dining-room table.

On the roof of the house Eufemia, the laundress, was washing the large pile of clothes which the Castro family soiled every day. When Eufemia had first come to work in this house she had been surprised at the quantity of clothing the family owned and by the fact that they changed their clothes every day. And the big cement sink on the roof, with its running water and built-in washboard, was impressive. But it was much more pleasant to wash clothes in her native village where the women gathered at the river, scrubbed the clothes with strong bar soap, and slapped them against the stones, all the while joking and gossiping with each other. Here it was more advanced but it was lonely. She stayed on because she was well paid, ate better than ever before, and slept in a bed (with the chamber-maid). In her village she had slept on a straw mat on the floor.

At eleven a bell rang twice in the kitchen, a signal that the Señores were awake and getting ready to come down for breakfast. Usually on holidays they got up a little earlier, at ten or ten-thirty, but David had come home late the night before, actually at five in the morning, and Isabel had a cold and was quite willing to stay on in bed. On school days Isabel had to rise at six-thirty to get the children under way for the day. They attended three different private schools, and the three schedules for breakfast, lunch, and the school bus in addition to her husband's independent routine, quite filled Isabel's mornings and afternoons.

Isabel had rung the bell from the master bedroom where she slept with her husband in a double bed. When they were getting along well together they used the double bed; but when they quarreled David sent the big bed down to the basement and had it replaced by twin beds. This bedroom was large and expensively furnished. The floor was covered with thick carpeting and the bed with a spread of gold satin. A gilt crucifix hung over the head of the bed.

"Shorty," David said to his wife, "you felt hot when I got in last night. Have you got a fever?"

"I don't know," Isabel answered, "but I've felt bad ever since last night. Now I'm going to wake up the children. Listen, why did you come home so late? Another party?"

"Are you beginning that again? I know what I'm doing and that's the end of it. You aren't to complain. Didn't we agree on that?" David spoke deliberately, as usual, pronouncing his words carefully and exaggerating the vowels. He was proud of his ability to speak well, but when he was angry he quickly lapsed into slang and vul-garities, revealing his lower class background.

"All right, but it's just too much. You're a terrible example to your children. That's why they don't respect me."

"They don't respect you because you don't know how to handle them. Where's your psychology? When I'm around they're lambs."

"Yes, you have a very special kind of psychology."

"What do you mean? Do you mean to say I'm an ogre to my children?" David had raised his voice to a yell.

"I didn't say that. But they're afraid of you because you can take a lot of things away from them and because you're a man. And what about when you're not home? You should train them to obey me. You haven't any idea how much trouble they give me. Especially Rolando. You'd never think I am his mother. But of course they see what goes on between us two."

"Look," David said, "shut up or we'll end up fighting the way we always do and I'm sick of it. I wish we could have a little peace in this damned house. When you're not fighting about money you're fighting because I get home late or for something else. You've always got something to complain about."

Isabel kept quiet. She stood up, putting on a pair of rose-colored silk slippers and a long white bathrobe of Spanish piqué and lace over her transparent pink nylon nightgown. Thirty-four years old and the mother of four children, she was still beautiful and young looking. She was small-boned and had delicate features, a light skin, large brown eyes, and short curly chestnut-colored hair. Fastidious about her person and clothes and careful of her diet, for she tended to gain weight easily, she worked assiduously to keep herself looking young. She never gave her true age when questioned.

Isabel went to her daughter's room where the little girl had been awake for over an hour and playing quietly with her dolls. Some time before she had started into her parents' room, but when she heard them quarreling she had crept back to bed. Lourdes' room was small but it, too, was expensively furnished with a carpet, a youth bed with a spring mattress, a bureau with drawers, a wardrobe, a night table, and two small chairs. It also had a closet where Lourdes kept all her elaborate toys. When her mother came in, the child began to jump up and down on the bed.

"*Mamacita,* last night I dreamed about a lot of little angels that were flying around in a lot of clouds. Why didn't you come to see me sooner?"

"I was talking to your papá, child. Why didn't you come in? Come on, put on your bathrobe and your slippers so we can go down to breakfast. It's very late."

"I was yelling for Josefina but she didn't come. I wanted her to bring me some water."

"Come on. Get up, baby. I'll be right back. I'm going to look in on your brothers to see if they're awake. They're too quiet. I don't know what mischief they're up to."

Just then there was a yell.

"That's Fatty," Isabel said. "They must have hit him." She ran to the boys' room and found a battle under way. Pillows and blankets had been thrown on the floor and the youngest boy, Juan, was sitting in a corner wailing bitterly.

"What's the matter, darling?" Isabel asked.

"Rolando hit me. He hit me hard on the back."

"Yes, I hit him. What of it?" Rolando said. "But just ask him to tell you why. Go ahead, coward, sissy, tell mamá why I hit you. He opened my present, mamá, and if I hadn't seen him he would have taken it out of the box. He's a bastard. He can't take it."

"It's not true. It's not true." The little boy was crying desperately.

Perplexed, not knowing which one to believe, Isabel turned to Manuel, who was hard-of-hearing and wore a hearing aid.

"Tell me, son, you're the most serious one of all. Whose fault was it?"

"Look, mamá, it's true that Fatty unwrapped the present. We were still sleeping and he got up quietly and went to look at all the presents. He opened up his and then he started in on ours, but Rolando saw him and got up and hit him. Fatty's a hypocrite. He wasn't hit that hard."

Isabel went to the closet and saw that there were indeed several boxes on the floor. One of them was open and its contents, a red sweater, an undershirt, and two pairs of cowboy pants, could be seen; another was half unwrapped. She went back to Juan who was crying more quietly.

"Now, now, son. But what did you do that for? I worked so hard to wrap up the presents and now you can't wait. Be quiet, because

*300*

if your father hears you he'll come in and beat you all. He's in a bad mood and if he gets angry he won't give us any money to buy a Christmas tree."

"Yes, brother," Manuel said to Juan, "keep quiet or the innocent will suffer with the guilty and papá will take it out on all of us. Let's see if he won't let us play with the train he bought us."

All three boys stopped talking immediately and were quiet in their beds. In addition to the three beds there were two wardrobes in the room, two bureaus with drawers, three cushioned chairs, and an easy chair. The floor was covered with linoleum because the boys would be too rough on a carpet. In the closet all manner of toys were stored haphazardly.

It was eleven-thirty when David Castro got up. He put on a red corduroy bathrobe over his silk pajamas, slipped his feet into leather slippers, and went into the bathroom where he locked himself in to take his daily bath. He soon called to Isabel that there was no soap, and she took him a bar of English lavender soap which he bought for his own personal use. Isabel also used a special soap which she kept out of the children's reach.

Isabel went downstairs to the kitchen to supervise the preparations for breakfast. Lourdes went with her, holding tightly to her mother's hand. The little girl wore a wool bathrobe over her flannel nightgown and red felt rabbit-shaped slippers on her feet. Lourdes was only six, a pretty and intelligent child, extremely attached to her mother and the favorite of both her parents. With this one of his children David Castro was consistently gentle, for he had always wanted a daughter. It was only after Lourdes was born that he had started giving a monthly personal allowance to his wife.

In the kitchen Isabel said to the cook, "Let me see the pancake batter. What's the matter with you, Juana? Every day I tell you how to make it and you always make it too thick. When are you going to learn? Well, it tastes good. Look, this is how it should be." Isabel added a little more milk to the batter, and Juana watched her because she knew her mistress could cook well. "Is the griddle good and hot?"

"Yes, Señora. Everything is ready. Excuse me, but I thought the batter was all right like that. You'll see, it won't happen again. Listen, daughter," she said to Concepción, "call Josefina because the Señores are coming down for breakfast."

Concepción went out and returned in a few minutes with Josefina who pushed open the swinging door between the dining room and the kitchen. Isabel, with Lourdes just behind her, went into the dining room and inspected the table. When she saw that everything was in order she went upstairs again and into the boys' bedroom. The children, still in their pyjamas, were yelling and jumping from one bed to another. They did not stop when their mother came in even though she called to each of them in turn. At last she went to her own room and came back with an old leather belt. The boys stopped playing as soon as they saw the belt in her hand.

"Hurry, boys, your father is going to come out of the bathroom and if he sees you still like that he's going to get angry."

The boys put on slippers and bathrobes and ran yelling down the stairs. The youngest one, Juan, slid down the banister in spite of Isabel's efforts to prevent him. Lourdes again stayed close to her mother, holding tightly to her mother's bathrobe.

"Wash your hands," Isabel shouted at the boys from the top of the stairs. "When I come down I want you sitting at the table ready for when your father gets there."

Just then David came out of the bathroom. He had trimmed his small mustache and was perfectly shaved (he used an electric razor) and now smelled of his favorite Yardley cologne. He had carefully combed the longer hair over the bald spot on the top of his head. In the bedroom Isabel was laying out his underclothes. In five minutes he was completely dressed in pearl gray trousers, a blue sport shirt, a tweed sport jacket, black leather and buckskin suede shoes, and blue striped socks. He placed a white and blue handkerchief, which Isabel had carefully folded for him, in the breast pocket of his jacket.

David Castro was a man of forty-seven who tried to conceal his age by dressing youthfully. He was rather short, about five feet five, and his skin was dark and blotchy. His hair was still black, however, and he was healthy and active, an attractive man if not handsome.

His clothes were expensive but tended to be loud. With an English tweed suit he sometimes wore a bright-colored turtle-necked sweater and two-tone suede shoes as well as jewelry. David was lavish in spending money on himself; he owned a few dozen suits and jackets and many pairs of shoes which the huge wardrobe in the bedroom could hardly contain.

Holding Lourdes by the hand, David and Isabel started down the stairs. "Listen, old man," Isabel said, "the boys want us to put up a Christmas tree for them. It's the eighteenth now and they are pestering me for it."

"Well, why haven't you bought one?"

"Because I don't have any money. Do you think the household money is enough for that too? Everything is very expensive and more so in this neighborhood. Come on, don't be stingy. Give me at least fifty pesos."

"Fifty pesos? Are you going to buy fifty trees?" David asked with a smile.

"Fifty trees! Since they've forbidden the cutting of trees, the ones who have some sell them very dear. They're sky-high."

"Don't bother me. I'll give you the money later. Let's have breakfast first. I'm starving."

"Papá," said Lourdes, "don't be mean. My cousins have their tree and we haven't any. It's so pretty, with lots of lights and ornaments. Aunt Elena put a star up on the top. She says it's the star of the Three Kings and that if I don't put a star on my tree Santa won't come."

"Who is Santa?" her father asked.

"Santa Claus? Don't you know about him?"

"Well, in my time the Three Kings were the ones who came and I never even got a present from them. Of course since I was so poor and didn't even have any shoes—"

"Oh, papá," Rolando said, "you didn't really not have any shoes!"

"Of course I didn't. Do you think every child has what you all have? That's why you don't know how to appreciate it. You see, you don't pay any attention to the electric train and it cost plenty of money."

"How much did it cost you, papá?" asked Manuel.

"What difference does it make? A lot of money. Isn't that right, old girl?"

"I don't know," Isabel said. "When do you ever tell me how much anything costs?"

"All right, all right, let's have breakfast."

David Castro was proud of the fact that he was a self-made man and had risen out of the slums. He never lost an opportunity to remind his children of how poor he had been. He and his brother had grown up in the worst neighborhoods of Mexico City, supported by their mother who ran a house of ill-fame. David did not remember his father but his mother and his aunts kept an image alive for him with bitter and hostile words. His father had abandoned his legal wife and two daughters to live with David's mother. But when the Revolution broke out he went off to fight and was never heard from again. David's mother was left in utter poverty, and to support her children during the war she turned to the only lucrative business that was open to her. Thus David grew up in the company of prostitutes, criminals, drunkards, and dope addicts.

His mother was self-sacrificing, affectionate, and indulgent with her children. She had nursed David until he was five and once laughingly told Isabel how David would demand her breast, calling her daughter-of-a-whore if she didn't accede at once. She had also permitted David to complete elementary school, an unusual privilege for a child of his class. But he resented the way she made a living and never got over his hostility to her.

For a short period he was a member of a gang of toughs, took dope, and earned money by hiring out dance-hall girls; then he broke away from this kind of life and apprenticed himself to a carpenter. He was energetic and ambitious and got ahead. Later he set up his own woodwork and lumber shop where he employed his brother and his mother, and slowly expanded his business by means of credit established at banks on the basis of business contracts. His big chance came when his brother, who later died of an overdose of marihuana, somehow managed to lend him a large enough sum of money to go into the cement business. Isabel suspected that David's brother had stolen the money or won it gambling because always before he had been penniless.

As David's business flourished, he attempted to satisfy his literary ambitions through a part-time job writing advertisements. He enjoyed this new role for he had facility with words, but as soon as he had proved his ability he quit and gave full attention to business where his energy, daring, and shrewdness, which bordered on unscrupulousness, served him well.

At twelve o'clock the family sat down at the table. Isabel rang a little silver bell, and Josefina, who waited on the table, came in with a platter of pancakes.

"Mamá," said Lourdes, "just give me one."

"You'll eat as many as your mother gives you, baby," her father said. "I don't know why you all fuss so much about eating. It would be a good thing if you knew what it is to be really hungry."

"I bet you don't know, papá," Manuel said.

"Why shouldn't I know? Do you think I've always had money? I've pulled myself up to where I am today but it's meant plenty of hard work. But I always took home money to my mother no matter what. And I never answered her back the way you all do to your mother. Now shut up and eat, fast and well. You, Juan, what do you think knives and forks were made for? Don't you have a knife? Why are you breaking the hotcakes with your hands?"

"Because Manuel hid the knife on me."

"It's not so, papá," said Manuel. "This crybaby complains about everything. We can't even lay a finger on him because he yells so much."

"That's because you both treat him the way you do," Isabel put in. "You bother him."

"That's not true, mamá," said Rolando. "He's just a pest. Isn't that so, Deaf One?"

"Don't call your brother that," Isabel said irritably. "He's not deaf.

And you don't have any right to bother him. Shut up and eat. Look, you spilled the syrup on the tablecloth. Pig! You act as though you'd never eaten at a table before!"

David said, "Let the boy alone, Isabel, and you eat up too. Don't tell me you're trying to reduce. At your age," and he winked at his children, "nothing you do can keep you thin."

"Oh, of course," Isabel answered, "I seem old to you, but don't think that you're any chicken. Besides, I don't seem so old to others."

David laughed aloud and calmly ate a great number of pancakes. These had become a standard breakfast for the family ever since Isabel had bought a box of pancake mix at a neighborhood supermarket five years before. David no longer missed the breakfasts of *tortillas*, fried beans, and chile. Like other members of the new middle and upper class in Mexico, he was a great admirer of the United States and unquestioningly accepted many of its standards and customs as superior to his own. Actually, Santa Claus, the Christmas tree, and pancake mix, until recently so foreign to Mexico, were rapidly becoming "traditional" in this segment of Mexican society.

Josefina stood beside Isabel ready for orders.

"Listen you, stupid," Juan said to her, "bring me more hotcakes. Don't just stand there like an idiot."

"You see what these boys are like, David?" Isabel said. "They don't respect anybody."

"Leave them alone, woman. That's what we pay for."

Josefina went at once to the kitchen but she could be heard weeping. When she came back with a platter of pancakes her eyes were still wet. She placed the platter near Isabel and returned to the kitchen.

For a moment no one spoke. Suddenly Lourdes gave a yell which made everyone jump.

"What's the matter, baby?" David asked.

"Rolando kicked me under the table, papá," she said and began to cry.

"It's not so, papá. I just stretched out my leg and touched her accidentally."

"Accidentally!" said Isabel, "I don't know what's the matter with

that boy. You'd think the devil was in him. He won't stop for anything. He has no consideration for anybody."

"Ay! mamá, don't be that way, it's not true, it's not true," Rolando said petulantly.

"All right, all of you shut up. You're going to make me angry,"
David said. "If you keep on making trouble I'll take back the train
and good-by Christmas presents."

"That's what you should do, old man," Isabel said. "Let's see if
these little fiends will understand that. But you only threaten—"

"They'll see that it won't be just a threat this time. You just tell
me how they behave and they'll see."

Manuel spoke up. "No, papá! It's not our fault. You see, mamá?
It's going to be your fault if my papá takes the train back. You're
mean."

"Do you hear how they talk to me, David? They don't respect me.
Not until I strap them with the belt! You'll see."

"No, no, mamá, right away you get the belt. We aren't animals."

David finished his breakfast, went upstairs to brush his teeth, and
came down again in a few minutes.

Lourdes had stopped crying and now said to her father in a whin-
ing voice, "Papá, is Santa Claus going to bring me a doll house?
That's what I want, but I don't know."

"Yes, my darling, you at least know how to behave yourself, not
like these devils. I'm going to write to Santa Claus so he'll bring
you your doll house. But why don't you write him yourself, sweetheart? You know how."

"Yes, papá, I know how but I just scribble. You'd better write it."

"All right, all right, we'll see."

The telephone rang and Manuel, who was the nearest to the telephone table, answered it.

"Hello, who's speaking? It's for you, mamá."

"Who is it?"

"It's Aunt Elena. She wants you to come over soon."

Isabel took the receiver, David waited expectantly, and the children fell silent at a sign from him.

"Hello? Yes, yes, it's me. . . . That was Manuel. . . . No, we're just having breakfast now, but we're almost through. . . . Of course I want the car. . . . No, I won't keep it long. I'm just going downtown to buy some boots and a pair of pants for the baby. . . . All right, if you're going out with Mauricio why do you want the car? He'll take you and bring you back. . . . Yes, yes, of course I'll fill it with gas. When have I ever returned it without gas? . . . All right, it's all set then, I'll be by for it in an hour at the latest. . . . Listen, how's the baby? . . . Oh, how cute. But he's better, isn't he? What milk are you giving him now? . . . Well, but you make it up, don't you?"

"Listen, old girl," David interrupted, "hang up. After all you're going to see her in a few minutes."

"No, nothing, nothing happened," Isabel continued. "David's going out. No, no, I won't call you, we'll see each other in a minute. . . . Well, if you leave before I get there leave the keys for me with Bertha. All right, yes, good-by."

Isabel hung up the receiver and the whole family went outside to see David off.

"Hurry up, Shorty," David said, "it's twelve-thirty already. I'm going to get to the office late and they're a lazy bunch. If the boss doesn't show up they don't work."

"What are you worrying about? Doesn't your son get there early?" Isabel was referring to David's son by a first wife with whom he had lived briefly in "free union." David had never supported the son or the mother, but when the latter died he helped the boy by giving him a job.

"Yes, my little woman, even he can't be trusted. Everyone's just looking to see what they can get out of you. Good-by, children. Be nice with your mother because if you're not, Santa Claus won't come."

"Papá," Manuel said, "will you take us to the movies tonight? I want to see *The Unknown Planet*."

"We'll see, we'll see, if I get home early."

"Oh, yes, don't let us down," Isabel said. "You said you were going to take us yesterday and just look at what time you got home. Come on."

"Yes, papá, yes," the children shouted in a chorus.

David climbed into the car, and Isabel called to Rolando, "Open the gate. The key's in the flowerpot over there." She turned to say to her husband, "Listen, are you coming home for lunch?"

"I think so. Why? Ah, I know, since you're going out. . . ."

"No, that's not the reason. Because sometimes we wait and wait for you and you don't come at all. I'm going out but I'm just going nearby. I'm going to take the baby with me and leave Rolando at Elena's house because if they all stay here together, there's the devil to pay."

"All right. I'll be seeing you. Good-by, Shorty." David put his head out the window and kissed his wife on the cheek. "Be good, eh?"

"I'm always good, what do you think?"

David backed the car toward the gate. He drove with great aplomb and was soon lost to sight at the end of the street. Isabel stood looking in the direction he had gone. Her husband puzzled her. She truthfully could not tell whether he loved her or hated her. Sometimes he was pleasant and affectionate, "so sweet he swallows me in one gulp." But at other times he was brutal and took pleasure in belittling her. He made her beg for money, he struck her with little provocation, and he flaunted himself before her as a Don Juan. He had once gone so far as to ask her to give him an injection which she discovered to be testosterone, a male hormone that he took to stimulate his sexual powers. Since he made sexual demands of her only once a month, she knew he must be taking the hormone "so that he could be more of a man with his sweetheart." She was so angry that she jabbed him too hard and the needle broke and had to be removed by surgery.

Isabel complained that she could never have a discussion with David because he insisted that he was always right and did not think her opinions worth listening to. "He never gives me credit for the things I do well. He never makes me feel secure." Whenever she took an interest in his personal or business affairs or expressed tenderness for him, she would be rebuffed. "It is as though he has a barrier around him which he lets no one penetrate."

Isabel believed David tried to isolate her from the society of people she enjoyed. In the past they had invited guests to dinners and parties at their home and Isabel had often been asked to play the guitar. "But," she said, "David couldn't bear to hear people compliment me and didn't want parties any more." She had had to give up her friends and was limited to visiting only her own family. She often went to the movies and did a great deal of shopping. It was now many years since she had played the instrument.

Occasionally David would take her with him when he went out with his friends, most of whom were businessmen and politicians. He liked to go to night clubs or to expensive restaurants and thought nothing of footing the bill for everyone. Isabel had seen him spend as much as two thousand pesos in one evening. He also spent as much betting on bull fights and baseball, his favorite sports. With friends he drank heavily and became noisy and aggressive. He liked to wrestle and had a trick of embracing some friend tightly and then lifting him up from the floor to show the strength of his arms. He had once cracked a friend's ribs doing this.

Isabel had at one time tried to improve David's manners and taste, "to civilize him," as she put it. Although she had had no training in the arts, she enjoyed them and urged her husband to take her to the opera and the theater, to concerts and art galleries. These "cultural" outings bored David, however, and he put a stop to them.

Isabel noticed that Rolando had shut the gate and had gone into the house. She called to the other boys. "Look, children, go play in the garden behind the house so I'll be free to order lunch and get ready."

"Mamá, are you going out?" Juan asked.

"Yes, little Fatty, but I'm only going to take the baby with me. You and Manuel are going to stay here quietly."

"No, mamá, why are you taking just the baby? Take me. You're telling lies because you're going to take Rolando too." Juan began to cry.

"Shut up, Juan! You're going to make me get angry and then I

*310*

won't bring you any comics. Keep quiet and go along with your brothers."

Juan went up to his room to change his clothes, for he was still in his pyjamas. Isabel, remembering suddenly that the boys were not dressed, shouted from the foot of the stairs.

"Rolando! Manuel! I want you all to take a bath before you get dressed. But be careful not to fool around because you'll see. One by one, so as not to mess up the bathroom."

Then she called in the direction of the kitchen, "Josefina, come quickly." The servants were eating breakfast, but the girl came at once.

"At your service, Señora," she said.

"Did you lay out the boys' clothes? I have to keep after you all because if I don't you don't pay attention to anything."

"Yes, Señora, all their clothes are ready on top of their beds. I laid it out just as you told me—shorts, undershirt, shirt, socks, and pants. Everything's there."

"Good. Go back and finish your breakfast so you can clean the house soon. I'm going out and I want you to press some clothes for me."

"Tell me which clothes right now, Señora, because then you scold me later if they're not ready."

"What talk! I want that green checked skirt that my sister lent me and the black sweater with the high neck. Press them carefully and don't burn them the way you did my white blouse when you scorched the whole collar. Good for nothings!"

"It wasn't me, Señora," the maid said, now almost in tears. "It was Eufemia. She let the iron heat up because she was talking to Juana and didn't notice it."

"And why didn't you tell me?"

"Because she's so spiteful. She said she'd punch me in the nose if I told you anything, and I'm afraid of her. She's so strong. She's an Indian! Please don't tell her I told you because—who knows?"

"Don't worry," Isabel said, "but you must tell me these things. Otherwise how am I going to know who does things wrong?"

"Because I'm the new one they blame everything on me."

"Go on. Tell me when everything's ready. Call Juana so I can tell her what to get for lunch."

Josefina went back into the kitchen. Lourdes had sat down on the piano bench and was tentatively touching some of the keys with her fingers. Isabel patted her daughter's cheek.

"Do you like the piano, baby? Would you like to study like your cousin does?"

"No, mamá, the teacher scolds a lot."

"But look, my darling, then you'll be able to play very nicely for your papá and for your aunts too. Now you're little and you can learn quickly. Don't be foolish. You'll be sorry later for not having studied in time."

"No, no, mamá, I don't want to. Rolando would hit me because he says the piano is his and that my papá bought it for him. The other day he hit Manuel because he began to play on it."

Juana came in. "Josefina told me you called me, Señora."

"Yes, I want you to tell me what you've thought of having for lunch."

"Ay! Señora. You must tell me. I don't know any more. The children don't like anything and sometimes they even throw the food at me. Tell me what you'd like."

"Look, make some vegetable soup, white rice, banana cakes, breaded cutlets in chile sauce, and a lettuce salad."

"And what about dessert?"

"I'll pick up some ice cream along the way."

"Are you going out, Señora? Don't leave all of the children. They start to fight and don't pay any attention to us and sometimes they even kick us. Take them with you. Some day something's going to happen to them. It frightens me."

"Don't worry, woman, go get your work done. I'm just going out for a little while and I'll be right back. Manuel and Juan are the only ones who are going to stay. Go right now or lunch won't be ready on time."

"Do you know, Señora, I think it would be better if you'd tell me the night before what you want to eat. Then while you're all getting up I can go to the supermarket and get everything because otherwise there's such a hurry to get things done."

"All right. I'll do that. Later on you can give me an accounting of the fifty-peso bill I gave you. Go easy, eh?"

Juana went back to the kitchen. Just then a great hubbub broke out upstairs followed by wailing, and Isabel ran up the stairs calling, "Now, Manuel, let's see what's happened."

Upstairs she found that the boys had locked themselves in the bathroom. She knocked on the door but no one opened it. She knocked harder shouting, "If you don't open the door there'll be trouble. You damned boys! You, Rolando, open up because if you don't you'll all get it."

She pounded on the door with her fist and at last it was opened. She saw that the bathroom floor was a lake of water, and in one corner Manuel, nude, sat crying.

"And now. What happened? Who hit you? Tell me, boy," Isabel said.

"It was Rolando, mamá. He hit me because I didn't want to give him the soap."

"Yes, mamá, but he was throwing soap in my eyes and wouldn't let me rinse off in the shower and then he pushed me and I slipped."

"Didn't I tell you to bathe one by one? You'll see."

Isabel was angry now, brought out the belt, and hit Rolando with it twice. The boy, furious, began to mutter under his breath.

"Listen, mamá," said Juan, "he is talking back to you."

"Tattle-tale, gossip, old woman. It's not true, mamá. I didn't say anything."

"All right, for the love of God," Isabel said. "None of you loves me. You'll be the death of me. I don't know how to put up with you. You're taking months off my life every day. But you'll see. Next year you're all going to be sent to boarding school. That's going to be your punishment for your bad behavior. I can't stand you any longer. You'll see. I'll give you five minutes to dry yourselves and get into your room."

She slammed the door angrily and went back to her bedroom, saying aloud, "Of course, how can these bastards respect me, with the example set them by their father. Wretched miser! Everything he gives me hurts him. I wish I were dead because these kids are going to kill me off soon anyway. Now I can still manage them, but later? They see how he treats me all the time. Always after women! He even lets the children see him with other women and that is why they don't respect me."

Isabel was thinking of a time three years before when her husband had taken his mistress to Acapulco and had also taken his children. One night Rolando had slipped out of bed and spied on his father. When he saw his father in bed with the woman, his instant reaction had been to slam the bedroom door with such force that the mirror inside fell and smashed into bits. His father came out in a rage and whipped the boy so hard with a leather strap that the bruises made by the strap buckle left permanent scars. When Isabel saw the bruises on her son's body she forced him to tell her what had happened. He consented only after she had promised not to tell his father. Isabel then wrote herself an anonymous letter which told of her husband's escapade in Acapulco. She mailed it to herself and showed it to David. They quarreled bitterly about it, but David did not give up his mistress.

When five minutes were about up, the boys came out of the bathroom one by one, each wearing a towel tied around his waist. They went quietly to their room where they began to dress.

"If you haven't finished dressing by the time I'm through bathing the baby there'll be trouble. It won't take long because I'm not going to take a bath. Hurry up."

While Isabel undressed Lourdes the child tried to comfort her. "Don't be angry, *mamacita*. Tell my papá so he can punish the boys. Write to Santa Claus so he won't bring them anything. But don't get angry. It's not good for you and you get sick. Come on, give me a little kiss. Don't be angry, mamá."

"No, daughter, I'm not angry. It's just that those damned boys drive me crazy." Isabel held her daughter close to her, aware of the great comfort she received from this child. She was the only one of the children who seemed normal and agreeable and gave her no cause for worry. The other three were disrespectful, ill-mannered, and cruel, not only with each other but also with their mother and sister and especially with the servants. In school they were poor students and behavior problems. Rolando and Manuel had already been expelled from several schools. Rolando, only fourteen, had begun to develop effeminate mannerisms, and the principal of his present school had alarmed Isabel by advising her to take him to a psychiatrist. David, however, would not believe that the situation was serious and flatly refused to discuss family affairs with anyone. He said that psychiatrists made people crazier and only fools sought their advice. He considered himself well able to handle his children without outside help.

Isabel bathed her daughter with a plastic sponge, rinsing her off in the shower, and drying her body and her hair with two thick towels. The towels were kept in a closet next to the bathroom where bed and bath linens, soap, rolls of toilet paper, and household cleaning equipment were also stored. She rubbed the little girl with Helena Rubenstein bath lotion, sprinkled talcum powder on her, and left her wrapped in a bathrobe while she went to the bedroom for her clothes. A little wool undershirt came first, then some white panties trimmed with lace, a blue slip also lace-trimmed, and a blue cotton dress with colored embroidery. Blue socks matched the dress, and the child's shoes were white. Finally Isabel brushed her daughter's hair with a nylon brush and then combed it. Lourdes pulled away while her hair was being combed, but Isabel held her gently and talked to her affectionately, "Now, baby, now. If you won't let me we'll be late. Don't you see we have to go out and it's getting late?"

"Am I going with you, mamá?"

"Of course, my baby. Unless you'd rather stay with your cousin, but your aunt is going out and she's sure to take Rosalba because your uncle doesn't like her to be left alone and the nursemaid isn't very bright."

"Yes, but if Aunt Elena stays home may I stay with her? I want to play with the dolls like the other day."

"Yes, my pretty one, but now be quiet so I can get ready."

Juan knocked on the bathroom door. "We're all through, mamá," he said. "We're going to go out front for a little while. May we take the bikes out?"

"Yes, yes, go wherever you want. Just leave me in peace for a minute. Don't go far because it won't take me more than half an hour."

The boys ran down the stairs, that is, all but Juan who tried and finally succeeded in sliding down the banister on his stomach, head first. They opened the door into the garden and ran out yelling and shrieking. When they reached the iron gate at the entrance to the house Isabel called to them from an upstairs window.

"Be careful because the workmen just fixed that gate yesterday. Don't pull it down again. You, Rolando, raise it up a little bit and let Manuel open it carefully." She watched them while they took out the bicycles carefully so as not to scrape the gate. "That's right," she said then. "Now close it again and bolt it."

The boys mounted their bicycles and began to race each other in the street, which, since it lay well inside the Lomas colony, had little traffic. Isabel watched them for a few minutes, then called, "Be careful," before she turned away from the window. Taking Lourdes by the hand she went to her own bedroom to dress; her cold was a bad one and she had decided to omit her daily bath.

From the bottom part of her dressing table, which was covered with a gold silk curtain, Isabel took jars of cosmetic cream and began applying them to her face and neck, first a cleansing cream which she wiped off with a paper towel, next a skin refresher lotion, and finally her daytime cream. She also smoothed on some rouge and liquid make-up that matched the color of her skin. With a brown eyebrow pencil she outlined her eyebrows thinking that it was time again to go to the beauty parlor to have them thinned. With a second pencil she traced a line along her lower lids, ending with a stroke which lengthened the line of her eyes. She applied blue eye shadow to her eyelids and touched up her eyelashes with mascara. Her eyelashes were false ones which she herself put in place every two weeks and because of which she could never wet her face.

The heavy make-up gave Isabel a theatrical air which was accentuated by the tight, provocative dresses and the dramatic jewelry she usually wore. She had been taught by her mother to use her physical charms to make her way in the world. Isabel's mother, hampered by an ineffectual husband who was a Civil Service clerk, had made the most of connections with wealthy relatives to keep up a front. She managed to give Isabel's oldest brother a professional education and to send the two younger brothers through secondary school. For her three daughters she had quite correctly counted on their beauty to catch rich husbands, and not one of the girls had gone beyond the third grade. The mother taught them domestic skills at home, but her greatest concern was with their appearance and their virginity. From the time they were fifteen, she had had them examined each month by a midwife. Since Isabel lost her virginity soon after her coming-out party, she was forced to bribe her examiner to keep silent.

When Isabel was sixteen she was seduced by an older man, a trusted friend of the family, and gave birth in great secrecy to a daughter. This child was immediately adopted by Isabel's mother, and no one outside the family knew her real parentage. Isabel had met David at a dance and had found him attractive. Encouraged by her mother who was dazzled by his weath, Isabel permitted him to seduce her in a back room in his office. They went to Acapulco and informed their families that they had eloped. David had promised to marry her but once she had yielded to him he would not go through with the ceremony. She had to be content with his assurance that he would support her in style. She worried about living in sin and stopped going to confession but David did not have religious scruples and was untroubled at not being able to confess. He had never been a church-goer. Instead he went once a month to the Villa to pray to the Virgin of Guadalupe for help, for he believes that otherwise he would not continue to prosper. Isabel solved her problem by praying at home every morning and evening. She accompanied her husband to the Villa and went alone only when she "needed a miracle." But she had resolved to give her children a strict Catholic upbringing.

The first five years of the union were happy ones for Isabel. She was embarrassed by their sex life and did not take much pleasure in it, but her husband seemed satisfied and was attentive and charming even though he left her periodically to go on long "business" trips. She did not learn until later that these trips were always taken in the company of a woman. He had resumed this bachelor practice just five days after their honeymoon in Acapulco and almost always had a mistress whom he supported in a *casa chica*.

Later David began to neglect his wife and children, sometimes not coming home for two weeks and leaving Isabel without money for food and expenses. During these periods she pawned or sold household silver or furnishings (but never her personal jewelry or clothing), or she borrowed money from her family. When she complained, David would threaten to leave her or he would put an end to the matter by striking her.

Isabel bore all this "for the sake of the children," until on one occasion David overstepped himself. He came home late at night, a bit drunk, and told Isabel to move over to make room for him in the bed. She said she couldn't because Lourdes was sleeping with her. He then pushed her with such force that she and the child both fell off the bed. Lourdes awoke crying and Isabel angrily called him a brute. David, always enraged when his wife became aggressive, fell upon her with his fists and kicked her as she lay on the floor. Her screams woke up her sons who came running to help her. Rolando picked up a vase and threatened to hit his father with it but David pushed the boys out of the room. Without looking at his wife who was screaming with pain, he left the house and did not return for three weeks. Isabel was hospitalized with a broken collarbone.

This time David's behavior had gone beyond Isabel's (and her family's) limits of endurance and she consulted a lawyer about a separation and a settlement. She found, however, that her husband had arranged his affairs in such a way that his money could not be touched, and she would not be able to sue him for support. Isabel had considered taking Lourdes and going to live with her mother. She was willing to get a job which might support the two of them, but she could not bring herself to abandon her sons. It was for them, she believed, that she had martyred herself and stayed on with her husband.

## The Castro Family

After a reconciliation Isabel, at her husband's suggestion, underwent a sterilization operation and at the same time had vaginal plastic surgery to repair the stretching and tearing caused by five childbirths. She had hoped that, thus rejuvenated, her husband would
find her more attractive than his current mistress, a motherly woman
to whom he had been faithful for the past five years. But he had not
changed, and, in despair when she learned that his mistress was
pregnant, Isabel followed David to his *casa chica,* burst in, and
slashed hysterically at the furniture and the walls with a knife that
she had taken from home. When she went to the extreme length of
threatening the woman herself with the knife, David stopped her
and took her home in his car. His wife's behavior subdued him for
a while, but it did not cause him to give up his mistress.

Isabel now and then permitted herself to have a brief affair with
a casual acquaintance, usually with a man of the lower class. Her
last lover had been a motorcycle policeman whom she had met
when he gave her a ticket for speeding. Isabel told herself many
times that she was resigned to her marital situation and that it was
her sons who made her unhappy and anxious, but her hostility toward her husband remained intense.

As she hurried with her dressing, Isabel thought of all the Christmas shopping she had yet to do and wondered how she could
stretch her allowance to include everyone on her list. "To think that
with so much money he is stingy with me! I'll bet he's not like that
with his mistress. Fat chance! These damned men refuse their wives
what they give their mistresses. And that woman is so ugly. She
looks like a worm. I don't know what David sees in her. He keeps
promising to leave her but he doesn't. She must have given him
some kind of love potion. The truth is that at times one even has
to believe in witchcraft when one sees the stupid things some men
do. I don't know what's the matter with him, the brute! If he would
only leave me alone once and for all, but no, if he's not bothering me
he's not happy. But I know how to get even with him. When he
wants to make up to me I pretend to be asleep and then he's stuck
with his desires. And when I let him, I feel no pleasure. It is like
holding my nose to take castor oil. I have to get back at him some

way. Let him go where he has to pay for it. He only gives me enough for the bare essentials."

While she waited for her mother, Lourdes played with a large toy dog one of her uncles had brought her from the United States. The servants went about their work. Josefina was trying to put the bathroom in order, and the cook's daughter Concepción was helping her. "Just look," Josefina said. "Those boys are pigs. It's easy to see that money isn't everything. If we ever did this in my house my mother would make us clean it up with our tongues. As soon as I can I'm leaving. The truth is I can't stand them any longer."

"That's why I don't let them get away with anything with me," Concepción said. "I'd be a fool. If they hit me I just answer them back. After all, my mother said that if they fire us they have to give her three months' pay because she'll speak right up."

Isabel entered the bathroom unexpectedly, and the servants fell silent. Isabel hadn't heard what they had said but even if she had she might have pretended that she had not. "Servants are so difficult to get and I dislike housework so much," she would say. She asked the two girls to leave the bathroom and then locked the door. Concepción went to find Lourdes, who was still playing with her dog.

"Shall we play, child?" she asked.

"All right. Just for a little while because my mamá won't be long and then we're going. Let's play house. You pick up the things after I've gone." With the dog in her arms Lourdes went to her room. Concepción followed, carrying a large vinyl doll that could walk when held by the hand. Concepción took a brush out of one of the bureau drawers and began to brush the doll's hair.

"Don't pull her hair," Lourdes said. "How rough you are. You're going to pull it all out."

"Of course I'm not going to pull it out," Concepción said. "These dolls can be bathed and combed and everything. Haven't you seen them on TV? Pull the chair over so we can make a house."

"Listen, children," Josefina said looking in on them from the hall, "don't make so much of a mess for me. I'm going to do the Señora's room and I want you to play quietly."

The girls paid no attention to her. They hung a sheet over two chairs, making a covered place, and went inside with the dog, the doll, and other toys to play house. Josefina started to make the bed in the master bedroom. She spread the bed with two fresh sheets, a woolen comforter that had a silk cover, a blue blanket with silk borders, and finally the satin spread. She folded David's pyjamas and put them away in a compartment of the wardrobe kept especially for night clothes. Next she picked up all the newspapers strewn on the floor and put them into a wastepaper basket. She went downstairs to return in a few minutes with the skirt and sweater Isabel had asked for.

Isabel came out of the bathroom dressed in her underclothes. She wore a girdle and an uplift brassière that held her small breasts high. Her underwear was nylon, trimmed with lace, made to order in an expensive specialty shop. Glancing at her wrist watch she saw that it was one-thirty. "Good Heavens, I didn't think it was so late! I don't know what time we'll get back. Come on, Josefina, give me my clothes quickly."

Josefina handed her the sweater which she put on hurriedly, next the skirt, and then a patent leather belt which she buckled very tightly around her waist.

"What shoes shall I give you, Señora?" Josefina asked.

"The patent leather ones, the pumps, but quickly. Come on."

Josefina opened the closet door. Inside the closet a shoe rack held twelve pairs of shoes, shoes for dancing, sports, and street wear. Underneath the rack many boxes held still more shoes. Josefina picked out the patent leather pumps which had very high and startlingly thin heels. As she handed the shoes to Isabel she asked, "Señora, excuse my curiosity, but won't these heels break?"

"No, silly, they have a steel core."

"What's that?"

"That means that there's a steel rod in the center of the heel that keeps them from breaking."

"Ah, well, I see."

Isabel put on the shoes and began to brush her hair. Some time before she had had her hair dyed a mahogany color but she was changing back to the original color, and now at the roots and for over an inch along the part it was dark chestnut. She combed it back loosely, trying not to disturb the set which she had been given a few days before at a beauty parlor. When she was ready Isabel called to Lourdes.

"I'm not going, mamá," Lourdes answered. "I'm having so much fun playing."

"Of course you're going. I'd be foolish to leave you with those devils. And if your father found it out he'd get angry. Come on. When you get back you can play some more. Let's go quickly because your aunt must be out of her mind by now. Wait a minute. I'm going to call her on the telephone to see if she's already left."

Isabel went to the telephone extension in her room and called her sister's number.

"Hello," she said. "Who's speaking? Is that you, Bertha? Call the Señora. . . . Listen, Elena, what time are you leaving? . . . All right. I'm on my way right now. The boys want to come play with your Arturo. . . . No, goodness, just Rolando. The others are going to stay here. All right. I'm on my way. . . . I'll see you."

She grabbed Lourdes' hand.

"Ay! Mamá, don't pull me."

"Come on. It's late. Listen, Josefina, give me my bag. It's over there on that chair."

Josefina gave her a patent leather handbag shaped like a portfolio and Isabel put some paper handkerchiefs into it. She went downstairs and back to the kitchen where she spoke to the cook, who had returned from shopping.

"I'm leaving, Juana. I'll be back about three o'clock. Don't forget to put plenty of garlic in the chile sauce for the cutlets. I'll be back."

She went outside. Eufemia, the laundress, was behind the house hanging out clothes. Isabel called to her to come hold the gate while she opened it and to close it again after her. Then she called Rolando. "Let's go, son." She turned to Juan and Manuel. "Behave yourselves. Don't fight with the maids. I'll bring you some comics."

"Good-by, mamá."

Rolando rode off on his bicycle. "I'll wait for you there," he said.

"Be careful," Isabel called after him, but he could no longer hear her. "Let's go, baby," she said to her daughter. "It's almost two o'clock."

They walked along without talking. Although Isabel was short she walked rapidly. Lourdes pulled at her hand from time to time for she could hardly keep up the pace. They walked several blocks, and arrived at Elena's where two 1953 De Sotos were parked in front of the house. Isabel rang the doorbell and a servant in uniform answered. "Listen, Bertha," Isabel said, "tell my sister I'm here and tell her to send me out the keys. I won't go in because it's very late."

"Very well, Señora, I'll be right back."

But Elena herself came to the door. She was a pretty young woman with brown hair, taller than Isabel, but otherwise resembling her sister markedly.

"Listen, crazy one," she said, "why don't you come in? We're almost ready to go, but come on in so you can see the baby."

"No, sister, I won't come in. It's almost two o'clock." Isabel looked at her watch. "I won't have enough time. Listen, what are you going to give your husband for Christmas?"

"I don't know yet. I wanted to shop at the Palace today, but everything here is upside down because they called to say that Jorge, Mauricio's brother, is sick and we have to go see him. I'll go to the Palace tomorrow. Later on today we're going to buy the things for the children. Wouldn't you like to go with me?"

"All right, sister. I'll see you then. I'll bring the car right back."

"Don't worry. I'm not going to need it all day. But don't forget to bring it back with a full tank. I just filled it this morning."

"Now, now, don't worry. Good-by. Call me when you get back to see if we can get together in the afternoon."

"Auntie," Lourdes asked, "are you going to take Rosalba with you? Because mamá says if she stays I can stay with her."

"No, dear, you can't stay. I'm going to take her because Bertha can't take care of everybody and even less now that the chambermaid has left. When we get back I'll see if I can send her over to your house for a while, eh?"

"Well, then, mamá, let's go," Lourdes said.

Isabel took the keys her sister handed to her, went to Elena's car, and lifted Lourdes onto the front seat. She got in on the other side and drove to the Reforma, where she turned right toward the center of the city.

"What shall I buy David?" she thought. "The truth is I don't want to buy him anything, he's such a mule, but what's the use? I've bought him a cashmere sweater, but I'd better take it back. I'd be a fool to spend so much. Then I won't have anything left to buy the other presents. Ah, I know. I'm going to buy him that jacket he liked the other day. It won't cost me any more than three hundred pesos and he doesn't even deserve that."

Lourdes had been silently staring out of the window watching the cars go by. Now she turned to Isabel. "Mamá, what color pants are you going to buy me? I want them yellow. Manuel told me they had to be cowboy pants but I don't like boys' pants. I want girls'."

"We'll buy whatever kind you want, but don't talk to me right now because you'll distract me and we might have an accident. Be quiet for a second, baby."

They were crossing the Diana circle where the traffic was heavy and, although Isabel was an expert driver, she was always afraid of this spot. Beyond the circle she continued down the Reforma as far as Niza where she turned to the right and drew up in front of a smart-looking shop. This shop, which specialized in children's clothing, sold only original designs that were of course very expensive. Isabel locked the car before entering with Lourdes.

The owner of the shop, smiling, at once came forward to meet Isabel. "Now, what are you going to buy for the little girl? Hello, Lulu, how are you? How pretty you look. Short hair suits you very well."

Lourdes didn't answer. She was timid and talked easily only with someone she had known for a long time.

"We'd like to see some cowboy boots and some little pants in yellow corduroy for my little girl, but American corduroy because the Mexican doesn't last any time at all," Isabel said.

The saleswoman who was now waiting on her said, "Don't worry, Señora, we only sell American corduroy. Look, here are the boots. Size 20, isn't that right, like the little shoes you bought yesterday?"

"No, give me size 21, because these boots are hard to break in and it's better to have them too big. Besides, she won't wear them out so soon and I won't have spent the money for nothing."

Lourdes chose a brown pair with white trimming. "These, mamá, these fit me well. I like these. Let me keep them on."

"All right, dear, but don't be impatient. How much are they, Señora?"

"Ninety pesos. We sell them to you at this price because you're our client."

"Very well, although they seem a little expensive to me, but all right. What about the pants?"

The saleswoman helped Lourdes into a pair of pants which Isabel thought were a little short. "The first time they're washed they'll shrink," she said.

"No, Señora, they won't shrink. This is American corduroy. Take them and you won't be sorry. I'm going to give them to you for forty pesos. They're worth forty-five, but we always give you a special price."

Isabel smiled incredulously. She agreed to the price, however, and then looked at a woolen sweater for Manuel. He had outgrown one sweater and another had torn sleeves. "What can one do!" Isabel thought. "I have to buy him clothes because his wretched father doesn't buy them anything. Imagine giving me only a thousand pesos for the children's clothing for the whole year. It's the limit. But it would have been worse if he'd gotten stubborn and hadn't given me anything. At least this will be enough for the first half of the year, and then if they go to that exclusive boarding school he'll have to buy them more clothes. He expects me to work miracles with the stingy six hundred pesos he gives me every month."

Next Isabel asked to be shown Mickey Mouse socks for Lourdes, bought six pairs at four and a half pesos a pair, and asked for her bill. The owner of the shop added it up. "What you've bought today comes to two hundred and two pesos and what you owe from before is one hundred and ninety-eight pesos, a total of just four hundred pesos. If you like you may leave part of the money. You needn't pay it all now."

"No," Isabel said, "I'd rather pay it all now because I still have to come and buy presents for my nephews and nieces." She gave the woman a five-hundred-peso bill. Lourdes in the meanwhile had been admiring herself in front of a mirror. The saleswoman accompanied them to the door, thanking Isabel and patting Lourdes. Isabel placed the boxes inside the car and locked it again before going to a men's store for David's jacket. She didn't expect a present from him. They had been quarreling lately and she knew that this would be his way of getting back at her. It had been difficult even to convince him that she needed an advance of three months' allowance to cover her Christmas expenses.

As she walked to the store she figured silently: "I've already spent almost eight hundred pesos on the boys' presents. I have to make a part payment at the beauty parlor because I owe almost five hundred pesos. And then the dressmaker—Ay, Dios! It's not going to be nearly enough. Well, after all, mamá and the family aren't here in the city. I'll give them their presents when they get back. There's just Elena and her family. I'll have to see what I can do to make it go around. As a last resort I can buy the presents for Elena's children at this store and pay later. I wish David would give me money for Christmas but instead he'll probably buy me some silly present or an expensive jewel that he won't let me wear and then when he feels like it he'll take it back."

At the men's store she asked to be shown the jacket. This store was one of the most fashionable in Mexico City, and Isabel was convinced that everything was better here. A salesman brought the jacket to her: it was of black leather, lined with lamb's wool, and had deep side pockets closed by zippers.

"How much does it cost?" she asked.

"Only four hundred and twenty-five pesos. It's a bargain for an imported garment, I assure you."

"Uy! It's very expensive. Imagine, I only wanted to spend three hundred pesos at the most."

"No, that's an impossible price, but let me speak to the Señora. She may be willing to give you a discount."

The salesman went to an adjoining office while Isabel waited and

Lourdes found another mirror in which to look at herself. When the salesman came back he said, "Look, Señora, the owner says that you can have it for four hundred pesos, but that's the lowest price. We have a lot of expenses. I'd advise you to take it. Later on there won't be any left."

Isabel thought for a minute. "All right. I'll take it. But wrap it as a gift, very nicely wrapped, eh? I want to make a good impression." In a short time she was handed the package wrapped in paper printed with Christmas trees. "Thank you very much," Isabel said as she paid for it.

"Thank *you* very much, Señora," the salesman answered. "You'll see how happy your husband will be when he sees this wonderful present."

"Is that jacket for my papá?" Lourdes asked. "Then what's Santa Claus going to bring him?"

"Look, baby. Santa Claus doesn't have time to bring presents for grownups and he gave me the money to buy a jacket for your papá. That's why I came to buy it."

"Ah, I see," was all Lourdes said.

Isabel left the store and headed for a shoe store on the corner. She looked first into the display window and thought, "I wish I could buy at least three pairs for myself. I need those black satin ones for the black dress I'm going to wear to the dinner tomorrow. Satin shoes are the only ones that will go with it because of the trimming on the dress. I could wear the velvet ones, but they wouldn't go with my bag. These are beautiful, and I like the transparent heels, but if I buy them I won't be able to buy any more because they cost one hundred eighty pesos. Well, but I like them. I hope they have my size."

Isabel went into the store and tried to bargain for the shoes, but the saleswoman was firm and she had to pay the regular price. She handed the saleswoman another five-hundred-peso bill and received the box and her change.

"And now let's go," she said to Lourdes. "It's awfully late and I've spent all the money."

"But the comic books you said you'd buy for us, mamá? Come on.

Don't be mean. Buy them. Let's get the ornaments too. Don't be like that. Then you won't put up a tree for us."

"We'll come back in the afternoon. Your aunt said I could have the car all day. We'll buy the comic books some place along the way, but hurry up, baby. It's almost three o'clock and your papá will be home soon."

She took Lourdes by the hand and almost ran to the car. When she had lifted the child inside and put all the presents in the back seat she climbed in and started up the car.

"You'll see," she said. "With this traffic it will take us a year to get out of here and your father told me he'd be home early. Ay, Dios! It's very late."

It was three o'clock when Isabel pulled into the driveway at home. Eufemia opened the door for them.

"Did anyone come? Is anything new?" Isabel asked.

"No, Señora. I asked Juana for a box of Fab because the soap flakes were all gone."

"But, Eufemia, just the day before yesterday I gave you money to buy a box. How you use soap! Since it doesn't cost you anything!"

"Ay, Señora, I'm mortified, but there's so many dirty clothes and with the sheets and everything! And I also gave some to Josefina to wash the entrance with. I do take care of it, honestly."

"Ah, well! Now make this box last because I won't give you any more for the rest of the week. Here, help me with the packages." Isabel was thinking, "These damned alley cats act big since it doesn't cost them anything. But what can I do? If I scold them more they'll leave and then what can I do? They really have a strangle hold on us."

In the house she discovered that Manuel had found a board which he was using to sit on and slide down the stairs. "You damned brat!" Isabel said. "I no sooner leave you alone for a minute than you're up to your deviltry and a half. Can't you see you're going to tear your pants? And just look at your shoes. They're all wet and you're as dirty as a monkey. You look as though you'd never had a bath. Where's Fatty? He must be up to some mischief."

"Ay, mamá! You get mad at everything. Fatty has really been

acting up. Ever since you left he's been eating and eating. He ate a *jicama* with sugar and two oranges and now he's in the kitchen fighting with Juana because she doesn't want to give him any more fruit. Go there and you'll see."

Isabel left her packages in an easy chair in the hall and started toward the kitchen. She could hear her youngest son arguing with the cook even before she reached it.

"Why won't you give me any more fruit?" Juan was saying. "You act like it's yours. I'm going to tell my papá so he'll kick you out. You give your daughter, all right, don't you? I saw her eating an apple. My mamá doesn't buy them for this little brat to eat. I'm going to tell on you, you bloody bitch."

"Look, child," the servant said, "it's one thing for your parents to pay me and another for you to insult me. I bought the apple for Concepción. Now keep quiet because if I leave we'll see where you'll find another fool to put up with you."

"Listen," said Concepción, "do you think you're the only one with money to buy apples? We're poor but we have some money."

"Shut up, you wretched cat."

"I won't shut up. Why should I? Who are you to shut me up? I won't even let your mother order me around because I'm not your maid."

Everyone stopped talking when Isabel entered the kitchen. "What's going on here?" she asked aggressively.

"Mamá, mamá, Juana doesn't want to give me fruit but she gives it to this brat. Look! She's eating an apple and she doesn't want to give me any."

"Señora," said Juana in a firm voice. "Concepción is eating an apple I bought her when I went to the supermarket. I was telling the boy that you didn't tell me to buy any apples today but he won't pay any attention to me. He kicked me and spilled the milk that was on top of the table. I can't stand them any more. Fatty has acted terrible today. If it keeps up like this I'm going to leave. You're nice and the Señor is too, but frankly, I can't stand the boys."

"Don't pay any attention to them, Juana," Isabel said, "and you, Juan, you keep quiet. We're going to eat in a few minutes. You all have no consideration for me. Go outside with your brother and be quiet while I supervise lunch. Go on," she added, giving Juan a slight push. "Get out."

"Let's go, baby," the boy said, turning to Lourdes. "Let's see your boots. Mamá, they're like mine, exactly, exactly. But those pants aren't cowboy pants. Isn't that true, mamá, they're not cowboy pants?"

"No, no, they aren't cowboy and what about it?" Lourdes asked angrily. "I'm a girl, can't you see? And I'm not going with you because you'll hit me. I'd rather stay here with my mamá."

"Yes, leave her alone. Get out," Isabel said. When the boy left she went to the stove and began to inspect the meal. "What about the bananas, Juana, why aren't they cooked?"

"Were they supposed to be cooked, Señora?"

"Of course. You never do what you're told to do. But don't boil them now," she said when she saw Juana was about to put them in a pan of water on top of the stove. "Just serve them fried with the rice. Let's see what my husband says to me because they aren't the way he ordered them. Call Josefina so she can call my sister's house and tell Rolando to come back right away because his papá won't be long now. You, baby, take the packages upstairs and put them in my bedroom closet. Let Concepción help you because you won't be able to do it alone."

Josefina came in to telephone. "Hello," she said, "who's speaking? The Señora says Rolando is to come home. . . . What Señora? Señora Chabela. He's to come home because his papá is going to be here soon. . . . Yes, the boy from here. Is the Señora there? . . . All right, that's all. . . . What? . . . Yes, I'll call her right now." She turned to Isabel and said, "Señora, it's Bertha. She says the baby's crying and how should she make his milk?"

"Give me the receiver," Isabel said. "What? . . . Look, put three ounces of milk. . . . What? It's powdered milk? Well, I don't know how to prepare that. Look up Jorge's number in the telephone directory and call the Señora. She's there. If you don't find it call me back and tell me and we'll see what we can do."

"Elena's awful," she said as she hung up. "What an idea to leave without having the baby's milk all ready and without telling me anything about it. Who knows what powdered milk is or how it's prepared. How awful! She's still just as irresponsible as ever."

Isabel quickly inspected the table to be sure that nothing was lacking, then went upstairs to wash her hands and to change her high-heeled shoes. "I'm going to call David at the store to see if he's already left," she thought. "The truth is I'm starving and if he's going to be any later we'll start eating." She was told, however, that her husband had already left. "He won't be long, then. I hope Rolando comes home soon so we can begin to eat right away. I feel quite sick with this grippe. When David comes I'll try to get him to give me permission to send to the drugstore to buy a bottle of Desenfriol and some Alivin. Otherwise I'm going to be really sick for tomorrow's dinner. Right now I'm going to take an aspirin to see if that will help me."

She brushed her hair back and covered it with a blue silk scarf. She heard a noise downstairs and went down to find that Rolando and Manuel were talking with some friends at one side of the garden. Rolando was doing most of the talking. He said that right there his father was going to build a room to install the electric train, and besides that he was going to widen the living room because "this garden isn't good for anything and it's just wasting the lot. That way the living room will be a lot better. When we have a lot of guests we won't be all squeezed in. Now we can never have any parties with all my papá's friends."

The other boys were impressed, and Isabel smiled as she watched from the balcony. "I wish they'd always be like that," she thought, "calm, nice, and acting like little gentlemen, but that's like asking an elm tree to give pears. I don't know what I'm going to do when they grow up. They're going to be the death of me."

In the living room Juan was talking to Lourdes. "Listen, baby," he said, "those pants look real ugly from behind. Look, turn around."

"That's not so," the girl insisted even though she was visibly chagrined. "They don't look ugly. Isn't that true, mamá?"

"Of course not," Isabel said. "Leave her alone, Juan. Like she says, she's a girl and that's why she likes these pants that are for girls."

"Yes, mamá, but there are cowboy pants for girls, too, closed in the front. The little girl across the street has some and they look nice, tight. But these bag in back."

"All right, leave her alone. What nuisances you are! Look out and see if your father is coming. And anyway tell the boys to come in to eat."

Juan went out and called to his brothers. They came in clamoring, "What did you bring us, mamá? What about the comics?"

"Guess what, mamá," Rolando said, "we were playing just swell at my cousin's house. We made a tent house in the garden and we took out all the toys and the things from camping trips. My aunt gave us permission. You should have left me there."

"Yes, and then what would you have eaten? You know your aunt doesn't like you to stay to eat because she says you get into mischief and your father gets angry if you're not all here. You can go back in the afternoon. I'll buy the comics for you later, when we go to buy the things for the tree. Get after your father and let's see if we can get the money out of him for the tree. I don't have any money."

"Here, mamá," Rolando said, "I'll give you these ten pesos for the ornaments." Manuel wondered whether he too should contribute "to buy lots of things."

"Come on, Manuel, don't be stingy. Give mamá the ten pesos you took out of your piggy bank."

Manuel handed a ten-peso bill to his mother. "But this is for the ornaments, eh?" he said. "If we don't have a tree you give them back to me."

"Now, now," Isabel said with a smile, "how suspicious you are. When have I ever double-crossed you in anything? I give you money and lend you and you never pay me. Now go upstairs and wash your hands and then come and sit down. So that there won't be any fights Manuel and Juan will wash their hands down here."

The boys did as they were told, but Juan picked up an empty box, carried it halfway up the stairs, and then threw it down into the living room. His mother cried out, "Who threw this box down? I've already picked it up several times. This is the last time I'm going to pick it up. If you throw it again I'll get even with the one who does it."

On his way to the table Juan pushed Lourdes. She fell down because he had taken her by surprise, and began to cry. Isabel went up to Juan and cuffed him on the head. He began to cry. "You'll see," he said, "I'm going to tell my papá on you—that you're mean and always hitting us and that you went away alone and didn't take us. You'll see."

Isabel hit him again, but this time she hit him hard. "Go ahead," she said in fury. "So you're going to tell him. Tattle-tale! But if you don't tell him I will and you'll see. I'll make sure that Santa Claus doesn't bring you anything, you son-of-a-gun. You'd think I wasn't your mother. You act like my enemies."

Just then Rolando, who had been looking out from the upstairs balcony, yelled, "My papá, my papá!" and raced down the stairs and outside to meet David who was pulling up at the gate. It was almost four o'clock.

"Hi, children. Were you going to eat without me?" he asked smilingly as he patted Lourdes who also had come to meet him. He picked her up and went into the house with her in his arms. When he saw Isabel he went up to her and kissed her on the mouth. She half turned away as though to avoid him. "What's the matter, golden girl?" he said. "Are you still angry? You know I like to find you smiling when I get home."

"No, old man," she said. "It's just that those boys drive me crazy. I can't manage them. This can only be straightened out by boarding school. Otherwise you'll be a widower very shortly."

"What more could I ask for?" David said jocularly. "My luck isn't that good."

"What do you mean your luck isn't that good?" Isabel answered, going along with his joke. "You had all the luck when you married me."

"Yes, you can see what kind of luck. Four children who drive you crazy. But now seriously, children, don't do things to worry your mother any more. If she complains again to me you'll see what you'll get."

David turned to his wife. "Do you know, old girl, you came out very well in the picture. You look gorgeous."

"What picture?" Isabel asked, but David was on his way up to the bathroom and did not answer.

"Ay! mamá, why the one of the inauguration of the factory, of course. The one they took the other day."

"Of course. When your papá comes down we'll ask him. Sit down so you'll be ready."

David came down again, rubbing his hands together. "Aren't you going to give me a drink, old girl?"

"What kind do you want?"

"Cognac."

Isabel served Cognac Courvoisier to her husband and herself in two large amphora-shaped crystal glasses, pouring out just enough to cover the bottoms of the glasses. David said, "Your health, little treasure," clinked his glass with hers, and kissed her again. This time she accepted the gesture more amiably. When they had drunk the cognac Isabel asked, "What were you telling me about the picture?"

"Ah, yes. Well, that you looked very beautiful. I wanted to bring it, but I would have had to bring the projector too because the one we have here isn't any good for that size."

"Ay, papá," Rolando said, "you should have brought it. We haven't seen how it turned out. Will you bring it tomorrow?"

"Yes, if Mr. Rojas has it ready for me I'll bring it. If not we'll go to the office in the afternoon to see it. You'll see, you'll see how beautiful your mother is in it."

The family sat down at the table, and Josefina came in with plates of vegetable soup on a copper tray. She served the family according to age, first David, then Isabel, then Rolando, until she came to Lourdes who was last. She asked if she should bring cold drinks and all of the children shouted "Yes!" She then brought Pepsi-Colas for everyone except David, who took *Chianti de Misión de Santo Tomás.* The family began to eat and to talk about the holidays, the *Posada,* and the Christmas parties.

"Papá, I want my tree," Lourdes said to her father. "Aren't we going to buy one?"

"Yes, dear, why hasn't your mother bought it for you?"

"Because you haven't given her any money, papá," Juan said. "Give her some now. Otherwise she won't buy it."

"But, Shorty, you should have bought it and I would have given you the money later."

Rolando, who dared be most insolent to his mother, broke in, "I told you so, mamá, but you always say that my papá won't give you any money. If you don't get the tree give me my money back."

Isabel ignored her son this time. "Yes, I buy it and then you don't give me the money," she said to David. "Besides, I don't have any money left. It was just barely enough for everything I had to buy."

"All right, before I go I'll give you money to buy it with. Come on now, eat up." David was speaking to Lourdes who was forgetting to eat. "You all are so fussy about eating and you don't know how lucky you are."

"I don't want any soup, papá," Lourdes whined. "It tastes awful. I don't like it."

"Come on, baby, eat. All right, let them serve you the next course."

Isabel rang the bell, and Josefina came in with plates of white rice covered with fried bananas. "Weren't you going to make cakes?" David asked Isabel.

"Oh, yes, but since I went out, when I got back I found that nothing was done. I tell you I can't leave them alone because they make all kinds of mistakes. But the rice doesn't seem to be too bad."

Manuel, who had been silent for some time now said, "Listen, papá, shall I put on the recording machine so we can hear what we recorded yesterday?"

"Wait till we finish eating," Isabel said, "or at least until you're through. Otherwise you just play and don't finish eating and in the afternoon you're dying of hunger."

Manuel made a move to get up anyway, and David spoke up firmly, "Yes, do as your mother says."

"You see, papá," Juan said. "Manuel never obeys and he's always bragging about how he's the one who behaves the best."

"Now keep quiet and eat," Isabel said and rang the bell again.

Josefina brought in broiled steak covered with chile sauce and garnished with lettuce, and radishes and potatoes. When he caught sight of the meat Rolando screamed, "I didn't want the meat with chile. I won't eat it."

"What happened?" Isabel asked angrily. "I told you to set aside his meat. I put it aside myself. Call Juana."

Juana came in looking repentant, but her daughter Concepción followed her and spoke up quickly before her mother could say anything. "It was me, Señora. I thought my mamá had forgotten the two steaks that you left on the plate, and I put chile on them. It wasn't her fault."

"But who told you to put your nose into this? And you, Juana, why do you let her help you? Don't you see she fools around with the food?"

"I won't eat it. It must be filthy," Rolando said.

"Well," his father said to him, "you should be thanking the little girl because she's going to save you the trouble of eating, and instead you're getting angry. Come on, thank her and don't yell any more."

"Don't joke, David," Isabel said. "He wanted the meat without chile. Now what is he going to eat?"

"Don't worry, Señora. I'm going to wash the meat with stock and it will be all right."

"All right, but if it isn't any good *you* can eat it," Rolando said insultingly.

Juana said nothing and went back to the kitchen. The other children ate quickly without speaking because they wanted to finish and be free to leave the table. David asked, "Aren't there any *tortillas*? This doesn't taste good with bread, frankly."

"Of course there are," Isabel said and called for Josefina. "Bring in some hot *tortillas*, but don't burn them."

Josefina went out to return a few minutes later with Rolando's meat and a plate of hot, thin *tortillas*. The boy examined his meat with exaggerated care, but finding nothing unusual he began to eat it. David took the *tortillas* and also a piece of meat from Isabel's plate. He had finished his own. She not only didn't object but gave him the last piece on her plate, saying, when he was about to refuse it, "Go ahead, eat it. I don't want it, with this grippe that's taken my appetite away. By the way, may I order medicine at the drugstore?"

"Yes, of course. Order what you need. You'll have to take care of yourself or else we'll have you in bed all week."

"God help me! I'm going to have an injection and take some Desenfriol today. Will you give me some money?"

"When I leave. Tell the maids to bring the coffee now."

"Aren't you going to have any ice cream? It's very good."

"No, who thought of making ice cream in this cold weather?"

"Give me some," yelled all the children almost in unison.

"It's coming, it's coming. Wait just a minute," Isabel said and rang the bell. Juana's daughter came in carrying the ice cream. Josefina brought in steaming cups of coffee which she placed in front of Isabel and David.

"It's the coffee I brought you, isn't it?" David asked Isabel. "The good coffee?"

"Yes, this is it. As though what I give you every day is bad!"

"I don't say it's bad, but it's not like this. This cost me twenty-five pesos the kilo."

"Ya, ya, since you have so much money. . . ."

"No, Shorty, it's not that I have money, but for a few cents more you can drink something better," David said. He lit a cigarette, an American brand, and asked, "Aren't you smoking?"

"No, little one, I don't want to look for trouble. I haven't smoked all day and I don't intend to until I feel better."

David and Isabel drank the coffee which had already been sweetened. Manuel and Rolando ate their ice cream very quickly and went to connect the recording machine. Immediately they heard commercials advertising their father's company and everyone listened. "Where did you record that from? From the television or the radio?" David asked.

"From the TV, papá. Listen to how clear it is," Rolando said.

Following the commercials a popular song began which was repeated over and over. The children did not seem to tire of hearing it. "Really, what more can these children wish for?" David said. "How many children have what they have. Imagine, old girl, television, recording machine, piano, train, accordion, and I don't know what else. But I don't think they even appreciate it. It must be because they have it all without having to work for it. If they had the hard times I did they'd think more of what they have given to them."

"Ay, David," Isabel said with a smile, "they're so young, and what greater satisfaction could you have than to give them all the things you give them. I'm happy that they don't have a hard time and that they lack nothing. Although at times I think that this is bad for them, but no, it's better for them to have everything. It's so hard to want something and not have it. . . ."

Isabel paused because she heard a voice on the recording machine that apparently was making a speech. "And what's that?" she asked.

"Ay, mamá," Manuel said, "it's my papá. Don't you recognize his voice?"

"Ah, of course. Let's see, what's he saying?"

The voice said, "I still recall those nights spent in Acapulco when our great friend and advertising man David Castro began his career. . . ."

"Listen," said Isabel, "how can that be you?"

"Shorty, I'm reading Señor Villa's speech, the one he gave on the day of the inauguration. The boys recorded it, don't you remember?"

"Listen, I didn't see when you recorded it and that's why I thought it was strange."

Finished with his coffee, David went upstairs to the bathroom and returned a few minutes later. "I'm going now. Call me on the telephone to tell me how you feel and to see if I can take you all to the movies. Are you going out?"

"Yes, I'm going with the children to get the things for the tree, and speaking of that, give me some money for the tree."

"Yes, papá, yes. Give it to mamá," said Juan. "If you don't she won't buy anything for us."

David made a motion as though to take out his wallet, but it was only a motion. He left without giving Isabel any money. "Damned miser," she said half to herself, "now the children are going to try to make me pay for the tree but I won't do it."

"You see, mamá, what papá is like?" Rolando cried. "Give me back my ten pesos. I'm not going to buy anything. He just says he will and then nothing."

"Don't worry, son, he'll give it to us tomorrow."

"No, no, mamá," the boy said almost hysterically. "Give me my ten pesos. I don't want a tree or anything else any more."

"All right, son. I'll give them to you, but remember that you said you would help me with your cousin's present. I'll give them to you later, eh?"

"Yes, yes, give them to me."

The telephone rang and Juan, the only one who had stayed in the living room, answered it. The other children had gone out to see their father off. "Hello, who is speaking? . . . Mamá, it's Bertha. She wants to speak to you."

Isabel went to the phone. "Yes, it's me. All right. I'll wait. . . . Listen, sister, don't be an ass, you didn't leave a bottle for the baby. . . . What? But Bertha told me. . . . Ah, well, what a dumb girl. I was all upset and told her to look for you at Jorge's house. . . . Listen, will you lend me the car for a while longer? The children want to go buy the things for the tree. . . . Yes, yes, I'll return it to you at seven at the latest. I have to get back early because if David doesn't take us to the movies he's sure to go to bed early. Last night, or rather today, he got home almost at five. . . . Yes, in the morning, of course. . . . Nothing. What did you want me to say to him? I'm fed up, but I don't want any more fights. I'm the one who always loses. Let him go wherever he wants, what difference does it make to me? . . . What happened? How did you find your brother-in-law? . . . That's good, yes, there's nothing like maids to get you all excited. And the house? Did you find something? . . . Yes? You did? Then that's because I prayed to the little Virgin to help you find a house. It's a miracle. She never fails me when I ask help for someone else. . . . That's good. If I have time when I get back this afternoon maybe you could take me to see it. . . . All right, yes, good-by. Kiss the children for me. I'll be there early with the car. . . . Yes, yes, I won't forget. While I'm out I'll take it to be filled up. I'll return the tank just as it was. Good-by, Elena."

"Poor Elena," Isabel thought as she hung up the receiver. "With five children and now this having to move. But that's what happens for not having her own house. When you least expect it the owners ask for the house back and there's nothing to do about it. And with my mamá so far away, who's going to help her with the moving? Of course it will be me. It's God's will. What are we going to do about it? I hope at least it's a good house and she's happy. But her poor husband, what he's going to have to spend and he's so good! He really is a good husband, I'm always telling Elena. Out of thirty million Mexicans she got the best one of all. That really is luck, good luck. I have luck too, but it's bad."

Isabel went upstairs to get ready, for the children wanted to leave immediately to buy the Christmas tree ornaments. She remembered that she needed medicine from the drugstore and called to Rolando. "Son, dial the drugstore and order me an Alivin and a bottle of Desenfriol, but tell them to bring them right away because I'm going out." Rolando did as he was told. When he hung up he said, "Get ready, mamá. I'm going out to play for a while."

Isabel quickly brushed her teeth, cleaned her face with a paper towel, and retouched her make-up. Lourdes asked her a little anxiously, "Am I going with you, mamá?"

"Of course, my baby. You go where your mother goes."

Lourdes was satisfied and sat down in a small easy chair covered with gold-colored silk to read some Walt Disney comic books. Isabel took off her scarf, brushed her hair, and combed it. She was changing her shoes when Josefina came in with a package wrapped in manila paper. "They brought this from the drugstore."

"Very well, go down and tell them to give you the bill for me to sign." Isabel unwrapped the package immediately and took a pill with some water. Josefina came upstairs again. "It can't be signed for, it has to be paid."

"Well, who do these people think they are? We'll see. Dial the drugstore number for me and give me the receiver. Hurry up or I'll be late."

Josefina obeyed and when the store answered gave Isabel the receiver. Isabel spoke with some heat. "Listen, Señorita, this is Señor

Castro's house calling. My husband has gone out and didn't leave me any money for the medicine, but I'm going to sign the bill and pay it later. . . . What? . . . Call the owner's brother, please. . . . But, Señorita, this isn't the first time and we trade a great deal. . . . What's that? . . . All right, I'm going to send it back."

She banged down the receiver. "*Caramba!* After the hundreds of pesos we've spent at their store! But I will never buy anything else in that drugstore. Take this," she said, turning to Josefina. "Give it to them. I've already opened the Desenfriol, but that they can worry about."

"Listen, mamá, why don't you pay for it? Don't you have any money?"

"Yes, yes, I have some, but now for spite I won't pay for it. Besides, if I pay for it your father won't make it up to me later on. I'll buy some later in the *Farmacia de Dios*. I only wish they had delivery service there."

Josefina took the package without saying anything and went downstairs with it. Isabel was now ready to leave. "Come on, baby," she said to Lourdes. "Let's go." Downstairs she called to Juana, "I'll be back soon, but buy the bread early and fix supper. Make some kind of snack for us. When I get back we'll go over the accounts. You won't have spent all the money, eh?"

"No, Señora, but everything's very expensive."

"Very well. I'll be back. Fatty and Manuel will stay here. I'm only going to take Rolando and the baby with me. If anyone asks for me tell them I'll be back about seven."

When Isabel walked out of the house at five-thirty she found all her children at the gate. Rolando was already in the car and Juan and Manuel were waiting expectantly. She told Juan and Manuel that they were not going with her and they began to protest. Manuel soon fell silent, but Juan kept on talking angrily. "You're mean. You don't love us. You leave us and go off with the rest. Just tell me, why won't you take me?"

"Because if I take you, Manuel will want to go too, and all of you together drive me crazy and we'd all be killed. Stay, son, you'll see what I'm going to bring you."

"You won't bring me anything, you won't bring me anything," Juan whimpered.

Manuel had meanwhile climbed up on the front of the car and was trying to tear off the radio antenna. Rolando yelled, "Look at him, mamá, look at him! Damned deaf one. But just let me at him and I'll fix him right now."

Isabel held Rolando back forcibly while she spoke to Manuel, "You'll see. I swear you won't have any Christmas. Get down from there because I'll kill you, you wicked boy."

Manuel got down laughing and ran toward the house. He stopped suddenly and looked back at the car. Then he went to the gate, pulled at it, and made one of its posts fall down. Isabel said nothing to him but she thought, "These sons of mine, I'm fed up with them. I feel like hanging them, I swear." But in a moment or two she calmed down and said, "Please, children, don't talk to me. I'm very nervous and I might have an accident. Ride quietly."

Rolando sat in the front seat with his mother, Lourdes was in the back. They were on the point of starting when a man dressed in blue overalls came up to the car. "Do you want a tree, little lady?" he asked. "I'll sell it cheap."

"Go ahead, mamá, go ahead," Rolando said. "Don't be mean. Let's go."

"Where are they?" Isabel asked the man.

"Just up ahead a little bit. We don't carry them with us because they'd take them away from us. But if you want we can go there."

"All right. Get in back and tell us how to get there."

The man got in and gave directions to Isabel. Soon they arrived at a little hidden alley. Some way down the alley there was a gate with a tiny room made of boards at one side of it. A number of small children, dirty and poorly dressed, were playing outside; they did not seem to mind the cold although none of them had sweaters. Isabel and her children got out of the car and walked through the room into a corral where Christmas trees were lying on the ground. The man showed them one tree after another until Rolando found one he liked. "This one, mamá, this one," he said. "See how pretty it is."

"How much do you want for it?" Isabel asked.

"Fifty pesos, Señora. Look, you won't get one any cheaper. We work hard to bring them here."

"On Liverpool Street there are some imported ones almost this size for nineteen fifty. I'll give you thirty pesos."

"No, Señora, at least forty pesos. You won't find anything cheaper."

"Mamá, yes, yes, later we won't have any tree at all. Come on, don't be mean," Rolando said, jumping up and down, frantic for fear his mother wouldn't buy the tree.

"No, thirty pesos and no more," Isabel said decisively and made a motion to leave. The man agreed to her price. "All right," Isabel said, "take it to the house and tomorrow I'll pay you, because I don't have any money with me right now."

"No, Señora, we may be leaving today. We have only a few trees left, and we're just waiting to sell these before we go because we don't come from around here."

"All right. Then bring it tomorrow if you're still here."

"That would be better, Señora," the man said humbly. Isabel went back to the car, the children following her. Lourdes said nothing, but Rolando was in a rage. "You see, you refuse us everything," he said. "Just because you say papá won't pay you. Give me my ten pesos. I don't want anything. I'm going home."

"Go then, you damned boy, go and take your ten pesos. You won't go with me," Isabel answered furiously and held out a ten-peso bill to him. Now the boy was frightened. His mother was angrier than he had ever seen her. He climbed into the car without speaking and without taking the money. Isabel drove to a gas station where she asked the attendant to fill the tank. She was nervous and still angry and didn't speak to the children, nor did either of them speak to her.

"Everything's all right, Señora. That will be ten pesos forty-five."

Isabel gave him eleven pesos. "Keep the change. Thank you very much." She headed downtown on the Reforma toward the stores in the *Medellín* market where she had bought ornaments before. She planned to buy three more boxes to complete those they already had. "But I don't feel like buying anything," she thought. "The boys don't deserve anything. They're exactly like their father."

At last Lourdes dared to speak. "Mamá, won't it be closed? It's late."

"No, all the stores close at eight every day and if it isn't open we'll go tomorrow."

"They close at eight! We'll go tomorrow!" Rolando muttered.

"What did you say?" his mother asked, ready to flare up again.

"Nothing. I didn't say anything."

"Yes, mamá," said Lourdes. "He was grumbling."

"Shut up, you brat, or I'm going to hit you."

"Look, if you don't keep quiet I'll go home and there'll be no tree or anything. It's up to you." Isabel stopped the car.

"No, mamá," Lourdes said conciliatingly. "We're going to keep quiet, aren't we?" Rolando stubbornly said nothing.

"All right," Isabel said, "I'm telling you. At the first word we'll go home." The children were quiet while she drove through the city's traffic, which was very heavy at this time of day. "I hope David will send the boys to boarding school," she thought. "I don't know if I've let them get the upper hand, but I can't control them. I think a boarding school is the only thing that could subdue them a little. That way I can rest and everything will be different. I haven't had time today even to go to the beauty parlor to have my nails done. All day with these wild animals. They drive me crazy and no wonder. I'm not strong enough to beat them."

Reaching the market, she parked the car in front of a large hardware store and said to the children, "You stay here. I'm going to get out alone and I don't want any more discussions or fights."

Inside the store Isabel waited for someone to take care of her, but the store was crowded and she waited for about five minutes without being noticed. She grew impatient and went up to a clerk. "Well, sir, are you going to wait on me or no?"

"Yes, Señora, what do you want?"

Isabel gave him her order and the clerk went to the back of the store to fill it. Again Isabel was kept waiting. From time to time she looked out to see if her children were behaving themselves. At last she went out.

"What else do we need?" she asked. "I've ordered the ornaments, the lights, and the cut cellophane paper, and the star for the top of the tree too."

"Mamá," Rolando said, "we need hay and cotton, but we'll buy that somewhere else. And the two separate lights for the other string too." Rolando was in good humor now, for he saw that they really would have a tree after all.

Isabel went back into the store, completed her purchase, and paid the bill, which was thirty-five pesos. She took the packages out to the car, then said to the children, "Come with me. We're going to the market."

As they walked along, Rolando said to his mother, "Excuse me, *mamacita*, but it made me mad to think we might not have a tree. You saw how my papá fooled us and didn't want to give us any money and then you didn't want to buy that nice tree."

"Look, son, you must understand that I don't do this out of self-ishness. Your father has money, but I have to force him to give you these things. He likes us to beg him for it and that's not right. One hundred or two hundred pesos are nothing to him, and they mean a lot to me because I don't have any income of my own. What he gives me is just barely enough. You should all help me and instead of that you make things more difficult for me. You're the oldest and you're the one who should set an example for your brothers. How can you ask them to respect me if you don't?"

"No, *mamita*, forgive me. I promise I'm going to behave well, but don't get mad at me. It makes me very sad," Rolando said and kissed his mother.

Inside the market they went to a stand where hay, moss, and pine boughs were sold for the crèches which traditionally were set up on December twenty-fourth in every house in Mexico City. They bargained for the hay, finally buying a small heap for three pesos. Rolando carried it out to the car. It was a little after seven o'clock and completely dark now, and Isabel remembered that she still had to return the car to her sister.

"All right, son, we're going home now." Isabel settled Lourdes on the back seat where she promptly fell asleep. "Don't suggest anything else because I don't have any more money and it's very late."

Isabel headed the car for the Reforma, and pulled up in front of her house fifteen minutes later. No one had said anything on the way home and Isabel was anxiously wondering whether David had called while she was out.

She honked the horn for the servants to come and help her. She didn't want to get out of the car because she had to take it back to her sister. She felt really ill, and tonight, she thought, she would rather stay at home than go to the movies. Not for anything would she miss the *Posada* dinner the following night. It was to be held in a fashionable night club and promised to be a brilliant affair.

At the sound of the horn Eufemia came out drying her hands on her apron. "You're back, Señora?"

"No, Eufemia, not yet," Isabel answered with a laugh. "Help us with the packages and come back for the baby so you can carry her in. Bring a blanket to wrap her in so she won't get a chill."

Eufemia took the packages that Rolando handed her, carried them into the house, and came back a little later with a blue blanket. She and Rolando wrapped Lourdes in it and Eufemia carried her into the house. "You get out too," Isabel said to Rolando. "Close the gate and put back the bricks the way they were. Tomorrow the workmen can fix it again. Your father is going to be good and angry. I hope he won't hit Manuel." Rolando followed his mother's instructions, then got back into the car which she drove to Elena's house.

When they arrived Rolando got out and rang the bell beside the red gate which was locked with a chain and padlock. In a few minutes a tall, stout maid came out. "Come in, Señora," she said pleasantly. "I'm going to open up for you."

"No, Maria," Isabel said. "Don't open the gate. Ask Elena if she wants me to leave the keys or if she'll come down to take me back to the house."

The maid went back to the house and soon returned to say, "The Señora says for you to leave the keys and lock the car well. She can't come out just now because she's bathing the baby. She wants to know if you won't come in."

"No, it's very late. Tell her I'll call her tomorrow to see if we're going to the Palace. I think I'll go lie down now because I have a devilish case of grippe. Good-by, Maria. Here are the keys. And you, Rolando, lock the car up well. Tell Elena thanks a lot. I filled up the tank and had the water and oil checked and the air in the tires. Good-night."

Isabel took her son's arm and they began to walk back to their own house. When they reached the corner of Reforma she said, "How pretty the Christmas lighting looks. At least this regent takes care of the city."

"What's a regent, mamá?" the boy asked.

"He's the mayor, the one who governs the city of Mexico, like the state governors, or like the president in the whole Republic, except that he just rules the city of Mexico, that is, the whole federal district. Don't tell me you don't know what the federal district is?"

"Of course I know. They taught me that in the third grade. And who is the regent?"

"His name is Uruchurtu, but I don't remember his first name. He is also called the governor of the federal district and chief of the central department. He did a lot for our city. He tore down the filthy old markets and built new ones and took the peddlers and beggars off the streets. See how beautiful the city is now with the flowers he planted—and the fountains. Your papá says he wants to be president."

"Uy, he must have a lot of money, no, mamá?"

"Of course, son, all these big men have money. They steal a lot and make all kinds of dirty deals."

"And my papá isn't a friend of this Uruchurtu?"

"No, son, he has other friends."

"And my Uncle Mauricio? He knows everybody."

"Well, who knows? I don't know about that."

Isabel took no interest in politics, not even exercising her vote. But David had friends among government officials and he was prominent in a manufacturers' organization. He had been urged to take part in politics, and because of his speaking ability, to run for office. But he had refused. His civic feeling took the form of a wish to leave something of value to his city. He had once told his wife that he intended to leave all the buildings he owned to the people of

Mexico City as a kind of monument to him. This statement had alarmed Isabel because it sounded as though David did not plan to leave anything substantial to her and the children. But she had not had the courage to question him about it.

When they arrived at their house they found the gate was open. Rolando locked it carefully after them. Inside the house Manuel came to meet them and said, "My papá says you're to call him, but right away because he's ready to leave the factory. It's almost eight o'clock." Isabel ran to the phone to call her husband. When David answered she said, "No, I went to return the car to Elena. . . . Just as you like, but I think it would be better if I stayed here because I think I even have a fever. I'll send the boys to you in a cab instead and you take them. I'll take some medicine and stay here in bed. . . . No, don't be mean, you promised them. . . . In a cab from the stand, of course. I'll send them just as soon as they've had their supper. Wait for them there. . . . Without their supper? You'll take them somewhere afterwards? . . . All right, bring me some sandwiches. . . . All right, yes, good-by. They'll be there within half an hour."

She hung up the receiver and told Manuel what had been decided. "Call Juan and Rolando. I think they're upstairs, I just heard them yelling. Tell them to get ready to go to the movies with their father."

"Ay, mamá, aren't you going? Then I won't go either."

"No, son, I have a bad case of grippe. I'd rather go to bed early and that way I'll be all right tomorrow for when we put up the tree. Go on, call your brothers."

Manuel ran upstairs while Isabel went out into the kitchen. "What have you been doing all afternoon?" she said to Juana. "It's eight o'clock and you haven't finished cleaning the kitchen. Look at that stove. You go up to your own rooms and the devil take the housework. Make me a cup of tea and bring it to me upstairs, and prepare the chocolate milk for the baby who's asleep and take that up too. I'm going upstairs because I can't stand this headache."

The cook only moved her head in assent and Isabel went upstairs and into the boys' bedroom. It was in complete disorder. Toys

*348*

had been thrown around, pillows lay on the floor, the beds were unmade, and a Venetian blind had fallen to the floor.

"Ay, Dios Mio! What's happened here? You'll see, you two aren't going to the movies."

"No, mamá, don't be mean. We were playing and the blind got tangled and fell down," Juan said.

It occurred to Isabel that if she kept the boys home the punishment would be hers. If she let them go she could rest peacefully for a while and she could read the novel she had just borrowed. So she said, "All right. I'll forgive you once more, but the next time you'll see. Ring the bell, Juan, for Josefina to come and pick up this mess. Get ready. I'm going to call the stand for a cab. Or you'd better call, Rolando."

"Mamá," Juan asked, "aren't we going to have our supper?"

"No, stupid," Manuel said, "Papá is going to take us for sandwiches for supper where he always takes us. Come on, the cab will be here soon."

They heard a horn at that moment and the three boys ran pell-mell down the stairs. "Who's going to pay for the cab?" Rolando yelled to his mother.

"Let your father pay for it when you get there. Be very careful and tell your father you're not to make noise when you come in because I'm going to be asleep."

From the balcony of her bedroom Isabel watched the boys get into the cab and drive off. She rang the bell and Juana soon appeared carrying a bottle with chocolate milk and a porcelain cup of tea on a tray. Isabel undressed Lourdes, put on her flannel pyjamas, and covered her with blankets. Then she gave her the bottle, which the child took almost asleep, kissed her, and turned out the light, leaving only a night light. She tiptoed into the bathroom, where she brushed her teeth and took off her make-up with cleansing cream. In her own bedroom she undressed and put a white wool bed jacket over her nightgown. Before she got into bed she put night cream on her face. Then she called for Josefina to serve her the tea. Josefina turned out the bright lights—Isabel had already turned on her bed light—and gave her mistress two aspirin tablets which she took from a dressing-table drawer.

Isabel turned the radio on very softly and took up her book, *The Egyptian*. One more day had ended for her. Her husband and her children would return at almost one in the morning of the next day, but she would be asleep by then. She began to read. For a while she would live in the fantasy of the book and then she would sleep. She only hoped that by tomorrow she would have recovered from the grippe and would be able to attend the party. It promised to be amusing. She had eaten no supper because, whatever David said, she meant to try to keep her figure.

# BIBLIOGRAPHY

Bermudez, Maria Elvira, 1955: *La Vida Familiar del Mexicano*. Mexico, Robredo.

Firth, Raymond, 1956: *Two Studies of Kinship In London*. London, Athlone Press.

Hoggart, Richard, 1957: *The Uses of Literacy: Changing Patterns in English Mass Culture*. Fairlawn, N.J., Essential Books.

Lewis, Oscar, 1951: *Life in a Mexican Village: Tepoztlan Restudied*. Urbana, Ill., University of Illinois Press.

———, 1952: "Urbanization Without Breakdown," *The Scientific Monthly*. Vol. LXXV, No. 1, July 1952.

Malinowski, Bronislaw, 1922: *Argonauts of the Western Pacific*. London, Routledge and Kegan Paul Ltd.

Slater, Eliot, and Woodside, Moya, 1951: *Patterns of Marriage*. London, Cassell and Co.

Spinley, B. M., 1953: *The Deprived and the Privileged*. London, Routledge and Kegan Paul Ltd.

Steward, Julian, 1957: *The People of Puerto Rico*. Urbana, Ill., University of Illinois Press.

Stycos, J. Mayone, 1955: *Family and Fertility in Puerto Rico*. New York, Columbia University Press.

Zweig, F., 1949: *Labour, Life and Poverty*. London, Victor Gollancz Ltd.